DEVELOPMENT CHALLENGES
(Afflicting Uttar Pradesh)

DEVELOPMENT CHALLENGES

(Afflicting Uttar Pradesh)

Editors

D.M. DIWAKAR

SANATAN NAYAK

MANAK

PUBLICATIONS PVT. LTD

First Edition 2007

Published by

MANAK

PUBLICATIONS PVT. LTD

B-7, Saraswati Complex, Subhash Chowk,
Laxmi Nagar, New Delhi-110092
Phone: 22453894, 22042529
E-mail : info@manakpublications.com
manak_publications@hotmail.com
Website: www.manakpublications.com

ISBN 81-7827-169-9

Layout by
Sudhir Kumar Vatsa

Laser Typeset by
Arpit Printographer, B-7, Saraswati Complex,
Subhash Chowk, Laxmi Nagar, Delhi-110092

Printed in India by
Nice Printing Press, New Delhi

Dedicated to
Deprived and Discriminated Masses,
who suffered Injustices of Development
Challenges most

CONTENTS

PREFACE

Uttar Pradesh, as one of the major states of India by size of population and area, compounded with syndrome of backwardness in terms of infrastructure development, natural resource management and structural inequality, occupies significant place in the development of the country. In order to address dimensions of challenges towards development with distributive justice for the masses of this state, mapping resources for effective and optimum use and identifying gaps in infrastructure have been concerns of academics and policy makers, reflected in formulation of planning and implementation.

In conformity with the national planning, this state has also witnessed ten five years plans and Approach Paper to 11th Five Year Plan has been outlined towards formulating strategies for development with distributive justice. Although, gradual realisation of various dimensions of ground realities has been very much reflected with better articulation in successive plans, still much is left to be desired. Efforts have been made to minimise hardship of common masses and reduce regional disparities. Mobilisation and allocation of resources in a defined investment framework has been crucial strategy to determine growth processes and performance of the economy. Towards finalising strategies for the Eleventh Five Year Plan with public and private partnership in development process, there is imperative need of the labour to address the issues of development and identifying priority area, people at large and poor and historically disadvantaged groups and community in particular who remained yet at the margin.

This exercise presents a broad assessment of the direction of development of different sectors of the economy of Uttar Pradesh. This study is a collective output of a team of experts from various institutions: Professor A.K.Singh, Director, Professor D.M.Diwakar. and Dr. Sanatan Nayak, members of the faculty, Giri Institute of Development Studies, Lucknow, Professor Y. Tyagi and Dr. M.K. Agarwal from the Department of Economics, and Dr. D.R. Sahoo from the Department of Sociology, University of Lucknow, Dr. N.M.P.Verma from the Department of Economics, BB Ambedkar University, Lucknow, T.N. Dhar I.A.S. (Rtd.) from Indian Institute of Public Administration, U.P. Regional Branch and Dr. A.N. Pandey from the Institute of Entreprenur Development, Lucknow have spared their valuable time for this exercise. We express our gratitude to expert contributors for their valuable contribution despite their busy schedules and preoccupations. Publication support extended by M/s Manak Publications, New Delhi and secretarial assistance provided by the Giri Institute of Development Studies, Lucknow are acknowledged with appreciation.

Views expressed in chapters are of respective authors. Despite our best efforts, needless to mention that responsibilities of shortcomings left unattended regarding editing, rest on us. Hopefully this exercise will attract readers for enriching debates on development of Uttar Pradesh.

D.M. Diwakar
Sanatan Nayak

CONTRIBUTORS

1. Dr. A.K. Singh, Professor and Director, Giri Institute of Development Studies, Lucknow, Uttar Pradesh.
2. Dr. Y. Tyagi, Professor, Department of Economics, University of Lucknow, Uttar Pradesh.
3. Dr. D.M. Diwakar, Professor, Giri Institute of Development Studies, Lucknow, Uttar Pradesh.
4. Dr. N.M.P. Verma, Professor and Head, Department of Economics, Babasaheb Bhimrao Ambedkar University, Lucknow, Uttar Pradesh.
5. Dr. D.R. Sahoo, Reader, Department of Sociology, Lucknow University, Lucknow.
6. Shri T.N. Dhar, IAS (Retd), Hon. Secretary, Indian Institute of Public Administration, U.P. Regional Branch, Lucknow, Uttar Pradesh.
7. Dr. A.N. Pandey, Senior Faculty Member, Institute of Entrepreneurship Development, Lucknow, Uttar Pradesh.
8. Dr. M.K. Agarwal, Reader, Department of Economics, University of Lucknow, Uttar Pradesh.
9. Dr. Sanatan Nayak, Fellow, Giri Institute of Development Studies, Lucknow, Uttar Pradesh.

INTRODUCTION

D.M. Diwakar

Addressing the issues of 'development with distributive justice' has been a major challenge in order to ensure descent living conditions with basic amenities to common and deprived masses in India in general and its heterogeneous regions of backward states like Uttar Pradesh, Bihar, Madhya Pradesh, Orissa, Assam, Jharkhand, Chhattisgarh, and other states and union territories in particular. Judicious dissemination of the fruits of development among unequal regions and strata of the society therefore attaches utmost importance. It needs not only material development but also evolving institutional agencies of delivery mechanism for development with distributive justice. Therefore, identifying challenges to wards material and institutional development have been major concerns for academicians, policy makers and sensitive development agencies. Irrespective of the level of challenges to development, structural planning and execution has acquired a decisive role in development of an economy, polity and society. It has achieved special significance in case of a backward economy in which majority of the people is still dependant on primary sector mainly on agriculture. In Indian economy as a whole and Uttar Pradesh as one of the most populated developing states of this country in particular, mapping of challenges and resources has significant role to reorient its priorities and strategies of development as per the need of the people at the centre stage.

Process of development and planning in this regard has been enriched in due course by its experiences gained through various Five Year Plans. In conformity with the national planning Ten Five Year Plans have already been executed and implemented for the economy of Uttar Pradesh and the Eleventh Five Year Plan is to be finalised. Gradual realisation of various dimensions of ground realities has been very much reflected with better articulation in successive plans. In the era of reforms now the economy is expected to grow with public and private partnership in development process. In order to address the need of development and identifying priority area, it is claimed that people remained at the central point. It is also claimed that efforts have been made to minimise hardship of common masses and reduction of regional disparities. But the question is whether mobilisation, allocation and utilisation of resources in a defined investment framework has been crucial strategy to determine growth processes and performance of the economy. Emerging results are almost contrary to the claims of reforms with human face. Regional disparity has widened. Deprivation and exclusion is on the rise.

Basic objectives of this exercise is to present a general review of the progress in different sectors of the economy and indicate possible corrective measures towards achieving development goals—growth with justice. Assessment of the targets has also been undertaken in the light of constraints and challenges for the growth of the economy. Although the reference point for the assessment has been, *inter alia,* identified priorities and objectives of the plan, resource allocation, investment pattern and requirement and status of its mobilization and physical targets set in the plan proposal, this study pursues to assess whether the over-all economy of the state is moving towards desired direction and the targeted investments are being made accordingly. The deficiency in the physical targets has been ascertained and correcting measures have been suggested for the overall development of the economy.

We all know that Uttar Pradesh is one of the most populated states with a volume of 16.62 crores population and about 66 per cent of the workforce dependent mainly on agriculture, which contributes about 32.7 per cent of the state income with a structure of above 90 per cent marginal and small farmers. Birth rate is about 31.6 per thousand and literacy level is about 57.4 per cent, which ranks this state with poor infrastructure at 14 and 13 in the country respectively. Estimates of growth performance through sector wise domestic products and its per capita distribution at factor cost suggests that net state domestic product (NSDP) between 1960-61 to 2002-03 has grown annually at 3.79 per cent where as per capita NSDP has grown merely by 2.54 per cent (Table 1). Plan wise annual compound growth rate at constant prices suggest that seventh plan could achieve highest ever growth rate to the tune of 6.61 per cent. However, this rate of growth could not be sustained in subsequent plans. Similarly, rate of growth of per capita NSDP registered 4.25 per cent in the Seventh Plan, which came down to 2.87 in the Eighth Plan and it reached at the lowest level to 0.93 per cent during the Ninth Plan. Data suggest that average growth rate of state income during two years of the Tenth Plan is higher than that of the Ninth Plan. However, it is far behind than the growth rate of National Income. Moreover, contribution of state in National income has been declining. This suggests that the relative position of state performance is sliding down from the average contribution in the Ninth Plan

Sector wise annual compound growth rates during 1960-61 to 2000-01 for Fishery and Mining & Quarrying has registered impressive performance, i.e., 7.54 and 7.55 per cent respectively among the sub sectors of the primary sector (Table 1). Manufacturing as a whole could achieve 6.41 per cent growth rate in which registered sector grew by 7.37 per cent but unregistered had lower rate of growth (i.e., 5.19 per cent). There has been significantly double-digit (11.23 per cent) growth rate for electricity, gas and water supply. Similarly banking and insurance has also grown by 9.97 per cent. Transport storage and communication could grow by 5.06 per cent. Remaining sectors have however, lower values of growth rates but still higher than that of agriculture. Agriculture could grow at very low level by 2.63 per cent and forestry had a negative score (-) 3.85 per cent. Negative trend of growth rate in forestry and lower trend in agriculture are matter of serious concern. If we take the growth performance in 1980s and 1990s into account, growth rates of Mining and Quarrying, Construction, Transport, Storage and Communication sectors have registered higher growth rates in 1990s than 1980s. Growth rates in remaining all the sectors have been with lower score in 1990s. As a result, growth rates of NSDP and per capita NSDP have also been lower in 1990s than that of 1980. This study is an attempt to take a brief account of an overall indicative view of the economy of Uttar Pradesh. Sector and problem specific in depth analysis in details has been presented by the expert contributors in subsequent chapters.

Agriculture remains mainstay for the workforce of the economy of Uttar Pradesh, which attaches significance of the development of this sector. D.M. Diwakar intends to examine the performance of agriculture and its growth linkages and constraints, options and strategies. This exercise tests whether agriculture has significant direct relation with land and water management, modernisation of agriculture and price structure. For land and water management, cropping intensity, and status of irrigation has been taken into account. Fertiliser consumption has been considered as a proxy of the use of modern inputs and income deflator price relatives of agriculture and non-agriculture have been taken for price behaviour. Assumptions for this study carry irrigation as the king pin for development, which promotes intensive use of land reflected in cropping intensity through using traditional as well as high yielding varieties of seeds, chemical fertiliser. Price relatives reflect price received and paid in the process of transaction by the farmers. Thus, this study examines the effects of irrigation, fertiliser consumption, cropping intensity, and price relatives. While doing so it adds the contexts of structural challenges, initiatives and lessons. Needless to mention that this exercise has an indicative value to examine various factors to begin with.

It was revealed that contribution of agriculture has come down from 64.87 per cent in 1960-61 to 32.7 in 2004-05. Sector wise analysis of state income at constant prices suggests that annual average growth rate for agriculture during Ninth Plan was merely 0.85 per cent and total primary sector was 1.99 per cent. However, during first year of the Tenth Five Year Plan it turned negative due to severe drought. During second year it could register an impressive growth rate due to favourable monsoon with lower base value of the growth rate in previous year. But over all growth rate for the first two years remained negative. Severe drought in successive year might have resulted in further decline. Agriculture being a major component of Primary sector the growth rate of this sector turned negative. Manufacturing sector has performed better in the Tenth Five Year Plan and could register 6.5 per cent growth rate. Other sectors grew by 4.3 per cent, which is higher than the growth rate of previous plan.

If one attempts to review the targets set for broader sectors for the Tenth Five Year Plan as mentioned in Plan Document, annual growth rate target for agriculture was set to the tune of 5.17 per cent, manufacturing as 12.36 per cent and remaining sectors (services) as 8.06 per cent (see vol. I Part I p. 35). In the first year of the Tenth Five Year Plan (2002-03) agriculture and allied sectors registered negative growth rate to the tune of (-) 6.03 per cent because of unfavourable monsoon. However, in the year 2003-04 it recovered to 5.28 per cent, as monsoon was favourable. This recovery appears mainly on the lower negative base value of the growth rate in previous year. If one takes average of the two years, annual growth rate remained negative (- 0.37 per cent). In view of the wide spread drought in the year 2004-05 and intermittent uncertainty of monsoon thereafter, possibility for further reconsolidation remained weak.

Subsistence agriculture dominating by food grains has been facing declining area production and productivity amidst uncertainty of monsoon. Irrigation network remained ineffective because of fluctuating and scanty rainfall. Despite the fact that the use of chemical fertilizer has significantly contributed in enhancing production and productivity, disproportionate use of NPK has not only exposed the hard facts about ineffective extension services but also created environmental crises in agriculture, which will have far-reaching consequences on agricultural production. Even if attracted to value added agriculture, market induced production has made the farmers more vulnerable than ever before. Small and marginal farmers remained capital constrained and deprived of effective credit flow. This needs to be addressed on priority basis. Thus, it appears that agriculture needs special attention to protect from uncertainty of the monsoon and to provide proper infrastructure support for transformation and development.

Inequality in agrarian structure remained major concern for the transformation of agriculture in Uttar Pradesh. Despite the fact that land to the tillers emerged as basic slogan from the freedom movement in India and this state got credit for championing the cause of land reforms, implementation of land reforms remained a major challenge. In order to understand the present status of land reforms in this state D.M. Diwakar has attempted an exercise towards understanding the issues of land reforms and exploring the possibility of acquiring sustainable basic needs through access to land resources. This study is primarily intended to examine as to how far access to land has been instrumental in facilitating basic needs on sustainable basis. Primary data for this purpose have been collected from rural households through census survey in ten sample villages spread over five districts representing different regions and climatic zones of Uttar Pradesh. This chapter deals with the process of redistribution and possessions of ceiling surplus (CS) and gram samaj (GS) land and underlines the impact of land reforms on basic needs and social development in Uttar Pradesh (UP).

Land reforms, which could have addressed the issues of rural unemployment and poverty, remained at the back seat. As a result, question of fulfilling basic needs through crash programme remained unsatisfactory. New form of tenancy as advance rent in cash has aggravated unemployment situation of poor peasant. Witnessing faster pace of liberalization in 1990s in the Indian economy, agriculture did not remain isolated. Employment elasticity has turned to be insignificant. National Agricultural Policies have accommodated corporate farming, which have necessary implications on employment and income of poor peasantry who are potentials to be alienated from subsistence employment base in agriculture without any substantial alternatives. The above analysis, thus, suggests that the question of inequality in land distribution has not lost the ground and much is yet to be done to restore the land to the tiller not only to remove the qualitative inequality in distribution of land but also to improve production, productivity of agriculture and employment and earnings status of the poor peasants. Therefore, substantial investment to prepare agriculture to meet challenges remains the main concern in the syndrome of general indifference and gradual withdrawal of state from its responsibility of welfare status in the interest of market, which is in fact a challenge before the economy, polity and society.

Irrigation plays an important role in transformation and development of agriculture. Sanatan Nayak has focused on the role of irrigation as physical infrastructure for the development of the agriculture economy. He found increasing trend in expansion of irrigated area. The net irrigated area has been increasing from 62.55 lakhs hectares in 1966-67 to 128.28 lakh hectares in 2001-02. The proportion of net irrigated area to net cropped area has increased from 36.12 percent to 76.30 percent in 2001-02. However, the net irrigated area by private sources such as private tube-well/ pump sets constitutes nearly 87.09 lakh hectares, which is 68 percent of the net irrigated area, whereas major and medium sources through canal irrigation possesses at 27.19 lakh hectares, which is nearly 21 percent of the net irrigated area. However, there was disproportionate growth of irrigation by sources with disproportionate distribution of public investment in various five-year plans among sources. The proportion of actual expenditure on irrigation and flood control out of total planned expenditure during 9th and first three years of 10th plan remained almost constant. The irrigated area under various sources shows an increasing trend over the years. However, both the potential and utilization of potential have increased continuously in reference period. It has been summarized that the biggest single malady in the major and medium irrigation sectors right from first plan has been the continued tendency to start additional new projects resulting in proliferation of projects, thin spreading of resources leading to time and cost overruns. There is need to complete those projects on priority basis for which sufficient resource allocation and proper monitoring needs to be ensured. Despite this expansion of irrigation network intermittent droughts have been experienced by the agriculture sector of state economy. This reflects the degree of effectiveness of irrigation networks of the state.

Secondary sector in U.P. contributes about 20 per cent of the state income and manufacturing alone contributes about 12 per cent with 5.6 per cent absorption of workforce. Growth rate of this sector in the Ninth Plan was negative. However, in the Tenth Five Year Plan this sector has grown considerably by 6.5 per cent per annum. Industry is one of the important sectors, which facilitates and determines the growth prospects of other sectors of the economy through forward and backward linkages. By implications the pace of the development of this sector determines progress of other sector. Besides small and cottage industry medium and heavy industries have grown significantly. Altogether 1370 IEM/LOI have been issued in the Ninth Plan for medium and heavy industries, i.e., about 274 per annum. In case of Tenth Plan IEM/LOI issued for two years were 497, i.e. 248.5 per annum. Investment in previous plan was on an average 4077.22 crore and employment about 46251 per annum. In the first two years of the Tenth Plan, investment has been to the tune of average Rs. 1755.94 crore and employment generated about 40837.5 per year. These figures are lower than that of the Ninth Plan and therefore need to be addressed effectively so that this sector can progress better than that of the previous Plan. Recent data of Economic Census 2005 suggest that concentration of rural enterprises have outnumbered urban entrepreneurs. In Uttar Pradesh percentage of enterprises in rural area was 54.63 and 45.36 per cent enterprises are in urban area constituting 9.53 per cent of total enterprises in India. Tamil Nadu emerged highest in terms of number of industrial units (44.5 lakh), whereas Maharashtra registered itself as largest employer with 1.18 crore jobs. Andhra Pradesh, Maharashtra, Tamil Nadu, Uttar Pradesh and West Bengal together accounted for 50 per cent of the total enterprises in the country.

Hopes for generating employment have been pinned on micro and small enterprises. A study (Singh, et.al., 2004) suggests that during last two years employment in this sector has increased by 5.7 per cent. Women workers have increased by 8.4 per cent, men by 4.9 per cent, and child workers by 71.4 per cent. This also suggests that preference for employing women and children, as cheap casual labour remained higher than man. Employment in general has grown faster in the industry (having 6 to 9 workers), i.e., by 7.4 per cent than small scale (having 10 to 19 workers) by 5.2 per cent. However, the study also suggests that 60.7 per cent female family workers and 75 per cent family child labour are unpaid. Proportion of female worker is very small. Every enterprise does not employ at least one woman.

A.N. Pandey in his chapter on industrial development focuses on the strength of the industrial base and yet pervasive backwardness in industrial sector. Pandey underlines reasons of backwardness *inter alia* political instability, shift in priorities from industry to social sectors, gap between outlay, allocation and utilisation of resources and low public investment, less developed infrastructure, low power consumption, lack of modernisation, pervasive traditional methods and technology of production and lower participation rate of workforce. Pandey apprehends that this syndrome may continue even in future also if proper remedial measures are not initiated. Industry may hardly achieve its unrealistic target of 12 per cent growth rate in the Tenth Five Year Plan. This indicates absence of coordination between Planning and functioning of Industry Departments, which needs to be addressed.

There has been growing realisation that infrastructure

building is one of the major segments to promote employment, growth and quality of life. Infrastructure has been classified broadly in three categories: Physical, Social and Financial. Further segregations of these categories into irrigation, power and transport as economic physical infrastructure have been categorical to identify contribution in reducing transaction cost of production and generating employment, income and growth of the economy. Social infrastructure enhances human capabilities through education, health, housing, and recreation facilities leading towards improvement in productivity of labour and quality of life. Financial infrastructure like postal, banking, and tax capacity of the people determines the financial performance of the state. All these together constitute income generating capability of a state. On the contrary, it has been observed that differential infrastructure facilities across the states are primarily responsible for the widening of income disparity (Ghosh and De, 2004). Study suggests that in U.P. all three categories of infrastructure, i.e., physical, social, and financial remained almost stagnant in their relative positions. However, physical infrastructure displayed better position than financial and social infrastructure. Ninth and Tenth Five Year Plan have laid emphasis on infrastructure building in the state.

Energy is considered as one of the key components for growth of agriculture as well as other sectors. To meet the growing demand of energy is a major challenge. Energy sector involves basically, generation, transmission and distribution. Technical losses during transmission remained to be addressed till date, which may reduce the scarcity of energy to a certain extent. Expansion of network in rural areas still remains a major task. As per CMIE estimates, compound annual growth rate of the percentage of village electrified in 1980s was 7.61 per cent, which was declined to 0.90 per cent in 1990s. However, road length for the same period has gone up from 0.22 per cent to 4.03 per cent. In terms of per capita power consumption U.P. is ranked 15th among selected 18 major states of the country. With regards to electrification in rural areas, Uttar Pradesh stands 11th among major states. Moreover, in terms of electrification of the households in the electrified villages, which shows the true picture of the economic strength of an economy, Uttar Pradesh stands as one of the backward states at all India level. Latest data show only 20 percent of the rural households electrified in Uttar Pradesh against 44 percent at the all India level. Nayak found huge gap in demand and supply, lack of proper renovation and modernization activity, huge distribution and transmission losses and lack of sufficient stand on tariff reforms. These need to be addressed on priority basis.

An efficient transport system, which is a pre-requisite for sustained economic development, plays crucial role in promoting national integration, increasing productivity, enhance the competitive efficiency of the economy in the world market, development of backward regions and integrating them with the mainstream economy by opening them to the trade investment. However, Nayak discovered huge gap in supply and demand, regional disparity in the road construction, low maintenance standards, no better regulatory framework and high environmental pollution in the transport sector. These issues have been raised for the consideration on priority basis.

Reduction of regional disparity has been one of the major challenge for the development of state in Five Year Plans. Chapter on regional disparity analysed by Yashvir Tyagi covers various dimensions in terms of demographic structure, social development, infrastructure, agriculture and industrial development, income disparities, and intra-regional disparities. Analysis of this chapter could identify a few important reasons for regional disparities such as, lack of industrialisation in backward regions, inadequate irrigation facilities in eastern and Bundelkhand regions, large flood prone areas in the eastern region, largely rain-fed agriculture in Bundelkhand region, and low cropping intensity, etc. Tyagi concludes that despite many efforts intra-regional disparities appeared to have widened over time. There is a need to dovetail special area programmes with other developmental programmes at the district level to avoid duplication of efforts and synergies among programmes to harness and optimize the use of resources. Infrastructure facilities in the backward districts should be augmented to give impetus to development. There should be evaluative studies to determine the effectiveness of various special area programmes in reducing regional disparities. There is a need to have augment capacity and capability to formulate, plans/ programmes in time to take advantage of centrally sponsored schemes to avoid delay in implementation. Moreover, for balanced regional development, agro-climatic conditions, special problems and potential of development of different districts/regions should be assessed properly and taken into account while formulating area development plans.

Poverty and unemployment are two major concerns for any developing economy. In this study two chapters have been devoted to analyse these issues. Tyagi deals mainly with official data which suggest that the level of poverty has declined significantly in U.P. but relative position in terms of share of poor in U.P. with respect to India has increased. Data from Annual Plan 2004-05 suggest declining trend in poverty from 29.5 per cent in 2001-02 to 27.8 per cent in 2003-04, 26.97 per cent in 2004-05 and assume further decline to 25.4 per cent in 2006-07 despite all sorts of unfavourable situation (Annual Plan 2004-05, vol. I, p. 79). Using indirect method of poverty estimation the Central Planning Commission estimated the incidence of headcount poverty for rural U.P. during 1999-2000 to be 31.22 per cent that corresponds to the monthly per capita expenditure of Rs. 336.88. Major concentration of poor has been found in rural area. Further regional break up indicates that central U.P. has highest concentration followed by eastern U.P. Moreover, OBCs and SCs constitute highest concentration to the tune of 47.6 and 34.6 per cent respectively. There is hardly any difference in the level of poverty between Hindu and Muslim in rural areas but there has been significant difference in urban areas where Muslims are more poor than that of the Hindu. However, Tyagi did not deal with alternative estimates of poverty based on direct method. Another chapter on poverty with an alternative estimate from the same round of NSS data worked out by Diwakar (2005) suggests much higher level of calorie deficiency and poverty in Uttar Pradesh. Using direct method of poverty estimation with NSS 55th Round data for the year 1999-2000, the incidence of headcount poverty for rural

Uttar Pradesh based on the calorie norm of 2400 kcal is estimated to be 64 per cent that corresponds to monthly per capita expenditure of Rs. 455. Thus, we get a difference in the estimates of headcount poverty by these two methods for rural U.P. at a magnitude of 30 per cent. Taking 2200 kcal norm the estimates turned out to be 27.5 and 47 per cent respectively and associated monthly per capita expenditures are 325 and 400 respectively.

Considering interstate variation in the estimates of poverty into account one can hardly escape the conclusion that incidence of poverty estimated through direct method has been much higher than official indirect estimates. So long, we accept calorie intake as criteria for deciding poverty line it will be difficult to escape from this hard reality. Moreover, if we add up drinking water, sanitation, health and education in basic necessities, estimates of deprivation will touch even higher level than this one. Thus, under estimation of poverty has definite implication in terms of policies and allocation of resources for poverty eradication.

It will not be out of place to mention here that rural income of U.P. is largely dependent on agriculture and allied activities. This sector has therefore significant influence on poverty. Agricultural economy of state has not been performing satisfactorily as Diwakar has dealt in his chapter on agriculture. Nayak has questioned effectiveness of irrigation, which is a crucial input for agricultural production amidst vagaries of monsoon. It is a matter of investigation as to how poverty could be reduced significantly when agriculture, which remained shelter of larger number of the people of the U.P. did not grow satisfactorily. Recent Census data of 2001 do not suggest significant shift of workforce in industry or other sectors. Therefore, working out strategies for reducing the level of poverty has remained and will remain a challenge before policy makers and implementing agencies.

The backlog of unemployment in state in 2004-05 is 25 lakh persons. The total under employed in the state has been estimated 99 lakh persons. In addition, new entrants in 2004-05 will be around 14 lakhs. Thus, number of unemployed would be 39 lakhs and under employed would be 99 lakhs for whom employment has to be provided during the tenth plan. Generation of employment is linked to growth of income. On the basis of employment elasticity (0.45) it has been estimated that targeted growth of 8% per annum would generate employment for about 14.64 lakh during annual plan period (Annual Plan 2004-05, vol. I, p. 84). But with a lower growth rate of 3 per cent per annum, employment generation could be quite lower than expectations added with the problems of under employed for which extra effort is required in the remaining years of the tenth plan. Therefore the problem of unemployment will further be aggravated. However, one can expect some kind of let up from implementation of Employment Guarantee Act subject to the level of efficient implementation.

Rising open as well as disguise unemployment is another dimension of concerns that emerged from analysis of a chapter on poverty and unemployment. Tyagi found sharp increase in marginalisation of workforce indicating deterioration in quality of employment. Agriculture still remains the mainstay but shift in occupation towards non-agriculture has also been found. Although live register shows declining number of unemployed in employment exchange, it does not necessarily indicate decreasing unemployment. It might suggest indifference of educated youth for inconsequential registration for employment in organised public sector. In view of the disappointing and jobless growth, situation of unemployment would have aggravated further. Recent announcement and distribution of unemployment allowances to live registered has again showed swelling effect in the volume unemployment. Tyagi suggests to expedite necessary measures for achieving growth to higher level, identify labour intensive opportunities for public and private investment, improve social infrastructure, enhance capabilities of poor, strengthen social security measures, create income generating assets, diversify agriculture, initiate and strengthen special drive for employment of weaker section, and involve local bodies in implementation of the employment and anti poverty programmes.

Besides investment in physical infrastructure,

industrialisation, and region specific schemes, investment in poverty alleviation programmes in rural and urban areas for creating employment and employable assets, remains major component for development and distributive justice. Chapter on 'Rural Development and Poverty Alleviation' by N.M.P. Verma presents scheme wise assessment of important rural development programmes and their physical and financial targets and achievements. Besides these, this chapter deals with specific schemes on infrastructure and employment. Some of the schemes have been able to achieve their targets. However, this chapter also indicates towards some missing links in implementations and coordination besides undesired political interferences and suggests future strategies. Coordination among various departments is also imperative for fast execution and success. Panchayati Raj institutions may be made transparent in order to solve problems at the local level. Emphasis may be given on deciding priorities at the local level. Local planning may be cost effective also. Regional balancing is equally missing during target setting and fund allocation. This needs to be corrected through inter departmental coordination. Establishment cost may also be reduced and rationalized time to time. Mere formation of SHG may not be helpful SHGs may be supported with motivation and basic infrastructure and liberal credit with due screening of cases. This will enhance success rate of beneficiaries. After construction of awaas there should be quick distribution to beneficiaries. This may reduce maintenance cost as well.

Witnessing high growth of urban population in U.P. in recent census 2001 has compounded challenges before the housing, urban development, and employment and poverty alleviation programmes during the Tenth Plan. Addition of dwelling units remained a challenge amidst non-availability of funds in the first two years of the Plan. National Capital Region, Nagar Vikas Yojana, and Integrated Development of Small and Medium Towns, are the major programmes for urban development. A.N. Pandey found disproportionate and skewed allocation of resources away from the basic priorities. In order to address the issues of urban employment and poverty alleviation, Swarn Jayanti Shahari Rojgar Yojana (SJSRY), and National Slum Development Programme (NSDP) have been in operation. SJSRY has many components of self and wage employment, training and rehabilitations of urban poor. Plan outlay for these schemes have been lower than that of the Ninth Plan. Moreover, gap between outlay and proportionate annual allocation remained in the case of SJSRY also. A great deal of systematic and transparent efforts are required to make the impacts of these schemes visible on urban poor.

Social Development is a major challenge for the development and qualitative transformation of Uttar Pradesh. CMIE estimates suggest that elementary education has been strengthened in 1990s in comparison to 1980s. Compound annual rate of growth of primary school per lakh population in 1980s was -1.79 per cent, which was improved to 0.88 per cent in 1990s. CARG for Middle and Higher School for the same period has was -1.44 and 2.62 per cent respectively. Many new experiments have been initiated for controlling dropouts. Mid Day Meal has been introduced for retaining boys and girls in education. However, experience of Sarva Siksha Abhiyan and mid day meal remained much to be desired. Availability of teacher has been addressed to some extent through Shikshamitra. Quality of Mid Day Meal needs to be improved substantially. Expansion of Primary Health Centres slowed down in 1990s compared to 1980s. Its growth rate was 18.03 per cent in 1980s, which was decelerated to 2.28 per cent in 1990s. Hospital and dispensary beds witnessed even negative rate of growth from 0.9 per cent to -1.39 per cent. Therefore, education and health need special care in order to build an educated and healthy society.

Chapter on Social Development discussed Education, Population, Health, and Voluntary Sector in which Manoj Agarwal deals with emphasis on elementary and female education and underlined indifference in specific initiative for literacy drive for the girl child. This chapter also raises concerns for highest birth and death rates in the state and emphasised that in absence of clear-cut targets for welfare, awareness, and facilities the Tenth Plan might not achieve the desired goal towards reduction in birth and death rates. Lack of strong policy on health may result in despair despite having emphasis on health sector. Voluntary sector has got wider acceptance for major role in social development and increased allocation of resources has also been made but mapping of good organisations and data bank on their track record of performance and social acceptability are yet to be done. Therefore, mere allocation of resources without proper exercise may not help in drawing any conclusion.

In order to ensure social justice, initiatives for empowerment of the weaker and historically disadvantaged section of the society—agriculture labourer, SCs, STs, OBCs and women have been main thrusts of development A chapter on ' Living Condition and Survival Strategies of Agricultural Labour in Uttar Pradesh' is an endeavour of D.M. Diwakar to examine the basic condition of livelihood of agricultural labourers and their survival strategies amidst depressed wage, unrewarding employment, burdened with debts and informal bondage, coercion and often subhuman treatment in the syndrome of abject poverty. Development of technology and infrastructure has created some avenues and space to supplement income through non-farm earnings but still inadequate to meet their basic needs. Common property resources (CPR), access to which is although getting restricted gradually by the dominant section of the society, remain a significant relief for their survival. However limited accessibility to CPR is not free from informal bondage and unpaid work to please the so-called masters, farmers cum moneylender, who virtually control the CPR. Prominence of market strategy and role of State in globalised finance has made them worse and there does not seem any letup. They are yet to get mobilised and organised as class in themselves towards consolidating class for themselves to repose their confidence to create favourable condition for their freedom and self-respect, which may appear rhetoric but perhaps an answer to get away from exploitative syndrome. Dealing with the issues of social justice and empowerment relating to gender and weaker sections, D.R. Sahoo in a chapter on empowerment and social justice discusses various initiatives for empowerment of women, SCs, STs, and OBCs to end discriminations, raise consciousness, enhance capabilities, fix corporate social responsibility and efficient management and utilisation of funds. This chapter also enumerates various social security measures for weaker sections of the society but proper implementation remains real challenge. Social justice is still far away. Only increased participation associated with training can provide practicable solution. Before initiation of any programmes in a given area, consciousness boost up initiatives are required not only for SCs, STs, and OBCs but also for general population so that space for acceptance may be created.

There has been general agreement that investment is the function of growth. In order to examine this functional relation for Uttar Pradesh, plan document (Annual Report 2004-05, vol I-I, p. 14) suggests that incremental capital output ratio for the year ending Ninth Plan, i.e., 2001-02 was 4.08. Growth rate of the state income for this year was 4.5 per cent (ibid, p. 72). Thus, saving/ investment rate can be worked out as 18.4 (4.08 x 4.5) per cent. Target set for the Tenth Plan was 8 per cent. With a given ICOR saving/investment required for 8 per cent growth rate of the economy could be 32.64 (4.08 × 8) per cent. Thus, target to rise saving was about 77.4 per cent more than that of the base level of 18.4 per cent in order to achieve 8 per cent growth rate. For the first two years about 3 per cent growth per annum could be achieved. Thus, this appears to be a big challenge rather unachievable and unrealistic as this required investment rate of 32.64 per cent for this state. This rate is even higher than the central government, which has higher rate of investment than that of U.P.

It is worth noting here that the Tenth Plan of the government of India has set a target of 8 per cent along with recommendations of positive policies and programmes for changing the sectoral pattern and technology in favour of labour intensive production (GOI, 2002b: 144). Needless to mention that in order to achieve this growth rate a higher rate of investment is needed. Average rate of investment during 1992-93 to 1999-2000 was 24.4 per cent and average growth rate was around 6.5 per cent. This implies an incremental capital output ratio (ICOR) of 3.75 per cent. Thus, in order to achieve a growth rate of 8 per cent would require an increment in the rate of investment to 30 per cent of GDP. This will further require increased domestic savings and foreign investment (GOI, 2002a: 83). However, we all know that achieving 8 per cent growth rate remained unattainable except one year for the Indian economy also (Diwakar, 2003).

Plan document of U.P. suggests that 29.4 per cent of aggregate investment required (Rs. 364645 crore) to achieve 8 per cent at given ICOR would be mobilized by the public sector and 70.6 per cent by private sector (Tenth Five Year Plan, GoUP, vol. I, p. 14). Therefore the target growth rate is largely dependent on private sector investment. Looking at the growth rates of two years it appears that investment by private sector could not be mobilized substantially to accelerate the growth rate of the economy. Data on private investment are not available for analysis. Moreover, Plan document did not have technical notes on calculating various figures, for example on ICOR. In such a situation, assessing growth targets and resultant figures remain a difficult proposition without a separate study.

There is hardly any disagreement that development has direct relation with *inter alia* resource mobilisation, allocation and investment. Allocation of resources for the Tenth Plan suggests that percentage share of agreed outlay for General Economic Services has been placed in top priority. Other sectors got lower percentage outlay than that of the Ninth plan. Utilisation of funds *inter alia* decides the level of effective implementation of the programmes. Mid Term Appraisal (MTA) of the Tenth Five Year Plan suggests that over all annual utilisation of funds for 2002-03 to 2004-05 (including anticipated and proposed) is to be only 26.57 per cent. Proportionately it should have been 60 per cent. General Economic Services, which is on the top priority of the Tenth Plan with 31.26 per cent of agreed outlay could utilise only 1.47 per cent of funds in three years. In most of the cases the level of utilisation is below 40 per cent (Diwakar and Nayak, 2005). However, Special Area Programme could achieve ideally above 63 per cent but this amount is insignificant in view of non- utilization in other heads. Provisions and allocations have seldom matched. MTA suggests that over all annual utilisation of funds in the year 2002-03 was to the tune of 90.55 per cent of the allocation for the year, which is quite lower than the proposed one. Out of which capital expenditure also remained to the level of 93.43 per cent. Second year of plan suggest that expected expenditure was quite lower than allocation. It is expected to come down to 79.26 per cent and capital expenditure earmarked for the year is also to be about 86.04 per cent. But annual slot itself is much below to the proportionate level. This needs to be addressed on priority basis

Actual fiscal deficit of this state at the end of the Ninth Five Year Plan was at the tune of Rs. 9898.13 crore in 2001-02 which was reduced to Rs. 9496.9 in 2002-03 but revised estimate in 2003-04 indicate staggering increase to the tune of Rs. 20413.89 crore because of payment of arrears of central public sector units by U.P. Electricity Corporation, however, in 2004-05 it was estimated to be reduced to the level of 10398.46 crore. Interstate comparison of gross fiscal deficit as a ratio to net state domestic product (NSDP) in selected states suggests that position of U.P. in 1999-2000 (6.7 per cent) was better than Bihar (9.7), West Bengal (9.5), Rajasthan (9.1), and Orissa (11.4) and worse than other states. Fiscal deficit as percentage of SDP, which was 5.3 in 2001-02 decreased to 4.9 per cent in 2002-03 and 2003-04 and increased to 5.9 per cent in 2004-05 (R.E.) and 5.3 per cent in 2005-06 (B.E.).

Plan expenditure (at constant prices) during the entire Eighth Five Year Plan fell short of the outlay by 26.3 per cent in U.P., which happened to be much less than Bihar (67.8%) and Orissa (46.9%). This situation continued in Ninth Plan and first two years of Tenth Plan also. The per capita plan expenditure also showed a decline with some fluctuations over the years. This was because of heavy shortfall in total plan expenditure as compared to the outlay during the years. The huge gap between the approved outlay and expenditure in U.P. was alarming. U.P. provided more funds for energy sector at the time of allocation but it could hardly be implemented. The expenditure on irrigation was less than what was provided.

Dealing with sector wise break up suggests that in the Ninth Five Year Plan year 2002-03 special area programme, transport in general and capital expenditure in agriculture and rural development have over scored whereas irrigation and flood control, industry, science and technology, and general economic and social services have lagged behind in terms of utilisation of funds. In the year 2003-04 also special area programmes, agriculture, rural development, energy, and general services remained satisfactory whereas irrigation and flood control, general economic services, science and technology, and social services remained under spent. Approval for the year has been much higher than the previous years but the question of utilisation remains to be handled with care. There is need to expedite finance administration and utilisation to use this scarce resources prudently and efficiently.

Outstanding liabilities of state of Uttar Pradesh have been mounting year after year which need to be addressed. During 1990-91 it was Rs. 17966 crore, which increased to 41768 crore by 1996-97 and by the end of Ninth five year Plan it was mounting to 83011 crore. During Tenth Five Year Plan also the trend remained alarming. During 2002-03 outstanding liabilities went further higher level to the tune of Rs. 91182 crore, in 2003-04, 106407 crore , in 2004-05 Rs. 116794 crore and it was estimated to the tune of Rs. 129155 crore. State borrowings expected to rise to 1, 37, 914.92 crore during 2006-07. State borrowings as percentage of GSDP, which was 44.4 per cent at the end of the Ninth Five Year Plan increased to 50.2 per cent in 2004-05. However, this ratio has declined marginally to 49.2 per cent during 2005-06. Thus, liabilities of the state have alarming trend.

A. K. Singh in his chapter on plan financing, resource mobilisation and private investment has attempted to assess the trend and behaviour of plan expenditure, fiscal health of the economy and their relationship with growth. Areas of concerns have been identified as declining plan investment, widening gap between plan outlay and expenditure, increasing market borrowing, plan expenditure mainly based on loan (to the tune of about 75 per cent, half of which becomes revenue

Table 1

Growth Rates of NSDP (with SD Error) of Uttar Pradesh at Factor Cost by Industry of Origin at 1993-94 Prices

Sector	*1960-61 to 1980-81*	*1960-61 to 1970-71*	*1971-72 to 1980-81*	*1981-82 to 1990-91*	*1991-92 to 2000-01*	*1960-61 to 2000-01*
1. Agriculture	1.73±. 0034	1.29±. 0086	2.45±. 0102	2.96±. 00303	2.15±. 00376	2.63±. 0011
2. Forestry & Logging	1.90±. 0051	5.75±. 0054	(-) 2.65 ± .00477	(-) 11018± .0142	(-) 2.33± .028	(-) 3.85 ± .00442
3. Fishing	5.52±.0028	7.97±. 0061	4.44±. 001608	12.48±. 01345	6.87±. 0042	7.54±. 0019
4. Mining & Quarring	1.12±. 012	6.35±. 036	6.34±. 025531	3.67±. 024	8.23±. 0174	7.55±. 00576
5. Manufacturing	4.52±. 0027	4.5±. 0051	6.94±. 007579	10.15±. 0072	3.68±. 011	6.41±. 00183
5.1 Registered	5.12±. 0038	5.84±. 0119	5.98±. 009134	14.05±. 0132	3.32±. 017	7.37±. 00258
5.2 Unregistered	4.04±. 0035	3.35±. 0029	7.73±. 008766	5.57±. 00325	4.04±. 0046	5.19±. 00135
6. Construction	4.69±. 0057	2.99±. 01987	4.26±. 006503	1.3±. 0050	7.76±. 00975	3.5±. 0020
7. Electricity, gas & Water Supply	12.34±. 0090	16.89±. 009	16.99±. 02768	18.64±. 00923	0.3±. 0078	11.23±. 00495
8. Transport Storage & Communication	4.43±. 00149	3.85±. 00179	5.32±. 004473	5.03±. 0030	6.35±. 0054	5.06±. 00076
8.1 Railways	4.07±. 0020	4.27±. 0035	4.83±. 006618	3.46±. 0093	4.18±. 0158	4.02±. 001511
8.2 Transport by other Means & Storage	4.59±. 00212	3.06±. 0021	5.72±. 004983	6.03±. 00255	5.97±. 0037	5.49±. 00093
8.3 Communication	5.23±. 0021	6.24±. 0058	5.32±. 004231	3.69±. 00285	12.81±. 0156	5.65±. 022
9. Trade, hotels, & Restuarent	2.70±. 00226	2.07±. 0058	3.72±. 006583	3.97±. 0026	3.94±. 00385	3.59±. 0009

10. Banking & Insurance	7.48±. 0035	6.26±. 0058	9±. 011378	16.89±. 0111	11.97±. 0139	9.97±. 0024
11. Real Estate, Ownership of Dwelling's & Business Services	2.43±. 0028	1.51±. 00001	4.99±. 008032	4.46±. 0016	1.86±. 00099	3.69±. 0012
12. Public Administration	2.45±. 0012	1.85±. 003	1.81±. 003089	9.4±. 00557	6.05±. 0065	4.81±. 0019
13. Other Services	3.12±. 0010	3.9±. 00166	2.18±. 000747	8.78±. 00713	4.86±. 00395	4.25±. 0013
Net State Domestic Product (Net State)	2.60±. 0022	2.1±. 0057	3.53±. 006301	5.09±. 0033	3.86±. 0027	3.76±. 00099
Per Capita NSDP (Rs.)	2.21± 0.0013	1.8± 0.0001	3.17± 0.00433	2.73± 0.0033	1.64± 0.00257	2.63± 0.0007

Source: Calculated from data generated by Economic & Political Weekly Research Foundation, Mumbai.

expenditure), unsustainable debt trap (as major resource - about 46 per cent - spent on debt servicing in which 30 per cent goes to payment of interest only), implications of recommendation of the Twelfth Finance Commission and indifference of financial institutions resulting into declining share of loan amount for U.P. Lower Tax GDP ratio remains the hope for mobilisation of resources besides initiating measures to restore and promote better investment environment for the private sector. Singh concludes that U.P. government has to make bold and imaginative efforts for raising investment in infrastructure and other priority areas in the public sector and to attract large private domestic and foreign investment, if the goals of stepping up economic growth and reduce poverty are to be met.

Governance occupies key role in translating policies into action at the ground, which is an uphill task. T. N. Dhar in this chapter on governance and reforms deals with various challenges before the government of U.P. including political, economic, administrative, deprivation, manpower planning and corruptions. It has been argued that many reform measures to improve governance in order to address these issues have been initiated in terms of policies, programmes and implementations. Certain positive results have also been witnessed but still there is a long way to go. Gaps between policies, programmes and implementations need to be bridged up. Imperative need of the hour is to evolve a clean and competent political management, efficient, honest and accountable bureaucracies, transparent and sensitive judiciary and administration with compassion and outreach, sound and equity oriented economic and fiscal policies, ethics led business, rule of law, strong democratic and decentralised institutions for participatory development and informed citizenry, so that state of U.P. may move ahead amidst the challenges of globalisation, free market and poverty and disparity.

Thus, it emerged from the above description that challenges to bring the economy on the track of development is an uphill task. Target to improve productivity in agriculture remained a serious challenge amidst vagaries of monsoon. Utilisation of funds was restricted through punched allocation.

One has to look into the process of implementation of various schemes as under utilisation of funds and decelerating growth rates, which is a challenge towards achieving the targets and goals set. Expansion of economic and social infrastructure particularly irrigation and electricity remained the crux of the problems. Growing unemployment in the situation of lower growth rates is obvious. Mounting debt burden and fiscal deficit is another area of concern for financial discipline. Estimates of poverty need to be straighten out to capture real picture of inequality in this state, as many of the studies show declining poverty amidst decelerating growth rates in 1990s. If these findings are any indicative there is an imperative to reprioritise allocation of resources and reorient implementation of programmes and ensure effective utilisation of resources for accelerating growth of U.P. economy, so that set goal of reducing unemployment, poverty and inequality may be covered at least partially.

Reference

Ghosh, B. and P. De (2004): How do different categories of Infrastructure Affect Development: Evidence from Indian States, *Economic and Political Weekly*, vol. 39, No. 42, October 16-22, pp. 4645-4657.

Diwakar, D.M., (2003): Employment Generation: A Shift from Commitment to Popular Prescriptions, A critical analysis of the Tenth Five Year Plan in India, *Mainstream*, December 27, 2003, pp. 51-60.

Diwakar, D.M., (2005): *Avibhajit Uttar Pradesh Maen Vyapt Garibi ka Smikshatmak Vishleshhan* (Hindi), First Annual Conference Volume, UP-Uttaranchal Economic Association, pp. 97-119.

Diwakar, D.M. and S. Nayak (coordinated): Mid Term Appraisal of the Tenth Five Year Plan of Uttar Pradesh, Department of Planning, Government of Uttar Pradesh, 2005.

Economic and Political Weekly Research Foundation, Mumbai,

Government of India, National Sample Survey Organisation, 55th Round, 1999-2000.

Government of India (2002a): Report of Taskforce on Employment Opportunities, Planning Commission, Academic Foundation, New Delhi.

Government of India (2002b): Tenth Five Year Plan 2002-07, Planning Commission, New Delhi.

Government of U.P. (2002): Tenth Five Year Plan, Planning Department, Lucknow.

Government of U.P. Annual Plan 2004-05, Department of Planning.

Government of U.P., Statistical Diary, 2004, Department of Planning.

Singh, A.K. et. al. (2004): Indian Journal of Labour Economics, Conference number, 2004.

Government of U.P., *Uttar Pradesh ke Krishhi Ankre*, Directorate of Agriculture.

1

GROWTH LINKAGES IN AGRICULTURE OF UTTAR PRADESH
Constraints, Options and Strategies

D.M. Diwakar

I. Introduction

There has been an increasing rate of growth in agriculture of Uttar Pradesh (UP) from 1960s until 1991 and thereafter growth rate of this sector in 1990s has declined. Growth rates of cropped area, production and productivity for all crops and food crops have indicated similar trend. However, non-food crops have shown increasing trend in area expansion but production and productivity have shown declining trend. Despite the fact that share of agriculture in state domestic production of Uttar Pradesh has considerably declined, agriculture still remains dominant shelter and provides livelihood for 66 per cent of workforce (Census of India, 2001) and their dependents. It contributed about 33.7 per cent of the state income in 2003-04 (GoUP, 2004). *Pro rata* estimates of per capita income at constant prices (1993-94) from agriculture and allied sectors with regard to rural population as proxy for this sector's population in 2003-04 suggest that per capita income from agriculture is very low (about Rs. 2426). Whereas per capita total income of state is about Rs. 5702. Average expenditure of the rural population as per 55th round of NSS is about Rs. 467 and average consumption in terms of calorie intake is about 2327 Kcal. NSS estimates suggest that about 64 per cent of the rural population survives with 2375 calories intake. Calorie intake as proxy to deprivation could be debatable but these data show that despite sizeable contribution in the state income large number of households is surviving in miseries. So long we accept calorie intake as a measure of deprivation and poverty there is need to examine the process of deprivation of the majority dependent on rural economy and work out strategies accordingly.

This exercise intends to examine the growth performance of agriculture and comprehend growth linkages. It is hypothesised that agriculture has significantly direct relation with land and water management, modernisation of agriculture and price structure. Value of agriculture output at constant prices 1993-94 has been considered as indicator of agricultural growth. For land and water management, cropping intensity and status of irrigation has been taken into account. Fertiliser consumption has been considered as a proxy of the use of modern inputs and income deflator price relatives of agriculture and non- agriculture has been taken for price behaviour. Assumptions for this study carry irrigation as the king pin for development, which promotes intensive use of land reflected in cropping intensity through using traditional as well as high yielding varieties of seeds, chemical fertiliser. Price relatives reflect price received and paid in the process of transaction by the farmers. Thus this study examines the effects of irrigation, fertiliser consumption, cropping intensity, and price relatives. While doing so it will add the contexts of structural challenges, initiatives and lessons.

This study is divided into four parts. First part deals with the introduction, brief methodology and data sources. Second part analyses growth profile of UP in general and of agriculture in particular which receives and contributes for the development of agriculture and non-agriculture as well. Third part deals with linkages and constraints, and fourth part is an endeavour to consolidate findings towards suggesting strategies. This exercise is mainly based on secondary data. In order to estimate growth rates splicing or income deflator method has been applied for constructing a common series of data at 93-94 prices. Non-linear regression model has been used for estimating growth rates and linear regression with dummy variable technique has been applied for exploring functional relation of various factors with agricultural growth. Needless to mention that this exercise has an indicative value to examine various factors to begin with. Therefore, it may not serve the purpose to suggest finer details for policies.

II Growth Profile of Economy

Growth performance of an economy can generally and customarily be comprehended through estimated domestic products and per capita distribution at factor cost by industry of origin. If we take a longer view through estimates of annual compound growth rate of net state domestic product (NSDP) with reference to time for the state economy of Uttar Pradesh (U.P.), it is evident that NSDP between 1960-61 and 2002-03 has grown annually at 3.79 per cent (Table 1). Economy could achieve highest ever rate of growth of NSDP in 1980s to the tune of 5.1 per cent per annum. However, in 1990s it was declined to 3.86 per cent. Per capita NSDP has grown merely by 2.54 per cent during 1960-61 to 2001-02. Highest score of growth rate was in 1970s (3.17 per cent) and thereafter started declining in successive decades. It has touched its lowest rate (1.64 per cent per annum) during 1990-2001-02.

Plan wise annual compound growth rates at constant prices suggest that seventh plan could achieve highest growth rates to the tune of 6.61 per cent. This rate of growth could not be sustained in subsequent plans. It declined to 5.22 in Eighth Five Year Plan, which further decelerated to 4.34 per cent in the Ninth Five Year Plan. Similarly rate of growth of per capita NSDP registered 4.25 per cent in Seventh Plan which came down to 2.87 in the Eighth Plan and it reached at the lowest level to 0.93 per cent during Ninth Plan (Table 2). Declining growth rates of NSDP and per capita NSDP is a matter of serious concern as these reflect declining per capita purchasing power of the economy. Agriculture as one of the major players of the state economy is supposed to be affected adversely in this context.

Share of NSDP of agriculture at constant price of 93-94 for the economy of U.P. has come down from 64.87 per cent in 1960-61 to 57.21 per cent in 70-71, 50.89 per cent in 1980-81, 40.97 per cent in 1990-91 and 35.7 per cent in 2000-01. However, Statistical Diary 2003 of U.P. suggests that share of agriculture and allied activities in 2000-01 have reduced to 36.3 per cent of state income, which has further reduced to 32.7 in 2004-05. Value of agricultural production per hectare at constant prices 93-94 has increased from Rs. 8125 in 1960-61 to Rs. 9381 in 1970 -71, 11538 in 1980-81, 15723 in 1990-91 and 19567 in 2000-01. Per capita production of food grains, which was on an average 511 gram per day in 1950-53, has been raised to 723.3 gram per day in 2003-04. Apparently, it seems that the progress remained upward.

Area, Production and Productivity

Claims and indicators of agricultural development suggest that economy of Uttar Pradesh has substantially grown from the position it has inherited at the time of the transfer of power from the colonial British Rule. In terms of land resources, net sown area (NSA) has increased from 162.3 lakh hectares in 1950-51 to 174 lakh ha. in 1995-96 but later declined to 168.12 lakh hectares in 2001-02 (Table 3). Perhaps this decline is because of creation of new state Uttaranchal. About 10.3 lakh ha. land area is current fallow and 6.24 lakh ha. is other fallow land. Besides this, about 5.18 lakh ha. cultivable land is yet to be brought into cultivation. Altogether 21.7 lakh ha. land area is lying unused. One may be tempted to guess that perhaps unfavourable and unpredictable monsoon might have driven the farmers to turn indifferent in absence of adequate assured irrigation. However, percentage of area irrigated to NSA for corresponding period indicates substantial expansion of irrigation infrastructure. Percentage Area irrigated has increased from 29.8 to 76.3 per cent. Irrigation intensity has been raised from about 108 per cent to 142 per cent. As a result, cropping intensity has also increased from 123 per cent to 151.4 per cent during reference year. However, micro study also suggests that cropping intensity in many parts of the state has remained constant (Saith and Tankha, 1997:86). Moreover, cropping intensity is quite low in U.P. compared to other states such as, Punjab (192), Haryana (173), and West Bengal (171).

Besides irrigation, technological progress in the form of farm implements has also been witnessed. Introduction of iron plough and then use of tractors, which has replaced the draught cattle in post green revolution period (Ray, 1996: 621-27) has resulted into structural change significantly. Introduction of energized pumping sets, thresher, crusher, harvesting combined devices, added with the application of HYV, etc., has changed the cropping pattern. Nevertheless, technological development was generally confined to a few regions, which were endowed with infrastructure facilities like irrigation, credit, market, etc, (Sharma and Haque, 1996: 639-44). Use of chemical fertilizer, pesticides, and weedicides have induced agricultural production and productivity particularly of rich peasantry whereas poor peasant remained constrained due to lack of input and credit at the right time of the season of the crop.

Performance of agriculture may be examined in terms of area expansion, volume of production and productivity. It may further be categorized in food crops and non-food crops. Data provided for different crops by the Directorate of Agriculture of Uttar Pradesh form basis to analyze the facts. Average annual rate of growth of the area under food grains production has been declining and turned to be negative in 1990s (Table 4) and in the case of production rate of growth has declined from 3.05 per cent per annum during 1970-71 to 1990-91 to 1.78 per cent in the 1990s. However, overall production during 1950-51 to 2000-01 has increased by 2.59 per cent per annum. Productivity has increased in post green revolution period until 1991, which subsequently could not be sustained later and witnessed declining trend. However, if one takes accounts of triennium ending average at two points of time it suggests differently. Data for triennium ending 2002 suggests that nearly 80 per cent of total cropped area in U.P. is under food grains production. If one compares this situation with triennium ending 1976, (72.6 per cent) there is an increase of about 8 per cent. Another state, which has similar trend, is Punjab. Punjab registered 8.8 per cent increase. At the all India level, there has been decline in general in area of food grains. However, 64.4 per cent of total cropped area in India is still under food grains production (Vyas, 2004: 5577). This indicates that value added agriculture is yet to make dent and market driven production in this sector is yet to dominate over subsistence agriculture.

Growth rates of non-food crops reveal decline of area until 1990-91 and subsequent increase in coverage of non-food crops. This explains about substitution of the area under food crops. So far production of non-food crops was concerned there was increase in productivity until 1990-91 and subsequently it registered significant declining trend. As a result, productivity had a negative trend during 1990s. This needs to be explained and examined in details about access to technology, credit, input and production markets. Non-food crops particularly. Potato and sugarcane growers have been facing critical situation. At the time of harvest, price of potato touches the lowest point quite below the level of minimal cost. In absence of retaining capacity, proper storage, credit and insurance farmers are left in lurch. Limited accessibility of inadequate facilities and infrastructure further aggravate the situation of majority of farmers belonging to small and marginal groups. In such a precarious condition, farmers prefer to leave the crops in the field itself to avoid further aggravation of crisis. Thus, in absence of proper infrastructure development it appears that technological effects of green revolution could not be sustained in either food grains or non-food crops, which resulted into declining area, production and productivity of entire agriculture in 1990s in Uttar Pradesh. Moreover, supply elastic nature of agricultural prices due to lack of sufficient supporting infrastructure such as storage, credit, insurance, etc., amidst unmet pressing need resulting into distress sales even by the net buyers worked as disincentives in absence of retaining capacity of the farmers

If one considers latest accounts at the ending year of the Ninth Five Year Plan total food grains production was 44187 thousand tones, out of which 15877 tones were of Kharif and 28310 tones were of Rabi crops. However, in the beginning of the Tenth Plan the production was reduced by 13.5 per cent because of the failure of monsoon. Kharif crops were most severely damaged, and production was reduced by 24.46 per cent and production of Rabi crops were damaged by 7.38 per cent. Monsoon was normal in the year 2003-04, therefore negative rate of growth of production was offset, and food grains could increase by 0.55 per cent recovered by 16.26 per cent increase in production. Sharp increase was registered in kharif crops, i.e., 33.31 per cent and 8.47 per cent in rabi crops (Table 5). This sharp increase was because of lower base in 2002-03. If one compares with the production of 2001-02, the increase was merely 0.55 per cent in total production and 0.71 per cent in kharif and 0.47 per cent in rabi production. In the light of the past experience this year in 2004-05 the production of food grains is bound to come down as 61 districts of the state has been declared under drought hit region. Thus, anticipated production of food grains for the year 2004-05 will be lower than that of the level of 2003-04.

Estimates of sectoral net state domestic product of agriculture and allied activities available at different constant prices have been spliced at 93-94 prices and their growth rates have been calculated. Result suggests that agriculture of U.P. has grown on an average of 2.63 per cent per annum between 1960-61 and 2000-01. During 1960s, agriculture grew by merely 1.29 per cent, 2.45 per cent in 1970s and touched its highest rate of 2.96 per cent in 1980s. During 1990s, growth rate has decelerated to 2.15 per cent. Fishery has maintained its impressive growth rates at 7.5 per cent per annum but forestry has registered negative rate of growth. Value of standard error attached with estimated growth rates suggests that possibility of variation in estimated rate of growth has been nominal (Table 6).

III Linkages and Constraints

Growth process of an economy is largely a reflection of the production structure. In order to understand linkages of production structure of agrarian economy of U.P., here a few indicators are discussed. Land as a prime resource for production other factors, such as level of irrigation, cropping intensity, use of fertilised and other modern inputs, access to credit, relative prices of output, allocation of resources and investment, etc. decides the growth process. In this section, an effort has been made to consider a few important factors influencing growth of agriculture in U.P.

Status of Irrigation

Net irrigated area of agriculture of U.P. has been increasing from 62.55 lakhs hectares in 1966-67 to 94.53 lakh hectares in 1980-81 and further to 128.28 lakhs hectares in 2001-02. However, the net irrigated area remained almost constant during 1998-99 to 2000-01 and again increased to 128.28 lakh hectares in 2001-02. The proportion of net irrigated area to net cropped area has increased from 36.12 percent in 1966-67 to 54.89 percent in 1980-81, 73.70 percent in 2000-01 and 76.30 percent in 2001-02. However, compound rate of growth of gross irrigated area has declined marginally from 2.91 in 1980s to 2.57 in the 1990s. Net irrigated area by private sources such as private tube-well/pump sets constitute nearly 87.09 lakh hectares, which is 68 percent of the net irrigated area, whereas major and medium sources through canal irrigation possesses at 27.19 lakh hectares, which is nearly 21 percent of the net irrigated area. Despite this expansion of irrigation, network intermittent droughts have been experienced in the agriculture of state economy. Needless to say, that repeated occurrence of flood and lack of effective water management has been major deterrent for this stagnation. This also reflects the degree of effectiveness of irrigation networks of the state. Beginning of the Tenth Plan, i.e., 2002-03 was badly affected by failure of monsoon. So was the case for the year 2004-05 also. About 61 districts of this state have been declared drought hit in the year

2004-05. Often occurrence of drought in Uttar Pradesh is also an excuse to have its implication on water recharging capacity, which in turn affects water table and efficiency of irrigation. However, having normal monsoon in previous year should have less aggravating impacts on agriculture if irrigation network is effective. Moreover, declining percentage of resource allocation on the head of irrigation and flood control affects operation and maintenance of irrigation networks. Shallow private tube wells and pump sets for irrigation, which covers large proportion of net irrigated area are affected by scanty rainfall and therefore expansion of deep tube wells becomes an imperative to counter the problems in irrigation. Role of public investment in irrigation may have necessary bearing.

It is evident from data (Table 3) that NSA remained almost constant and later declined in 1990s. There is possibility that even with given strength of irrigation declining NSA might have improved the percentage of net irrigated area. Increasing percentage indicates expansion of irrigation networks. Data suggest that until 1990-91 there was tendency to improve irrigation intensity also but in 1990s despite increasing irrigation cover no significant impact is found in irrigation intensity. Even if one takes face value of irrigation percentage during 1999-2000, this state was far behind to many states (for example, Punjab 94. 5 per cent and Haryana 81.3 per cent). This needs further examination of the factors responsible in this regard. Moreover, upward movement of cropping intensity was also slowed down. It will be pertinent to draw the attention of the readers that this state has utilised only 64.3 per cent of surface water and 68.9 per cent of ground water against ultimate potential by 2001-02. However, utilisation in strict technical sense is simply the creation of irrigation utility and not irrigation to the field as such. If an irrigation network and source is created say for 100 hectares it does not necessarily imply that 100 hectares land of farmers are irrigated. Gaps are always there in between creation of capacity and availability to the farmers. This indicates about the level of effectiveness of the irrigation network for the farmers. This partly also answers about the recurring impacts on drought and ineffectiveness of irrigation structures.

Fertiliser Consumption

Volume of fertilizer consumption in agriculture of U.P. has been increasing along with increasing coverage of irrigation despite decline of NSA. Total fertilizer consumption in U.P. has increased from 410.54 thousand tones in 1970-71 to 3352.13 thousand tones in 2001-02. In terms of per hectare consumption there is an increase from 23.72 kg/ha to 199.39 kg/ha (Table 7). However, estimates of compound annual growth rate suggest that there has been a declining trend in the rate of growth from 6.72 in 1980s to 3.8 percent in 1990s.

If one goes further to analyze proportionate use of fertilizer ingredients ineffectiveness of extension services are exposed. Desirable norm of the use of fertilizers—Nitrogen (N), Phosphate (P) and Potash (K) is recommended as 4:2:1 respectively. Mid Term appraisal of the Ninth Five Year Plan of the Government of India suggests that national proportion of NPK has been 8.5:3.1:1 in 1998-99 (GOI, 2000: 57). Situation in U.P. is more vulnerable than that of national level. Moreover, disproportionate use of NPK has been increasing fast. During 1990-91, it was 18:5:1, which has increased to 25:8:1 in 2001-02. Regional variation was even worse (Table 7). In Central U.P, this ratio was 42:15:1, in eastern U.P. it was 27.5:7:1, in Bundelkhand it was 431:280:1 and in Western U.P., it was 20:6:1. One of the most plausible explanations of this kind of disproportional could be absence of effective extension services and lack of awareness among the farmers. Another reason is linked with rain fed agriculture, where farmers use mostly nitrogen fertilizer for two reasons—one, when there is rain they use fertilizer to see the crop greener and second, subsidy content in Nitrogen fertilizer makes it cheaper than other ingredients. Majority of marginal and small farmers practice this disproportional. Dry land farming generally has consumption of Nitrogen, Phosphates and Potass. This imbalance has affected fertility of soil adversely and environmental problems have cropped up. There is an urgent need to address this issue to restore environmental balance in agriculture. Potential farmers may be sensitized at the grassroots level and training for preparing organic manure and vermi—culture at participatory level need to be expedited. Even for present level of ad hoc unmanaged agriculture, they are constrained by non-availability of timely credit.

Agricultural Credit

Agricultural credit has widened its horizon and many new instruments have entered to facilitate farmers of Uttar Pradesh in recent past. Besides crop loan, kisan credit card and national Agricultural Insurance Scheme have been introduced. However, comparative picture of agricultural credit between 1980s and 1990s are not encouraging. CMIE estimates suggest that compound annual rate of growth of per capita credit to agriculture was 16.01 per cent in 1980s but this was decelerated to 8.36 per cent in 1990s. However, latest data published by the CMIE Monthly Review of U.P. Economy, January 2005 for Uttar Pradesh suggest that a total sum of Rs. 1912.01 crore have been distributed till September 2004 as crop loan for Kharif season 2004, which 95.6 per cent of the target achievement. Of this cooperative Bank, distributed Rs. 586.63 crore that was 90.2 per cent of the amount earmarked for it. Commercial Bank distributed Rs. 1325.38 crore during the season almost closer to the target amount of Rs. 1350 crore. There had always been shortfall in achievement with respect to target. During the Rabi season 2003-04, crop loan worth Rs. 699.21 crore were distributed by cooperative banks, which were 80 per cent of the target of Rs. 875 crore. Commercial banks distributed Rs. 1842.68, which was more than the target. However, in total there was shortfall in achievements with respect to target for last two years of the Tenth Plan. To facilitate farmers with better credit, Cooperative and Commercial Banks have introduced Kisan Credit Card. During 2002-03, Rs. 32 lakh was distributed against target of Rs. 35 lakh, which was subsequently reduced to Rs. 27.23 lakh against Rs. 35 lakh in 2003-04. This has further reduced to 15.56 lakh against 25 lakh until 30.11.2004. Therefore, implementation and coverage need to be evaluated further as it has to go a long way to become a helping hand for small and marginal farmers.

National Agriculture Insurance Scheme covered 3.59 farmers against 5.35 lakh ha. and 414.42 crore insured amount with a premium of 7.61 crore in Kharif of 2003 which was raised to 7.7 lakh against 17.06 lakh ha. in addition, 765.05 crore with premium of 15.95 crore for the kharif of 2004. For Rabi crops, 5.72 lakh farmers have been covered in 2002-03 against 8.29 lakh ha. and Rs. 475.45 crore with premium of Rs. 8.63 crore. Coverage has increased to 6.41 lakh farmers in 2003-04 against 10.21 lakh ha. and Rs. 558.95 crore with premium of Rs. 9.51 crore. Majority of farmers are loaner and of category of marginal and small-holdings. With this speed of credit coverage U.P. may need to go a log way. Moreover, credit transaction cost and complicated procedure to get access to credit has diluted the effectiveness of these instruments in rural areas (Singh, 2003). Credit deposit ratio in the state is about 33 per cent. If one takes district wise analysis, only 11 districts have more than 60 per cent credit deposit ratio. About 33 districts have below 50 per cent and about 26 districts have below 29 per cent in which some of the districts have as low as 16 to 21 percent, for example, in Ballia, Ouraiya and Pratapgarh. There is possibility of assessment of viability of loan as one of the factors responsible for low credit deposit ratio, but one can hardly deny that proactive role of commercial bank is also missing. Therefore, official presentation of data need cross checking of the ground realities that poor farmers have been facing. Effectiveness of the agricultural insurance and coverage need to be analyzed with care and sensitivity.

To facilitate farmers with better credit facilities Cooperative and Commercial Banks have introduced Kisan Credit Card. During 2002-03, Rs. 32 lakh was distributed against target of Rs. 35 lakh, which was subsequently reduced to Rs. 27.23 lakh against Rs. 35 lakh in 2003-04. This has further reduced to 15.56 lakh against 25 lakh until 30.11.2004. National Agriculture Insurance Scheme covered 3.59 farmers against 5.35 lakh ha. and 414.42 crore insured amount with a premium of 7.61 crore in Kharif of 2003 which was raised to 7.7 lakh against 17.06 lakh ha. and 765.05 crore with premium of 15.95 crore for the kharif of 2004. For Rabi crops 5.72 lakh farmers have been covered in 2002-03 against 8.29 lakh ha. and Rs. 475.45 crore with premium of Rs. 8.63 crore. Coverage has increased to 6.41 lakh farmers in 2003-04 against 10.21 lakh ha. and Rs. 558.95 crore with premium of Rs. 9.51 crore. Access to credit cards and efficient delivery to farmers remain a major challenge as in the case of other credit support system. Moreover, sustainability of the credit cards in absence of related superstructure is always a big question.

Infrastructure

There has been growing realisation that infrastructure building is one of the major segments to promote employment, growth and quality of life. Infrastructure has been classified broadly in three categories: Physical, social and Financial. Further segregations of these categories into irrigation, power and transport as economic physical infrastructure have been categorical to identify contribution in reducing transaction cost of production and generating employment, income and growth of the economy. Social infrastructure enhances human capabilities through education, health, housing, and recreation facilities leading towards improvement in productivity of labour and quality of life. Financial infrastructure like postal, banking, and tax capacity of the people determines the financial performance of the state. All these together constitute income-generating capability of a state. On the contrary, it has been observed that differential infrastructure facilities across the states are primarily responsible for the widening of income disparity. In case of U.P., all the three categories of infrastructure, i.e., physical, social, and financial remained almost stagnant in their relative positions in the country. However, physical infrastructure displayed better position than financial and social infrastructure (Ghosh and De, 2004). However, during Ninth and Tenth Five Year Plan emphasis have been laid on infrastructure building in the state. In order to remove critical gaps in infrastructure at the district level Rashtriya Sam Vikas Yojana (RSVY) that was sponsored by the central government. However, proper implementation remains a challenge. Public private partnership is another dimension to improve infrastructure. However, to maintain welfare states feature is a challenge as paying capacity of the majority of the small and marginal farmers need to be improved to enter in the market for infrastructure.

Relative Prices

Agricultural Prices have general tendency of becoming supply elastic and technical progress in agriculture has contributed significantly in strengthening supply of agricultural production (Singer, 1950:473 -85). In Uttar Pradesh after the Green Revolution, introduction and expansion of irrigation network, high yielding varieties of seeds, chemical fertiliser, etc., has improved production and productivity. Data suggest that movement of relative income deflator prices of agriculture and non-agriculture has also moved upward in U.P. in 1960s at the rate of 0.46 per cent per annum. During 1970s it registered a declining trend (-0.671) and in 1980s it improved in favour of agriculture until 1990-91 (0.233). Rate of change in 1960s and 1980s remained positive but statistically insignificant and not different from zero (Table 8). During 1990s relative prices has moved against agriculture (-0.864). Role of administered prices and protection might have played a positive role to neutralise negative movement against agriculture in 1960s and 1980s. However, during liberalisation and reforms in 1990s there was significant decline in relative prices against agriculture in U.P. Supply elastic nature of agricultural prices including non-food crops might have significant bearing besides the role of declining international prices to influence internal market and price mechanism, which needs to be examined in this context. Now with the emergence of new trade regime under WTO to which India is a signatory member, commitment to free market access will have its own implication to agriculture of Uttar Pradesh also. Needless to mention that U.P. is the largest producer of sugarcane, wheat, potato, guava, and mango and second largest producer of rice in the country with considerably backward agriculture. However, majority of farmers are of marginal and small-holdings that are engaged in subsistence agriculture and constrained with capital and technological access. Therefore, to switch over to value added production may be an attractive proposition for the time being but it will be a hard proposition to sustain because of limited access to infrastructure, credit and insurance, which often result into losses and non-viability syndrome. Therefore, creation of effective infrastructure and ensured access to these facilities for small and marginal farmers is one of the major challenges for faster growth of agriculture. Moreover, access to international market is further restricted due to poor capital content resulting into lower level of competence to cross non-tariff barrier and overcome SPS measures. This needs to be addressed by sufficient resources allocations on priority basis.

Structural Challenges

In order to comprehend growth process in an agrarian economy land has been the basis of productive organisation and rural assets. Transformation in productive organisation, assets and structure is an important indicator to comprehend transition process which a rural society experiences. Forms of agrarian structure are reflected in distribution of operational holdings of a society and economy. In an agrarian society of Uttar Pradesh it indicates iniquitous pattern of distribution of land to the tillers (Diwakar, 2000). Persisting inequality in distribution of land reflects the existing relations. Although land reforms were decided to be implemented effectively, partly it contributed also in narrowing down inequality in distribution of land, it remained incomplete and neglected in absence of political commitment and will (Mishra & Diwakar, 2005). Even medium-cum-big farm holdings could manage land allotment reflecting procedural lapses of the scheme. A sizeable non-deserving beneficiary household were selected at the cost of genuine potential households, because of lapses in procedure, bribery, lack of awareness and sensitive implementing agencies, etc.

Subdivision and fragmentation of landholdings was witnessed in the process of natural attrition caused by division of family consequent upon growing population. As a result, landholding size in fifty years has decreased and therefore it is also argued that inequality in distribution of landholdings has lost its relevance to some extent. So far latest data available on distribution of operational holdings (Table 9) indicates that about 75.6 per marginal holdings have possessed only 34.1 per cent of the land area whereas top ten per cent of the households possessed about 43 per cent according to the latest data available so far. Data suggest that only 0.2 per cent of the landholders owning above 25 acres of land have about 3.2 per cent of the total operational area in their possessions. If we add the households above ten acres of land they amount to 2.6 per cent of the total number of holdings above ten acres. But the area of operational holdings that they possess amounts to 19 per cent of the total area of operational holdings. Quantitatively it may appear less iniquitous for many of us but it needs a fresh assessment of the facts. Land holding size in the process of natural attrition has decreased but the question of land controlled by the same privileged class still persists. Access to land resources enabled them to avail better opportunity and access in secondary and tertiary sectors. However transfer of land has widened the land base among middle caste/class and other section of the society also. Moreover family participation irrespective of caste/class has also increased. As data suggest, majority of the farmers in state is marginal holders followed by small holdings. They together constitute about 90.1 per cent and possess 57.9 per cent of operational area. Semi-medium farms have almost equal proportion of holdings and area in their possession. Even if one ignores concealed tenancy, which is pervasive in Uttar Pradesh, there is apparent inequality in distribution of land, which explains the need for redistribution of land in Uttar Pradesh.

Concentration of landholdings measured in terms of Gini Coefficient for Quinquannial census data of agriculture suggest that Gini ratio for land concentration of operational holdings has been declining from 0.567 in 1980-81 to 0.505 in 1990-91 and 0.461 in 1995-96. However, macro data of Uttar Pradesh remained almost unchanged[2] irrespective of ownership and operational holdings with marginal increase in the coefficient in 1982 (Sharma, 1994: A-14 & A-17). Moreover the gap between ownership and operational holdings may be explained through tenancy and fluctuation in it suggests the prevalence of tenancy at will. However, individual research studies based on primary data and longitudinal studies show that Gini coefficient with respect to land concentration in Moradabad district of West Uttar Pradesh has rather increased from 0.49 in 1957-58 to 0.52 in 1993. Although, value of coefficients remained unchanged when landless households is excluded (Dreze, 1997). Similarly another longitudinal study of Aligarh district of West U.P. suggests that percentage of households owning up to 25 *bigha* lands has increased from 36.4 in 1970 to 67.6 per cent in 1987. Of course, percentage of land owning households more than 50 *bigha* lands has declined. Overall Gini coefficient in 1970 was 0.73 for the distribution of owned land on a household basis, and 0.63 on a per capita per household basis whereas corresponding figures for 1987 were 0.74 and 0.65 (Saith and Tankha, 1997; 100). Major concentration of land areas in Allahabad and Muzaffar Nagar lies with Hindu upper castes and Muslims (Srivastava, 1997).

Decades ago the government of U.P. declared complete elimination of intermediaries in this state. However, concealed tenancy is very much pervasive here in agriculture, which is a basic feature of pre capitalist land relations in agriculture. Sharecropping remains the dominant form of tenancy in Uttar Pradesh (Mishra & Diwakar, 2005) with considerable variations in terms and conditions in the lease market particularly with respect to process of production (such as cropping pattern, use of inputs, etc.), assured supply of labour, sometimes at lower wage than the market rate and sometimes free labour as well, seasonal and crop specific in view of the intensity of labour, caste network and linkages, etc. Besides 50:50 sharing of crops, rents vary in degree say 1/4, 3/8, and 2/3 of the output. It is worth mentioning that exception apart big farmers generally do not pay more than 50 per cent of the output as rent to the lessers. However the vice versa is not found. System of contract rent in cash has also emerged to minimise the risk of uncertainty towards returns through rents. There is hardly any significant let up in the intensity and extent of tenancy. However the change is perceived with respect to creating balance between land and labour in order to cope with insufficient progress in mechanisation and deficiency of working capital. A shift from leasing out as a means of appropriating rents to leasing out as a form of securing control over labour power and the appropriation of its produce has also been witnessed (Srivastava, 1997; 214-16). Those households, who are not operating their land personally and are absent from the field as it did not remain their main occupation, behave as absentee landowner in order to exercise control over the lands through different mechanism and they keep on changing of their tenants, execute bonds to treat them as their servant not tenant so that the tenant may not prove their tenancy right over the land, if situation demands. The tenants are generally at their (landowners) will and also remains at lower profile to avoid the complication and ejection from the land, which remains the only option for their survival strategy due to lack of other opportunities in non-agricultural sectors. Ruling class biases towards landowners have often been compounding the uncertainty of the tenants in the lease markets and has sometimes intensified their hardships (Kripashankar, 1997).

Tenancy market relations are found very strong and despite the fact that intermediary status has formally lost its legal ground, this class still exists strongly between state and peasants and exploitation of surplus continues through various forms of tenancies such as share cropping, contractual fixed produce, money rent, money rent in advance, etc., are pervasive in Uttar Pradesh. Rent in advance has been driving out poor peasants gradually from lease markets which have been an important source for their livelihood, employment, income and repayment of loan in absence of viable alternative. Thus, tenancy relations are of compulsive nature and mainly share of 50:50 is the modal terms of tenancy. However pre-cultivation advance rent payment system is emerging effectively, which is driving poor out of the tenancy market. Cost sharing mainly in terms of fertilizer seed and occasionally irrigation cost has been found (Diwakar, 2000a). The above analysis, thus, suggests that the question of inequality in land distribution has not lost the ground and much is yet to be done to restore the land to the tiller not only to remove the qualitative inequality in distribution of land but also to improve production, productivity of agriculture and employment and earnings status of the poor peasants.

Allocation of Resources

There has been general agreement that investment is the function of growth. In order to examine this functional relation for Uttar Pradesh, allocation of resources through plans suggests that percentage share of agriculture for investment in public sector has been declining. There has been growing realisation that sustainability of private investment depends much on the level of public investment in agriculture. Data suggest that public investment in agriculture has been declining at the state level. Plan wise allocation of resources suggest that there was sharp decline in allocation in the Fifth Plan and Sixth Plan onward it remained at the lower key. Expenditure on irrigation and flood control witnessed substantial cut in expenditure and remained at less than half of the expenditure of the previous plans. It was highest in the Fourth Plan (52.63 per cent) and in the Fifth Plan; it was reduced to merely 19.5 per cent. In the Eighth and Ninth Plan, it was further reduced to 11 to 12 per cent. One can explain it as proportionate decline in terms of expansion of irrigation networks. This may appear reasonable also. However, ineffectiveness of irrigation during drought and recurring devastating flood has made the agriculture rather more vulnerable and dependant on vagaries of monsoon. This needs further examination to explain the root cause of stagnating agriculture. Utilisation of funds *inter alia* is considered as proxy of the level of effective implementation of the programmes and set targets. Needless to mention that quantity and quality judgement of expenditure is another dimension to decide quality of expenditure. In the year 2003-04 also special area programmes, agriculture, rural development, energy, and general services remained satisfactory whereas irrigation and flood control, general economic services, science and technology, and social services remained under spent. Approval for the year has been much higher than the previous years but the question of utilisation remains to be scrutinised carefully. Provision in the budget to avoid unpopularity does not always ensure its utilisation. It appears that lip services towards allocation of funds are made to avoid unpopular controversy but deliberate indifference remained undeclared thumb rule. Various interest groups of ruling class have successfully been manipulating decisions in their interest. As a result, under utilization of funds for various programmes go to the tune of 40 to 80 per cent or even more than that. For example, initiatives for seed development could use merely 10 per cent of approved outlay, organic and chemical fertiliser 20 per cent and agricultural engineering could spend only 5 per cent in Ninth Plan. Situation in the Tenth Plan is not different. Approved outlay for new initiatives in agriculture could not spend even a rupee so far after two years of plan execution. Capital expenditure per ha. NSA in public sector of agriculture per annum of U.P. has declined and it is substantially lower than Punjab (Table 10). However, it was higher than all India average. Private fixed capital formation in agriculture of U.P. during 1980s has shown marginal increase unlike Punjab, which has indicated decline (Table 11).

A simpler exercise to understand the linkages of growth in agriculture is to estimate correlation, functional relation to examine the effects of inputs like, irrigation, fertilizer consumption per ha and cropping intensity on value of agricultural output. All these variables are highly correlated among themselves and therefore it would not be appropriate to run a single model of multiple regression with these variables to estimate coefficients of change per unit of value of output. Hence, in order to comprehend effects of these three factors on value of production of agriculture simple regression has been run separately. For periodical analysis, multiple regression with respect to intercept and slope dummy was estimated. Results (Table 12) suggest that effects of irrigation, cropping intensity and fertiliser consumption remained significant and positive during 1960-61 to 2001-02. Per unit rate of change because of each factor remained 0.9. However, per unit rate of change in value of output with respect to fertiliser consumption per hectare was higher than others and closure to unit value (0.977).

When we took periodical analysis by using slope dummy with respect to time, we found that fertilizer consumption had significantly positive effect on value of production until 1980. it implies that with use of fertiliser agricultural output has been increasing. Thereafter fertilizer consumption has lost its significance in promoting agricultural output in 1980s and 90s. This insignificance of the coefficients with respect to slope dummy suggests that the role of fertiliser in increasing production remain stagnant in 1980s and 1990s. It is worth mentioning that desirable norms of NPK (i.e., 4:2:1) have been worsening from 7:2:1 in 1970-71 to 11:3:1 in 1980-81, which were further aggravated to 18:5:1 in 1990-91 and 25:8:1 in 2001-02. However, overall estimates of fertilizer consumption appeared to have positive and significant influence over agricultural production. In case of irrigation, except 70s all the periods have positive and significant effects of irrigation on value of production. In 70s, the relation was found negative. When we compared 80s and 90s, results suggested that coefficient of slope (rate of change) during 1980s was higher than 1990s. So far cropping intensity is concerned, results suggested that until 1980, its effects on value of agricultural output remained significantly negative and later it turned positive and significant in 1980s but again it turned insignificant in 1990s. This suggests that during 1960s due to severe drought and uncertainty although irrigation had positive influence on production but could not remain adequately protective which explains negative value of cropping intensity. During 1970s, irrigation itself had negative relation with value of output. Hence negative relation with cropping intensity was obvious. During 1980s irrigation and cropping intensity both had positively significant relation with production. Despite insignificant coefficient (rate of change) of fertiliser consumption per unit of land area with respect to value of production of agriculture, this was the period when agriculture and the economy of Uttar Pradesh witnessed highest growth rates. However, this could not be sustained during 1990s. Rate of change in value of production with respect to irrigation turned lower than that of the previous decade. As a result cropping intensity has lost its teeth over agricultural production. This suggests another dimension to be examined with regard to the extent of effective irrigation and diversification of agriculture and its impacts on production.

Effects of relative price behaviour with a time lag of one year on value of agricultural production suggests that price relatives have negative influence over price relatives of agriculture and non- agriculture. If one takes periodic effects, results suggest that relative price has negative influence on value of agricultural production until 1990. During 1990s however, it has turned with positive influence on value of agricultural production (Table 12). Although. periodic annual rate of change in terms of trade suggests that it remained either negative or insignificant (Table 8). Thus, consideration of the movement of relative price is important while analysing growth of agriculture and strategies for its development. It becomes more important than ever before specially in the age of market dominating development strategies, globalisation and new regime of trade. Acreage response to market price behaviour could be another area of research to explain the linkages and work out strategies for development of agriculture. Thus, linkages of irrigation fertilizer consumption, cropping intensity and time lag of price relatives explain declining production and productivity. This again raises question against effective irrigation, diversification and extension services and market regulation mechanism in the marginal and small holding agriculture of Uttar Pradesh.

Technological advancement amidst massive loss of production not only because of recurring flood, due to lack of proper and effective water management but also because of the absence of proper infrastructure, as it was witnessed in the recent past in the case of potato and onion. Frustration of sugarcane growers reflected in their action of burning their crops are the indications which pose question for other parts of the country as well where farmers are getting frustrated, committing suicides in this form of productive organisation.

Recently even garlic, which is a value added crop was reported to be the victim of distress sale in one of the districts of U.P. Undoubtedly symptoms of transitions are reflected in terms of increasing production and productivity, introduction of machine, displacement of labour through machines, marginal increase in wages, use of modern inputs, family participation, etc. Corporate farming guarded with National Agricultural Policy is the new dimension to alienate poor households further from land as means of production for their employment and livelihood. There has been deliberate indifference on the part of ruling class to keep the land reforms initiatives at lower key to serve their interest. Study suggests that land reforms has not been effective but beneficiary of land reforms with limited access to redistributed land could improve their residential facilities, overcome food security, liberated from bondage, and started investing for development of human capital even sending their girl child to school. Thus, there has been an indication of overall improvement in their living condition despite having taste of partial implementation of land reforms (Mishra & Diwakar, 2005).

Policies to address the problems of landless labourers, marginal and small farmers need an altogether different package and thus there is an urgent imperative for reorienting policies through effective mobilization of poor so that the policy makers and implementing functionary do not have any excuse and option but to work in favour of deprived masses. If the functionaries are not sensitised properly there is every possibility that persisting neglect of the deprived majority may create a difficult objective conditions as U.P. is the abode of highest percentage of poor of the country with increasing share of poverty (Sen & Himanshu, 2003). Moreover, incidence of poverty has inverse relation with the size of land ownership.

IV Options and Strategies

Consolidating discussions of the dynamics of development of agriculture one can hardly escape the fact that the growth rate has witnessed a declining trend and lack of effective infrastructure remains the major challenge. More specifically, ineffective irrigation network keeps farmer dependent on vagaries of monsoon and cropping intensity is almost stagnant. Sizeable land area to the tune of 21.7 lakh hectares is lying unused. Therefore, an effective land and water management strategy may prove a positive step towards solution. Homogenous participatory mechanism need to be evolved to sensitize farmers in order to create sensitive *Kisan Mitra* who will take care of their concern on sustainable basis. Subsistence agriculture dominating by food grains has been facing declining area production and productivity amidst uncertainty of monsoon. Irrigation network remained ineffective because of fluctuating and scanty rainfall. Despite the fact that the use of chemical fertilizer has significantly contributed in enhancing production and productivity, disproportionate use of NPK has not only exposed the hard facts about ineffective extension services but also created environmental crises in agriculture, which will have far-reaching consequences on agricultural production. Even if attracted to value added agriculture, market induced production has made the farmers more vulnerable than ever before. Small and marginal farmers remained capital constrained and deprived of effective credit flow. This needs to be addressed on priority basis. Infrastructure building has been a big challenge for which sufficient allocation of resources on priority basis is necessary. Land reforms, which could have addressed the issues of rural unemployment and poverty, remained at the back seat. As a result, question of fulfilling basic needs through crash programme remained unsatisfactory. New form of tenancy as advance rent in cash has aggravated unemployment situation of poor peasant. Witnessing faster pace of liberalization in 1990s in the Indian economy, agriculture did not remain isolated. Employment elasticity has turned to be insignificant. National Agricultural Policies have accommodated corporate farming, which have necessary implications on employment and income of poor peasantry who are potentials to be alienated from subsistence employment base in agriculture without any substantial alternatives. The above analysis, thus, suggests that the question of inequality in land distribution has not lost the ground and much is yet to be done to restore the land to the tiller not only to remove the qualitative inequality in distribution of land but also to improve production, productivity of agriculture and employment and earnings status of the poor peasants. Therefore, substantial investment to prepare agriculture to meet challenges remains the main concern in the syndrome of general indifference and gradual withdrawal of state from its responsibility of welfare status in the interest of market, which is in fact a challenge before the economy, polity and society.

Table 1

ANNUAL AVERAGE GROWTH RATES OF NET STATE DOMESTIC PRODUCT AND PER CAPITA NSDP OF U.P. DURING 1960-61 TO 2002-03

Period	*1960-61 to 1970-71*	*1971-72 to 1980-81*	*1981-82 to 1990-91*	*1991-92 to 2002-03*	*1960-61 to 2002-03*
NSDP	2.1	3.53	5.1	3.86	3.79
Per capita NSDP	1.8	3.17	2.73	1.64	2.54

Source: Calculated from the data published by EPW Research Foundation.

Table 2

ANNUAL AVERAGE GROWTH RATES OF NET STATE DOMESTIC PRODUCT AND PER CAPITA NSDP OF U.P. DURING FIFTH FIVE YEAR PLAN TO NINTH FIVE YEAR PLAN

Plan	*Fifth Plan*	*Sixth Plan*	*Seventh Plan*	*Eighth Plan*	*Ninth Plan*
NSDP	5.99	4.29	6.61	5.22	4.34
Per capita NSDP	2.36	1.84	4.25	2.87	0.93

Source: Calculated from the data published by EPW Research Foundation.

Table 3

Net Sown Area, Irrigation, Intensity of Cropping and Productivity in Agriculture of Uttar Pradesh during 1950-51 to 1996-97

Description	*1950-51*	*1960-61*	*1970-71*	*1980-81*	*1990-91*	*2001-02*
1. Net Area Sown (in Lakh hect.)	162.3	171.9	173.1	172.2	173.0	168.12
2. Percentage Net Area Irrigated	29.8	30.5	41.4	54.9	61.6	76.3
3. Gross Area Sown (in lakh hect.)	199.6	221.5	232.1	245.7	255.0	254.5
4. Percentage Cropping Intensity	123.0	128.1	134.1	142.7	147.3	152.0
5. Percentage Irrigation Intensity	107.6	109.6	115.8	120.3	138.6	142.0
6. Productivity at constant Price (1993-94) Rs./hect	—	8125	9381	11538	15723	19567
7. Per capita Availability of Food Grain (gram/ day)	511	538	604	622	710	719

Source: 1. Statistical Abstract, U.P., Economics and Statistics Division, State Planning Institute, Government of U.P., Lucknow, various issues.
2. SDP Estimates, CSO, Ministry of Planning, Govt. of India, various issues.

Table 4

Average Annual Growth Rate of Area Production and Productivity during 1950-51 to 2000-01

Period	*Average Annual Growth Rates (per cent)*		
Food Crops	*Area*	*Production*	*Productivity*
1950-51 to 1970-71	0.65	2.55	0.95
1970-71 to 1990-91	0.23	3.05	2.88
1990-91 to 2000-01	(-)0.14	1.78	1.91
1950-51 to 2000-01	0.33	2.59	2.26
Non-Food Crops			
1950-51 to 1970-71	2.19	3.16	1.88

1970-71 to 1990-91	1.77	3.43	2.82
1990-91 to 2000-01	3.03	2.65	(-)0.38
1950-51 to 2000-01	1.69	2.77	1.07
All Crops			
1950-51 to 1970-71	0.79	3.00	1.18
1970-71 to 1990-91	0.42	3.33	2.85
1990-91 to 2000-01	(-)0.07	2.10	1.16
1950-51 to 2000-01	0.47	2.72	2.20

Note: Food Crops include cereals, pulses and non-food crops include sugarcane, oilseeds, potato and other crops.

Source: Calculation is based on data from *Uttar Pradesh ke Krishhi Ankre*, various issues.

Table 5

Changes in Production of Food Grains during Tenth Five Year Plan in Uttar Pradesh

Season	*2002-03 over*	*2003-04 over*	*2003-04 over*	*2004-05 over*
	01-02	02-03	01-02	03-04
Kharif	(-) 24.46	33.31	0.71	12.27
Rabi	(-) 7.38	8.47	0.47	13.39
Total	(-) 13.51	16.26	0.55	12.98

Source: Calculated from Annual Plan 2004-05, Vol. I (Part II)

Table 6

Annual Average Growth Rates of Agriculture NSDP of Uttar Pradesh at Factor Cost by Industry of Origin at 1993-94 Prices

Sector/ Period	*1960- 61 to 1970-71*	*1971-72 to 1980-81*	*1981-82 to 1990-91*	*1991-92 to 2000-01*	*1960-61 to 2000-01*
Agriculture & Animal Husbandry	1.29 + .0086	2.45 + .0102	2.96 + .00303	2.15 + . 00376	2.63 + .0011
Forestry & Logging	5.75 + .0054	(-) 2.65 + .0048	(-) 11018 + .0142	(-) 2.33 + . 028	(-) 3.85 + .0044
Fishing	7.97 + .0061	4.44 + .00161	12.48 + .01345	6.87 + .0042	7.54 + .0019

Source: Calculated from the data published by EPW Research Foundation

Table 7

Region wise Fertilizer Consumption in Uttar Pradesh (000' tones)

	Year	*Total Fertilizer*	*Nitro-genic*	*Phospha-tic*	*Pota-ssic*	*Ratios*
Uttar Pradesh	1970-71	410.54 (23.72)	291.43	74.51	44.61	7:2:1
	1980-81	1150.59 (66.82)	860.64	209.34	80.61	11:3:1
	1990-91	2240.91 (129.53)	1690.66	453.98	96.26	18:5:1
	2000-01	2961.82 (176.04)	2206.5	662.09	93.24	24:7:1
	2001-02	3352.13 (199.39)	2503.54	749.76	98.83	25:8:1
Central	1970-71	27.51	20.32	4.47	2.73	7:2:1
	1980-81	97.15	75.21	15.47	6.47	12:2:1
	1990-91	207.06	156.72	41.79	8.54	18:5:1
	2000-01	304.24	216.51	80.84	6.9	32:12:1
	2001-02	388.48	282.03	99.7	6.76	42:15:1
Eastern	1970-71	151.71	104.18	28.31	19.22	5:1.50:1
	1980-81	399.91	295.55	71.89	32.45	9:2:1
	1990-91	696.46	496.27	163.69	36.51	14:4.50:1
	2000-01	913.54	684.52	196.51	32.53	21:6:1
	2001-02	1024.96	784.65	211.8	28.53	27.5:7:1
Bundel-khand	1970-71	7.45	4.83	1.89	0.75	6.5:2.5:1
	1980-81	27.76	17.56	9.13	1.06	17:9:1
	1990-91	58.99	36.88	21.61	0.52	71:42:1
	2000-01	79.11	45.3	33.63	0.21	215:160:1
	2001-02	92.51	56.09	36.31	0.13	431:280:1
Western	1970-71	195.2	141.61	35.05	18.58	8:2:1
	1980-81	546.57	416.51	96.07	34.01	12:3:1
	1990-91	1020.24	762.74	220.78	36.7	21:6:1
	2000-01	1367.89	1051.34	270.91	45.61	23:6:1
	2001-02	1544.32	1156.92	329.53	57.83	20:6:1

Source: Various Volumes of CMIE.
Note: Figure in parenthesis indicates Kg/ha NSA.

Table 8

ANNUAL AVERAGE RATE OF CHANGE IN TERMS OF TRADE BETWEEN AGRICULTURE AND NON- AGRICULTURE OF UTTAR PRADESH

Years	*Annual Average Rate of Change in Terms of Trade between Agriculture & Non Agriculture*
1960-61 to 70-71	0.46
1970-71 to 80-81	-0.671*
1980-81 to 90-91	0.233
1990-91 to 2000-01	-0.864*

Note: Calculated from Sectoral NSDP at 1993-94 Prices.
* indicates that the rate of change is significant.

Table 9

PERCENTAGE DISTRIBUTION OF OPERATIONAL HOLDINGS OF INDIA AND UTTAR PRADESH

Size of Holdings	*India*				*Uttar Pradesh*			
	Number		*Area*		*Number*		*Area*	
(Acre)	*90-91*	*95-96*	*90-91*	*95-96*	*90-91*	*95-96*	*90-91*	*95-96*
> 2.5	59.0	59.4	14.9	15.1	73.8	75.6	31.4	34.1
2.5 - 5.0	19.0	18.8	17.3	17.4	15.6	14.5	24.4	23.8
5.0 – 10.0	13.2	13.1	23.2	23.2	7.7	7.3	23.4	23.1
10.0 - 25.0	7.2	7.1	27.2	27.0	2.7	2.4	16.9	15.8
Above 25.0	1.6	1.6	17.4	17.3	0.2	0.2	3.9	3.2
Average size (acre)			1.6	0.55			0.9	0.9

Source: Statistical Diary, State Planning Institute, Department of Planning, Govt. of Uttar Pradesh

Table 10

CAPITAL EXPENDITURE IN PUBLIC SECTOR OF AGRICULTURE OF U.P. PER HA. OF NSA AT CONSTANT PRICES, FROM 1974-75 TO 1996-97

(Rs. Per annum)

State/Period	*1974-5 to 1978-9*	*80-81 to 84-85*	*85-86 to 89-90*	*90-91 to 91-92*	*92-93 to 96-97*	*Av. 74-5 to 1996-97*	*Trend rate of growth (per cent)*
U. P.	337	363	243	292	228	299	– 2.8
Punjab	853	713	355	128	618	616	– 5.39

Source: Chand, 2001.

Table 11

PRIVATE FIXED CAPITAL FORMATION IN AGRICULTURE

State	*Total at Current Prices (Rs. Lakh)*		*Per ha at Constant Prices (Rs./ha of NSA)*	
	1981-82	*1991-92*	*1981-82*	*1991-92*
U.P.	26663	68484	132	145
Punjab	12854	19804	262	173

Source: Chand, 2001.

Table 12

EFFECTS OF IRRIGATION, FERTILISER CONSUMPTION AND CROPPING INTENSITY ON VALUE OF AGRICULTURAL PRODUCTION PER HA AT CONSTANT PRICES 1993-94

Factors/Period	*1960-61 To 1969-70*	*1970-71 To 1979-80*	*1980-81 To 1989-90*	*1990-91 To 2001-02*	*Adjusted R Square*	*1960-61 To 2001-02*	*Adjusted R Square*
Net Irrigated Area (%)	0.072*	-0.099*	3.459*	1.624*	0.975	0.927*	0.855
Fertiliser Consumption (Kg/Ha)	1.12*	1.01*	1.081	1.202	0.981	0.977*	0.953
Cropping Intensity (%)	-9.248*	- 7.618*	1.517*	1.699	0.952	0.911*	0.825
Price Relatives (Ag/Non-Ag) TL(1)	-0.892*	-0.725*	-0.173*	0.253*	0.901	- 0.420**	0.155

Note: * indicates the level of significance at 0.001 per cent and above and
** for 0.007 per cent.

References

Chand, Ramesh (2001): Emerging Trends and Issues in Public and Private Investments in Indian Agriculture: A Statewise Analysis, *Indian Journal of Agricultural Economics*, Vol. 56, No. 2, April-June.

Diwakar, D.M., (2000): Agrarian Transformation in Uttar Pradesh, Journal of Social and Economic Development, Vol. 3, No. 1, January-June.

___ (2000a): Purvi Uttar Pradesh ke Kheti mein Poonji ka Vikas, *Lokyuddha*, November-December.

Dreze, J: Occupational Change, Land Ownership and Social Inequality in Breman, J. Et. Al. (Ed.) The Village in Asia Revisited, Oxford University Press, 1997, pp. 129 and 148.

Ghosh, B. and P. De (2004): How do different categories of Infrastructure Affect Development: Evidence from Indian States, *Economic and Political Weekly*, Vol. 39, No. 42, October 16-22, pp. 4645-4657.

Government of India (2000): Mid Term Appraisal of the Ninth Five Year Plan.

Government of U.P. Annual Plan 2004-05, Department of Planning, Yojana Bhavan, Lucknow.

Kripashankar, (1997): Bataidari ki Samsya (Hindi), paper presented in the Workshop on Social Mobilisation and Effective Land Reforms in U.P. at Gandhian Institute of Studies, Varanasi, December 19-20,

Mishra, G.P. & D.M. Diwakar, (2005): *Land Reforms and Human Development*, Manak Publications Pvt. Ltd., New Delhi.

Saith, A., et. al., "Longitudinal Analysis of Structural Change," in Breman, J. et. al., (eds. 1997): *The Village in Asia Revisited*, Oxford University Press, and New Delhi.

Sen, A. and Himanshu (2003): Poverty and Inequality in India: Getting Closer to the Truth, Centre for Economic Studies and Planning, Jawaharlal Nehru University, New Delhi, mimeo. Quoted in Dev, S. Mahendra (2004): How to make Rural India Shine, *Economic and Political Weekly*, Vol. 39, No. 40, October 2-8.

Sharma, V.K., and T.K. Haque, (1996): "Perspective of Technological Change in Indian Agriculture—A Case of HYV Technology," *Agricultural Situation in India*, December.

Singer, H.W., (1950): The Distribution of Gains between Investing and Borrowing Countries, *American Economic Review*, Vol. 40, May, pp. 473-85.

Singh, A.K., (2003): Institutional Finance and the Rural Poor, paper presented in a national seminar of Deprivation and Inclusive

Development, Giri Institute of Development Studies, Lucknow, March.

Shrivastava, R.: *Change and Resilience in Producer Strategies in Uttar Pradesh Agriculture in Breman*, et. al. (ed.), op. cit.

Vyas, V.S. (2004): Agrarian Distress: Strategy to Protect Vulnerable Sections, *Economic and Political Weekly*, Vol. 39, No. 52, December 25-31.

2

LAND REFORMS TOWARDS SUSTAINABLE BASIC NEEDS IN UTTAR PRADESH

D. M. Diwakar

I. Introduction

Generally the issues of basic needs have been focussed through crash programmes to ensure their fulfillment, such as, public distribution system (PDS) in general and now with focus on Below Poverty Line (BPL) households target groups for food security, housing schemes—*Nirbal Avas Yojana, Indira Awas Yojana*, etc., for providing shelter and piecemeal package for providing intermittent employment opportunities for enhancing purchasing power to secure other basic needs. National Programme for Minimum Needs got such articulation in the Approach paper of the Fifth Five Year Plan. Approach Paper mentioned home-sites for rural landless under basic needs. Realisation was further deepened towards expansion of employment opportunities and minimum standard of living.

> "Even with expanded employment opportunities the poor will not be able, with their level of earnings, to buy themselves all the essential goods and services which should figure in their reasonable concept of a minimum standard of living. The

> measures for providing larger employment and incomes to the poorer sections will, therefore, have to be supplemented up to at least certain minimum standard, by social consumption and investment in the form of education, health, nutrition, drinking water, housing, communications and electricity" (GOI, 1973: 9).

Thus, besides food, shelter and clothing, which were initially identified as basic needs, education, health, nutrition, drinking water, communication and electricity were added in the basic needs basket. Needless to emphasise that, these initiatives are necessary interventions. But the question arises whether these can be sustained without sustainable base for livelihood. It goes without saying that overcoming food insecurity and access to nutritious food, housing materials and clothes are by and large dependent on the produce of land and therefore, fulfillment of these basic needs is primarily dependent on access to land resources. Outlining strategies for fulfillment of Basic Need Approach to Fifth Five Year Plan document clearly mentioned:

> "Home-sites are as important as employment opportunities for ensuring to the rural landless a minimum standard of well being. The problem can be dealt with most economically as part of land reform and consolidation of holdings. Home-sites for the landless may be treated as the first charge on any surplus land that theses measures yield. The surplus land may be transferred to an appropriate location by exchange and allotted as home sites to the landless" (GOI, 1973: 10).

Thus, measures initiated by the government for redistribution of ceiling surplus and gram sabha land for housing, cultivation, fishing, plantation, pottery, etc., are pointers to examine whether these initiatives have been instrumental towards achieving sustainable basic needs through access to land resources. This paper is an exercise towards understanding and exploring the possibility of acquiring sustainable basic needs through access to land resources. This study is primarily intended to examine as to how far access to land has been instrumental in facilitating basic needs on sustainable basis. Primary data for this purpose have been collected from 1126 households through census survey in ten villages—one from each sample block spread over five districts namely, Chandauli, Gorakhpur, Rai Bareli,

Muzaffar Nagar and Hamirpur representing different regions and climatic zones of Uttar Pradesh. Households with different size of land holdings and with different operational status have been considered for this examination. Distribution and possessions of ceiling surplus (CS) and Gram Samaj (GS) land and the impact of land reforms on basic needs and social development in Uttar Pradesh (UP). This study is divided into four parts: Part one deals with agrarian structure, whereas part two discusses agrarian reforms, part three analyses access to land towards fulfillment of basic needs and social development followed by part four as an attempt to consolidate the findings along with policy advocacy forwarded by the rural households.

II. Agrarian Structure

Land has been the basis of productive organisation and rural assets in any agrarian economy. Transformation in productive organisation, assets and structure is an important indicator to comprehend transition process which a rural society experiences. Forms of agrarian structure are reflected in operational holdings of a society and economy. It indicates iniquitous pattern of distribution of land to the tillers. Persisting inequality in distribution of land reflects the existing relations in an agrarian society of Uttar Pradesh (Diwakar, 2000). "Caste—land—occupational relations are inextricably inter-meshed and this character of agrarian relations is favourable to those who operate large holdings and belong to the dominant caste." (Mishra, 1982: 79). Studies provide a basis to argue that in fifties distribution of land ownership holdings in Uttar Pradesh was highly iniquitous (Singh, et. al. 1964; 28, in which 4340 zamindars spread over 81 villages were studied).[1] Sen Committee Report (RBI, 1984; 76-84, 384-393) categorically underlined skewed distribution of land as one of the major constraints for agrarian transformation of the region of the Permanent Settlement. After the abolition of zamindari system two generations elapsed since then. Although land reforms were decided to be implemented effectively, partly it contributed also in narrowing down inequality in distribution of land, it remained incomplete and neglected in absence of political commitment and will. Meanwhile subdivision and fragmentation of landholdings was witnessed in the process of natural attrition caused by division of family consequent upon growing population. As a result, landholding size in fifty years has decreased and therefore it is also argued that inequality in distribution of landholdings has lost its relevance to some extent. However, percentage distribution of operational holdings shown in Table 1 indicates that about 74 per cent of the households have possessed only 31 per cent of the land area whereas top ten per cent of the households possessed about 44 per cent according to the latest data available so far. This table shows that only 0.2 per cent of the landholders owning above 25 acres of land have about 4 per cent of the total operational area in their possessions. If we add the households above ten acres of land they amount to 2.9 per cent of the total households. But the area of operational holdings that they possess amounts to 21 per cent of the total area of operational holdings. Quantitatively it may appear less iniquitous for many of us but it needs a fresh assessment of the facts. Land holding size in the process of natural attrition has decreased but the question of land controlled by the same privileged class still persists. However transfer of land has widened the land base among middle caste/class and other section of the society also. Moreover family participation irrespective of caste/class has also increased.

Concentration of landholdings measured in terms of Gini Coefficient for macro data of Uttar Pradesh remained almost unchanged irrespective of ownership and operational holdings, although marginal increase was registered in the coefficient in 1982 (Sharma, 1994: A-14 & A-17). Moreover the gap between ownership and operational holdings may be explained through tenancy and fluctuation in it suggests the prevalence of tenancy at will. Quinquannial census data of agriculture suggest that Gini ratio for land concentration of operational holdings has been declining from 0.567 in 1980-81 to 0.505 in 1990-91 and 0.461 in 1995-96. However, individual research studies based on primary data and longitudinal studies show that Gini coefficient with respect to land concentration in Moradabad district of West Uttar Pradesh has rather increased from 0.49 in 1957-58 to 0.52 in 1993. However, value of coefficients remained unchanged when landless households are excluded (Dreze, 1997). Similarly another longitudinal study of Aligarh district of West U.P. suggests that percentage of households owning up to 25 *bigha* lands has increased from 36.4 in 1970 to 67.6 per cent in 1987.

However, percentage of land owning households more than 50 *bigha* lands has declined. Overall Gini coefficient in 1970 was 0.73 for the distribution of owned land on a household basis, and 0.63 on a per capita per household basis whereas corresponding figures for 1987 were 0.74 and 0.65 (Saith and Tankha, 1997; 100). Major concentration of land areas in Allahabad and Muzaffar Nagar lies with Hindu upper castes and Muslims (Srivastava, 1997). The above analysis, thus, suggests that inequality in land distribution has not lost the ground and much is yet to be done to restore the land to the tiller in order to remove the qualitative inequality in distribution of land.

Data from districts level distribution of operational land holdings from select districts given in Table 2 reveal that average size of operational holdings in Gorakhpur and Rae Bareli is lower than the state average (0.90 ha.). Majority of the farmers in state as well as in sample districts is marginal holders followed by small-holdings. In Uttar Pradesh marginal and small-holdings together constitute about 89.35 per cent. Marginal holders possess only 31.4 per cent of area whereas small holders possess about 24.4 per cent of operational area. Altogether they possess 55.8 per cent of operational area. Semi-medium farms have almost equal proportion of holdings and area in their possession. However, 2.9 per cent medium and large landholders possess 20.8 per cent of operational area. Even if one ignores concealed tenancy, which is pervasive in Uttar Pradesh, there is apparent inequality in distribution of land. Situation of sample districts are not different. This also explains the need for redistribution of land in Uttar Pradesh.

There could be many analytical categories for understanding agrarian structure in terms of distribution of land ownership, operational structure, social caste hierarchy, labour use including family and female participation in agriculture, but this is not the focus of this study therefore it appears prudent to stick to the official category of operational holdings. However, we have used caste-class continuous for this analysis. Data collected from sample villages at the household level suggest (Table 3) that SCC constitutes highest percentage (56.48) followed by OMC (28.6), MSM (6.04), UPC (5.77) and UMC (3.11). Distribution of operational holdings reveals that MRG constitutes highest percentage (51.95 per cent) followed by LL (37.66), SML (5.86), SMED (3.46) and MED+BG (1.07). Marginal holdings along with landless constitute over 89 per cent and caste-wise also OMC and SCC are the major constituents of the social and agrarian structure. In order to understand regional variation in distribution of households by castes and operational holdings we have analysed the households further by sample districts as shown in Table 4. It is evident that the villages of Muzaffarnagar have the highest percentage of SCC households (70.85) followed by Chandauli (69.96), Hamirpur (57.08), Rae Bareli (45.75) and Gorakhpur. Except Gorakhpur, where OMC has the highest percentage of households (44.83), in every sample villages SCC have the highest number of the households followed by OMC. In Gorakhpur and Rae Bareli, UPC stands third position so far number of households is concerned. However, percentage in former districts is higher than that of the later one. If one takes distributions of operational land holdings into account, we find that highest percentage of landless households is in Chandauli (64.38) followed by Muzaffarnagar (46.64), Hamirpur (31.42), Gorakhpur (24.14) and lowest in the sample villages of Rae Bareli. However, marginal holdings are highest in Gorakhpur (71.98 per cent), followed by Rae Bareli (67.45), Hamirpur (51.33) and Muzaffarnagar, whereas, the lowest marginal holdings among the sample villages are found in Chandauli district, which have the highest landless households. These two categories constitute major proportion about 90 per cent and above in most of the sample villages.

Besides the fact that majority of households in this agrarian structure is of marginal and small farmers, tenancy remains a major source to supplement income of the households. Tenancy market relations are found very strong and despite the fact that intermediary status has lost its legal ground, this class still exists strongly between state and peasants and exploitation of surplus continues through various forms of tenancies such as money rent, fixed produce are pervasive in Uttar Pradesh. Rent in advance has been driving out poor peasants gradually from lease markets, which have been an important source for their livelihood, employment, income and repayment of loan in absence of viable alternative. Thus, tenancy relations are of compulsive nature and mainly share of 50:50 is the modal terms of tenancy. However pre-cultivation advance rent payment system is emerging effectively, which is driving poor out of the tenancy market. Cost sharing mainly in terms of fertilizer seed and occasionally irrigation cost has been found (Diwakar, 2000a).

III. Agrarian Reforms

In agrarian societies, land has been the most important means of production, status of power and prestige and therefore changes in agricultural institutions would have far reaching effects on land based social order. When land reforms emerged as one of the most important development strategies in the post-World War period, India was not an exception to this phenomenon; rather it added yet another dimension along with peasant struggle, i.e. through peaceful mobilization and persuasion—Bhoodan (Joshi, 1982: 88-89) however, it could not sustain and achieve significance. Needless to mention here that history of land reforms in different parts of the country was not a liberal gift from enlightened government rather it was an outcome of historical process necessitated by protracted peasant struggle (Radhakrishnan, 1989:13). It was an outcome of growing consciousness and realization, irrespective of geographical boundaries and ideological variations, that agrarian reforms would unleash productive forces, enhance productivity, erode feudal struggle, address distributive justice and thereby contend resentment towards bringing a peaceful social order.

Land reforms basically aimed at releasing productive forces of agriculture across the globe to spread up growth rate of agriculture on the one hand and enhance the capabilities of poor towards human development on the other. This development Strategy emerged in the post-World War period. Many colonies achieved their political freedom and the aspirations of major anti-colonial forces mainly peasantry compelled their national government to enact and implement land reforms. Therefore, land reform measures appeared as State initiatives (from above) in consonance with peasant's aspirations. However, Occupational Forces (General Mac Arthur for example in Japan and Taiwan) were also forced to take active part in agrarian reforms to do away with feudal hurdles of agricultural development (Dorner, 1972:21; Joshi, 1982:36; Radhakrishnan, 1989: 14). Thus, State initiatives were also the outcomes of peasant struggles (from below). Evidences from various countries suggest that France, Netherlands, China, Japan, Russia and many other countries could bring qualitative change in production relations and development process through land redistribution. It is also seen that land reforms provides savings out of conspicuous extravagant consumption and leakages of landlords. Tenants are liberated from illegal exaction and non-market coercion and constraints. This provides surplus to invest in agriculture to increase production and productivity and also works towards diversification of agriculture and non-agricultural activities and thereby changes occupational structure (Bagchi, 2000).

Creating institution for revenue collection was probably the first step towards institutional reform that Indian agriculture witnessed. Imposition of revenue farming as an institutional arrangement dates back to Mughal India, which were not only the root of inequality and poverty but also the seed of the growth of the Zamindar class (Tandon, *et.al.*, 1936: 2). Land revenue in Mughal India was fixed on the basis of produce and not on size of land area. It was not the rent but taxes, the burnt of which was felt by both lower and upper strata of the peasantry. However, upper strata had to pay less per unit of land than the lower strata. Moreover, intermediaries were authorized to collect excess over the fixed revenue to be paid to the king. Thus, there were inherent regressive tendencies to aggravate inequality between the rich and poor in the countryside (Raychaudhuri and Habib, 1982, Vol. I, Ch. IX, see also Ch. VII). This mechanism of revenue collection was further reinforced by the company government, which entered into agreement with Zamindars (Tandon, *et.al.*, 1936: 2-3). In this process small peasantries were subjected to exploitation, which led to ejection of large section of small peasantry who lost their right of ownership on land and forced to be subordinated, as tenants at will to Zamindars. Rampant exploitation of the peasants during colonial rule resulted into a series of peasant movements during national freedom struggle. Champaran, Bardoli, Khera, Malabar, Agra and Avadh unrest of peasants, etc. were to name a few among them. "The efforts of larger landholders to bring rents more into line with prices touched off the wave of agrarian unrest that swept eastern and south-eastern Avadh in 1920-21" (Dharmakumar, 1982: 83). Consequent upon peasant unrests in different parts of country, there was growing realization among national leaders that land reforms were necessary to initiate process of development in India. This was very much reflected in the planning, legislation and enactment regarding abolition of the then land revenue system, abolition of Zamindari and intermediaries, etc. Basic documents that shaped their initiatives were Congress Agrarian Enquiry Committee Report 1936, Congress Economic Programme Committee Report 1948 and the Congress Agrarian Reform Committee, 1949. However, Sampurnanand (1936) had better clarity than other leaders on these issues. He was of the view: "no radical improvement in the condition of peasantry is possible without the abolition of the Zamindari System." He apprehended and warned a note of caution and further emphasised: "we must take care, while eliminating one set of vested interests, not to create another set which might have equally hostile to our ultimate goal, viz. social ownership of the land and its produce" (p.xv).

In independent India, undoubtedly, abolition of Zamindari and intermediaries was a radical step to change agrarian relations. Concern of reducing disparity of ownership of land was very much recorded in Plan documents for structural reforms and agrarian efficiency (Government of India, 1956, pp. 178-179). If enactment would have been the yardstick for commitment and realization it was the largest body of legislation that India could pass after Independence (Thorner, 1976: 18). But "there was apparent unwillingness of the rulers to do anything concrete about changing the production relations in Indian agriculture, which ensured that in most part of India even tenancy reforms and land ceiling laws, enacted in however diluted a form, would never be implemented" (Bagchi, 1988: 2).

Since Lucknow session of the Congress and Congress Agrarian Enquiry Committee Report 1936 Land Reforms was widely debated till 1950, this gave enough time to the Zamindars, Talukdars and other intermediaries to dispose off their land or manipulate through benami transfer. However, Uttar Pradesh got credit of enacting Uttar Pradesh Zamindari Abolition Land Reforms (ZALR) Act, 1950 (Das, 200). Subsequently, Rampur Thekadari and Pattadari Act of 1953, the Kumaon Land Act, 1954, etc. followed and supplemented ZALRA 1950 were enacted. These acts eroded the base of feudal structure and direct relationship between peasants and state was established (Mishra, 1996: 2). However, Zamindars were also confirmed as landholders along with Bhoomidhars, Sirdhars and Asamis (Thorner, 1976: 27). Thus, the term Zamindar was of course eliminated instead of Zamindar as such. As a result, there was hardly any significant change in land distribution pattern (Mishra, 1996P: 2; Singh & Mishra, 1964). Subsequently, Ceiling on Land Holding Act of 1960 was introduced to address the resultant lapses of ZALRA. But this Act was self-defeating in purpose because of provisions of exemptions and other in-built loopholes. This Ceiling Act 1960 was further amended in 1971 and 1973, which provided enough time and opportunities for the landlords in killing the main spirit and objectives of land reform in Uttar Pradesh (Mishra, 1996: p. 4).

First Backward Class Commission was set up on 29th

January 1953 headed by Kaka Kalelkar. It submitted its report on March 30, 1955. This committee extensively recommended on land reforms and reorganization of rural economy. However, this report could not be placed for discussion before the Parliament. In 1975 Most Backward Classes Commission was set up in U.P. headed by Sri Chedilal Sathi, which submitted its report in 1977. Another Backward Class Commission Report was submitted in 1980 headed by B.N. Mundle. Among many other recommendations this Commission strongly recommended for effective land reforms.

> "Until the stranglehold of the existing production relations is broken through radical land reforms, the abject dependence of under privileged on the dominant higher castes will continue indefinitely. In fact there is already a sizeable volume of legislation on the statute book to abolish zamindari, place ceiling on landholdings and distribute land to the landless. But in actual practice its implementation has been halting half hearted and superficial" (GOI, 1980: 13.33, p. 60). "It is the Commission's firm conviction that a radical transformation of the existing production relations is the most important single step that can be taken for the welfare and upliftment of all backward classes. Even if this is not possible in the industrial sector for various reasons, in the agricultural sector a change of this nature is both feasible and over due."(GOI, 1980: 13.34, p. 60). "The Commission, therefore strongly recommends that all the State Government should be directed to enact and implement progressive land legislation so as to effect basic structural changes in the existing production relations in the countryside." (GOI, 1980: 13.35, p. 60) "Apart from social traditions, the dominance by the top peasantry is exercised through recourse to informal bandage, which arises mainly through money lending, leasing out small plots of land and providing house sites and dwelling space to poor peasants. As most of the functionaries of government are drawn from the top peasantry, the class and caste linkage between the functionaries of government and the top peasantry remain firm. This also tilts the socio-political balance in favour of the top peasantry and helps it in having its dominance over others." (Prasad, 1980, quoted in GOI, 1980, p. 60).

Besides these, legislative measures regarding abolition of tenancy, distribution of ceiling surplus and Gram Samaj land, consolidation of holdings, etc., were taken to address the problems of land reforms. Distribution of Gram Samaj patta land with implementing emphasis by the government is an added reinforcement. Moreover, in order to remove gender based discrimination in accessibility of land ownership a 'Committee for Gender Equality in Land Devolution in Tenurial Laws' 1998 was set up headed by Bina Agrawal which reviewed the gender inequality in land laws of five northern states (Haryana, Himachal Pradesh, Punjab, Jammu & Kashmir, and Uttar Pradesh). The Committee has submitted its report waiting for consideration.

State came into direct relation with the tenants after abolition of intermediary tenure. However, it proved mere change of nomenclature and there was hardly any substantial change in agrarian structure. To cover up this limitation Land Ceiling Act, 1960 was introduced with further modification in 1973 in order to acquire ceiling surplus land and redistribute among the land-poor households. Another significant dimension of the UPZALRA, 1950 was the lease of the government land vested in the Gaon Sabha (GS) for agriculture, fishery, poultry, plantation and residence. It is intended to discuss redistribution of ceiling surplus and Gaon Sabha land—its official status of implementation and micro ground realities going through household survey of the sample village in order to understand the status of implementation and possessions of land to the beneficiaries.

Distribution of Ceiling Surplus Land

Ceiling on Land Holding Act 1960 was introduced in Uttar Pradesh so that an upper limit of land holdings could be fixed and surplus land would be taken away from surplus farmers for redistribution among land poor peasantry. A limit of 40 acres of land of fair quality was fixed for a family of five members subject to increase in land area up to 24 acres in case of additional family members. However, this Act exempted a few categories of land from ceiling on land holdings used for grove, industrial purposes, cattle shed, compost pits, thrashing floor, residential houses, cremation ground/graveyard area under plantation of rubber, tea, coffee, land with religious/charitable trusts, poultry and dairy farm, land covered farm roads, etc., (Mishra, 1996: 4). Cut off date for reference was fixed as May 1959. This Act was further amended in 1973 and the cut off date was fixed on 24th July 1971. Under this amendment upper limit and exemption was reduced. Land areas under grove, used for poultry and dairy farm and farm roads were removed from exemption. Upper limit was brought down to 7.3 hectares in case of irrigated and from 10.95 to 18.25 hectares for un-irrigated land.

Land declared ceiling surplus and process acquire land was initiated by the government. But the process was not smooth. Disputes on settlement of land brought the matter into court of law. Many of them are still subjudiced and to be settled. Details of official records relating to these facts are shown in Table 5. Official data suggest that about 91.6 per cent of land area declared surplus in Uttar Pradesh was under possession of the government. About 70 per cent of the declared ceiling surplus land was redistributed among the landless poor. About 7.9 per cent area is still sub-judice. Data relating to sample districts display that Rae Bareli is one of the districts where 100 per cent area was acquired. About 78.9 per cent area was distributed to the landless and about 94.3 per cent area of ceiling surplus land was settled till March 2002. In Chandauli only 58.2 per cent area was brought under possession and as high as 41.8 per cent of declared ceiling surplus land was subjudice followed by Gorakhpur (23.9 per cent) and Hamirpur (20.9 per cent). Thus, data suggest that special effort is needed to expedite the judicial process to benefit the poor peasantry.

In order to comprehend the ground reality regarding distribution of ceiling surplus land findings from field survey, suggest that about 8.9 per cent households in sample villages were the beneficiaries of redistribution of ceiling surplus land. Beneficiary while reporting quality of land in terms of fertility and irrigation shows that all the land areas are not fertile and irrigated. Moreover, all the beneficiary households do not cultivate their land. There is gap between the households of beneficiary and self-cultivator beneficiary.

Distribution of Gram Sabha Land

Normal prescribed procedure of leasing GS land to leaseholders is ideal and democratic. Land Management Committee of the village Panchayat in confidence with Gram Sabha recommends the list of beneficiaries to the SDM through circle officer and the land is allotted to leaseholders. Land vested in Gram Sabha is leased out to the peasants for different purposes by the Sub Divisional Magistrate on the proposal of Land Management Committee. In Uttar Pradesh this scheme was launched in 1975-76 in order to improve economic condition of the SC/ST/ OBC and weaker section of the society. In this scheme under Article 198 of UPZALR Act, 1950 maximum 1.26 hectare area of cultivable land is leased out to the land poor households. The land is leased out on the joint name of wife and husband. Under Article 126 there is also provision to include the name of adult unmarried daughter, divorced, deserted and widow. According to the availability of land annual targets are set. Land is also allotted for fishery, plantation, and pottery. Under Article 122(c), Circle Officer, ADM himself or on the proposal of Land Management Committee, allots land as on recorded order of preference mentioned in sub-article (3). For the people of SC/ST community in rural areas, 100-150 yards square area is given for residence purposes if she/he does not have own residential facility (Citizen Charter, Land Revenue Department, Government of U.P., pp. 5-7).

Official details about district-wise distribution of GS land in Uttar Pradesh since 1975-76 to March 2002 is displayed in Table 6. Data suggest that about 54.8 per cent area of Gaon Sabha Land has been distributed among SCs followed by 25.9 per cent to BCs and 19.2 per cent Other Castes. Remaining area has been distributed among STs and Army personnel. District-wise distribution of GS land suggests that Rae Bareli has allotted highest area among the sample districts (3.5 per cent) followed by Muzaffarnagar (1.6), Hamirpur (1.4), whereas Gorakhpur could distribute only 0.5 per cent of total GS land distributed and Chandauli is still worse (0.2 per cent). However, inter-caste distribution of GS land among sample districts suggests that

Chandauli has the highest percentage of GS land area distributed to SCs (67.6 per cent) and BCs (30.3 per cent) followed by Hamirpur (60.6 and 28.7 respectively). Sizeable beneficiary of GS land other than SCs and BCs were found in Muzaffarnagar (27.5 per cent) followed by Gorakhpur (22.4 per cent).

Findings emerged with regard to ground reality of the households of sample villages, suggest that about 41.8 per cent of the households are beneficiary of GS land lease. Out of these households about 11.6 per cent are from Hamirpur followed by Chandauli (9.3 per cent), Rae Bareli (9.0 per cent) and Muzaffarnagar could score 5.7 per cent. Gorakhpur registered lowest spread of beneficiaries (only 0.6 per cent). So far the quality of land redistributed is concerned, 15 per cent of the households reported fertile and 19.4 per cent accepted that the land was irrigated. About 22.6 per cent of the households among 42 per cent were self-cultivating the land redistributed under GS lease. Reported reasons for non-cultivating households mainly two: one, they mainly work as non-agriculture labour; and, two, the households do not have male working member. Mere allotment does not ensure possessions. Even they got papers regarding allotment, possessions remain a difficult task. Hence there is always question of under-possession. With regard to gap of allotment and non-possession in case of ceiling surplus and GS land, non-possession in case of ceiling surplus land is about 52 per cent. Implementation status is almost nil in sample villages of Gorakhpur and Chandauli. In Hamirpur non-possession was to the tune of 10.3 per cent and it was nil Muzaffarnagar. So far the lease of GS land is concerned over all non-possession was around 5.7 per cent. However, Chandauli registered about 17.14 per cent. Clubbing these two categories of beneficiary, i.e., ceiling surplus and GS land overall non-possession was around 14 per cent, whereas, Gorakhpur registered a high as 80 per cent of the beneficiary households. Other districts had 2 to 5 per cent non-possession.

One can also take an overall view of possession in terms of caste distribution and farm size category. Major beneficiary of ceiling surplus land was Scheduled Castes as high as 85 per cent. However, possession was with 79.2 per cent of the beneficiary households. In case of farm size category about 65 per cent households were the recipient of ceiling surplus land by marginal farm size, but interestingly there is over-possession by this category of farm size. Over-possession is reported in case of small and semi-medium farm size also. So far area is concerned, under possession is reported on the whole. Although, UPC and UMC have complete possession on allotted land. SCC suffers from under-possession. Under-possession becomes clearer in farm size category. LL could not acquire possession at all, and marginal holding suffers from under-possession. However, other categories have complete possession. Thus, it appears that landless is the worst sufferer and marginal farm holdings and SCC remained under-possession. Distribution of the beneficiary household of the residential land suggests that SCC is the major beneficiary (about 65 per cent) followed by OMC. In terms of farm size category marginal holdings was benefited to the extent of 83 per cent followed by small-holdings with 12 per cent of households. Landless households remained at the lowest level, i.e. 1.9 per cent of the beneficiary households.

Possession status of beneficiary of ceiling surplus, GS lease and residential land distribution with respect to allotment in sample villages of Uttar Pradesh brought some gaps. Dealing further with GS land in terms of allotment and possession for various purposes, such as, cultivation, residence, fishery, pottery and plantation, findings explain gap by caste and farm size in implementation of land reforms. There is hardly any over-possession in case of SCC irrespective of various uses for which land was allotted rather there is under-possession in case of residential allotment. Secondly LL households have no possession on allotted land at all. Over-possessions are found with OMC, MRG and SML category of the households. In case of pottery and plantation there is ideal situation. Picture becomes clearer if one dwells into the gaps of allotment and possession in terms of area of leaseholder. In terms of average area allotted and possession with leaseholder by caste and farm size of the households in sample villages, findings reveal that except plantation, there has been over-possession in case of pottery and under-possession in allotment of residential, cultivable and fishery land area. Looking into caste-wise details it is evident that: there is hardly any under-possession of lease area in case of UPC, MSM and UMC. Rather in case of cultivation and pottery there is indication of over-possession. However, in case of SCC also over-possession is reported for cultivable area and under-possession in case of residential and fishery area. Considering farm size category landless households have been allotted land for cultivation, residence and fishery but they do not have possession. Marginal holdings reported under-possession in case of cultivation, residence and fishery and over-possession in case of pottery. Even medium-cum-big farm holdings could manage land allotment and showing under-possession. This gives clue for the procedural lapses in identifying beneficiaries. Thus, it is clear that under-possession is mainly with OMC and landless and marginal farmers for cultivation and OMC, SCC, landless and marginal farmers for residence and fishery.

This shows that despite having an explicit mechanism of distribution, procedure adopted for distribution of land has many distortions. Findings suggest that the Committee exists in villages but hardly known to everybody. Only 30 per cent of the beneficiary households knew about the committee in existence. Procedure adopted for recommendation and preparation of a list of beneficiary is very flexible. Generally, it is done by the Lekhpal and Village Pradhan, in consultation with other a few influential persons of village. However, about 49.5 per cent of the households of beneficiary acknowledged the role of PRI and Land Management Committee in selecting beneficiary of GS land. Findings suggest dominant and decisive role of Lekhpal, Pradhan and a few influential persons. This makes the process complicated and at the will of these persons in the helm of affairs. In this process the beneficiary has to run pillar to post to get the land allotted, at the cost of his wage employment and he is forced to borrow from the moneylender to bribe the Lekhpal and Pradhan. Findings suggest that about 9.1 per cent households of beneficiary admitted that they have lost their man days. About 15 per cent have been trapped in a money-lending usury network. This is not the end of the misery.

Despite all the complications about 13.8 per cent of the beneficiary households reported that they could not get possessions of the allotted land. The land is in the parcels of big farmers and influential persons. The reason behind is explained by the articulated villagers: at the time of consolidation individual land was consolidated but the land of Gram Sabha and Government remained scattered and fragmented, as patches in the consolidated area of the big landholders. Therefore, even if the land is allotted it has been difficult to take possessions of the land. This is one of the significant disincentives to the potential beneficiary to persuade Lekhpal and Pradhan to allot such land, as it is almost impossible to take possessions on it.

Besides these there are many other reasons as to why deserving potential beneficiary could not get land. It is evident from table that as high as 92.8 per cent of the non-beneficiary households have accepted that deserving beneficiary could not get land because non-deserving beneficiary have been identified and they wrongly got the land allotted. A sizeable households, i.e. 30.8 per cent of non-beneficiary admitted that many of them could not get land as nobody came forward to help them. Secondly, they lacked money to offer bribe to the concerned persons. Those who could afford to bribe they got the land. This shows the seriousness of wrong implementations and lapses on the part of concerned agencies and authorities. This is a challenge also as to how this can be overcome to ensure land to the tillers. Is it possible without changing this non-sensitive superstructure in implementing role? To one it appears that there is need of concerted efforts of sensitive officials and agencies and there is need to create awareness among the potential and bona-fide beneficiary to acquire their proper place and positions.

IV Land Redistribution towards Sustainable Basic Needs

Needless to repeat that basic objectives of the land reforms across the globe was to release productive forces to spread up growth rate of agriculture on the one hand and enhance the capabilities of poor on the other. Evidences from various countries suggest that France, Netherlands, China, Japan, Russia and many other countries could bring qualitative change in production relations and development process through land redistribution. It is also seen that land reforms provides savings out of conspicuous extravagant consumption and leakages of landlords. Tenants are liberated from illegal exaction and non-market coercion and constraints. This provides surplus to invest in agriculture to increase production and productivity. This also works towards diversification of agriculture and non-agricultural activities and changes occupational structure (Bagchi, 2000).

In India, abolition of intermediary tenurial system was one of the major institutional reforms. Although this could not produce desired result, in select pockets where peasant mobilization was effective, land reforms could improve productivity and growth rates in agriculture and liberate tenants from illegal exaction, non-market coercion and bondage. Kerala and West Bengal could witness encouraging results. Kerala could protect civil, political and substantive freedom through egalitarian land reforms (Bagchi, 2001). Operation Barga in West Bengal could improve the status of sharecropper and redistribution of land resulted into higher level of productivity and growth (Sanyal, Biswas and Bardha, 1998; Gohh, 1998). This led to better participation in education, health and development.

In Uttar Pradesh also, land reforms created space for economic security, reduced landlessness, and generated income despite several lapses and shortcomings in implementation. This section is intended to examine relationship between access to land and sustainable basic needs for better quality of life and over all social development. We have considered income, employment, GS land, net operated area, workforce, level of literacy, health status and schooling of girl child for this purpose. We attempted to discuss the role of land redistribution towards fulfilling basic needs and promoting human capital resources taking distribution of ceiling surplus land and GS land into account. Interesting results are visible despite many shortcomings in the implementation of land reforms and redistribution from the study of the beneficiary and non-beneficiary household survey of sample villages. In case of redistribution of land for residential purposes suggests that there was indication of liberation of poor from bondage as they could acquire their ownership of homestead land (Table 7). About 5.33 per cent of households reported their liberation from bondage as they got ownership of residential land. Majority among them were of SCC social group.

Farm size category in this context suggests that larger beneficiary were of marginal holdings. As they could acquire ownership of homestead land their position in society was elevated. Particularly SCC and marginal holders could construct their houses and to a certain extent they could enjoy comfortable living. Thus, it is evident from table that redistribution of land for residential purpose could liberate the beneficiary from bondage, elevated their social status and they were enjoying comfortable living in a house constructed for their family. Redistribution of land for cultivation is another dimension where tangible benefits were reported. Data suggest that about 28 per cent of the households were the beneficiary of cultivable land in sample villages and majority of them were from SCC followed by OMC (Table 8. In case of farm size category marginal holdings were reported as major beneficiary followed by the landless households. Findings suggest that production of food grains of the beneficiary households has increased which made them comfortable at food front.

Their dependence for borrowing from moneylenders has been reduced. Since, they can afford security before public financial institution getting credit from has become relatively easier than earlier situation. Now they can rear cattle to supplement their income and initiate other income generating activities. Cumulative results of all these stated above placed the households with better income level. However, this can be examined further with detailed study of the economics of cultivation and other income generating activities of the households. Table also suggests that there are gaps in the beneficiary households and the households reporting benefits from redistribution of cultivable land. This also suggests that mere distribution of land is not sufficient condition to pull out the households from the quagmire of poverty. However, it reveals that land ensures access to other benefits necessary for the households.

Another dimension of benefits can be examined in this context is from the point of social development. A few indicators have been selected to understand the potential benefits of social development emanating from redistribution of land. Health and schooling are two major areas where responses are very encouraging. Findings as shown in Table 9, about 13.7 per cent of the households accepted that health status of their children has improved as now they can afford proper food to their children. It is consistent that SCC remains larger beneficiary of health followed by OMC. Similarly marginal holdings followed by landless labourers reported major benefits of land redistribution to improve the health status of their children. They could afford proper clothing. Besides health, they could send their children to school as now they could afford initial cost of food, clothes and basic materials required for. Most significant is the impacts on schooling of girl child. Thus, basic indicators of social development such as health and education displayed significant impacts which beneficiary and non-beneficiary households have acknowledged.

However, findings suggest that impacts of the redistribution of land were marginal. Land is basis in transformation of rural society. As we have seen that land redistribution although with limited results is of instrumental importance to generate employment and income in order to have access to the resources for basic minimum needs and better quality of life. Here we would like to examine certain causal relations for employment, income and quality of life. In case of employment a hypothesis can be constructed that per capita employment (PCEMP) can be increased with increasing per capita net operated area (PCNOA), which enables household to withdraw workforce for capacity building or in other words for human development. Therefore, dependency ratio (DR) may be increased. Precisely it can be said:

PCEMP = f (PCNOA, Dependency Ratio).
Regression result:
PCEMP = 85.528 + 0.11 PCNAO + 0.39 DR
(43.85) (4.283) (14.168)
Adjusted R^2 = 0.181, F-Value = 124.447

Findings suggest that PCNOA has significant positive causal relation with PCEMP. It implies that with the increase in per capita employment households can afford higher level of dependency. Although adjusted R^2 explains only 18 per cent the model is highly significant revealed in F-Value in this model. Another model we have examined further including policy variables, such as, total workforce in agriculture (TWA) per capita ceiling land (PCCL) per capita GS land (PCGSL) and dependency ratio (DR) for explaining PCEMP. Thus, the model is:

PCEMP = f (TWA, PCCL, PCGSL, DR).
Result:
PCEMP = 01.095 — 0.467 DR + 0.155 PCGSL — 0.005 PCCL — 0.24 TWA
t-value = (40.158) (-16.579) (5.857) (-0.210) (-8.666)

Findings suggest that except per capita ceiling land other co-efficients are highly significant. Interestingly DR has negative relation. PCGSL has positive and significant causal relations. Therefore, if PCGSL is increased PCEMP will also increase. PCCL has no significant relation with PCEMP. With a given space of employment TWA has inverse relation with PCEMP. This model explains over 24.3 per cent of variation significantly. Thus, this model explains higher level of variation than earlier. Thus, to increase employment, there is need to increase per capita GS land to rural poor. Employment is important because it provides opportunities to generate income, which gives purchasing power to the households. Therefore, if we have to analyse the quality of life per capita income (PCINC) is one of major constituents. Per capita income can be explained through availability of per worker employment (PWEMP), per worker income (PWINC), Dependency Ratio (DR), PCNOA, per worker land (PWL), PCGSL, PCCL, and PCEMP. Thus, model is:

PCINC = f (PWINC, DR, PCNAO, PWL, PCGSL, PCCL, PCEMP, PWEMP)

Results: PCINC= 1099.568 + 0.884 PWINC — 0.138 DR + 0.552 PCNAO —0.318 PWL

t-value = (7.52) (60.45) (-6.348) (17.747) (-11.745) — 0.189 PCGSL —0.141 PCCL + 0.296 PCEMP — 0.215 PWEMP

(-12.908) (-10.231) (12.899) (-9.299)

Findings suggest that the model explains about 84.6 per cent as adjusted R^2 is 0.846, which is highly significant as F-ratio is 767.371. Obvious finding is that per worker income has significant positive relation with PCINC. Similarly PCNAO has significant positive relation. This is true with PCEMP also. Since DR has negative relation, here other relations have also turned negative. It is evident that if PCEMP is increased PCINC will increase. Therefore, simply increase per worker employment is not enough to increase the purchasing power of the household. In order to understand implication and impacts of land redistribution on social development, literacy level can be examined with a couple of related variables. Basic assumption is that access to land will widen employment base and level of income, which will be instrumental to higher level of access in education. Percentage literacy of household (PCLH) is explained through DR, PCGSL, PCCL and TWA. The function is:

PCLH = f (DR, PCGSL, PCCL, TWA)

Result = PCLH = 17.714 — 0.053 DR + 0.090 PCGSL + 0.030 PCCL + 0.094 TWA

t-value = (1.375) (-1.667) (2.996) (0.995) (3.002)

Findings suggest that constant and PCCL are not different than zero, whereas DR is weakly significant reflecting still inverse relation with literacy. But PCGSL and TWA have significantly positive relation with the level of literacy. Value of adjusted R^2 is significant but it explains very little so far the level of literacy is concerned. Excluding PCCL we have tried to estimate another model as follows:

PCLH =19.506 — 0.057 DR + 0.088 PCGSL + 0.093 TWA
t-value =(1.529) (-1.781) (2.952) (2.962)

Value of adjusted R^2 is still very low but significant (i.e. 2.3 per cent). The result suggests that constant is insignificant and not different than zero. DR has weakly significant inverse relation. However, PCGSL and TWA have significant positive relation. It implies that level of literacy can be enhanced through effective GS land distribution to the workforce in agriculture. It also suggests that literacy level for rural poor is not primary concern but it is employment and income for which GS land distribution has important role. It may be recalled that Bahujan Samaj Party (BSP) led government tried to sensitise bureaucracy for effective implementation, but the campaign lost its spirit in the middle itself. In order to comply the pressure, implementation was manipulated through dubious records, as we could encounter in the field. There was apparently general reluctance from the side of bureaucracy and its allies. This is because of over presence of land owning social groups and class in the bureaucracy.

In fact this is not new at all. Even pre-independence slogan of 'land to the tillers' by the political parties could not be sustained for long after independence. Although Zamindari Abolition Act and other Acts related to ceiling surplus land were promulgated but in every stage there was enough time lag to allow the land owning intermediary to legalise the ownership status of land. Thus, the hope was ultimately pinned down in the particular ruling class who could identify with the interest of the rural poor at the lower rung of the society. However, this was also not realised even after BSP usurping to power in Uttar Pradesh. Despite apparent willingness to some extent leadership has to compromise with ruling allies against the interest of rural poor. Since the bureaucratic structure is over represented by the anti-poor elements, it has been difficult for BSP government to sideline the anti-poor interest. Rather it has compromised to retain power at the cost of the interest of the poor at least in the case of land reforms and redistribution of land to the poor. Michael Kalecky has rightly observed "History has shown that lower-middle class and rich peasantry are rather unlikely to perform the role of the ruling class. Whenever social upheavals did enable representative of these classes to rise to power, they invariably served the interest of big business (often allied with the remnants of the feudal system)" (Kalecky, 1976:30). History also suggests that social mobilization has been creating compelling situation for the ruling class in order to contend the resentment of the peasantry and ruling class has been trying its best to convert the effects of mobilization in terms of land reforms from above. And U.P. has not been an exception in this context. Therefore, unless superstructure is radically transformed it is difficult to enforce effective implementation. There is enough evidence that redistribution of land to the tiller has enormous potential to transform the quality of life of rural poor and contribute significantly towards fulfilling basic needs promoting human development, non-compromising political will is the first and foremost essential condition. Unless the class interest is represented substantially in the ruling class this 'Political will' would remain a far fetched dream. Hopes still lie in consistent social mobilization in the line of class in itself to be transformed gradually into class for themselves.

V Findings for Policy Advocacy

Summarising the analysis and discussions in order to arrive at conclusions regarding access to land for sustainable basic needs in Uttar Pradesh we have tried to understand the process of land reforms and various initiatives taken-up by the governments, particularly after independence with special reference to Uttar Pradesh. We found that in order to overcome the shortcomings of UPZALRA, ceiling on land-holdings was imposed and surplus lands were acquired. However this process was also not free from manipulative syndrome. Exemption on various categories of land and subjudiced status on sizable ceiling surplus land provided a significant cover to and in favour of land-owning castes and class. More than 8 per cent of declared ceiling surplus land (i.e. 30,391 acres) is yet to be taken in possession. Moreover, all the land distributed to the peasants is not fertile and irrigated and therefore all the beneficiaries of ceiling surplus land did not cultivate land themselves.

Land vested in Gram Sabha (GS) is leased to poor peasants of different social groups i.e., SC/ST, OBC and army men, since 1975-76 in Uttar Pradesh for residence, cultivation, plantation, fishing and pottery. About 26,52,263 acres land have been distributed among SC (54.8%), BC (25.9%), and other castes (19.2%) and remaining to ST and army personnel. However, mere allotment of land did not serve the purpose. Possession over allotted land remained a difficult task. Non-possession was reported on account of influence and control of big farmers. Landless households were still waiting for possessions. Under possession in terms of area was also found in case of marginal holdings, SCs and Muslims. Over possessions were found with OMC, MRG and SML households. Status of possession became explicit in case of purpose-wise segregated details. Even medium-cum-big farm holdings could manage land allotment reflecting procedural lapses of the scheme. A sizeable non-deserving beneficiary household were selected at the cost of genuine potential households, because of lapses in procedure, bribery, lack of awareness and sensitive implementing agencies.

Even political powers with this given superstructures remain ineffective. Despite ruling of effective implementation with a declared deadline by the state government land reforms remained on the same ground with a marginal difference, as superstructure did not correspond because of their anti-dalit and anti-poor attitude. This suggests that unless superstructure is radically transformed in favour of poor and landless peasants mere usurpation of political power does not empower in real sense to implement the agenda of poor, may be land reforms or basic needs. Vicious nexus of land owning social groups and class embedded with their bureaucratic connivance because of their common interest, all sorts of manipulations of record have been done to foil the efforts of implementation of land reforms. Majority of functionaries from village to secretariats are represented and controlled by the landowning class and its natural allies in politics. Indifferent attitude towards implementation of land reforms and to ensure possession has been quite obvious. Now the land reforms have been pushed to back seat.

Despite the fact that there has been obvious indifference in implementation of redistribution of land and limited implementation, land reforms measures could bring positive and visible results. To the extent of limited implementation, land redistribution could create space for economic security, reduced landlessness, and initiated income generation. Indications of liberation from bondage on account of ownership of residential land, were found. Poor could erect houses and enjoy relatively comfortable living elevating their social status. In case of the beneficiary households of cultivable land, production of food grain increased which placed them relatively comfortable at food front. Land as collateral security provided access to public institutional network and credit. These could reduce their dependence on exploitative usury network of moneylenders. Allied activities such as cattle rearing to supplement their income became possible. However, due to lack of comprehensive follow-up package much is left to be desired. Findings also suggest that there were considerable differences in terms of indicators of social development, particularly in the areas of health and schooling. It is sad on the part of implementation that land reforms measures, which have enormous potential for fulfilling sustainable basic needs for human development, have become victim of neglect of ruling class and its natural allies. There is an urgent demand of reorienting policies through effective mobilization of poor so that the policy makers and implementing functionary do not have any excuse and option but to work in favour of deprived masses. But unfortunately advocacy and policy for corporate farming has been accepted which prove a drag on accessibility of land for sustainable basic needs for poor.

People's Voice and Advocacy

Based on responses of the rural households, discussion and analysis of this study following suggestion are thrown up for consideration of the implementing agencies and functionaries in order to achieve effective targets of land reforms: (1) There is need of ensuring effective possession of redistributed land through direct accountability of concerned functionaries. A land management committee at village level with proper representation of poor peasants should be formed to verify the implementation status. Undistributed scattered land parcels should be consolidated and redistributed through co-operative ownership. Poor peasants co-operative should be formed and follow up packages, access to credit, etc. should be rooted through co-operative. Pending cases on sub-judiced land should be disposed off on the priority basis and a separate legal committee should be constituted for technical support of the poor peasants. Poor peasant committee should be provided legal support to identify *benami* transfer of land. The benami land should be declared surplus and those surplus lands should be redistributed among poor households on the recommendation of poor peasant land management committee. Wasteland should be acquired and transferred to landless through their co-operative ownership and follow up assistance should be rooted through co-operative in reference. Assured irrigation co-operatives of landless peasants should be formed to provide irrigation on distributed and other lands. Effective insurance cover on crops should be extended through micro-finance co-operative of land beneficiaries. Ban on individual purchase of redistributed land should be executed effectively. A provision for direct institutional loan on land should be extended to the beneficiary of land directly on producing *kisan passbook*. Subsidised inputs should be provided to the beneficiaries of land. Indifference and negligence in implementation of land redistribution and possession by functionaries should be treated as cognisable non-bailable offence. Administration and Policy implementing agencies should be made accountable directly for non-possession and should be punished in terms of career of service. Best implementing functionaries should be given incentives. Minimum wages should be implemented effectively. Poor households should be organised and proper support should be extended to safeguard the interest of the beneficiary of land. Participation of poor in co-operatives, PRI and land management committee should be ensured. Illegal possessions of redistributed land by influential persons should be liberated on priority basis. Pro-poor social activists should be involved in organizing poor. Effective flood control measures should be initiated. Rural industrialisation, functional education and women participation should be encouraged. Micro-financial credit groups should be formed and self-help women cooperatives should be promoted. PRI should be empowered to form women co-operatives and Functional Education Groups. Technical support should be ensured to promote women participation. Land Records should be computerized, updated and easy access to the records should be ensured for information. Above all unless poor friendly environment is ensured any amount of attempts or initiatives with pious intention can hardly make substantial dent towards saturating basic needs on sustainable basis.

Table 1

PERCENTAGE DISTRIBUTION OF OPERATIONAL HOLDINGS IN INDIA AND UTTAR PRADESH DURING 1995-96

(%)

Size of Holdings (Acre)	*India*		*Uttar Pradesh*	
	Number	*Area*	*Number*	*Area*
Less than 2.5	59.4	15.1	75.6	34.1
2.5 - 5.0	18.8	17.4	14.5	23.8
5.0 - 10.0	13.1	23.2	7.3	23.1
10.0 - 25.0	7.1	27.0	2.4	5.8
Above 25.0	1.6	17.3	0.2	3.2
Average size (acre)		0.55		0.90

Source: Statistical Diary, State Planning Institute, Department of Planning, Government of Uttar Pradesh.

Table 2

OPERATIONAL LAND HOLDING OF U.P. AND SAMPLE DISTRICTS (%)

S. N.	*Description of land holding*	*Total U.P.*	*Gorakh-pur*	*Chan-dauli**	*Muzaffar-Nagar*	*Hamir-pur*	*Rae-Bareli*
1.	Average holding	0.90	0.58	n.a.	1.09	1.96	0.64
2.	Marginal holding						

S. N.	Description of land holding	Total U.P.	Gorakh-pur	Chan-dauli*	Muzaffar-Nagar	Hamir-pur	Rae-Bareli
	(up to 1.0 hec.)	73.82	85.07	85.01	64.56	46.06	80.83
3.	Small farms (1-2 hec.)	15.53	9.82	10.07	18.81	23.02	13.18
4.	Semi-medium farms (2-4 hec.)	7.69	4.16	n.a.	11.84	17.72	4.86
5.	Medium farms (4-10 hec.)	2.73	0.90	n.a.	4.59	11.46	1.09
6.	Large farms	0.22	0.05	n.a.	0.19	1.73	0.05
7.	Total	100.00	100		100	100	100

Source: For Uttar Prudish See Statistical Diary of Uttar Prudish year 2000 pg. no. 98,99 and for sample districts see Statistical Diary of: Gorakhpur 2000 pg. no. 61,62,63; Muzaffarnagar 2000 pg. no. 46,47; Rae Bareli 2000 pg. no. 59,60,61; Hamirpur 2000 pg. no. 48,49,50.

* Data relate to Varanasi as no land holding data are available for Chandauli, a carved out district from Varanasi

Table 3

PERCENTAGE DISTRIBUTION OF HOUSEHOLDS BY SOCIAL GROUPS AND FARM SIZE (OPERATIONAL HOLDINGS) AT THE SAMPLE VILLAGES OF UTTAR PRADESH

Size of Operational Holdings	UPC	UMC	OMC	SCC	MSM*	Total
Landless	0.98	1.15	10.21	23.71	1.60	37.66
Marginal	2.49	1.33	15.72	28.69	3.73	51.95
Small	1.24	0.27	1.15	2.58	0.62	5.86
Semi-Medium	0.71	0.27	1.42	0.98	0.09	3.46
Medium-cum-Large	0.36	0.09	0.09	0.53	--	1.07
Total	5.77	3.11	28.60	56.48	6.04	100.00

Source: Mishra & Diwakar, 2005.

Note: UPC =Upper Caste; UMC = Upper Middle Caste; OMC = Other Middle Castes; SCC = Scheduled Castes; MSM = Muslim.

* Muslim is not a caste but a religious classification, which has been used separately indicating entire Muslim Community as other castes are of Hindu community. However, most of them belong to OMC category.

Table 4

PERCENTAGE DISTRIBUTION OF HOUSEHOLDS BY SOCIAL GROUPS AND FARM SIZE OF NET OPERATIONAL AREA AND DISTRICT IN SAMPLE VILLAGES OF UTTAR PRADESH

Social Groups/ Farm Size	*Gorakh-pur*	*Chan-dauli*	*Muzaffar-nagar*	*Hamir-pur*	*Rae Bareli*	*Total*
I. Social Group						
UPC	14.22	3.86	3.59	3.54	3.30	5.77
UMC	2.59	6.87	--	4.87	0.94	3.11
OMC	44.83	19.31	25.56	33.63	18.87	28.60
SCC	38.36	69.96	70.85	57.08	45.75	56.48
MSM	—	—	—	0.88	31.13	6.04
Total	100.00	100.00	100.00	100.00	100.00	100.00
II. Farmers Category						
Landless	24.14	64.38	46.64	31.42	20.28	37.66
Marginal	71.98	28.76	41.26	51.33	67.45	51.95
Small	3.02	3.00	2.69	10.64	10.38	5.86
Semi-Medium	0.86	3.43	6.73	4.87	1.42	3.46
Medium-cum-Large	—	0.43	2.69	1.77	0.47	1.07
Total	100.00	100.00	100.00	100.00	100.00	100.00

Source: Mishra & Diwakar, 2005

Table 5

DISTRIBUTION OF CEILING SURPLUS LAND IN SAMPLE DISTRICTS OF UTTAR PRADESH 2003

Sample Districts	*Land declared ceiling surplus*	*Declared ceiling surplus land taken possessions by the state*	*Subjudice land stayed by the court order*	*Balance to be taken in possession*	*Allotted land area to the landless*	*Total area of settlement land*	*Area balance for settlement*
1	*2*	*3*	*4*	*5*	*6*	*7*	*8*
Gorakhpur	6024	4583 (76.08)	1441 (23.92)	1441 (23.92)	3611 (59.94)	4156 (68.99)	427 (7.09)
Chandauli	1311	763 (58.20)	548 (41.80)	548 (41.80)	570 (43.48)	688 (52.48)	75 (5.72)

1	2	3	4	5	6	7	8
Rae Bareli	4559	4559 (100.0)	00	00	3723 (78.93)	4298 (94.27)	261 (5.73)
Hamirpur	8749	6927 (79.15)	1822 (20.85)	1822 (20.85)	6297 (71.89)	6374 (72.77)	553 (6.38)
Muzaffar Nagar	6885	6581 (96.14)	304 (3.86)	264 (3.86)	3621 (51.02)	6454 (92.42)	127 (3.73)
Total U.P.	365584	335074 (91.62)	28969 (7.89)	30391 (8.38)	259000 (70.09)	313569 (85.31)	21505 (6.34)

Source: Land Revenue Board, Government of U.P., Nov 2003.
Note: Figures in parenthesis indicate percentage of land declared ceiling surplus (col. 3 + col. 5 = 100 per cent)

Table 6

DISTRIBUTION OF GAON SABHA LAND BY CASTE CATEGORY IN U.P. SINCE 1975-76 TO 2002 (ACRES)

Sample Districts	*Scheduled Castes*	*Backward Castes*	*Other Castes*	*Total Area**
1	2	3	4	5
Gorakhpur	7290 (55.4)	2933 (22.3)	2946 (22.4)	13168 (100.0)
Chandauli	3430 (67.6)	1539 (30.3)	104 (2.1)	5073 (100.0)
Rae Bareli	51510 (54.7)	18835 (20.0)	4112 (4.4)	94228 (100.0)
Hamirpur	22032 (60.6)	10432 (28.7)	3870 (10.7)	36332 (100.0)
Muzaffarnagar	21669 (51.3)	8977 (21.2)	11620 (27.5)	42268 (100.0)
Total	1454619 (54.8)	687213 (25.9)	508217 (19.2)	2652263 (100.0)

* Total includes ST and Army also.
Source: Land Revenue Board, Government of U.P., March 2002.
Note : Figures in parenthesis indicate percentage of the total households.

Table 7

IMPACTS OF REDISTRIBUTION OF LAND FOR RESIDENTIAL HOUSING ON THE BENEFICIARY HOUSEHOLDS BY SOCIAL GROUPS AND FARM SIZE OF THE SAMPLE VILLAGES IN UTTAR PRADESH

Social Group and Farm Size	*Percentage of Beneficiary Households*				
	Residential Land Bondage	*Liberated from Prestige*	*Enhanced Social House*	*Constructed*	*Acquired Comfortable Living*
I. Social Group					
UPC	0.18	0.09	0.09	0.00	0.18
UMC	0.36	0.27	0.27	0.18	0.36
OMC	2.31	0.98	1.24	1.78	2.04
SCC	6.22	3.55	3.82	4.00	4.53
MSM	0.53	0.44	0.44	0.18	0.36
Total BHH	9.59	5.33	5.86	6.13	7.46
Total	100.00	100.00	100.00	100.00	100.00
II. Farm Size					
Landless	0.18	—	0.09	0.18	0.18
Marginal	7.99	4.53	4.88	5.33	6.04
Small	1.15	0.53	0.62	0.62	0.98
Semi-Medium	0.27	0.27	0.27	—	0.27
Medium-cum-Large	—	—	—	—	—
Total BHH	9.59	5.33	5.86	6.13	7.46
Total	100.00	100.00	100.00	100.00	**100.00**

Source: Mishra & Diwakar, 2005

Table 8

IMPACTS OF REDISTRIBUTION OF CULTIVABLE LAND ON THE FOOD SECURITY AND INCOME OF THE BENEFICIARY HOUSEHOLDS BY SOCIAL GROUPS AND FARM SIZE OF THE SAMPLE VILLAGES IN UTTAR PRADESH

Social Groups and Farm Size	*Percentage Distribution of Households Accepted*							
	Beneficiary of Cultivable Land	*Production of Food grains increased*	*Confortable at food front*	*ML Borrowing Reduced*	*Public Loan Easier*	*Income increased*	*Easy cattle rearing*	*Other Income Gene-raing Initiative*
I. Social Group								
UPC	0.44	0.36	0.36	0.09	0.27	0.36	0.18	—
UMC	1.15	0.44	0.36	0.27	0.27	0.27	0.18	0.09
OMC	7.28	5.60	5.60	2.40	1.69	3.82	1.78	0.62
SCC	17.67	15.63	15.81	9.06	6.31	14.03	5.42	2.66
MSM	1.33	1.24	1.24	1.15	1.07	1.51	0.89	0.18
TOTAL BHH	27.89	23.27	23.36	12.97	9.59	19.98	8.44	3.55
TOTAL	100.0	100.0	100.0	100.0	100.0	100.0	100.0	100.0
II. Farm Size								
Landless	6.84	5.15	5.33	2.49	1.69	3.56	0.80	0.44
Marginal	18.47	15.72	15.63	8.97	6.39	14.21	6.93	2.40
Small	1.95	1.78	1.78	0.98	1.15	1.69	0.53	0.53

Semi-Medium	0.53	0.53	0.53	0.44	0.27	0.44	0.09	0.09
Medium-cum-Large	0.09	0.09	0.09	0.09	0.09	0.09	0.09	0.09
TOTAL BHH	27.89	23.27	23.36	12.97	9.59	19.98	8.44	3.55
TOTAL	100.0	100.0	100.0	100.0	100.0	100.0	100.0	100.0

Source: Mishra & Diwakar, 2005

Table 9

Impacts of Land Distribution on Social Development of the Beneficiary Households by Social Groups and Farms Size of the sample village of Uttar Pradesh

Social Group and Farm Size	Percentage of Beneficiary Households			
	Improvement in Health Condition of Children	*Proper Clothing for Children*	*Child Schooling*	*Sending Girl Child to School*
I. Social Group				
UPC	0.27	0.27	0.27	3.73
UMC	0.27	0.27	0.18	1.95
OMC	2.40	1.95	3.02	15.10
SCC	9.86	9.33	9.15	29.13
MSM	0.89	0.89	1.24	3.73
TOTAL BHH	13.68	12.70	13.85	56.64
TOTAL	100.00	100.00	100.00	100.00
II. Farm Size				
Landless	2.66	2.49	2.40	19.09
Marginal	9.06	8.35	10.12	27.71
Small	1.51	1.42	0.98	3.29
Semi-Medium	0.36	0.36	0.27	2.49
Medium-cum-Large	0.09	0.09	0.09	1.07
TOTAL BHH	13.68	12.70	13.85	56.64
TOTAL	100.00	100.00	100.00	100.00

Source: Mishra & Diwakar, 2005.

References

Bagchi, A.K. (1988): *Economy Society and Polity*, Oxford University Press.

Das, Sukumar (2000): A Critical Evaluation of Land Reforms in India in Sinha B.K. and Pushpendra (eds.), *Land Reforms in India*, Vol. 5, Sage Publications, New Delhi.

De Silva, G.V.S., et al (1988): *Towards Theorisation of Rural Development.*

Dharmakumar (1982): *The Cambridge Economic History of India*, Vol. II, Orient Longmans.

Diwakar, D.M., (2000): Agrarian Transformation in Uttar Pradesh,

Journal of Social and Economic Development, Vol. III, No. 1, January-June.

___ (2000a): "Purvi Uttar Pradesh ke Kheti mein Poonji ka Vikas," *Lokyuddha*, November-December.

Dorner, P. (1972): *Land Reforms and Economic Development*, Penguin, Harmondsworth.

Government of India (1980): Report on the Backward Class Commission, Vol. I.

Government of India (1973): Approach to the Fifth Five Year Plan 1974-79, Planning Commission.

Joshi, P.C. (1982): *Land Reforms in India*, Allied Publishers, New Delhi.

Mishra, G.P. (1996): *Distribution of Surplus Land and Rural Poor*, APH Publishing Corporation, New Delhi.

Mishra, G.P. & D.M. Diwakar, (2005): Land Reforms and Human Development, Manak Publications, New Delhi.

Neale, W.C. (1962): *Economic Change in Rural India: Land Tenure and Reforms in Uttar Pradesh: 1800-1955*, Kennikat Press, London.

Prasad, P.H., (1980): Rising Middle Peasantry in North India, *Economic and Political Weekly*, Annual Number.

Radhakrishnan, P. (1989): *Peasant Struggles Land Reforms and Social Change*, Sage Publications, New Delhi.

Raychoudhuri, R.C. and I. Habib (1982): *The Cambridge Economic History of India*, Vol. I, Orient Longmans.

Sampurnanand, B. (1936): *Agrarian Enquiry Committee Report*, Note of Ch. VI, p. XV.

Singh B. and Shridhar Mishra (1964): *A Study of Land Reforms in Uttar Pradesh*, Oxford Book Company, Calcutta.

Tandon, P.D. *et.al.*, (1936): *Congress Agrarian Enquiry Committee Report*, 1936, Prabhu Publications, Gurgaon (Haryana).

Thorner, D. (1976): *The Agrarian Prospects in India*, Allied Publishers Ltd., New Delhi.

3

PLIGHT OF IRRIGATION SECTOR IN UTTAR PRADESH
Investment, Environment and Management

Sanatan Nayak

I. Introduction

The development of irrigation along with fertilisers, HYV seeds and other modern inputs acts as a catalyst for agricultural development vis-à-vis economic development of the country. It brings numerous direct and indirect benefits to the society. Large number of studies have revealed irrigation enable to enhance land use intensity, crop productivity and production of various crops in different states in India since the evolution of planning (Dhawan, 1988; Shah, 1993; Vaidyanathan, 1994; Vaidyanathan et al, 1994; Subrahmanyam, et al. 2003). It also helps in reducing instability in crop production, changes the cropping pattern in favour of high valued crops, and reduces inequality in income among various section farmers in the society (Ray, 1983; Dev, 1987; Despande, 1988; Nayak, 2005). Indirect benefits of irrigation are creation of more rural employment, higher agricultural wages, and reduction in rural poverty, reduction of out migration and lower foodgrains prices (Bardhan, 1973; Rao, 1994; Narayanamoorthy, 2001; Sarmah, 2002; Narayanamoorthy, et al, 2004). However, irrigation is not certainly considered as blessings on the mankind, if it is not managed properly. Its side effect in the shape of waterlogging and salinity within the large canal commands have been considered as one of the important negative impact on the farms output (Joshi et al, 1984; Chopra, 1989; Datta et al, 2000, Nayak, 2002).

The net irrigated area has increased from 62.55 lakhs hectares in 1966-67 to 94.53 lakh hectares in 1980-81 and again increased to 128.28 lakhs hectares in 2001-02. The proportion of net irrigated area to net cropped area has increased from 36.12 percent in 1966-67 to 54.89 percent in 1980-81, again increased to 73.70 percent in 2000-01 and 76.30 percent in 2001-02. Total fertilizer consumption has increased from 4.12 lakh tones in 1970-71 to 33.53 lakh tones in 2000-01. This has lead to increase the total foodgrains production from 169.78 lakh tones in 1970-71 to 424.97 lakh tones in 2000-01 and the productivity has also increased from 1015 kg/hectare in 1970-71 to 2104 kg/hectare in 2000-01. However, numerous studies also revealed that irrigation also provide enormous indirect impact on generating employment, increasing wage rate, stabilizing prices, reducing poverty and disparity.

The tenth five year plan targets to irrigate the potential of 265.39 lakh hectares in order to achieve 5.17 percent of annual growth in agricultural sector vis-à-vis 8 percent overall growth of the state, which would enable to enhance the quality of life, reduce regional disparity, inequality and poverty. As the net sown area remains almost constant at 168 lakh hectares in the state, further expansion of irrigation including additional irrigation through modernization/ renovation can make agriculture vibrant to achieve food security mainly through multiple cropping and higher productivity of crops.

Keeping in mind the above mentioned problems related to agricultural and irrigation sector in Uttar Pradesh, this chapter attempt to assess the following aspects of the irrigation sector in recent years in Uttar Pradesh.

Firstly, to assess the pattern of public investment and its impact in irrigation sector during the recent years in Uttar Pradesh.

Secondly, to assess the physical achievements or diversification of irrigation sector towards more private irrigation and its impact on irrigation sector.

Thirdly, to assess the irrigation induced environmental problems and its impact of human well being.

Fourthly, to evaluate the financial performance or water rates of the public irrigation in the State.

Sixthly, to evaluate the extent and dimension of irrigation management or participatory irrigation management in the state.

Secondary sources data relating to public investment in irrigation and its sub-sectors, physical achievements, environmental degradation, water rates are collected from various volumes of Annual Plan Documents, Statistical Abstract, Statistical Dairy, NRSA Reports, Aaya-Vyayak Digdarshak of State Government and Central Government Reports.

This paper is divided into four sections. Section I deals with introduction, objectives and methodology of this study. While, Section II highlights the pattern of public investments and its impact, Section III describes the physical achievements and Public and Private irrigation in the state. Section IV analyses the extent and causes of irrigation induced land degradation, while section V deals with pattern and its impact on water rates in Irrigation sector. Section VI highlights the extent and dynamics of Irrigation Management, while section VII deals with Future Policy Direction. In the last, Section VIII deals with concluding remarks of this study.

II. Public Investment in Irrigation

The expenditure on irrigation and flood control was 12.64 percent of the total planned expenditure in 9th plan and restricted to 12 percent during the first three years of the 10th plan. On the other hand, total public investment in absolute terms in irrigation has increased continuously during 1980-81 to 2002-03 with the exception of few years and the same trend has been repeated in the 10th plan in the state. On the other hand, when we compare the real investment with current investment, the trend looks different during the same period. However, the real investment has remained constant since mid-eighties till late nineties and declined in the recent years (Figure 1).

Considering the distribution of public investment in intra-sector such as medium and major irrigation takes a lion share up to 83.81 percent during the 9th plan and it is anticipated to rise up to 84.45 percent by the end of 10th plan. The public investment on minor irrigation has declined drastically from 14.52 percent in 1998-99 to 1.37 percent in 1999-2000 and finally kept at 8.23 percent of the total by the end of 9th plan and it is proposed to decline to 7 percent in the 10th plan (Table 1). Development of command areas is considered an important sub-sector inter sectoral distribution of funds, which helps in maintaining effectively the already achieved irrigated lands. Unfortunately, the share under CAD is restricted to 5-6 percent and it declined to nearly 4 percent in the first three years of 10th plan. It shows the irrigation establishments have an overwhelming bias towards designing and construction of projects without commensurate concerns and budgetary share on the utilization of the potential created, operation and maintenance of the project completed.

Table 1

EXPENDITURE ON VARIOUS TYPES OF IRRIGATION DURING 9TH AND 10TH FIVE YEAR PLAN IN UP (RS. LAKHS)

Year/Sources	*Major & Medium Irrigation*	*Minor Irrigation*	*Command Area Development*	*Flood Control*	*Total*
1997-98	47387 (79.37)	8115.52 (13.59)	3057.8 (5.12)	1140 (1.91)	59700.32 (100.00)
1998-99	44840 (76.86)	8473.62 (14.52)	2514.63 (4.31)	2512.61 (4.31)	58340.86 (100.00)
1999-2000	63416 (87.17)	994.49 (1.37)	4249.53 (5.84)	4087.39 (5.62)	72747.41 (100.00)

Year/Sources	*Major & Medium Irrigation*	*Minor Irrigation*	*Command Area Development*	*Flood Control*	*Total*
2000-01	74198	5930.11	2876.96	3111.35	86116.42
	(86.16)	(6.89)	(3.34)	(3.61)	(100.00)
2001-02	71617	6102.26	2831.12	2229.94	82780.32
	(86.51)	(7.37)	(3.42)	(2.69)	(100.00)
Ninth Plan	301458	29616	15530.04	13081.29	359685.33
(current prices)	(83.81)	(8.23)	(4.32)	(3.64)	(100.00)
Ninth Plan (at 1996-97	246936.81	24912.43	12914.79	10715.73	295479.76
prices)	(83.57)	(8.43)	(4.37)	(3.63)	(100.00)
2002-03	82481	7026	3000	3853	96360
	(85.60)	(7.29)	(3.11)	(4.00)	(100.00)
2003-04	92032	8541	4000	5718	110295
(Anticipated)	(83.44)	(7.74)	(3.63)	(5.18)	(100.00)
2004-05	87750	10425	4000	4594.54	106769.54
(proposed)	(82.19)	(9.76)	(3.75)	(4.30)	(100.00)

Source: Annual Plan Document 2004-05, Vol. II, Government of U.P.
Note: Values in the Parenthesis are percent of the total.

When we assess the pattern of investment in surface irrigation with ground water irrigation, it looks substantial portion of public investment goes to surface irrigation. The

FIGURE 1
TREND OF CURRENT AND REAL INVESTMENT IRRIGATION SECTOR IN UTTAR PRADESH

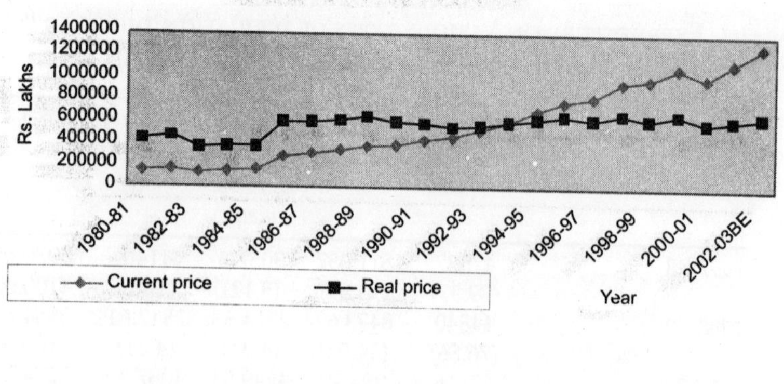

groundwater irrigation constitutes nearly 69 percent of the total utilised area during the 9th plan in the state, whereas surface irrigated area from all sources (minor, medium and major) constitutes nearly 31 percent of the total utilised area (Table 2). Similarly, the groundwater utilised irrigation is targeted to increase up to 71 percent of the total irrigated area in the 10th plan. It is clearly observed that nearly 80 percent of public investment is made on major and medium irrigation, which ultimately irrigate only 31 percent of the total irrigated area. Similarly, 4 percent of the public investment is meant for the overhead and maintenance of total canal irrigation sector. Hence, there may be rethinking of diversification of public investment in favour of development of minor irrigation in the non-canal and under developed regions in the state as well as on CAD of the canal irrigated area.

Distribution of Funds within O & M Costs

The share of operation costs (direction and administration) has been increasing over the years touching up to 82 percent in 2000-01 on the one hand and the share of maintenance and repairing has been declining up to 11 percent 2002-03. However, considering the entire period 1986-87 to 2002-03, the share on operation costs goes alone more than 50 percent and it declines to less than 30 percent on M & R over the years in the state. Most importantly, the share of direction and administration costs out of total O & M costs has been increasing on the one hand and share of M & R costs is being declining (Figure 2). It means a substantial part of the expenditure earmarked for O & M costs, goes to meet the expenditure on the staffs in the irrigation department leaving very little for maintenance and repairing work in the state. The diversification of fund within the O & M costs looks unfavorable for the sustainability of the irrigation systems. However, physical sustainability of a huge infrastructure like irrigation is very much dependant on judicious budget allocation. It may be suggested that there is a need for reallocation of budget to maintenance and repair works and reduction of expenditure on direction and administration.

Table 2
Source wise Irrigation during 9th and 10th Five Year Plan in UP ('lakh hectares)

Year	*Groundwater*	*Surface Irrigation*	*Major and Medium Irrigation*	*Total*
1997-98	140.18	4.57	60.34	205.09
	(68.35)	(2.23)	(29.42)	(100.00)
1998-99	143.74	4.66	61.09	209.49
	(68.61)	(2.23)	(29.16)	(100.00)
1999-2000	145.21	4.71	61.84	211.76
	(68.57)	(2.23)	(29.20)	(100.00)
2000-01	148.21	4.76	62.15	215.11
	(68.90)	(2.21)	(28.89)	(100.00)
2001-02	152.16	4.81	62.29	219.26
	(69.40)	(2.19)	(28.41)	(100.00)
Ninth plan	152.16	4.81	62.29	219.26
	(69.40)	(2.19)	(28.01)	(100.00)
Tenth plan (2002-07)	188.08	5.01	72.29	265.39
	(70.87)	(1.89)	(27.24)	(100.00)
(2002-03)	156.26	4.87	62.91	224.04
	(69.75)	(2.18)	(28.08)	(100.00)
(2003-04) Anticipated	159.13	4.94	64.35	228.42
	(69.67)	(2.16)	(28.17)	(100.00)
(2004-05) Proposed	162.31	5.01	65.65	232.96
	(69.67)	(2.16)	(28.18)	(100.00)

Source: Annual Plan Document, 2003-04, Vol. II, Government of U.P.

III. Physical Achievement

The net irrigated area has increased from 62.55 lakhs hectares in 1966-67 to 94.53 lakh hectares in 1980-81 and again increased to 128.28 lakhs hectares in 2001-02. The proportion of net irrigated area to net cropped area has increased from 36.12 percent in 1966-67 to 54.89 percent in 1980-81, again increased to 73.70 percent in 2000-01 and 76.30 percent in 2001-02. Moreover, the net irrigated area by private sources such as private tubewell/pump sets constitute nearly 87.09 lakh hectares, which is 68 percent of the net irrigated area, whereas major and medium sources through canal irrigation possesses

FIGURE 2

TRENDS OF O & M COSTS AND REVENUE IN UTTAR PRADESH (PER HECTARE)

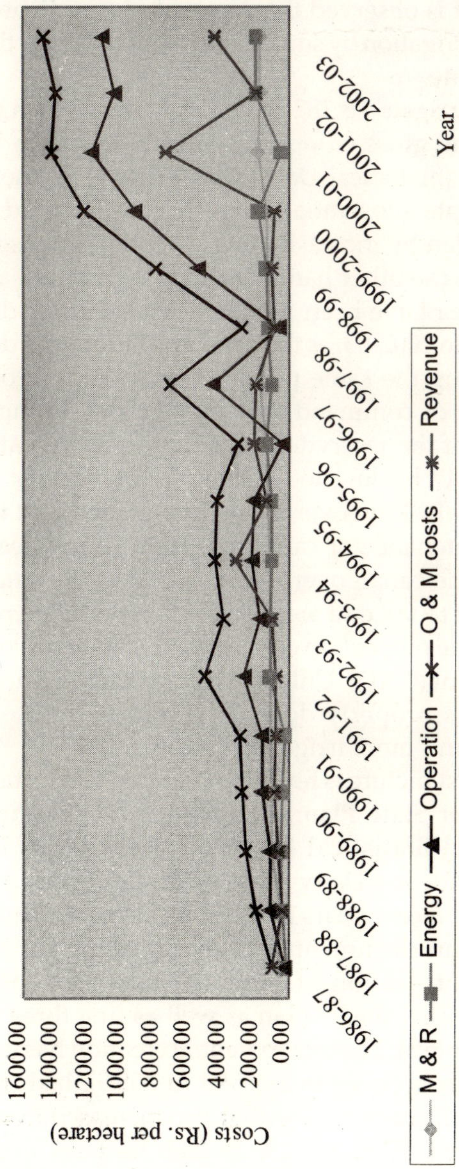

at 27.19 lakh hectares, which is nearly 21 percent of the net irrigated area. It is observed that there has been disproportionate growth of irrigation by sources developed during the study period in the state.

The gross irrigated is 182.20 lakh hectares, which is nearly 72 percent of the gross cropped area of 254.47 lakh hectares during 2002-03 (Statistical Dairy, 2003). It shows the state is enabled to irrigate substantial proportion of cropped area by the end of 9th plan by increasing the irrigation intensity up to 142 percent. On the other hand, both gross irrigated area and net irrigated area have been remaining constant or declining during 1998-99 to 2002-03, as the canal irrigation was declining constantly during the same period (Figure 3). It is observed that the decline of command area may be due to increase in sedimentation of the reservoirs causes more evaporation and less water supply leading to decline of water use at tail end areas of the canals. Moreover, it is apprehended that the poor quality of maintenance of canal irrigation causes leakage in upper part of the canal, over use of water in the same areas causes no water to tail end area. This has been happening due to declining of the proportion of budget allocation on command area development (CAD). Unless, the physical repairing of this infrastructure is properly done, it would be impossible to provide better and more irrigation facility.

The contrast picture is revealed between two data sources published under State Planning Institute, i.e., Annual Plan Documents and Statistical Dairy in recent years in Uttar Pradesh. The Statistical Dairy reveals a declining trend of canal irrigated area in recent years in the state as mentioned earlier, whereas the plan documents clearly pointing out both the potential and utilization of potential has been increasing continuously during the 9th plan as well as first three years in the 10th plan (Table 3). The total potential creation has increased from 285.80 lakh hectares in 1997-98 to 305.94 lakh hectares. Similarly, the utilization of potential also increased from 205.09 lakh hectares in 1997-98 to 219. 26 lakh hectares in 2001-02. However, the utilization constitutes nearly 72 percent of the potential creation in the 9th plan and first three years of the 10th

FIGURE 3
TRENDS OF VARIOUS TYPES OF IRRIGATION IN UTTAR PRADESH

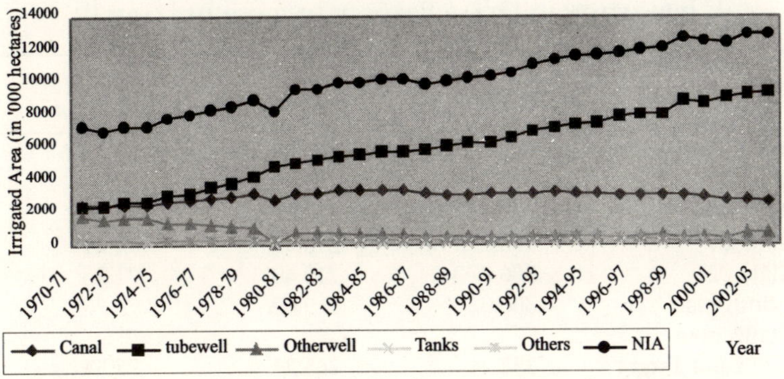

plan. Importantly, the lag of about 87 lakh hectares of potential creation is a matter of serious concern. It may be due to various reasons such as change in cropping pattern to more water intensive crops, low water use efficiency due to disrepair of the system and lack of reliable statistics on creation and utilization etc. (Government of India, 2002-07). Another mismatching exists between the gross irrigated area and utilization of potential in the two sources. The utilization of potential is always higher than the gross irrigated area, as both should be equal and near equal. It is apprehended that difference in the methodology of data estimation by the two documents is the prime reason for the difference in the data.

Public and Private Irrigation

The private and public irrigation is broadly classified under groundwater, minor surface irrigation, and major and medium canal irrigation. Groundwater irrigation mainly used both by private and public tubewell, shallow tubewells, dugwell and deep tubewells. Minor surface irrigation is mainly by both public and private sector consists of the development of tank irrigation. Finally, major and medium irrigation (canal irrigation) is mainly developed by public sources through the construction of dams over the rivers. It is urgently felt the role

Table 3

COMPARISON OF POTENTIAL CREATION AND UTILIZATION OF IRRIGATION IN UTTAR PRADESH (IN LAKH HECTARES)

Year	*Potential Creation*	*Utilization of Potential*	*Utilization as per-cent to potential*
1997-98	285.80	205.09	71.76
1998-99	290.65	209.49	72.08
1999-2000	293.32	211.76	72.19
2000-01	300.87	215.45	71.61
2001-02	306.07	219.60	71.75
Ninth plan	306.07	219.60	71.75
Tenth plan			
(2002-07) Target	352.24	265.39	75.34
(2002-03)	310.64	224.04	72.12
(2003-04)			
Anticipated	314.31	228.42	72.67
(2004-05) Proposed	319.16	232.96	72.99

Source: Annual Plan Document, 2003-04, Vol. II, Government of UP.

of both private and public sector irrigation under these major sources at the national and state level. However, the trend and nature of development of both private and public sector irrigation at the sate level is not far away from the national level.

It is observed that groundwater irrigation created by both private and pubic sector during 1997-2002 was nearly 126.49 lakh hectares; out of that private sector constitute 111. 42 lakh hectares, which constitute nearly 88 percent of the total groundwater irrigated area in the state (Table 4). However, the share of private sector in the groundwater irrigation during the first two years of the 10th five year plan remains constant in the state. Similarly, surface irrigation owned by both private and public sector during 9th five year plan is 4.53 lakh hectares, out of that private sector contributes 1. 64 lakh hectares, which is nearly 36.21 percent of the total surface irrigated area. Moreover, major and medium irrigation constitute a major share of the total irrigation comes from only public sector. In this way, when the private and public irrigation under the three broad sources are grouped, the share of private irrigation constitutes 113.06 lakh hectares, which is 58.49 percent of the total irrigated area in the 9th plan and it is anticipated that its share will increase up to 62.12 in the end of 10th five year plan.

Table 4

SOURCE WISE SHARE OF PRIVATE AND PUBLIC IRRIGATION
('LAKH HECTARES)

Year	*Groundwater*		*Surface*		*Major and Medium*		*Total*	
	Private	*State*	*Private*	*State*	*Private*	*state*	*Private*	*State*
1997-98	122.62	14.97	1.75	2.88	0	60.34	124.37	78.19
	(89.12)	(10.88)	(37.76)	(62.24)	(0.00)	(100.00)	(61.40)	(38.60)
1998-99	119.95	15.06	1.75	2.88	0	61.09	121.70	79.03
	(88.89)	(11.15)	(37.76)	(62.24)	(0.00)	(100.00)	(60.63)	(39.37)
1999-2000	115.48	15.07	1.72	2.88	0	61.84	117.20	79.79
	(88.46)	(11.54)	(37.36)	(62.54)	(0.00)	(100.00)	(59.50)	(40.50)
2000-01	113.07	15.07	1.67	2.89	0	62.15	114.74	80.10
	(88.24)	(11.76)	(36.65)	(63.35)	(0.00)	(100.00)	(58.89)	(41.11)
2001-02	111.42	15.07	1.64	2.89	0	62.29	113.06	80.25
	(88.09)	(11.91)	(36.21)	63.79)	(0.00)	(100.00)	(58.49)	(41.51)
Ninth plan	111.42	15.07	1.64	2.89	0	62.29	113.06	80.24
	(88.56)	(11.44)	(37.16)	(62.84)	(0.00)	(100.00)	(59.80)	(40.20)
Tenth plan	146.72	15.35	1.81	2.92	0	72.29	148.53	90.56
(2002-07)	(90.53)	(9.47)	(38.27)	(61.73)	(0.00)	(100.00)	(62.12)	(37.88)
(2002-03)	115.13	15.07	1.65	2.90	0	63.49	116.78	81.46
Anticipated	(88.43)	(11.57)	(36.29)	(63.71)	(0.00)	(100.00)	(58.91)	(41.09)
(2004-05)	118.79	15.06	1.67	2.91	0	64.93	120.46	82.92
Target	(88.74)	(11.26)	(36.40)	(63.60)	(0.00)	(100.00)	(59.23)	(40.77)

Source: Annual Plan Document, 2003-04, Vol. II, Government of U.P.
Note: Values in the Parenthesis is the percent of the respective total.

In the post green revolution era, heavy use of HYV seeds, fertilizer vis-à-vis diversification of agriculture led to large scale increase in the demand for private tube wells and pump sets. As a result, during the 9th five year the construction of actual tubewell was more than the targeted in the beginning of the 9th plan. In other words, the demand for private tubewells/pump sets has increased from 30.56 lakhs in 1997-98 to 32.84 lakhs in

2001-02 and ultimately 34.21 lakhs in 2003-04. Out of total private tubewells, the use of dieselized tubewell constitutes 82. 04 percent of the total, whereas the use of electrified tubewell constitutes only 17.96 percent by the end of 9th plan and 17.78 by the end of 2003-04 (Table 5). This has been occurring as a result of heavy power shortage, mechanical defects of the one hand and dieselized machines are more convenient on the other hand. This has been identified earlier in many other studies (Dhawan, 1982; Shanker, 1982; Pant, 2004). In case of diesel pump sets, it is found that there has been progressive increase in their number in the state during the 9th plan and first three years of the 10th plan. The proportion of diesel pump sets has increased 82.04 percent of the total because of shortage of power, the use of electric pump sets has declined and there has been an increase of diesel pump sets. This has been studied very closely in many other studies (Pant, 2004).

Table 5

Construction of Different Private Pump Sets during 9th and 10th five year plan in Uttar Pradesh (in numbers)

Year	Total private pump sets/ tube wells	Diesel Operated		Electrical Operated	
		Total	Percent of the total	Total	Percent of the total
1997-98	3055542	2499008	81.79	556534	18.21
1998-99	3122224	2557819	81.92	564405	18.08
1999-2000	3150249	2582916	81.99	567333	18.01
2000-01	3214560	2644673	82.27	569887	17.73
2001-02	3284044	2700173	82.22	583871	17.78
Ninth plan	15826619	12984589	82.04	2842030	17.96
Tenth plan	3866748	3255877	84.20	610871	15.80
(Target) (2002-03)	3356166	2767229	82.45	588937	17.55
(2003-04)					
Anticipated	3409645	2818500	82.66	591145	17.34
(2004-05) Proposed	3425163	2828742	82.59	596421	17.41

Source: Annual Plan Document, 2004-05, Vol. II, Government of UP.

IV. Irrigation Induced Environmental Degradation

Waterlogging

Waterlogging not only mean that the rise of water table above the surface areas but also it covers in the sub-surface areas. However, it is more problematic in the sub-surface areas. The definition of waterlogging differs among the various organization depending on the area and soil conditions. However, Groundwater Department, Government of Uttar Pradesh has defined waterlogging in the state based on the soil conditions and water level, which is more relevant for measuring the extent of waterlogging in the state. There are four categories of waterlogging area in the state (Government of UP, 2003). Firstly, wet lands include marshy land and pond areas, where water level may be above the ground surface or perched waterlogging conditions prevails. Secondly, critical waterlogged areas in clay loam soils within 2.0 meters below groundwater level in post-monsoon month and capillary rise of groundwater reaches the surface. Thirdly, semi critical areas fall between 2.0 to 3.0 mbgl and capillary rise reaches the root zones of cereal crops in clay loam to sandy loam soils. Fourthly, potential for waterlogging covers between 3.0 to 5.0 mbgl, where excessive surface water by irrigation and poor groundwater pumpage in such areas may create waterlogging problems. It is estimated that 45.84 lakh hectares of land coming under 0 to 2 meters below the groundwater level, whereas 38.09 lakh hectares are in the 2 to 3 meters range in the post monsoon of 1996. In other words, 83.93 lakh hectares, which is nearly 42 percent of the reported area of the state is waterlogged (Table 6). The level of waterlogging has declined marginally to 79.63 lakh hectares, which is nearly 40 percent of the reporting area during the post-monsoon of 2000 in the state. Waterlogging becomes a widespread problem especially in Eastern and Central region of the state not only due to recurrent floods but also rise of the water table above and very close to surface areas due to absence of well drainage system in the irrigated canal areas. It is estimated that just a little under one third of land area in the state is affected by surface and sub-surface waterlogging (Dhar, 2004).

Table 6

Region wise Waterlogged Area in Uttar Pradesh
(in lakhs hectares)

Region	*Reported area*	*Waterlogged Area (0-2.0 mbgl)*		*Waterlogged Area (2.0-3.0 mbgl)*		*Total*	
		1996	*2000*	*1996*	*2000*	*1996*	*2000*
Central plains	45.28	11.35	7.26	8.90	9.28	20.25 (44.72)	16.54 (36.53)
Eastern Plains	75.02	23.59	15.70	17.31	25.42	40.90 (54.52)	41.12 (54.81)
Western plains	80.77	10.90	9.81	11.88	12.16	22.78 (28.20)	21.97 (27.20)
UP Plains	201.07	45.84 (21.84)	32.77 (16.30)	38.09 (18.90)	46.86 (23.31)	83.93 (41.74)	79.63 (39.60)

Source: Groundwater Department, Government of Uttar Pradesh, 2003.

The key requirement is to reduce the water table in the waterlogging areas. That would possible by reducing seepage of recharge and use of shallow tubewells for irrigation. However, reliable data on sub-surface and waterlogging and appropriate water management strategies are needed. The appropriate water management strategies such as conjunctive use of water (reducing canal irrigation in such areas on the one hand and increasing shallow acquifer groundwater pumping on the other for such areas), proper drainage, appropriate crop rotations, and even use of water absorbing hydropaths (tree species that absorb water, i.e., eucalyptus). Various strategies are suggested for better implementation of conjunctive use of irrigation in the waterlogged areas. Firstly, it is recommended to go for a conjunctive use of surface and use of adequate quantity of groundwater from the tubewell irrigation, so that the pre-monsoon groundwater level should be around 10 meter below the land surface in such places where canal irrigation is in operation. Secondly, analysis of data from rainfall, canal water usage, groundwater use and the groundwater level in each canal command areas has to be done to decide the exact and most suitable conjunctive use of surface and groundwater to attain the maximum crop production. It is desirable to equip the officers of the irrigation department with computers and employ suitable staff to operate them and sue their analytical results. Thirdly, it is necessary that pizometers should be installed in all villages to watch the rise and fall of water table to monitor the use of canal and groundwater. Fourthly, in the areas where the water table has declined below 20 meters of land surface, it is desirable that the canal irrigation might be introduced and conjunctive use of surface and groundwater should be planned in such a way that the groundwater table is not allowed to rise beyond 10 meter below land surface. Fifthly, the farmers who use the groundwater in canal irrigated areas, where canals are not closed should be given incentives. Sixthly, each cultivator should be encouraged to have one piezometer installed in his filed. They should be advised to observe the water table regularly and to maintain the water table preferably below 4 meter in sandy soil and below 6 meter for silty and clay soils from land surface in Rabi season.

Salinisation

Saline soil 'which contains excess neutral soluble salts, chiefly chlorides and sulphate of sodium, magnesium and calcium in the quantities, which is sufficient to affect plant growth adversely. The salt affected soils are distinguished by three categories on the basis of chemical composition. Firstly, saline soils, which are characterized by chlorine and sulphate. Secondly, alkaline soils, which are preponderance of carbonate and bio-carbonate. Thirdly, saline-alkaline soils have both the contents, which are difficult to reclaim.

The origin of salinity directly or indirectly comes from waterlogging problems. The intensity of salinity also depends on the soil type, hydrogeology, climatic condition, and irrigation practices (Rai, 2003). Hence, the estimation of only saline soil is very difficult as salinity developed due to waterlogging in the flood affected and irrigated areas as well as non-irrigated areas due to the existence of salt content in the soil. Therefore, salinity/alkalinity occurs in the waterlogged areas as well as other fallow and wastelands. The major wasteland/ fallow lands can be mainly grouped under four categories such as *usar* and uncultivable wastelands, cultivable wastelands, current fallows and other fallows. In general sense, the current fallows and other fallows are not grouped in the category of sodic land but such areas are not in cultivation. So, it can be counted as unproductive lands and some of these areas are classified as wasteland. The experience indicated that most of these wastelands are closely related with waterlogging conditions (Rai, 2003). In most of these cases, sodic land is the consequence effect of waterlogging and wide areas of fallow lands fall in waterlogged zones. The usar soils of waterlogged areas can be categorized in three sub-groups, such as 'A' type usar with moderate pH 8.0-8.5 (double cropped but poor crop yield), 'B' type usar, with moderate to high pH 8.5-9.5 (mono-cropped and poor yield), 'C' type barren usar land with pH>9.5.

Uttar Pradesh Government has been undertaking serious measures for reclaiming degraded land even before the plan era. However, reclamation of degraded land has a long history in the state. In 1884, 1200 hectares of ravine lands were forested by the then collector of Etawah (Dhar, 2004). In 1870, the Reh committee suggested deepening of canals for reducing saline efflorescence area due to over-irrigation in the districts of western Uttar Pradesh. The use of gypsum arrived later towards the end of 19th century. In the post independence period, saline reclamation started in 1949 in the districts of Central and Western region of the state. In the last decade, many important schemes are being undertaken for the reclamation of saline land in the state. Most importantly, Uttar Pradesh Bhumi Sudhar Nigam (UPBSN) started reclaiming saline land with the support from World Bank in 1993. Moreover, the second phase of the same project was extended in 1999 to reclaim barren alkaline and other usar land in the severe affected districts of the state However, it is estimated that out of 12 lakh hectares of *Usar* land (Saline, Alkaline and saline-alkaline), only 1.6 lakh hectares of land are reclaimed (Government of Uttar Pradesh, 2004). The task is very much significant in the future years to reclaim the degraded land in the state. We can not forget the importance of food security in a growing populated state, where pressure on land is increasing.

Various methods are useful to control the salinity problems in the irrigated land. Firstly, the proper use gypsum in terms of quantity and periods are very essential to eradicate the salinity problems in the soil. Secondly, the consumption of chemical fertilizers can be reduced by using organic fertilizers. Biological control technique for pest and disease control etc. can be made easily available at a subsidized rate. Proper agricultural extension services to advise and educate the farmers on the application of fertilizers and pesticides. Thirdly, in order to reduce soil degradation, it is required that fertilizer of right type is applied in optimum quantity at the right time. For example, in the beginning of plant growth, requirement is low and therefore, level of application should be low.

Disproportionate Use of Fertilisers

Over the last 35 years, there has been a large increase in fertilizer consumption in India associated with the introduction of high yielding crop varieties. This has become major reason for increase in crop productivity. However, an inter related set of soil fertility problems has been reported, directly or indirectly associated with fertilizer consumption (Bowonder, 1981). Fertilizer use in the region is dominated by nitrogen; N: P and N: K ratios are higher than in the other parts of the world. The N: P: K ratio for India is 1:0.33:0.17 compared with 1:0.52:0.40 for the world (FAO, 1994). When fertilisers are first applied to a soil, high response is frequently obtained from nitrogen. The improved crop growth depletes the soil of other nutrients (FAO, 1994). Keeping the problems in mind, the balanced use of nitrogen (N), phosphorous (P) and potassium (K), the standard suitable mix of NPK has been estimated at all India level by keeping the soil, climatic condition, cropping pattern and other variables into consideration. Accordingly, the suitable mix of NPK in the country is 4:2:1 (Government of India, 2000-01). The use of NPK ratio in different sub-periods at aggregate level in Uttar Pradesh shows serious imbalance, viz., 18:4:1 during the green revolution period (Table 7). The ratio has increased from 7:2:1 in 1970-71 to 11:3:1 in 1980-81 and reached to the highest of 24:7:1 in 2001-2002. It shows the consumption of nitrogenous variety of fertilizer is quite higher than the standard mix. This excessive use of fertilizer could be a damaging factor for the environment and decline of productivity. However, the ratio of N and P with respect to K has been increasing over the study period in all the regions as well as the State level (Table 7). Moreover, the NPK ratio is observed unbelievable in Bundelkhand region due to the application of negligible amount potassium in the soil. As there is no availability of specific data of fertilizer consumption in irrigated land separately, but it is understand that irrigation plays an important role for increasing total fertilizer consumption and plays a big role for disproportionate use.

The impact of excess and disproportionate consumption of fertilisers has been explained variously. The crops and plants cannot take all the fertilizers applied and significant portion is lost in the soils. It means application of more than the required quantity of fertilizers remains in the field, ultimately leads to polluting the soils. The excess or inappropriate consumption of various fertilizers than the recommended quantity or ratio leads to polluting the soil, which ultimately causes for the decline of productivity of various crops. The excess amount of nitrogen applied in the soils automatically converts into nitrate. As nitrate is not observed by most soils, it remains in solution. If it is not taken up by plant roots, it is either washed into the drainage water or biologically reduced to dinitrogen gas. Nitrate that is washed out of the soil represents an economic loss to the farmers and possible health hazard if it reaches drainage water (Wild, 2003).

However, it was found that one of the effects of excessive fertilizer use is the contamination of groundwater. Rao (1994) found that the major source of environmental degradation in rural areas is the misapplication of yield increasing inputs like water, chemical fertilizers, and pesticides causing waterlogging, salinity and pollution of drinking water and loss of fish etc. The subsidy on urea has resulted in an unbalanced use of nitrogen, phosphorous, and potassium fertilisers in the state. This has led to decline in the productivity of fertilisers apart from depleting soil nutrients. However, chemicalization of

Table 7

REGION WISE FERTILIZER CONSUMPTION IN UTTAR PRADESH
(000' TONES)

	Year	*Total Fertilizer*	*Nitrogen*	*Phosphatic*	*Potassic*	*Ratios*
Uttar Pradesh	1970-71	410.54	291.43	74.51	44.61	7:2:1
	1980-81	1150.59	860.64	209.34	80.61	11:3:1
	1990-91	2240.91	1690.66	453.98	96.26	18:5:1
	2000-01	2961.82	2206.5	662.09	93.24	24:7:1
	2001-02	3352.13	2503.54	749.76	98.83	25:8:1
Central	1970-71	27.51	20.32	4.47	2.73	7:2:1
	1980-81	97.15	75.21	15.47	6.47	12:2:1
	1990-91	207.06	156.72	41.79	8.54	18:5:1
	2000-01	304.24	216.51	80.84	6.9	32:12:1
	2001-02	388.48	282.03	99.7	6.76	42:15:1
Eastern	1970-71	151.71	104.18	28.31	19.22	5:1.50:1
	1980-81	399.91	295.55	71.89	32.45	9:2:1
	1990-91	696.46	496.27	163.69	36.51	14:4.50:1
	2000-01	913.54	684.52	196.51	32.53	21:6:1
	2001-02	1024.96	784.65	211.8	28.53	27.5:7:1
Bundelkhand	1970-71	7.45	4.83	1.89	0.75	6.5:2.5:1
	1980-81	27.76	17.56	9.13	1.06	17:9:1
	1990-91	58.99	36.88	21.61	0.52	71:42:1
	2000-01	79.11	45.3	33.63	0.21	215:160:1
	2001-02	92.51	56.09	36.31	0.13	431:280:1
Western	1970-71	195.2	141.61	35.05	18.58	8:2:1
	1980-81	546.57	416.51	96.07	34.01	12:3:1
	1990-91	1020.24	762.74	220.78	36.7	21:6:1
	2000-01	1367.89	1051.34	270.91	45.61	23:6:1
	2001-02	1544.32	1156.92	329.53	57.83	20:6:1

Source: Various Volumes of CMIE.

agriculture may pose a greater threat to the rural economy at much higher levels of application of chemical fertilizers and pesticides. High doses of fertilizer lead to salinity in the soil (Singh, 1997). A change towards balanced use of NPK by raising both P and K per unit of N would raise output by 2 million tones in India (Rao, 2005).

V. Water Rates

Profile of Costs Recovery in Irrigation Sector

It is revealed in the earlier discussion that substantial part of the expenditure earmarked for O & M costs, goes to meet the expenditure on the staffs leaving very little for maintenance work in the state. On the other hand, the situation of costs recovery in the state is becoming totally burdensome. The costs recovery ratio has declined to the lowest up to 7 percent of O & M costs in 1999-2000 and remained at nearly 34 percent on an average basis during 1986-87 to 2002-03 (Table 8). In other words, when the average O & M costs is Rs. 621, only Rs. 179 is recovered through revenue collection during the period. Therefore, the financial health of this sector is becoming weak and the authority is facing serious financial crunch for is O & M. Various reasons are important such as the prices are fixed in nominal terms and are not revised for years, the pricing structure is based on crop area irrigated and not on volume of water consumed, there is hardly any link between the agency levying water charge and the agency that collects it, the cost of collection is itself high due to over-staffing (Gulati, 2005). Unless these problems are sorted out, there is hardly any chance of recovering the financial health of the sector.

Rationalization of Irrigation Price

The water rates in Uttar Pradesh have not been revised since 1995 and problems are complicated in many ways, which leads to low cost recovery ratio. There is no uniform set of principles in fixing the price of water rates. It varies from project to project and crop to crop. Moreover, the rate also varies for the same crop in the state on irrigation season, type of system etc. The price is fixed on annual basis instead of frequency of water used in the irrigated land. The serious problem lies, when equal rates are fixed for farmers residing at upper, middle and tail end part of the canal. It is well known fact that there has been wastage of water in the upper part and farmers at the tail end do not get water in right quantity in right time. This inequality of water distribution leads to instability in crop

Table 8

TREND OF REVENUE AND O & M COSTS OF IRRIGATION SECTOR IN UTTAR PRADESH

Year	*M & R*		*Energy*		*Operation*		*O & M Costs*	*Revenue*	
	Per hectare (Rs/ha)	*Percent to O & M*	*Per hectare (Rs/ha)*	*Percent to O & M*	*Per hectare (Rs/ha)*	*Percent to O & M*	*Per hectare (Rs/ha)*	*Per hectare (Rs/ha)*	*Percent to O & M*
1986-87	67.64	68.05	13.21	13.29	18.55	18.66	99.40	97.13	97.72
1987-88	52.16	26.06	38.67	19.32	109.34	54.63	200.17	39.54	19.75
1988-89	93.03	35.56	55.01	21.03	113.58	43.41	261.62	65.32	24.97
1989-90	94.71	32.77	38.36	13.28	155.92	53.95	289.00	91.39	31.62
1990-91	114.63	38.77	19.79	6.69	161.25	54.54	295.66	73.17	24.75
1991-92	113.53	22.62	114.96	22.90	273.51	54.48	502.00	77.95	15.53
1992-93	107.15	27.17	112.57	28.55	174.58	44.28	394.30	92.85	23.55
1993-94	116.45	26.32	101.99	23.05	224.07	50.64	442.51	316.63	71.55
1994-95	125.39	29.13	96.45	22.41	208.58	48.46	430.42	131.45	30.54
1995-96	131.39	42.34	136.28	43.91	42.66	13.75	310.33	208.65	67.24
1996-97	167.46	23.33	100.54	14.01	449.84	62.67	717.84	191.35	26.66
1997-98	112.16	39.16	118.42	41.34	55.85	19.50	286.43	90.83	31.71
1998-99	127.94	16.05	131.12	16.45	538.28	67.51	797.35	99.13	12.43
1999-2000	130.59	10.57	185.78	15.04	918.88	74.39	1235.25	91.67	7.42
2000-01	188.91	13.27	53.48	3.76	1181.17	82.97	1423.56	735.02	51.63
2001-02	168.28	11.98	192.72	13.72	1043.67	74.30	1404.68	199.67	14.21
2002-03	167.21	11.34	191.49	12.99	1115.41	75.67	1474.10	441.76	29.97
Average	122.27	27.91	100.05	19.51	399.13	52.58	621.45	179.03	34.19

Source: Estimated from Various Volumes of Aaya-Vyayak Digdarshak, Irrigation Department, and Government of Uttar Pradesh.

Note: O & M Costs are estimated excluding Interest and Depreciation charges.

production and eventually affected the revenue realization. Inefficient water distribution management may be one of the important reasons for lower rate of collection. Hence, both out dated water price and lower collection have affected the cost recovery ratio seriously.

The Vaidyanathan Committee (1992) emphasized not only the need to higher recovery of the costs of water supply (O & M costs plus one percent of capital cost and depreciation allowances) but also recommends eventually moving to a volume based rate structure and a group based distribution system for canal water. Irrigation commission, 1972 had recommended that the irrigation rates could be 5 to 12 percent of the gross value of the products. Moreover, Taxation Enquiry Committee, GOUP in 1980 also recommended the water rates should be kept at 8 percent of the gross value of the products with the exception of sugarcane at 4 percent. Keeping in mind these recommendations, there had been large gap between the recommended water rates and the actual collection from the farmers. Revenue collection varies tremendously from the lowest of 7 percent to highest 71 percent keeping average nearly 34 percent of the O & M costs during 1986-87 to 2002-03 in the state (Table 8). In other words, irrigation rate varies between 1-2 percent of the gross value of important crops, viz., wheat, paddy and sugarcane (Table 9). This may opined that there is vast scope for enhancing the water rates if efficient water facility is provided, which would not affect the living conditions of the farmers.

Table 9

Gross Value and Total Costs of Major Crops in Uttar Pradesh

Major Crops	*Gross Value (Rs/Ha)*	*Total Costs (Rs/Ha)*	*Irrigation Rates (IR) (Rs/Ha)*	*Percent of IR to GV*	*Percent of IR to TC*
Wheat	13750	4605	287	2.09	6.23
Paddy	14000	6304	287	2.05	4.53
Sugarcane	46200	8405	474	1.03	5.64

Source: Estimated from Bajaj Committee Report, 1996-97.
Note: IR is the irrigation rates and TC is the total costs.

In a toto, the irrigation sector is suffering from the ailments of low and out dated water rates, low rate of collections on the one hand and higher rate of construction costs, high escalation of O &M costs on the other hand. This leads to low recovery of costs causing high burden on the state exchequer. Inadequate cost recovery adversely affects the irrigation system performance, even funds are not available to undertake routine maintenance of canal and drainage works. It reflects the water rate structure does not bear any relationship to the costs of producing bulk water nor its scarcity value. The financial health of the irrigation department can be improved by reduction of expenditure or improvement in revenue collection through the revision of water rates and collection of huge old dues. The revision of water tariff would become acceptable, only when restructuring is done by reducing the establishment cost, better irrigation facility (timely and enough water to tail end), better technical management, shifting of power from irrigation authority to public and enhancing the involvement of the people in the irrigation management through efficient public participatory management system (PIM).

VI. Participatory Irrigation Management (PIM)

The efficiency of irrigation water can be developed possible by two critical factors, i.e., level of water users' organization and changes in the collection of irrigation fees. The former is necessary for better way of managing water resources, O & M of the systems by the users' and the latter is essential for reduction of state's fiscal deficit either through increase in revenue collection or participation by the user in term of labour. Both can be possible by adopting participatory approach by the users. PIM has be been adopted at the centre at different level since mid-seventies, while the level of success differ widely among state as water is a state subject. Tough Uttar Pradesh has not achieved substantially in transferring power to the farmers unlike Andhra Pradesh, Maharastra, Madhya Pradesh and Gujarat, yet the encouraging steps are noteworthy to mention in terms of institutional and legislative reforms at various levels to ensure the implementation of above objectives.

Institutional Arrangements

Realizing the disassociation and problems associated among the line departments, Government of Utter Pradesh has constituted "State Water Board" under the chairmanship of the Chief Secretary for better coordination and cooperation. Now the Board has to brought all the sectoral water demands and its management under one umbrella and promote the water related activities. However, substantial reforms have not been taken place by the Board and still the water resources planning for various uses are being carried out by the respective departments. Government Orders (2002) enable the creation of Water Users Association (WUAs) and its link with the Panchayat Raj institutions. The committees (water management committees) at the Panchayat level are to be represented in the WUAs and the representatives of the tail end are to head the WUAs. However, the policy is implemented through out the state but the real functioning of the committees and WUAs are challenging as mentioned by various case studies (Government of Uttar Pradesh, 2005).

Legislative

Even before independence, various legislative acts such as "Northern Canal and Drainage Act 1873 and its amendment Act in 1890" carried out in the state for equitable distribution of water and in case of disputes, the involvement of executive engineers were consulted respectively. Subsequently in the amended Act of 1963 provided active role of Gram Sabha for construction of watercourses and filed channels. The Command Area Development Authority (CADA) Act, 1976 provides for the participation of beneficiary farmers in irrigation management particularly below the outlet in case of projects covered under CADA. However, maintenance of the outlet system, implementations of physical works of development and enforcement of the cropping plan are handed over to the Chak

Samiti, which is constituted by many Chak Sabha under section 22 of this Act. Moreover, the provision for the constitution of Water Management Committee at the village Panchayat level has provided in February 1990 and finally provisions are made for these committees to be member of the WUAs in 2002.

Despite the state effort to prepare lot of legislative act, the devolution and participation in the management of irrigation water by the user is at preliminary stage. However, many efforts are being undertaken in term of mobilizing farmers to part with the WUAs. The minimal devolution is being taken place in few areas at below the outlet level. More ambitious devolution such as to take over minor canal commands with volumetric water charges is distance dream till yet. However, it may assessed the degree of involvement by the farmers in the context of water management, "although there is large amount of literature detailing the establishment of WUAs for operation, maintenance and distribution of irrigation water, there is very little literature on farmers participation in drainage management (Government of Uttar Pradesh, 2005)".

VII. Future Policy Directions

Expansion of Irrigated Area

Increase in irrigated area has been the single most important factor in achieving food security in a growing populated state like Uttar Pradesh. There is ample need as well as scope for both expansion and improvement in efficiency in the state. Emphasizing one and neglecting the other may have adverse consequence for growth and equity. Needless to say that in course of time as the remaining irrigation potential becomes smaller, gains from improvement in efficiency would assume much greater importance than expansion.

Stepping up public investment and judicious distribution of funds in the sub-sector of irrigation

The public investment in irrigation sector compared to other sectors such as power and transport has been declining since 7th plan onwards in Uttar Pradesh, which would essentially affect the addition to irrigated area from these sources in the current and next decade. As it is a matter of fact, irrigation plays crucial role for stabilizing foodgrains productions, generates employment, enhances wage rate and eventually catalyses in poverty reduction in the rural areas as well as protect food security for the entire nation. Therefore, there is a need for reallocation of budget for increasing the share of irrigation out of total planned expenditure in the years to come. Moreover, the budget has been allocated un-judiciously in intra sectoral basis among the subcategories, such as CAD and minor irrigation. Here, there is a need for enhancing the share of public funds towards O & M costs. The share of direction and administration is being increasing more than 50 percent of the O & M costs on the one hand and the share of maintenance and repairing is declining even less 30 percent of the O & M costs over the years. However, it may be suggested that there is a need for reallocation of budget to maintenance and repair works and reduction of expenditure on direction and administration.

The irrigation sector is being suffering from thin spreading effect of expenditure. It has two types of implications. Firstly, it has been observed that nearly 80 percent of the total budget allocated to the irrigation sector goes to construction of major and medium irrigation, whereas budget allocation on command area development (CAD) has been declining to nearly 3 percent. Hence, it is referred here that major focus is given to construction of new projects instead of providing better maintenance facility to the existing irrigation systems. Secondly, in many cases it is observed that newly projects were started construction instead of completing the existing projects. Hence, the existing projects should be completed in order to achieve the full benefits. There has been suggestion from different corners for revising the Gadgil formula by earmarking at least 10 percent of the central assistance as matching assistance to the state for the ongoing major and medium irrigation projects, which are at the advance stage of completion. A substantial part of the amount saved by the centre on amount of the reduction in fertilizer may be earmarked as grants to the states specifically for the development of irrigation.

Conjunctive Use of Irrigation

Conjunctive use of water resources acts as balanced factor between surface and groundwater irrigation by controlling environmental damages. It would be desirable to use adequate quantity of groundwater through tubewell irrigation in the pre-monsoon season, so that groundwater level would be around 10 meter below the surface in the places where waterlogging becomes severe by the canal irrigation in the rainy season. On the other hand, in the areas where the water table declines below 20 meters of the surface, it is desirable that the canal irrigation may be introduced or adequate rain water harvesting facility would be planned in such a way that the groundwater table is not allowed to fall below 10 meters.

Analysis of rainfall data, canal water usage, groundwater use and the groundwater level in each canal command areas has to be done to decide the exact and most suitable conjunctive use of surface and groundwater to attain the maximum crop production. It is desirable to equip the officers of the irrigation department with computers and employ suitable staff to operate them and apply the results in the filed. It is necessary that pizometers should be installed in all villages to watch the rise and fall of water table to monitor the use of canal and groundwater irrigation.

The farmers who use the groundwater in canal irrigated areas where canals are not closed should be given incentives. Each cultivator should be encouraged to have one piezometer installed in his filed and observe the water table. Moreover, in the sandy soil the water table should preferably below 4 meter of land surface in the time of Rabi crop and in silty and clay soils it should be below 6 meter from land surface.

Protect the Contamination of Groundwater

The groundwater sources has been becoming contaminated due to human intervention such as seepage of sewer lines, disposal of chemical effluents in natural water courses, salinity contains in the soil and also by nature such as arsenic, fluoride and iron. It is difficult to restore the groundwater quality once the acquifer is contaminated. In order to promote human health, there is urgent need to prevent contamination of groundwater and also promote and develop cost effective techniques for purifying contaminated groundwater for use in rural areas. Dilution of harmful chemicals can to a large extent be achieved by recharge. There is a need for master plan for the rainwater harvesting and recharge of the groundwater in the over exploitated areas of the state. The application of the model should be compulsory for all the urban areas of the state, as the Central Groundwater Board (CGWB) has recommended.

Encouragement of Participatory Irrigation Management (PIM)

Irrigation sector is being suffering from inadequacy of public investment, inefficient management of systems in operation on the one hand and the prevailing modes of management that are excessively technocratic and bureaucratic, to the politicization of cost recovery process by the political elite on the other hand. These problems are basically traceable due to non-involvement of the farmers using irrigation services in the decision making as well as implementation process. Hence, there can be tremendous development of the water sector by the paradigm shift of government owned and operated system to participation of beneficiaries in construction, operation and maintenance. There is need on the part of the State government to promote participatory irrigation management more vigorously, as currently only 15 percent of the net irrigated area is partially covered in the state. The sustainability and success of PIM depends on mutual accountability between the water user's association and the irrigation department, attitudinal change in the bureaucracy, autonomy for the water user's association, multifunctional nature of the water users association and choice of appropriate model for PIM with appropriate legal and institutional framework.

VIII. Concluding Remarks

Irrigation acts as a catalyst of agricultural development vis-à-vis overall growth of an economy by enhancing productivity, total production and generate employment, enhance wage rate, reduce poverty and regional disparity. Proper financial and institutional policy frame is essential for the highest degree of efficiency in the use of irrigation water. However, any loopholes in the management of irrigation systems lead to downtrodden situation of the system. The recent performance of the irrigation sector in the state looks disappointing in various ways. The net irrigated area has declined in the recent years during 1998-99 to 2000-01. The trend of productivity of cereals, foodgrains, groundnut and sugarcane shows a clear decline, except rice and wheat in the nineties. It has been observed that the proportion of surface irrigation is being declining on the one hand and groundwater irrigation has been increasing on the other hand over the years in the state. However, the groundwater can not replace totally to the surface irrigation, as surface irrigation acts as a catalyst for recharging the groundwater table. Hence, surface irrigation is very much important for the survival of the groundwater and irrigation system as a whole. Both are complimentary to each other for an efficient irrigation system.

The proportion of surface irrigation is declining due to the increase in the per hectare costs of construction and O & M costs on the one hand and the distribution of public funds in the irrigation sector remains stagnant or decline over various plans. Moreover, inefficiency in the systems is mainly due to inadequacy of public funds, non-judicious distribution of public funds among the sub-sectors. In addition to that the prevailing modes of management, which are excessive technocratic and bureaucratic, and politicization of the cost recovery processes by the political elite that leads to poor recovery of water rates in the recent years. This has lead to poor O &M of the canal systems. These factors affect the irrigation system unreliable and inequitable supply of water (over irrigation in upper part of the canal and less water in the tail end), the problem of waterlogging due to seepage of water from canal network. All the factors individually or jointly lead to decline the efficiency of water uses and eventfully affect the crop production. This can be improved substantially by the mechanism of participation of users in the management of the systems at different level.

References

Bardhan, Kalpana (1973): "Factors Affecting Wage Rates for Agricultural Labourers", *Economic and Political Weekly*, June.

Bowonder, B. (1981): *The Myth and Reality of High Yield Varieties in Indian Agriculture*, Development and Change, 12 (20).

Dhar, T.N., (2004): "Degraded Lands in Uttar Pradesh: Recovery Imperatives and Paths", in Dhar, T.N. (ed.), National Seminar on "Recovery of Degraded Lands in Uttar Pradesh", organized by SHERPA in collaboration with UP State land Use Board and IIPA, Lucknow.

Food and Agricultural Organization (1994): *Land Degradation in South Asia: Its Severity, Causes and Effects Upon the People*, World Soil Resources Report, Rome.

Government of India (2002-07): *10th Five Year Plan, Vol. II*, Planning Commission, New Delhi.

Government of Uttar Pradesh (2003): *National Symposium on Water Resources Management and Development with Reference to Ganga Basin*, Irrigation Department, Government of Uttar Pradesh.

Government of Uttar Pradesh (2004): *Basin Planning in Uttar Pradesh: Issues and Options*, State Water Resources agency, Lucknow.

Government of Uttar Pradesh (2005): Water Sector Restructuring Projects: Re-designing of Irrigation and Drainage Systems Under PROIDO", Main Report, Vol. 1, TAHAL Consulting Engineers Ltd.

Government of Uttar Pradesh, (2004-05): *Annual Plan (2004-05)*, Vol. I, Part II, State Planning Commission.

Gulati A.; Ruth Meinzen-Dick; K.V. Raju (2005): *Institutional Reforms in Indian Irrigation*, Sage Publication, New Delhi.

Narayanmoorthy, A. (2001): "Irrigation and Rural Poverty Nexus: A State wise Analysis", *Indian Journal of Agricultural Economics*, Vol. 56, No. 1.

Narayanmoorthy, A. et.al. (2004): "Can Irrigation Increase Agricultural Wages?: An Analysis Across Indian Districts", *Indian Journal of Labour Economics*, Vol. 47, No. 2.

Nayak, Sanatan (2002): "Extent and Costs of Environmental Degradation in Sriramsagar Project Command Area: Integration with Cost Benefit Analysis", *Artha Vijnan*, Vol. XLIV, No. 3-4.

Nayak, Sanatan (2005): Growth, Instability and Land Degradation in Andhra Pradesh Agriculture, *Journal of Rural Development*, Vol. 24, No. 2, April-June.

Pant, N. (2004): "Trend of Groundwater Irrigation in Eastern and Western Uttar Pradesh", *Economic and Political Weekly*, Vol. 39, No. 31, July 31.

Rai, Dhaneswar (2003): "Strategies of Irrigation and Water Resources Management for Optimization of Sustainable Agricultural Production in the Ganga Basin" in *National Symposium on Water Resources Management and Development with Reference to Ganga Basin*, Organised by Irrigation Department, Government of Uttar Pradesh.

Rao, C. H. Hanumantha (1994): *Agricultural Growth, Rural Poverty and Environmental Degradation*, Oxford University Press, New Delhi.

Rao, C. H. Hanumatha (2005): *Agriculture, Food Security, Poverty and Environment: Essays on Post-Reform India*, Oxford University Press, New Delhi.

Sarmah, Sasank (2002): "Agricultural Wages in India: A Study of States and Regions", *Indian Journal of Labour Economics*, Vol. 45, No. 1.

Shanker, Kripa (1982): "*Working of State Tubewells in Phulpur Block of Allahbad District*", G B Pant Institute of Social Sciences, Allahabad.

Shah, Tusar (1993): *Ground Water Markets and Irrigation Development: Political Economy and Practical Policy*, Oxford University Press, Mumbai.

Singh, A.K. (1997): *Land Use, Environment and Economic Growth in India*, MD Publications Pvt. Ltd, New Delhi.

Vaidyanathan, A. (1994): "Employment Situation: Some Emerging Perspectives", *Economic and Political Weekly*, Vol. 29, No. 50.

Vaidyanathan, A. et.al. (1994): "Impact of Irrigation on Productivity of Land," *Journal of Indian School of Political Economy*, Vol. 6, No. 4.

Wild, Alan (2003): *Soils, Land and Food: Managing the Land during the Twenty First Century*, Cambridge University Press, Cambridge.

4

INDUSTRIAL DEVELOPMENT IN UTTAR PRADESH

A. N. Pandey

I. Economic Backwardness

The economy of Uttar Pradesh is regarded as one of the backward economies of Indian states in spite of the fact that U.P. produces 19.00 per cent of India's food-grains, 20.00 per cent vegetables, 21.00 per cent fruits, 38.00 per cent potatoes, and its is the largest producer of milk and sugarcane. Besides, U.P. has the largest railway network and the second largest road network in the country. Even with regard to the number of schools and colleges per lakh of population, the position of U.P. is better than the national average of well comparable.

However, the economic backwardness of U.P. is very much obvious from the fact that while the state accounts for about 17 per cent of India's total population, its share in the national income is only 9 per cent. Also, the per capital income of U.P. is only about 54-55 per cent of the same at the national level. Even, the growth rate of Gross Domestic Product (GDP) as well as that of the per capital income of U.P. has been much below the same at the national level during the recent years. The growth rate of economy of U.P. during the 8th Five Year Plan (1992-97) was reported to be 3.20 per cent as against the same being 6.80 per cent at the national level. The same during the period of first four years of 9th Five Year Plan (1997-2001) was 2.30 per cent as against 5.40 per cent at the national level. Further, the industrial growth rate of U.P. during the first 3 years of the Ninth Five Year Plan was negative and it had picked-up and become positive in the last two years (i.e., 5.6 per cent in 200-2001 and 7.7 per cent in 2001-02).

Keeping in mind the above mentioned problems, the objective of the paper is to assess the performance of the industrial sector and its sub sectors in the state during the recent years. This paper is divided into six sections. Section I deals with introduction, objective and methodology of this study. Section II highlights about the industrial base in the state, while section III describes the backwardness despite considerable industrial base. Section IV analyses the strength of Industrial & Service Sector Policy, while section V deals with Allocation & Performance of the sub-sectors. Section VI deal with the connection of the chapter.

II. Considerable Industrial Base

As per the information made available by the Udyog Bandhu, U.P., the number of Industrial Entrepreneur Memorandum (IEM) and Letter of Intent (LOI) issued in U.P. for Medium and Heavy Industries during the Ninth Plan Period ranged between 233 in 2001-02 and 375 in 1997-98 with the amount of proposed investment ranging between Rs. 2381.98 crores in 2001-02 and Rs. 6316.80 crores in 1997-98 on the one hand, and employment generation possibility ranging between 22,379 persons in 2000-2001 and 67741 persons in 1997-98.

On the basis of these information, while it can be said that U.P. appear to be a favourable destination for investors, it is obvious that there has been a declining trend not only with regard to number of IEM/LOI, but also with regard to the proposed investment and employment. Besides, only 45.0 to 50.0 per cent of IEM/LOIs actually gets materialized. Even then the position of U.P. is better than many other states in this regard.

Similarly during the Ninth Plan Period, the number of SSI units established was reported to have ranged between 27566 in 1998-99 and 29689 in 1999-2000. While the investment in these units was estimated to have ranged between Rs. 270.00 crores in 2001-02 and Rs. 385.60 crores in 1997-98, the generation of employment ranged between 69,169 persons in 1998-99 and 97,155 in 2001-02, the value of production ranged between Rs. 635.04 crores in 2001-02 and Rs. 1409.00 crores in 1998-99 (Directorate of Industries, U.P.). Though the trend even in this regard was found to be declining during the period of five years, yet the establishment of 143160 SSI units, an investment of Rs. 1662.25 crores, employment of 385891 persons appear to be quite impressive.

As per the Third Census of SSI, there were a total number of 17, 07,977 Small Scale Enterprises in U.P., out of which only 162938 units (9.54 per cent) were reported to be registered. Further, 63.74 per cent of the SSI units were rural units. The total fixed investment in the SSI units was reported to be Rs. 17, 288.80 crores and the total gross output was reported to be worth Rs. 27423.19 crores. Also, a total number of 40, 02,375 persons were reported to be employed in the SSI units. Thus, even the 3rd Census of SSI gives an impressive picture of the industrial base of U.P. though there could be several debatable aspects.

Handloom Industries in U.P. are of considerable importance with 5230 societies and units, employing 3.79 lakh handlooms and 2.6 lakh weavers. The value of total export from the Handloom Sector in U.P. was over Rs. 500.00 crores. The value of annual export from the Handicraft Sector has been estimated to be around Rs. 3700.00 crores. Also, the total number of Khadi and Village Industries (KVI) units in U.P. was reported to 128405, producing goods worth Rs. 659.69 crores, and employing 436254 persons. The sales figures of theses units were reported to be around Rs. 786.35 crores.

The data made available by the concerned departments and corporations about the status of these traditional industries indicate an impressive and substantial base of such industries in U.P. Even otherwise, U.P. is well known for the traditional industries and it is said that U.P. accounts for almost 65.0 per cent of the craft industries in the country.

Value of the total exports from U.P. in the year 2001-02 was reported to be Rs. 20, 113.51 crores, out of which Software and Electronics accounted for 20.6 per cent. Art Metal Works for 10.4 per cent, Engineering & Building Hardware for 9.5 per cent, Hand-woven Carpets and Durries for 7.4 per cent, and Cotton Clothes and Readymade Garments for 5.5 per cent. Besides, 37.0 per cent of the export value was accounted for the other items that were not classified (Source: Export Promotion Bureau, U.P.).

As for the industrial infrastructure, U.P. has 134 developed Industrial Areas and 81 Industrial Estates covering an area of 39050 acres. Besides, 168 Mini Industrial Estates are reported to be there in the State (Source: Udyog Bandhu, U.P.).

On the basis of available information from the concerned departments/ organizations, it can be said that the industrial base of U.P. is considerable. However, it is difficult to ascertain the veracity of data. While some of the data are under consideration. Also, it is difficult to find data on the same aspect having similar time frame from other sources. It is also true that there are variations in data on the same subject collected by different agencies.

III. Backwardness despite Considerable Industrial Base

It is obvious from the above facts that the industrial base of U.P. was quite substantial. Even then U.P. continued to be an industrially base of U.P. was quite substantial. Even then U.P. continued to be an industrial backward state of the country. One of the reasons for continued industrial backwardness of U.P. has been the low growth rate. It may be noted that the growth rate of Secondary Sector in U.P. during the 8th Plan Period was only 3.3 per cent against the same being 8.8 per cent during the 7th Plan Period, 9.5 per cent during the 6th Plan Period, and 7.3 per cent during the 5th Plan Period, 9.5 per cent during the 6th Plan Period, and 7.3 per cent during the 5th Plan

Period. The 9th Plan Period had witnessed the lowest growth rate of 0.9 per cent only, and the manufacturing component within the Secondary Sector had negative growth rate to the extent of 3.4 per cent. Thus, there has been a continued decline in the industrial growth rate of U.P. after the 6th Five Year Plan.

While there could be several reasons for this, one of the key factors has been the political instability during this period. In order to gain short term mass support, the focus of development has shifted from industries to the social sector. While it is debatable as to whether the social sector has really benefited from the shift, it cannot be denied that the development of industrial infrastructure has suffered. Also, the overall industrial climate has been on the receiving end and the Governments have hardly been serious about the industrial development notwithstanding the ambitious policy pronouncement.

In addition to the industrial growth rate, there could be several other indicators of the industrial status of a state or a country. Even some of these indicators suggest that U.P. continues to be an industrially backward state. The average number of workers per day in the registered factories per lakh of population in U.P. in 1997-98 was only 365 while the same at the national level was 793, and it ranged from 1176 in Maharastra to 1680 in Tamil Nadu. The share of workforce in the manufacturing sector to the total work-force in State is another indicator of industrial development. It may be noted that the share of manufacturing sector in U.P. was reported to be only around 8.0 per cent while the same ranged between 11.0 to 16.0 per cent in the States, like West Bengal, Gujarat, Tamil Nadu, Maharastra, Punjab, Haryana and Karnataka. The same at the national level was about 10.00 per cent.

The industrial backwardness of U.P. is also reflected from the per capita consumption of power which was only 191 KWH in 2000-2001 as against 366 KWH at the national level. The 3rd Census of SSI revealed that only 35.8 per cent of the SSI units required electricity while as many as 42.9 per cent of the SSI units did not require power at all. The remaining 21.0 per cent of the SSI units required coal, LPG, Oil, firewood and nonconventional energy for their operation. This indicates that over 64.0 per cent of the SSI units were traditional units dependent on manual skills and solid, liquid and gaseous fuel. As such, the productivity and output level of such units must be quite low.

Even the plan outlay for U.P. appeared to be quite low, incapable of making a dent into the economic backwardness of U.P. It may be noted that the per capita plan outlay in U.P. for the year 2002-03 was only Rs. 431.00 as against the same being Rs. 981.00 at the national level.

The purpose of discussing the extent of economic and industrial backwardness of U.P. on the hand, and highlighting the economic strength and industrial base of U.P. on the other is to indicate the extent of efforts required for the industrial development of U.P. despite having a substantial base and large potential for industrial development. This would also help in understanding the adequacy of provisions made in the Xth Five Year Plan for accelerating the pace of industrial development in U.P. Also, the implementation of industrial component of the Xth Five Year Plan has been effective enough to give a sense of optimism for the future.

Tenth Five Year Plan

It has been stated that the Xth Five Year Plan (2002-07) was prepared with a two-fold mission: *(i)* achieving balanced industrial development and *(ii)* minimizing the problem of unemployment. Besides, the creation of infrastructure facilities so as to attract more and more capital investment in the State was one of the major objectives of the Xth Plan. However, the total plan outlays for industry and minerals do not seem to reflect the missionary concern. The very introduction of the Industrial and Service Sector Investment Policy, 2004, announced by the Government of U.P. begins with highlighting the major objective of the Xth Five Year Plan.

It has been estimated that there would be an investment of Rs. 45,565.14 crores in Large and Medium Industries during the 10th Plan Period and employment opportunities would be generated for 4,55,651 persons. It is also stated that the conversion rate of Industry Entrepreneur Memorandum (IEM)/ Letter of Intents (LOIs) in U.P. has been 45-50 per cent.

IV. Industrial & Service Sector Industrial Policy

It is expected that with the announcement of the Industrial and Service Sector Investment Policy-2004, it would be possible to generate the envisaged investment and employment during the 10th Plan Period. The Industrial and Service Sector Investment Policy 2004 aims at expediting the process of industrial development in the state with the promotion of private sector participation, development of village and small industries, promotion of export, and greater capital investment by attracting Non-Resident-Indians (NRIs) and Foreign Direct Investment (FDI). It is hoped that by improving the low and order situation, making the administrative structure of the state sensitive and responsive to entrepreneurs, restructuring of the tax regime, large scale deregulation, industry specific promotional package and deliberate encouragement of service sector would help rapid industrial development of the State.

Accordingly, the strategy of the State Government would be to nurture private economic activities and entrepreneurship, and meaningful partnership between private and public sector would be promoted in the formulation and actual execution and implementation of industrial policy. Regarding the infrastructure, the above policy promises to establish industrial infrastructure development fund, industrial infrastructure development authority and promote infrastructure facilities like travel and transport, electric energy, telecommunication, water supply, industrial estate/areas, special economic zones (SEZs), bio-technology research parks and gas pipelines, etc. Also, the Institute of Design is proposed to be set-up for which the necessary initiatives have already been taken. For the development of electric energy, the policy proposes to provide interest free loan, necessary land to the units at the acquisition cost, and lease its own land for 99 years at the rate of Rs. 100 per acre and so on. The policy proposes to provide uninterrupted power supply to the industrial units and industrial feeders would be exempted from power cuts. Such feeders as has 75 per cent of electricity for industrial supply would be defined as industrial feeders.

The Government would provide land for telecommunication and establish big trade centers in the State Capital in the private or joint sector. Similarly, display sales centers and urban hats are proposed to be developed. Also the financial grants and rebates would be provided to private sector by rationalization of stamp duty, registration fee, land exchange charges and land transfer charges.

Further, the rationalizations of trade tax rates and simplification of procedures, special incentives on establishment of pioneer units, as also rationalizations of interest and financial assistance are other features of the promotion of industries. Regarding rules and regulations, the policy proposes to make the Single Window System effective, simplify the labour lows, industrial laws and pollution laws. Also, there are proposals for the deregularisation of a variety of other rules such as approval of building maps, land acquisition, minimum freight rates for trucks, transfer of investment of UPFC and PICUP in various undertakings to the private sectors, dis-investment in the public undertakings and so on.

Similarly, the industrial policy highlights ways and means of promoting export, comprising master plan for export oriented cities, strengthening the offices of Export Commissioner, and freight subsidy etc.

The policy has special package for small scale and tiny industries, handloom industries, Khadi and Village industries, information technology, bio-technology, service sector and so on. Special policy for service sector lays emphasis on development of hospitals. Information Technology training centers, cinema halls and multiplex, development of high-tech townships and so on is also important. Policy has also specific provision for training of entrepreneurs and human resource development, NRI investment, rehabilitation of sick units and so on.

As such, the industrial policy is quite ambitious and aims at the rationalization and development of almost all aspects required for the rapid industrial development. The policy clearly outlines the vision of the Government of U.P. for industrial development but the most significant question is whether these policies would really be implemented, at least to a substantial extent. This would require a great deals of efforts, commitments and sincerity on the part of the departmental functionaries.

Meagre Plan Outlay

It may be noted that the share of proposed outlay for Industry and Mineral in the Xth Five Year Plan was the lowest one at 1.80 per cent Rs. 1485.76 crores) as against the same for agriculture and allied activities, rural development, special area programmes, and irrigation and flood control together being 27.10 per cent (Rs. 22901.90 crores). How much importance the Government of U.P. has been attaching to the industrial development of the State is very much reflected from the proposed plan outlay itself. Even a rather ambiguous sector, like the ecology and environment had the proposed plan outlay of Rs. 2355.25 crores (2.80 per cent share) as against Rs. 1485.76 crores for industry and minerals. As such, the 10th Plan does not focus upon the development of industry and minerals though it can be said that there was a net increase of 218.18 per cent in the proposed outlay of the Xth plan over the outlay for the 9th Plan and of 327.31 per cent over expenditure in the IXth Plan.

Even the proposed plan outlay for industry and mineral was further reduced and the finally agreed 10th Plan outlay was Rs. 1262.46 crores. Out of the total agreed outlay of Rs. 1262.46 crores, Village and Small scale Industries (VSI) accounted for 26.9 per cent, electronics 8.7 per cent, mining 1.0 per cent and the remaining 63.4 per cent for industries (large and medium). Within the VSI Sector, the outlay of 26.9 per cent (Rs. 339.46 crores), Khadi accounted for 6.3 per cent (Rs. 80.0 crores), sericulture for 1.69 per cent (Rs. 21.31 crores), and Handloom for 10.3 per cent (Rs. 130.0 crores).

Meagre Annual Allocations

The annual allocation of outlay for the first year (2002-03) of the 10th Plan period was only Rs. 56.98 crores (4.5 per cent) against which the anticipated expenditure was 54.18 crores only. Except in the case of Khadi (where the anticipated expenditure was Rs. 5.55 crores against the outlay of Rs. 8.064 crores) and Mining (where the anticipated expenditure was Rs. 0.71 crores against the outlay of Rs. 1.0 crore), all other sub sectors appeared to have spent the same amount as allocated.

The proposed allocation for the 2nd year (2003-04) was Rs. 61.06 crores and all the sub sectors had almost the same amount of allocation (with marginal variations over those in the year 2002-03) except in the case of Industries (Medium and large) where the proposed allocation was Rs. 23.0 crores against the allocation of Rs. 16.90 crores in the previous year, and Electronics, where the allocation had been substantially reduced from Rs. 7.0 crores in the previous year to Rs. 3.83 crores in the year 2003-04.

Thus, the total annual plan allocations for Industry and Minerals for the first two years of 10th Plan period was only Rs. 118.04 crores against the total plan outlay of Rs. 1262.46 crores, accounting for just 9.3 per cent. As such, it is obvious from the total plan outlay as well as from the annual allocations for the first two years that the development of Industry was not at all a major objective of the 10th Five Year Plan. If not even 10.0 per cent of the outlay could be utilized in the first two years, how could it be possible to make use of the remaining 90.0 per cent of the outlay during the remaining 3 years?

Meagre Allocations & Plan Expectations

Now the question arises as to why this state of affair in such a large state and which is industrially so backward and that too in the era of liberalization and globalization? For such a vital sector of the economy, like industry which is supposed to play a catalytic role in the so much desired structural change of the state economy, change in occupational structure of the State, and raising the living standard of the people of the State?

Can this pattern of plan allocations and expenditure help in reducing regional disparity in the industrial development, reducing unemployment, and creating world-class infrastructure to attract large scale domestic and foreign investment. Would this level of plan outlay, annual allocations and expenditure help secure the target annual industrial growth rate of 12.0 per cent? The obvious answer has to be in negative. Such a low level allocations can not succeed in creating conducive conditions for attracting large scale investment and rapid industrial growth of the State.

V. Sub Sector: Allocation & Performance

Industry and Mineral Sector of the 10th Five Year Plan consists of the following sub-sectors:

1. Small Scale Industries
2. Khadi & Village Industries
3. Handloom Industries
4. Sericulture
5. Industries (Medium & Large)
6. Information Technology & Electronics
7. Mining

1. Small Scale Industries (SSI)

The total outlay for SSI in the 10th Five Year Plan (2002-07) is Rs. 108.15 crores out of which only Rs. 8.45 crores was approved for the year 2002-03, Rs. 8.00 crores for the year 2003-04, and the proposed outlay for the year 2004-05 was Rs. 5.85 crores. Thus, only Rs. 22.30 crores out of Rs. 108.15 crores was allocated in the first 03 years amounting to only 20.62 per cent of the total outlay. The rest 79.38 per cent of the outlay (Rs. 85.85 crores) would have to be utilized in the remaining period of two years. The average annual utilization of plan outlay for the first three years was worked out to Rs. 7.43 crores only, and at this rate only about Rs. 14.86 crores could be utilized in the next two years. What would happen to the remaining plan outlays of Rs. 71.0 crores? Is there any special plan to make use of the remaining plan outlay in the next two years? If the same level of allocation and utilization of outlay continues in the coming two years as in the first three years, there is a grater possibility of the Xth Plan performance being lower than the IXth Plan.

Targets of the Xth plan for the SSI sub-sector are establishment of 150,000 SSI units and creation of 6 lakh additional employment opportunities through them. This means that 30,000 SSI units are to be established every year and 120000 employments are to be created through them every year. If one goes by the data available (provided by the Directorate of Industries, U.P.), targets for establishment of SSI Units had been achieved in excess during the year 2002-03 as well as 2003-04, and the achievement with regard to employment generation was 94.00 per cent and 98.0 per cent respectively for the two years. Also, an investment of Rs. 548.26 crores was reported to have been generated in this process during the period of first two years of the 10th Plan. If one goes by the data made available by the concerned Department, it can be said that the objectives of annual plans (and Xth Plan) in this regard had been largely achieved. It may also be noted that in the small scale sector the role of Government Agencies is only promotional and most of the investments originates from the private sector. As such, it can be said the SSI sector has succeeded in achieving the targets of Xth Plan to the Extent of establishment of SSI units, generation of investment and employment.

The performance under Prime Minister's Rozgar Yojana (PMRY), Entrepreneurship Development Programme (EDPs), and Single Table System is reported to be quite good in the first two years of the 10th Plan period. Under the PMRY, the achievement of target was reported to be 86.9 per cent for the year 2002-03 and 86.6 per cent for the year 2003-04. For EDP, the achievement was 106.10 per cent during the year 2002-03 and the same was 93.9 per cent during the year 2003-04. But the most surprising aspect was more than 3 fold increase in the target of EDPs during the year 2003-04 over that during the year 2002-03. It may be noted that the target number of EDPs increased from 716 (organized 750) in 2002-03 to 2249 (organized

2156) in 2003-04. Similarly, the target number of trainees increased from 29335 (21137 trained) in 2002-03 to 104510 (98182 trained) in 2003-04. How could this be accomplished without any significant increase in the allocation of plan outlay? Also, as to what could have been the impact of such an increase on the content and effectiveness of EDPs?

It is obvious that the number of long duration EDP (Standard EDP of six weeks duration) was substantially reduced and the number of short duration Entrepreneurship Awareness Programme (EAPs) or Campus (EACs) (duration being two weeks or less than that) were substantially increased. Such an approach to the promotion and development of entrepreneurs (particularly, first generation entrepreneurs) can hardly be effective in the long run. Efforts should be made to ensure that at least one standard EDP of six weeks duration is conducted in each district every year and with the help of proper follow-up and escort services majority of the trained potential entrepreneurs are enabled to set up their enterprises. Such trained successful entrepreneurs themselves would become a major motivation force for other youths who could opt for entrepreneurial careers rather than hunting for jobs in vain.

As far the Single Table System (STS), the achievement was reported to be 99.9 per cent for the year 2002-03, and 99.0 per cent for the year 2003-04 as 20014 applications out of 20034 complete applications received in 2002-03 and 21365 applications out of 21578 complete applications received in 2002-03 were reported to have been disposed off. However, these information are not sufficient for the evaluation of STS. There is a need to have these information purpose specific and the nature of assistance provided for. Mere disposing of application (Positive or negative) hardly serve any development purpose.

Performance under these select areas indicated that the SSI sub-sector had been doing quite well in meeting the targets of 10th Five Year Plan and there was hardly any major area of concern. And that too with a paltry amount allocated under the 10th Five Year Plan. But it must not be forgotten that the source of these performance related data is the concerned department only and the real picture of performance can emerge only with the help of independent studies conducted by the professional institutions/agencies covering a cross section of the stakeholders of the SSI sub-sector. The performance related areas of investigation aiming at improving the delivery system could be the quality of manpower, availability of information, data and reference materials, extent of facilities, treatment meted out to the clients, speed of service delivery, quality of assistance and so on. Any evaluation effort or appraisal based on the data furnished by the respective departments may not be able to capture the ground realities.

2. Khadi and Village Industries

The thrust areas of Khadi & Village Industries (KVIs) for the 10th Five Year Plan are stated to be *(i)* creation of sustainable employment opportunities for the rural unemployed youth, *(ii)* providing gainful employment to agricultural labour, small and marginal farmers during the lean season, *(iii)* Intensive Rural Industrialization through cluster approach, *(iv)* developing entrepreneurs exclusively for marketing of village industries products, and *(v)* development of Hand-Made Paper Industries and so on. Besides, the emphasis for Scheduled Castes/Tribes, Backward Classes, Women and Minorities, attempts are proposed to be made for common Trade Marks, Quality Control, Development of Designs, and development of infrastructure facilities for traditional village industries and so on.

All the above mentioned tasks are to be accomplished with the plan outlay of Rs. 80.0 crores only. Against the total plan outlay of Rs. 80.00 crores, only Rs. 8.06 crores had been allocated for the year 2002-03, Rs. 9.0 crores for the year 2003-04 and about Rs. 8.0 crores for the year 2004-05. Thus, only about Rs. 25.0 crores had been allocated during the period of first three years, accounting for just 31.3 per cent of the plan outlay. This means that the remaining 68.7 per cent of the outlay would be utilized in the coming two years of the 10th Plan Period. But the question to be answered is as to how? It may also be noted that only Rs. 5.55 crores had been utilized in the year 2002-03 against the annual allocation of Rs. 8.06 crores.

But even with this meager allocation and utilization of the plan outlay, the performance seems to be commendable as suggested by the data made available by the Khadi & Village Industries Board of U.P. It may be noted that the target for the 10th Plan is to establish 25000 village industries leading to the creation of employment opportunities for 2.5 lakh unemployed youth. This would mean 10 employment opportunities per unit which itself is of quite a high order. Against these targets, it has been reported that 3452 Khadi and Village Industry units had been established in the year 2002-03 with an investment of Rs. 103.32 crores. As such, the average investment per unit was over Rs. 299305.00. Also, these new units had created employment opportunities for 30213 persons, i.e., about 9 persons per unit. On the other hand, 2864 units had been established till the end of September 2004 with an investment of only Rs. 20.45 crores and these units had created employment opportunities for only 6882 persons employed. Thus, the per unit investment had subsequently gone down to Rs. 71, 404.00 and per unit employment to 2.4 persons. What could be the reason for such a drastic decline?

Even then, only 6313 units were reported to have been established with the employment opportunities for 37095 persons till September 2004. Could it be possible to establish the remaining 18684 units having employment opportunities for 212905 persons in the remaining period of the Xth Plan?

As far the other schemes like interest subsidy, rebate on sale of Khadi, industrial feasibility studies, project formulation and survey, product development of Hand Made Paper, designing and packaging development and others, there is neither any specific target nor any data available to assess the performance. Thus, the lack of specific target for a number of proposed developmental activities and allocation of funds against them could be one of the areas requiring necessary action for improvement. It is well known that KVIB has been operating on traditional pattern and not much innovative development initiatives have been taken. Though a number of initiatives are proposed in documents they are hardly implemented. Besides the field setting of KVIB is neither very efficient not effective enough to attract entrepreneurs in the rural areas. At the same time, need for the location of production enterprises in the rural areas also works as a constraint. Functioning of the staff of KVIB and its associated organizations are so lack-luster and could hardly attract new customers and consumers. It may also be noted that mere technical knowledge of production would not be sufficient either for the officials of Board or entrepreneurs to promote and manage technology by the officials, and suitable attitudinal changes in them. Also, there should be greater emphasis on business orientation of potential KVIB entrepreneurs and professional management of the existing enterprises and offices. Since the financial support for the banking sector has become vital for the success of KVIB Schemes, closer coordination and liasoning with banks is must for the future.

3. Handloom

Within the VSI Sector, outlay under the 10th Five Year Plan being Rs. 130.00 crores for the Handloom Sector is the largest one. Out of the total plan outlay, Rs. 17.31 crores had been allocated in the year 2002-03, Rs. 14.50 crores in 2003-04 and Rs. 14.50 crores for the year 2004-05. Thus, only Rs. 46.31 crores out of Rs. 130.00 crores could be allocated in the first three years of the 10th Five Year Plan, accounting for about 35.62 per cent. If the remaining outlay of Rs. 83.70 crores is to be utilized in the remaining two years of the 10th Plan, the annual allocations would have to be increased to three fold of what have been allocated during the first three years and the Handloom Sector would have to make three fold efforts. How could it be possible?

As for the physical targets, it appears that the Handloom Sector has the target of producing 510 million meters of cloths each year and generation of 25000 employment every year. Against these targets, achievement was to the tune of 97.6 per cent in 2002-03 and 91.0 per cent in 2003-04 with regards to the production of handloom cloths. As for the achievement of employment generation target, it was reported to be 32.7 per cent in 2002-03 and 77.3 per cent in the year 2003-04. During the year 2004-05, both the production of cloths and the generation of employment were reported to be 100.00 per cent of the annual target.

As for the Deen Dayal Hathkargha Protsahan Yojana, the total allocation for 03 years was Rs. 21.925 crores against the total plan outlay of Rs. 64.0 crores accounting for 34.26 per cent of the target. Against the outlay of Rs. 21.925 crores, the achievement was reported to be Rs. 18.81 crores, accounting for 85.79 per cent of the allocation. However, only Rs. 18.81 crores could be utilized against the total plan outlay of Rs. 64.0 crores accounting for just 29.39 per cent. Thus, the achievement with regard to the largest component of Handloom Sector was less than 30.00 per cent in the first 03 years of the Xth Five Year Plan.

Another interesting feature was the allocation and utilization of funds under the Marketing Incentive Scheme. As against the outlay of Rs. 4.5 Crores for the Xth Plan period, allocations in the first three years of the plan period was reported to be Rs. 8.4 crores, and the utilization was reported to be Rs. 15.56 crores. Thus, the total allocation was to the extent of 186.70 per cent of the total plan outlay and the utilization was 345.8 per cent of the same. As such, there was hardly any relationship between the plan outlay and annual allocations and utilization of funds.

As the installation of computers in the Directorate, restructuring of cooperative societies, strengthening of Directorate, assistance to Handloom Corporation and UPICA etc. are concerned, though outlay had been made, yet neither any annual allocation nor utilization of funds was reported in the last three years. In some cases, like establishment of Textile Centre, Development of Knitwear/Garment Centre, Preservation of arts and crafts though annual allocations for the first two years had been indicated, hardly any utilization was reported against the annual allocations. All these indicate that the planned development of Handloom Sector is yet to be established in the real sense.

4. Sericulture

Sericulture is an important industry and there is a good potential for this industry in the State of U.P. The Sericulture Department has a lot of innovative schemes by the physical and financial targets under the different schemes have neither been outlined nor are the target specific achievement figures available to afford their mid-term appraisals. The total outlay for the 10th Five Year Plan was Rs. 21.31 crores out of which only Rs. 1.73 crores had been allocated in the year 2002-03 and the same amount in the subsequent year of 2003-04. Thus, only Rs. 3.46 crores out of Rs. 21.31 crores, accounting for 16.2 per cent, had been allocated in the first two years. As such, 83.80 per cent of the allocations would have to be made in the remaining 03 years.

5. Large and Medium Industries

Major schemes for the industrial development are development of two Agro Parks at Lucknow (in Barabanki district), and Varanasi, 07 Growth Centres at Bijauli (in Jhansi district), Shahjahanpur, Moradabad, Jainpur (in Kanpur Dehat district), Dibiapur, Shataharia and Sahjanawan (in Gorakhpur district), and setting up of 05 Special Economic Zones (SEZs) in Bhadohi, Kanpur, Greater Noida Authority (GNA), NOIDA and Moradabad district. While the progress of Agro Parks and Growth Centres appear to be satisfactory, the same can not be said about the SEZs. Though the process of developing SEZs was initiated in the year 2002 itself, and U.P. is the first State in the country to have enacted Special economic Zone Act 2002, most of the proposed SEZs are still in the process of land acquisition and hardly any significant progress seems to have been made except in the case of SEZ at Moradabad. The only SEZ functioning in the state is at NOIDA which was converted from Export Processing Zone (EPZ) to Special Economic Zone (SEZ).

Other major instruments for industrial development are Industrial Development Authorities viz., New Okhla Industrial Development Authority (NOIDA). Greater Noida Authority

(GNA), Shataharia Industrial Development Authority (SIDA) in Jaunpur district, and Gorakhpur Industrial Development Authority (GIDA) in Gorakhpur district. Among these 04 authorities, while NOIDA and Greater NOIDA have been doing well, SIDA and GIDA appear to be still lagging behind. Therefore, it is high time that greater attention was paid to these two industrial development authorities located in the industrially backward regions of Eastern U.P.

Another important agency for industrial development is the U.P. State Industrial Development Corporation (UPSIDC). If the target and achievement figures are taken into account, it can be very well said that UPSIDC has been doing quite well. As against the target of acquiring 1000 acres land in the year 2002-03, the achievement was more than double at 2038 acres. Similarly, there was 100 per cent achievement in the development of industrial land of 853 acres. Also, against the target of 1000 acres, UPSIDC had succeeded in allotment of 1923.03, the achievement was more than double at 2038 acres. Similarly, there was 100 per cent achievement in the development of industrial land of 853 acres. Also, against the target of 1000 acres, UPSIDC had succeeded in allotment of 1923.23 acres of land. While 191 industrial units on the allotted land were already in production, 296 industrial units were under construction during the year 2002-03. In the year 2003-04, UPSIDC had succeeded in acquiring 1185.70 acres of land against the target of 1000 acres and had developed 870 acres of land against the target of 840 acres. Similarly, UPSIDC had succeeded in the allotment of 1207 acres against the target of 700 acres during the year 2003-04.

It may be noted that the total plan outlay for large and medium industries during the 10th Five Year Plan is Rs. 800.00 crores. Out of which only Rs. 16.9 crore had been allocated during the year 2002-03 and Rs. 23.0 crore during the year 2003-04. Thus, in the first two years of 10th Plan Period only about 39.9 crore had been allocated. At this rate how could it be possible to make use of the remaining 760 crores within a period of the remaining 3 years. Thus, not only the allocation of Plan outlay was low for the industrial development but even the annual allocations were meager and one doubts whether it would be possible to make use of more than Rs. 200.00 crores in the 10th Plan Period.

6. Information Technology and Electronics

The 10th Five Year Plan has an outlay of Rs. 110.00 crores for Information Technology and Electronics. However, only Rs. 7.00 crores had been allocated for the annual plan 2002-03, Rs. 3.83 crores for the annual plan 2003-04 and Rs. 6.00 crores for the annual plan 2004.05. Thus the total allocation for the first 03 years of 10th Five Year Plan was only Rs. 16.83 crore against a total outlay of Rs. 110.0 crores. As such it is hardly possible to make use of the remaining Rs. 92.17 crores in the last two years of the 10th Five Year Plan and the bulk of outlay for the 10th Plan is bound to remain unutilized. This is in spite of the fact that the Government of U.P. asserts in the Industrial and Service Sector Investment Policy—2004 that it is committed to bring I.T. to masses, accelerate the use of I.T. in schools, colleges and educational institutions, building electronic cities at NOIDA, as also Software Technology Park at NOIDA, Agra, Lucknow, Kanpur, Allahabad, Varanasi and Moradabad. As a whole, the policy for I.T. is quite ambitious and if implemented effectively a lot of additional funds would be required. But the question is whether the policy would be taken up seriously in a real sense. The progress made during the last 03 years does not give much scope for optimism.

7. Geology & Mines

The outlay of the 10th Five Year Plan is Rs. 13.00 crores out of which only Rs. 1.0 crore had been allocated in the year 2002-03 and Rs. 1.00 crore during the year 2003-04. Out of this only Rs. 54.83 lakh had been spent during the year 2002-03 though the sanctioned amount was 65.01 lakh. The same during the year 2003-04, was Rs. 68.47 lakh against the sanctioned amount of Rs. 68.60 lakh. Thus, the total expenditure during the first two years of the 10th Plan Period was only Rs. 123.30 lakh accounting for less than 10 per cent of the plan outlay. As such there are little possibilities that the plan outlay of Rs. 13.00 crores would be utilized during the Xth Plan Period.

VI. Conclusion

It is obvious from the above discussion that the plan outlay for industries and mining in the lowest among the major heads of Xth Five Year Plan, yet most of the departments involved in the industrial and mineral development has been unable to make use of the outlay to the fullest extent. If the trend witnessed during the first 2-3 years of Xth Five Year Plan is any indication, but of the plan outlay is bound to remain unutilized. What could be the reason for this? Is there lack of vision for the development of industrially backward state of U.P. or the concerned departments are rather incapable of making much efforts for the industrial development of the State? There is need to delve deeper in order to understand the industrial backwardness of the State of U.P. If this trend is allowed to continue, there is little scope to hope for making U.P. an industrially developed state of the country.

There is a need for a greater integration of planned provisions of industrial development and the departmental allocations of funds and execution of plan. One gets the impression that there is hardly any relationship between plan outlay and annual allocation of funds. Also, there is no mechanism for the collection of reliable data from the field. The data provided by the individual departments hardly reflect the ground realities. Keeping in view the policy for industrial development, there is an urgent need to orient the departmental and field staff and make them accountable for the achievement of targets. Besides, independent agencies should be engaged for the collection and analysis of data on a regular basis.

5

DEVELOPMENT OF POWER SECTOR IN UTTAR PRADESH
Physical and Financial Performance

Sanatan Nayak

I. Introduction

The role of energy is considered as one of the important indicators for economic growth of an economy. It has been considered as an essential infrastructure for industrial, commercial and agricultural development of an economy. However, the per capita power consumption, percentage of electrified villages, percentage of electrified households (both rural and urban), and electricity consumption per industrial unit are some of the true indicators for measuring the economic prosperity of the state. This is evident from the fact that the per capita consumption of power in 1998-99 was 195.58 Kwh in the state against all India averages of 359.57 Kwh (Government of Uttar Pradesh, 2002-03). The state is ranked 15th among selected major 18 states in the country in connection with per capita power consumption. This shows one of the lowest per capita power consumption states in India. In addition, electrification to rural areas is also considered as an important economic variable for the development of an economy. In this regard, Uttar Pradesh stands 11th position among some of the major states, as 79 percent of the villages are electrified in Uttar Pradesh as against 86.3 percent at all India level in 1999-2000, whereas some of the states, viz., Punjab, Haryana and all Southern States achieved 100 percent electrification of rural villages during the same period (Government of Uttar Pradesh, 2002-05). Moreover, electrification of the households in the electrified villages shows the true picture of the economic strength on an economy. In this regard, Uttar Pradesh stands as one of the backward states at all India level. The latest data shows, only 20 percent of the rural households in Uttar Pradesh as against 44 percent at the all India level are electrified (Agarwal, 2005). However, it is accounted that nearly 72 percent, 60 percent and 62 percent of the households are electrified in Gujarat, Andhra Pradesh and Madhya Pradesh respectively. When we considered the urban household, Uttar Pradesh also lags behind the all India average. It is estimated that nearly 80 percent of the urban households are electrified in the state as against nearly 88 percent at all India level (Agarwal, 2005). Moreover, the seriousness of the problem accounted, when we include the industrial sector. The availability of electricity was around 54,024 units in 1984-85 and it declined drastically to 16, 487.64 units in 1997-98 per unit of industrial output (Mohan, 2005). Considering all these factors, the Government of Uttar Pradesh in the 10th five year plan formulated major reforms in the power sector for increasing the generation of power, developing the transmission and distribution system, taking necessary steps for rural electrifications, tariff reforms, privatization in generation, transmission and distribution, renovation and modernization etc. Hence, thorough evaluation is essential by taking latest data in the state in order to provide right policy measures to enhance over all economic development in the coming years.

The major objectives of the paper are as follows. Firstly, to assess the physical performance considering capacity of installation, generation, total sales and transmission and distribution losses of the UPSEB in the State. Secondly, to evaluate the financial performance considering the cost and tariff structure of power generation of the SEB in the State. Thirdly, to evaluate the extent and dimension of rural electrification and privatization of electricity supply in the state.

The physical and financial performance of the UPSEB is estimated by taking installation capacity, gross generation, T & D losses, and cost and tariff structure and subsidy issues. The growth of various indicators during 1974-75 to 2001-02 is estimated on the basis of using compound annual growth rate (CAGR). Its main focus is on the comparison among three sub periods, viz., period covering from 1974-75 to 1981-82, i.e., period I. The latter phase is from 1981-82 to 1991-92, i.e., period II. The last phase is known as liberalization period covering from 1992-93 to 2001-02, i.e., period III (post liberalization phase).

Secondary sources data relating to installation capacity, gross generation, T & D losses, cost and tariff of electricity, losses of State Electricity Boards (SEB), with and without subsidy, subsidy for agricultural and domestic sector and cross subsidy are collected from various volumes of Centre for Monitoring Indian Economy (CMIE), Annual Reports of SEBs and Central Electricity Regulatory Commission (CERC).

This paper is divided into four sections. Section I deals with introduction, objectives and methodology of this study. Section II highlights the Physical performance containing installation capacity, gross generation, T & D losses of the SEB, while section III deals with the financial performance of SEB containing the cost structure, tariff structure and subside aspects. Section IV describes the issues related to rural electrification and section V deals with the issues of privatization of electricity generation in the State. Section VI analyses the demand side management. The last section VII briefs the concluding remarks of the study.

II. Physical Performance

The growth performance of installed capacity and gross generation has drastically declined in 90?s compared to that of

80?s. However, the growth performance of Hydro electricity is always lower than that of thermal power in case of both installed capacity and gross generation (Table 1). The CAGR of installed capacity has declined drastically from 5.12 percent during 80?s to 1.51 percent in 90?s. Similar observation is revealed that gross generation has declined from 7 percent in 80?s to nearly 3.5 percent in 90?s (Table 1). It shows that inadequate timely capacity additions have been inescapable long-run experience of under-utilization of the existing capacity itself in the country. One important causative factor of such low capacity utilization is the poor technical efficiency, reinforced by an inability to attain and assimilate significant technological progress over time.

Uttar Pradesh power sector has been suffering heavy deficit due to supply bottlenecks than the demand. The generation of gross electricity has declined heavily during the first three years of the 10th five year plan. However, it appears that the supply of electricity was lower by 2004-05 than that was achieved in the end of 9th plan. The 10th plan targets the power generation to 28,892 MU at the terminal year. In other words, in order to improve the power capacity an ambitious target of creating 4898.33 MW additional capacities has been proposed for the 10th plan (Government of Uttar Pradesh, 2004-05). However, only 22793.14 MU has been achieved by the end of 2003-04 and 23059 MU units are proposed during 2004-05. Hence, total generation is declining instead of increasing to capture the additional targets. The proportion of the own generation to the total demand has been declining gradually from 52 percent during the 9th plan to 44.54 percent in 2003-04. Hence, the gap between demand for electricity and state's own generation has been widening over the years in the state (Table 2). This enforces that the state is depending more and more on import of electricity. The dependency on import of the electricity is increased from about 63.24 percent of the demand (average) in the 9th plan to nearly 80 percent in 2003-04 and 67.11 percent during the 2004-05. Due to the inability of the state to meet the requirement through huge import, the eventual consequence is gradual huge deficit. The state is facing a huge deficit of electricity demand due to increasing/constant demand and sluggish or declining generation of electricity. This lead to an increase of the deficit from 16.13 percent on average basis of the demand during 9th plan to 24 percent during 2002-03 and 30.3 percent during the 2004-05 in the 10th plan. This may account here that in order to achieve the targets in the next two years; the state has to generate an additional 3161.5 MU on average basis. In other words, the state has to generate 26220 MU in 2005-06 and another 3161. 5 MU in 2006-07 in addition to the 26220 MU in 2005-06.

The trend of gross electricity generation in the 9th year plan was better than the first two years of the 10th plan. However, the own generation of hydel electricity has declined nearly 32 percent over its previous year and it again declined drastically to nearly 160 percent during 2002-03. Moreover, the annual growth of thermal power generation is moderated to 2.6 percent in the 9th plan and declined to 1.08 percent in 2002-03 and -0.03 percent in 2003-04. In toto, the gross generation of electricity has declined to nearly 10 percent over the previous year and the anticipated growth rate is 1.83 percent during 2003-04 (Table 3). On the other hand, the rate of import has been increasing over the years except 2002-03, as the deficit in that year is highest. The annual growth of demand for electricity is moderate during the 9th five plan and the first two years of the 10th plan.

Transmission and Distribution Losses

It is observed that during the last 20 years the proportion of T & D losses to the gross generation and total sales has been increased dramatically without any deviation. However, 1514 million kwh has been lost as T & D courses out of total 10190 million kwh gross generation. The T & D losses have been consistently increased to 15929 million kwh, which is nearly 68 percent of the gross generation (Table 4). Though the gross generation and total sales has been increases, yet the proportion of T & D losses has also increased in due course of time. These are very high by international standards compared with less than 10 percent in most of the developed economies and less than 15 percent in most of the developing economies (Kannan et al, 2002). The neglect of the T & D sector, especially the transmission sector, in terms of adequate investments in capacity and maintenance and the lack of systematic T & D planning over the years are the major technical factors contributing to the high level T & D losses. Defecting metering, un-metered supply and pilferage are the main non-technical factors. There has been a pronounced bias in investment in favour of augmenting generation capacity to the utter neglect of the 1:1 norm in investment in generation and T & D sectors. Increase in number of consumers vis-à-vis inadequate T & D capacity has resulted in heavy overload of the system, causing substantial losses.

Institutional and organizational inefficiency also causes the inefficiency of the SEB in the State. Excessive interference in the affairs of the SEB by the state government has resulted over employment in the SEB especially and more unwarranted in administration section. Institutional factors breeding inefficiency has been the lack of professional management with commitment, accountability, inclination and initiatives in decision making. Moreover, the socio-political dynamics of the state has led to a situation of wide-spread corrupt practices of nepotism at the cost merit, ability and efficiency.

However, some of the major reforms in T & D are essential to curb the losses.

1. Illegal tapping and meter tampering can be eliminated by using under ground cables.
2. Transmission losses can be reduced by a changing over to 400 KV transmission voltages.
3. Resistive losses can be minimised by using cooper conductor in the place of aluminum cables.
4. No load losses can be curbed by using low loss core transformers and switching them off when not use.
5. Peak load power shortage power shortage can be eliminated by switching on hydroelectric power during peak hours.

III. Financial Performance

Power sector reforms were expected to focus on two thrusts. One was the establishment of rational tariff structures through independent regulatory commissions. The second was the restructuring of the State Electricity Boards separating generation from transmission and distribution to bring about greater efficiency in each area. In this regard, U.P. Electricity reforms Act 1999 has come into force in January, 2000. However, under this Act for better tariff structures and to attract private investment in power, the Government of Uttar Pradesh unbundled the erstwhile U.P. State Electricity Board (UPSEB) into three corporations, viz., UP Thermal Generation Corporation, UP Hydro Generation Corporation and UP Power Corporation (for T & D works).

The establishment of State Electricity Regulatory Commission (SERC) had been envisaged by the State Power Ministers conference in December, 1996. The Central Electricity Regulatory Commission (CERC) was expected to set tariffs for ail generation and transmission utilities supplying power across several states (Government of India, 2002-05). However, SERC were expected to discharge a similar function for state utilities. Accordingly, the Electricity Regulatory Commission Act was passed in July, 1998. Under this Act, U.P. Electricity Regulatory Commission (UPERC) established in September, 1998 and subsequent tariff orders were prepared from 2000-01 onwards till the current financial year 2004-05. In the last report of UPERC, the determination of tariffs within the ambit of Electricity Act 2003 and important objectives were prepared (UPERC, 2004-05).

- Rationalization of Electricity tariff
- Ensuring transparent policies regarding subsidies
- Gradually removing the element of cross subsidy
- Promoting competition in the industry
- Protecting interest of consumers and supply of electricity

The revenue realized from the sales must be sufficient at least to recover the costs of supply is the basic prerequisite for the health of any industry (Kannan, et al, 2002). Starting from this premise and comparing revenue realized with cost incurred in the power sector serve the purpose of highlighting the parlous financial position of the UPPCL, which in turn is used to justify the clamour and claim for reforms. When we asses the tariff cost ratio, the picture may be more clear. At all India level, tariff cost ratio was 83.4 percent in 1974-75, declined to 77 percent in 1980-81, again declined to 75 percent in 1990-91 and slightly improved 81 percent in 1997-98 (Kannan, *et.al.*, 2002). It means SEBs is able to collect 81 percent of the cost of electricity trough tariff from all the sectors. The scenario in Uttar Pradesh is no way different from that of all India level. Total loss with and without subsidy has been increasing over the years of the UPPCL due to high cost involved and low revenue realization in the supply of power (Table 5). However, it may attributed here that high commercial losses are due to various reasons such as heavy power theft, large arrears in revenue collection, large gap between cost of supply and realization, high transmission and distributional losses. This may more transparent when we compare the cost of supply and realization in sector wise for better policy and perspective.

The financial health of the SEBs has been deteriorating over the years mainly due to higher level of technical and commercial losses and subsided sale of electricity to agricultural and domestic consumers. Category wise average tariff estimation in 1997-98 shows agriculture sector contributes at the lowest, i.e., 27.7 paise/unit as against 134 paise/unit in domestic, 333 paise/unit in commercial, 285 paise/unit in industry and as against average of 180 paise/unit at all India level. Average tariff cost ratio shows agriculture is the least paid, i.e. 12 percent followed by domestic, i.e. 59 percent, industry 125 percent and commercial 146 percent (Kannan et al 2002). However, the scenario at Uttar Pradesh is much worse than that of all India level. The domestic rural and agricultural sector contributes only 27 percent of the cost of supply of electricity, where as commercial and industrial sector contribute more than the costs involved (Table 6). This also reveals that highest amount of losses are incurred in the rural domestic and agricultural sector, as small medium, large industries, urban commercial units, railways and lift irrigations show profit for this sector.

Keeping in view of the above scenario, serious thoughts are to be given for the survival of the sector. However, recent decision in the meeting of the Power Minister to raise the tariff up to 50 percent of the cost involved need to be implemented carefully and very delicately without harming the poorest section of the society (Government of India, 2002-07). Moreover, tariff orders issued by the CERC and SERC need to be implemented fully unless stayed or set aside by court (Government of India, 2002-07). In addition, subsidies to be given only to the extent of the state government's capacity to pay. In order to make the market more competitive and vibrant, two steps are necessary to reformed. Firstly, there should be organizational and physical separation of agriculture and rural sector. Secondly, cross subsidy in tariffs should be eliminated for urban domestic consumers and replaced with lifeline rates for low income consumers in both rural and urban areas and subsidised extension of the network to high cost areas (Sinha, 2005).

IV. Rural Electrification

In the state, nearly 54,951 villages out of 97,135 were electrified by the end of 2001-02 and it was proposed that the rest 42,184 villages are to be electrified during the 10th five year plan. However, UP Power Corporation has to electrify rest 42, 184 villages in order to achieve 100 percent electrified villages during the 10th plan. In order to electrify all the villages, Rs. 316380 lakhs were required on an average of Rs. 7.5 lakhs per village. However, during 10th plan, only 132700 lakhs were sanctioned to electrify 17, 693 villages. Hence, on an average of 3371 villages per annum would be electrified. However, the situation took place differently. During the first two years of 10th plan shows that only 2164 villages were electrified out of 6742 villages. In order to electrify these 17, 693 villages, atleast 5176 villages per annum are to be electrified in the coming three years. However, 52.79 percent and 11.39 percent of the targeted villages are electrified during 2002-03 and 2003-04 respectively (Table 7). In order to achieve 100 percent electrified villages in the 10th plan, atleast 13, 340 villages are to be electrified in the forth coming three years. However, the remaining 40,020 villages are still un-electrified by the end of 2003-04 in the state out of total 97,135 villages. In order to avoid the risk of completing the project and due to other problems, the Government of Uttar Pradesh has extended the targeted year of achieving 100 percent electrified villages up to 2008-09. However, this is not end of the story. Due to sever shortage of power supply in the state, UPUCL is capable of supplying power to 12 hours per day to rural areas, 17 hours to districts head quarters and 21.5 hours per day to large cities in 2001-02 (Ahluwalia, 2005).

Similarly, the energisation of private tube wells was achieved 129.11 percent of target in the year 2002-03 and again come down to nearly 63 percent in 2003-04. In order to achieve 100 percent of the target, atleast 10,660 private tube wells per annum are to be energisized in the next three years. However, the performance of the all the three item during 2003-04 was poor compared to the earlier year. The electrification of Anusuchit village was only 37 percent of the target in 2003-04. In order to electrify all the 5742 Anusuchit villages, atleast 1389 villages are to be electrified per annum in the next three years.

V. Privatization

The demand for power has been increasing over the years due to growing industrialization, growing domestic and commercial needs, increasing the consumption in agricultural sector. However, the rate of generation of power has been remaining constant or declining over the years causing the increase of deficit. Hence, the percent of deficit has been increasing every year in the 10th plan. The deficit has increased from 15 percent in 2002-03 to 18.43 percent in 2004-05. Therefore, in order to control the increase in the deficit of power, the entry of private sector for generation activities has been allowed in the state. The issue is not only the gap between demand and supply but also the anomalies taking place in transmission, distribution, rural electrification, tariff collection by the public sector undertakings, which causes heavy power theft, large arrears in revenue collection, large gap between cost of supply and realization, high transmission and distributional losses. This ultimately remunerates huge losses to the State Electricity Boards (SEBS). Hence, the idea of private sector participation is being evolved in the field of generation, transmission, distribution of power in the country as well as the State level in order to develop the efficiency in power supply, smoothening distribution activities and increasing overall welfare of the state. Many of the states viz., Orissa, Maharastra, Delhi has been adopted privatization at various levels in the power sector. The success and failure stories are different for different states at different levels.

However, U.P. Energy Policy, 2003 has encouraged the private sector participation in all areas, viz., generation, transmission, distribution, trading and R & M to facilitate the consumers benefiting from competition. However, more emphasis was given on privatization of distribution business initially. The privatization activities have not been started but consultants have been engaged to carry out privatization process (Government of Uttar Pradesh, 2004-05). So far as the generation activities by the private sector are concerned, only four companies were agreed to establish the units. However, Rosa thermal, Vishnu Prayag hydro project may able to produce power by December 2006, where the state would get a share of 1594 MU by the same year (Government of Uttar Pradesh, 2004-05). It may be attributed here that the contribution by the private would be very much meager to enabling the deficiency in the power sector.

Few pertinent questions are raised in connection with the private participation in the field of generation, transmission and distribution etc. Firstly, jus a mere paradigm shift of ownership from public undertakings to private ownership in the field of generation, transmission and distribution, would it be really helpful for achieving the goal without improving the paying capacity of the majority of the people those who are living below the poverty line? Or in other words, throwing the fate of majority of the people to the market driven forces without changing the structure of the society, would the power sector be freed from all the anomalies it is being suffering since the inception of the planning era? The opinions of the few think tanks are portrayed as follows. The determination of tariffs and privatization in the power sector is mostly politically determined. However, this sector is technology driven and hence the reform process should not be judged ideologically. Privatization is not the only solution and has to be done selectively in places where we can show good results to inspire confidence in this process from a larger section (Probhu, S. 2005). However, Dhaul, H. (2005) expressed more aggressively, let the producers and consumers of power deal directly with each other and why there is a need of intervention. However, he has opined that greater private participation is just not happening because giving chance to generate only without transmitting, distributing and deciding the tariff structures.

VI. Energy Conservation and Demand side Management:

Some of the energy conservation and demand side management are suggested for better social and economic life.

Household Sector

- Change of incandescent bulb to compact florescent lamps (CFL).
- Florescent tube lights consume 53 watts where as T5 tube lights consume only 28 watts for the same.
- Electricity boilers in bathroom with solar water heaters. We may also use solar pumps to take water to overhead tanks. If the households do so, power consumption may come down to 90 percent with the same level of output (Firodia, A., 2005).

Public Sector

- Street light should be Sodium Vapor Lamps, Switching off automatically done at the morning.
- If the locality or society harvest its rainwater and

recycles its effluents for gardening, a municipality would no longer have to transport water over long distances or pump sewage out.

- Traffic lights and outdoor signals should use LED (Light Emitting Diodes), which would save 90 percent of power.

Agriculture Sector

- Drip Irrigation would save water consumption and watershed development would raise water level. Farmers would then need to use smaller pumps and then low power consumption.

Industrial Sector

- Six major industries such as Aluminum, Fertilizer, Chemicals, Steel, Petrochemical and Refineries consume nearly 65 percent of the power consume in the industrial sector. This would induce to reduce energy consumption according to international norms of ?energy cost of per unit of output?.

VII. Conclusion

Power sector not only enhance production and consumption directly but also create many direct and indirect benefit of the society. It is considered as one of the important indicators for economic growth of an economy. In due course of time, UPSEB succumbed to huge commercial loss, unable to maintain the demand and supply activity of power sector. Though, Electricity Supply Act, 1948 permits SEBs as autonomous bodies, yet States intervention to satisfy the socio, economic and political requirements caused tremendous financial weakness of the UPSEB. Apart from operational weakness, its differential price policy favoring few sections of the consumers, undesired employment policy of taking more non-skilled labour, highly inefficient collection mechanism caused mounting up the losses of the SEB in subsequent periods. Another important factor is that the financial situation of UPSEB could have been neutralized to some extent, had the State paid the required subside due to them for domestic and agricultural sectors regularly and exactly. Providing more autonomous by converting the SEB into SERC may be right a step for improving the financial health, improving generation, transmission and distribution capacity. But, will they succeed by breaking the strong socio-political nexus without sacrificing the welfare of the society at large?

Table 1

CAGR of various Physical Indicators in Power Generation in Uttar Pradesh

Indicators	*1980-81 to 1990-91*	*1990-91 to 2000-01*	*1980-2001*
Install Capacity	5.12*	1.51*	2.94*
	(14.58)	(2.31)	(10.60)
Hydro	2.22*	0.30 NS	1.10*
	(4.95)	(1.73)	(6.68)
Thermal	6.39*	2.02 ***	3.66*
	(10.23)	(2.16)	(10.05)
Gross Generation	7.03*	3.45*	4.91*
	(6.9)	(5.91)	(14.08)
Hydro	3.87*	1.20 NS	2.02*
	(5.77)	(1.01)	(5.61)
Thermal	8.43*	4.18*	6.07*
	(5.02)	(6.30)	(12.42)
T & D Loss	17.46*	7.68*	10.96*
	(17.23)	(5.59)	(14.88)
Total sales to Consumers	9.19*	2.83*	7.03*
	(25.13)	(3.26)	(15.63)

Source: Estimated from various volumes of CMIE.

Note: CAGR obtained by fitting the standard form $Y_t = Y_0 (1+r)^t$, where the time series data of above mentioned variables are regressed by time. The values in the parenthesis are t-values, where *, **, *** indicates 1 percent, 5 percent and 10 percent level of significance, whereas NS indicates not significant.

Table 2

TRENDS OF ELECTRICITY GENERATION IN THE STATE DURING 9TH AND 10TH PLAN (IN MILLION UNITS)

Year	Electricity Generation			Import	Import as percent of Gene ration	Demand	Gross Generation as a propor- tion of Demand	Deficit	Deficit as percent of Demand
	Hydel	Thermal	Gross						
1997-98	5428	18380	23808	14514	33.94	42761	55.68	-6336	-14.82
98-99	6196	18742	24938	15914	35.77	44488	56.06	-5503	-12.37
99-2000	5297.42	18960	24257.42	39864	82.72	48192	50.33	-8328	-17.28
2000-01	5305.78	19583	24888.78	40645	82.08	49521	50.26	-8876	-17.92
2001-02	4020.61	20464	24484.61	41838	81.69	51685	47.37	-9427	-18.24
9th plan (Average)	5250	19226	24475	30632	63.00	47329	52	-7694	-16
2002-03	1550.18	20687	22376.70	37060	75.83	48870	45.79	-11809	-24.2
2003-04 (Anticipated)	2111.90	20681	22793.14	40932	80.02	51153	44.56	-10220	-20.0
2004-05 (Proposed)	1759.00	21300	23059.00	42989	69.70	61681	37.38	-18692	-30.3
10th Plan (target)	1739	27103	28842	41817	59.06	70803	40.74	-28986	-40.9

Source: Annual Report 2003-04, Government Uttar Pradesh

Table 3

RATE OF CHANGES OVER THE PREVIOUS YEAR (GROWTH RATE) OF ELECTRICITY GENERATION, IMPORT AND DEMAND DURING 9TH AND 10TH PLAN

Year	*Electricity Generation*				
	Hydel	*Thermal*	*Gross*	*Import*	*Demand*
1999-2000	-16.96	1.15	-2.81	60.08	7.69
2000-01	0.16	3.18	2.54	1.92	2.68
2001-02	-31.96	4.31	-1.65	3.74	4.19
2002-03	-159.36	1.08	-9.42	-13.93	-5.76
2003-04 (Anticipated)	26.60	-0.03	1.83	9.46	4.46
2004-05 (Proposed)	-20.06	2.91	1.15	4.78	17.07

Source: Computed from Annual Report 2004-05, Government Uttar Pradesh

Table 4

T & D LOSSES AS PERCENT OF GROSS GENERATION AND TOTAL SALES OF ELECTRICITY IN UP

Year	*1980-81*	*1990-91*	*2000-01*
Gross Generation (Mil.KwH)	10190	18742	23598
Total Sales (Min KwH)	7846	20896	23266
T & D losses (Mil KwH)	1514	7505	15929
TD/ Gross generation	14.86	40.04	67.50
TD/ Total Sales	19.30	35.92	68.46

Source: Estimated from CMIE.

Table 5

COMMERCIAL LOSSES OF UP POWER CORPORATION LTD. (RS. CRORES)

Year	*Revenue Realization*			*Cost involved in Supply*						
	Revenue	*Subsidy*	*Total*	*Power Purchase*	*R & M*	*A & G*	*Debt Service*	*Total*	*Loss with subsidy*	*Loss without subsidy*
2000-01	5241	280	5521	5855	186	1023	553	7617	2096	2376
2001-02	5098	902	6000	6417	206	1027	594	8244	2244	3146
2002-03	5452	826	6278	6162	200	980	216	7558	1280	2106
2003-04	6133	1029	7162	6872	210	1105	580	8767	1605	2634
2004-05	6423	1056	7479	8306	248	902	784	10240	2761	3817

Source: UPPCL, 2005.

Table 6

SECTOR WISE LOSS OR GAIN IN UTTAR PRADESH

Category	*Cost of supply (Rs. Unit)*	*Average rate Tariff (Rs. Unit)*	*Energy Sales (MU)*	*Loss (Rs. Crores)*	*Gain (Rs. Crores)*
Domestic (Rural)	4.05	1.1	4394	1296.23	
Single Point for bulk Loads	4.05	3.01	20	2.08	
Other Metered Domestic Consumers	4.05	2.8	6998	874.75	
Commercial (Rural)	4.05	1.41	1011	266.90	
Other Metered Commercial Consumers	4.05	4.47	1227		51.53
Public lamps	4.05	2.69	350	47.60	
Institutions	4.05	3.71	1433	48.72	
Private Tubewells	4.05	1.08	3640	1081.08	
Small and Medium Power	4.05	5.5	1389		201.41
Public Water Works	4.05	4.26	643		13.50
State Tubewells	4.05	2.4	1477	243.71	
Temporary Supply	4.05	6.32	68		15.44
Dept. Employees and Pensions	4.05	1.14	114	33.17	
Large and Heavy Power	4.05	4.51	3925		180.55
Railways	4.05	4.37	584		18.69
Lift Irrigations	4.05	4.43	291		11.06
Total	4.05	2.81	27564	3891	493

Source: UPPCL, 2005.

Table 7

COMPARISON OF TARGET AND ACHIEVEMENT OF ELECTRIFICATION IN RURAL AREAS

	10th Plan (2002-07)		*2002-03*			*2003-04*		
	Targets	*Achievement*	*Target*	*Achievement*	*Percent of target*	*Target*	*Achievement*	*Percent of target*
Electrification of villages	42184		3372	1780	52.79	3372	384	11.39
Energization of PTW	50000		10000	12911	129.11	10000	6309	63.09
Electrification of Anusuchit Basties	5742		1148	1839	160.19	1148	428	37.28

Source: Annual Report, 2004-05.

References

Agarwal, S.K. (2005): "Uttar Pradesh...Challenges", A paper presented in the *National Seminar on Recommendations of the Twelfth Finance Commission and Their Implications for the States,* during 6-7th May, 2005 conducted by Giri Institute of Development Studies, Lucknow.

Dhaul, H. (2005): What Hubbles Electricity Reforms? *The Economic Times,* May 10, Tuesday, p. 15, New Delhi.

Firodia, A. (2005): No Sweet: Tackle Power Crisis by Reducing Consumption, *The Times of India,* April 25, Monday, Lucknow.

Government of India (2002-07): 10th Five Year Plan, Vol. II, Planning Commission, New Delhi.

Government of India (2005): *National Electricity Policy-2003,* Ministry of Power, February, New Delhi.

Government of Uttar Pradesh, (2002-03): *Tenth Five Year Plan (2002-07) and Annual Plan (2002-03),* Vol. I, Part II, State Planning Commission.

Government of Uttar Pradesh, (2003-04): *Annual Plan (2003-04),* Vol. I, Part II, State Planning Commission.

Government of Uttar Pradesh, (2004-05): *Annual Plan (2004-05),* Vol. I, Part II, State Planning Commission.

Kannan, K.P. et.al. (2002): *Plight of the Power Sector Reforms in India: Inefficiency, Reform and Political Economy,* Centre for Development Studies, Thiruvananthpuram.

Mohan, A. (2005): Myth of Rural Electrification for Growth and Development, *The Times of India,* May 17, p. 4, Lucknow.

Prabhu, S., (2005): What Hubbles Electricity Reforms? *The Economic Times,* May 10, Tuesday, p. 15, New Delhi.

Sinha, S. (2005): Introducing Competition in the Power sector: Open Access and Cross Subsidies, *Economic and Political Weekly,* Vol. XL, No. 7, February 12-18.

Uttar Pradesh Electricity Regulatory Commission, (2004-05), Tariff Report for UPPCL, Lucknow.

6

TRANSPORT SECTOR IN UTTAR PRADESH
Physical and Financial Performance

Sanatan Nayak

I. Introduction

An efficient transport system is a pre-requisite for sustained economic development. It plays crucial role in promoting national integration, increasing productivity, enhance the competitive efficiency of the economy in the world market. Moreover, it also helps in developing the backward regions and integrating them with the main stream economy by opening them to the trade investment. The transport system includes railways, roads, civil aviations, oceanic shipping, coastal shipping and inland water transport. However, roads and railways are considered as the important transport system in the state. During the planning process, the transport sector has been progressed both in quantity and in quality. With this impressive achievement, this sector also suffers from large number of deficiency and bottlenecks. The quality and productivity of the transport net work and resource base needs improvement.

Keeping in view of the importance of road transport sector,

the objective of the paper are as follows. Firstly, to assess the physical coverage of roads under different schemes of state and central government, and some International agency. Secondly, to assess the performance (physical and financial) of the Uttar Pradesh Road Transport Corporations.

Secondary sources data relating to physical connectivity and financial performance of this sector, data are collected from various volumes of Annual Plan Documents, Statistical Abstract, Statistical Dairy, various State Government and Central Government Reports.

This paper is divided into five sections. Section I deals with introduction, objectives and brief methodology of this study. Section II highlights the status of Uttar Pradesh in Road sector, while section III describes the physical achievements of road sector in the state. Section IV analyses the physical and financial performance of Uttar Pradesh Road Transport Corporation. While section V deals with conclusion and policy recommendation of this study.

II. Status of Uttar Pradesh in Transport Sector

Roads per one lakh of population and per 100 square kms area are some of the true indicators for measuring the strength of transport sector in the state. This is evident from the fact that roads maintained per one lakh population are 57.3 kms in the state against all India averages of 82.5 kms (Government of Uttar Pradesh, 2002-03). The state is ranked 12th among selected major 18 states in the country in connection with this indicator. It is revealed that Punjab and Rajasthan have 204 kms and 126 kms respectively per one lakh population. In addition, roads maintained per 100 square kms area is 30.8 kms as against 23.7 kms at all India level. In this regard, Uttar Pradesh stands 6th position among some of the major states, such as Punjab has 92.2 kms and Kerala has 53.5 kms (Government of Uttar Pradesh, 2004-05). Considering this background, it is necessary to have a thorough evaluation in the transport sector in the state keeping the 10th plan targets in mind.

1. Meeting the higher demand of transports due to growth process of the economy.
2. Ensuring the transport growth in all regions of the state.
3. Capacity augmentation, quality and productivity improvements through technology upgradation.
4. Emphasis on higher maintenance standards.
5. Internal generation of resources through rational pricing, user charges and increasing participation of private sector.
6. Better regulatory framework in order to curb the distortions like sunk costs, presence of externalities.
7. To develop an adequate transport data base comprising traffic flows and costs, this must be systematically collected and updated.
8. There is need of better and efficient safety network for curbing the accidental fatalities.
9. Environmental pollution is a serious matter of concern due to development of heavy traffic congestion and road construction. Therefore, serious steps need to be evolved to curb the environmental pollution due to these activities.

III. Physical Coverage of the Roads and Bridges

Construction of roads and bridges has both direct and indirect impact on the development of socio-economic condition of the people. The direct benefits constitutes savings in operating costs, time savings, increase comforts and convenience, whereas indirect benefits are to stimulate economic development and environmental improvements (Belli, Pedro *et.al.*, 2001). It helps in increasing agricultural production, increases the employment opportunities, decreases cost of travel and transportation, save the traveling time and provides a lot of indirect benefits to the rural community (Singh, et al. 2004); Kadiyali, 2003). However, the indirect impacts are much more than the direct impacts. The indirect impacts are a necessary pre-condition for commercialization and diversification of agriculture. Studies also show the rural roads have a noticeable effect on reduction in poverty levels and improvement in education levels and health conditions (Singh, et al. 2004); Kadiyali, 2003).

Keeping the importance of roads and transport on the socio-economic development of the economy, Government of Uttar Pradesh has set some of the objectives in the 10th five year plan. Some of the important objectives such as maximizing the benefits by completing the ongoing schemes, development of rural roads, upgradation of existing road networks and bridges, construction of flyovers and subways in important cities, improvement of urban roads, improvement of traffic safety measures, computerization of P.W.D secretariat, private sector participation etc. In addition, widening the roads, improvement in riding quality and strengthening, road safety measures and providing wayside amenities to cater to the growing demand for road services.

The share of transport sector has been improving over the various five year plans in the state. However, the share has been enhancing from 4 percent in the 1st plan to 15 percent of the total planned expenditure in the 9th plan. The investment under transport constitutes a lion share of the state budget under the infrastructure sector. However, budget allocation comes from state, central government and other international financial agencies for construction of roads and bridges in the state. In this connection, the Government of Uttar Pradesh started construction of roads under the Diversified Agricultural Support Project (DASP) undertaken by the support of the World Bank during 1998-99 to 2003-2004. Under the DASP nearly 2740 kms of rural roads have been constructed in the project districts of Uttar Pradesh and Uttaranchal at a cost of Rs. 4718.5 million.

However, keeping the objectives as an priority basis in the transport sector for construction of roads, bridges, villages roads, nearly 6008 crores has been allocated for this sector during 10th plan in the state. The proportion of actual expenditure to the allocated outlay is satisfactory during the first two years of the plan (Table 1). Most importantly, 100 percent of the allocated outlay is spent in 2002-03 and it is nearly 66 percent in 2003-04. The budget allocation is also same to the average allocation during last two years of the plan.

The physical achievement in reconstruction/upgradation of roads such as national high ways, state high ways and major district roads are not satisfactory during the first two years of the plan. The proportion of physical achievement to the targets is 0 percent, -76 percent and 5 percent for national and state highways, and major district roads respectively in 2002-03 (Table 2). However, the achievement of these roads is not mentioned during 2003-04 in the state. However, the connectivity of villages through surface village's roads has been satisfactory during the two years. During 2002-03, the achievement has crossed many times more than the targets. On the other hand, the proportion of achievement to target is nearly 87 percent during 2003-04. Similarly, the connectivity of the number of villages during the two years has been better compared 9th five year plan.

Village Connectivity

There are 98, 248 villages of all types covered through out the state. However, all the villages are connected through all weather mettle roads in different five year plan. There are 43,437 villages connected by mettle roads up to 9th plan in the state. It shows that nearly 56 percent of the total villages are still unconnected by mettle roads. In addition, 2920 and 1492 villages are added to list of mettle roads during 200-03 and 2003-04 respectively. However, 2289 villages are proposed to be connected by mettle roads in 2004-05. With all the efforts, still 49 percent of the total villages are remained unconnected by mettle roads by the end 2004-05. In order to cover all the villages, the state government has taken various schemes, such as Ambedkar Gram Vikas Yojna, Samagra Gram Vikas Yojna, Pandit Deen Dayal Upadhayaya Link Road Project and project by World Bank. Ambedkar Gram Vikas Yojna was launched in 2002-03 for construction of rural roads by connecting the villages predominated with scheduled caste population. Samagra Gram Vikas Yojna was started in 2004. The purpose was to connect 10 selected villages by each MLA in their respective constituencies. Similarly, Pandit Deen Dayal Upadhayaya Link Road Project was funded by NABARD and the purpose was to construct rural roads based on population of various categories. However, it was not restricted to construct only rural roads by different schemes during the plan period. The construction of railway over heads and bridges are also proposed to construct during the plan period. However, one railways overhead bridge is completed in 2002-03 and two is in progressive stage during 2003-04. Another 8 overhead bridges are proposed to be constructed during 2004-05. However, the proposal on rural rods to be completed by 2010 seems to be great task for the authority. Nearly, 49 percent of the rural villages have to be connected within five years.

Mobilization of Resources

Given the limitation of budgetary support for road sector projects, emphasis was given on generation of resources through levy of appropriate user charge and active participation of private sector in financing and maintenance activities. In this regard, no substantial progress has been achieved by the Government of Uttar Pradesh. The viability study for nearly 214 projects is under progress by the M/s RITES, New Delhi.

Employment Opportunity

The construction of rural roads not only integrate the rural economy with the main stream economy by increasing productivity of various crops, developing market facilities but also raise the employment opportunity at the rural areas during the construction of rural roads. It has been proposed to create 2024 lakh man days during the 10th five year plan by constructing rural roads in the state. During 2002-03, nearly 339 lakh man days were created and 334 lakh man days are anticipated to be created during 2003-04.

IV. Uttar Pradesh State Road Transport Corporation (UPSRTC)

UPSRTC came into existence on 1st June 1972 under the provisions of the Road Transport Act, 1950. It provides transport services in the state of Uttar Pradesh and adjoining states in North India. The corporation has been reconstituted on 31st October 2003 with the services in the state of Uttaranchal forming a separate state. The major task before the UPSRTC is to improve the physical and financial performance, rationalization of motor vehicle act and collection of taxes, technological upgradation, road safety, pollution control and upgradation of check posts.

Physical Performance

Various indicators such as fleet utilization percent of buses on road, vehicle production (revenue earning km per bus held per day), bus staff ratio, staff production and fuel efficiency are some of the important variables for assessing the physical performance of the State Road Transport Corporation. However, Uttar Pradesh shows a moderate performance among various states at the all India level (Government of India, 2002-03). According to the latest estimation at all India level, fleet utilization percent of buses on road, bus staff ratio, fuel efficiency in Uttar Pradesh are considered better than that of all India level, while vehicle production, staff production are lower in the state than that of all India level.

Financial Performance

Poor Financial performance by the UPSRTC, despite an improvement in the physical parameters is a matter of concern. However, it is argued that high rate of taxation, low fare structure, concession to meet social responsibility; over staffing, increasing interest burden and unhealthy competition in the private sector have put an extra burden on the corporation making operations uneconomic. The UPSRTC has been a perennial loss making corporation except for four years, when it had nominal profit between Rs 45, 000 to Rs. 1.21 Crores (Benerjee & Chaubey, 2004). The situation is quite grim, as the losses seem to increasing every year. Yearly loss rose from Rs. 1 crore in 1972-73 to Rs. 121 crores in 2001-02, though fluctuating in between. The corporation had an accumulated loss of Rs.

300 crores in 1992-93, Rs. 600 crores in 1999-2000 and Rs. 900 crores in 2002-03. In fact, the accumulated losses now far exceed the total external capital.

In order to reduce the cost recovery ratio, it is indeed true to reduce the cost drastically and increase the revenue considerable. Total revenue consists of traffic and non-traffic revenue. Major portion of the revenue consist of traffic revenue and it is more than 90 percent though the proportion of non-traffic has increased over the years. In fact, the absolute revenue collection fell in 2000-01 and 2001-02, while cost rose as usual. In case of UPSRTC, the costs are on the higher side as compared to many large corporations. Two factors such as higher compensation rates and higher bus-staff ratio are responsible for high cost recovery ratio. The bus staff ratio is found to be 8 in the UPSRTC. Hence, there is some scope for reducing it, as it has been attained in other corporations. The cost recovery ratio, which improved for a while in early 90's and reached 0.95 has been on continuous slide down and touched the low of 0.85 in 2002-03, which is an improvement compared to past two years.

Policy Measures

In order to make financially viable to the UPSRTC, it is needed to increase revenue earnings and at the same time reducing the cost. Some of the major avenues to increase earnings and reducing the costs are as follows.

1. To increase the occupancy rate without declining the comforts and efficiency.
2. Look for avenues to earn non-traffic revenues.
3. Bus staff ratio can be reduced.
4. The corporation can do away with the over aged buses on regular basis as they consume more fuel and repair and maintenance costs is higher.

Technological Upgradation

There has been some improvement by introducing computerization in the departments, i.e., nine out of seventy one offices are computerasized and there is plan for introducing a driving school in the state. However, there has been no progress in the field of road freight transport, i.e., extreme over loading of trucks, lax implementation of rules and regulations, unhelpful tax regimes and congested roads.

Road Safety

Safety on roads has become a major area of concern. In this regard, no special efforts have been taken by the government. Measures need to be taken to minimize road accidents through the introduction of road safety devices, training of drivers and instructors, awareness programme for the public and transport users, computerization of the licensing system, creation of pedestrian and cycle path, exclusive bus lane etc.

Pollution Control

The share of transport sector in total emission is increasing and is matter of concern. There is serious respiratory health problems associated with air pollution. The main causes of vehicular pollution are outdated engine technology in heavy motor vehicles, poor maintenance, large number of overage vehicles, over loading and traffic jams etc. In this regard, state government has to take serious efforts following the guidelines of the central government to control the air pollution.

V. Summing Up

Road transport plays crucial role in promoting national integration, increasing productivity, enhance the competitive efficiency of the economy in the world market, the development of backward regions and integrating them with the main stream economy by opening them to the trade investment. However, roads per one lakh population and per 100 square kms area are some of the true indicators for measuring the strength of transport sector in the state. This is evident from the fact that roads maintained per one lakh population are 57.3 kms in the state against all India averages of 82.5 kms. The state is ranked 12th among selected major 18 states in the country in connection with this indicator. In addition, roads maintained per 100 square kms area is 30.8 kms as against 23.7 kms at all India level. In this regard, Uttar Pradesh stands 6th position among some of the major states, as Punjab has 92.2 kms and Kerala has 53.5 kms. Moreover, poor financial performance by the UPSRTC, despite an improvement in the physical parameters is a matter of concern. The UPSRTC has been a perennial loss making corporation except for four years. The situation is quite grim, as the losses seem to increasing every year. Yearly loss rose from Rs. 1 crore in 1972-73 to Rs. 121 crores in 2001-02, though fluctuating in between. The corporation had an accumulated loss of Rs. 300 crores in 1992-93, Rs. 600 crores in 1999-2000 and Rs. 900 crores in 2002-03. In fact, the accumulated losses now far exceed the total external capital. This may be attributed here that there exist huge supply and demand gap, regional disparity in the road construction, low maintenance standards, no better regulatory framework and environmental pollution in the transport sector. However, high rate of taxation, low fare structure, concession to meet social responsibility; over staffing, increasing interest burden and unhealthy competition in the private sector have put an extra burden on the corporation making the corporation uneconomic.

Transport sector can be effectively managed by reducing the demand and supply deficits, ensuring the transport growth in all regions of the state, capacity augmentation, quality and productivity improvements through technology upgradation, emphasis on higher maintenance standards, internal generation of resources through rational pricing, user charges and increasing participation of private sector, better regulatory framework in order to curb the distortions like sunk costs, presence of externalities, To develop an adequate transport data base comprising traffic flows and costs, this must be systematically collected and updated. However, both physical and financial viability of the UPSRTC can be improved by increasing the occupancy rate without declining the comforts and efficiency, looking for avenues to earn non-traffic revenues, bus staff ratio can be reduced, the corporation can do away with the over aged buses on regular basis as they consume more fuel and repair and maintenance costs is higher.

Table 1

FINANCIAL TARGETS AND ACHIEVEMENT DURING THE 10TH PLAN (RS. CRORES)

Year	*Outlay*	*Expenditure*	*Percent of the outlay*
10th plan	6008.16	—	—
2002-03	921.23	921.23	100
2003-04	1225.22	806.68	65.84
2004-05	1264.97	—	—

Source: Annual Plan, 2004-05.

Table 2

PHYSICAL ACHIEVEMENT OF VARIOUS ROADS DURING 10TH PLAN (KMS)

Item	*10th plan (Targets)*	*2002-03 Target*	*2002-03 Achie-*	*2002-03 Percent of target*	*2003-04 Target*	*2003-04 Achie-*	*2003-04 Percent of target*	*2004-05 (target)*
National Highways	1000	100	0	0	100	—	—	100
State Highways	9000	100	-76	-76	100	—	—	100
Major District Roads	10000	200	10	5	200	—	—	200
Other District Roads	-20000	200	1323	661.5	200	—	—	200
Village Roads								
Surface	9236	1672	5011	299.70	2458	2127	86.53	2228
Un-surface	-4298	-710	-629	88.59	-330	-320	96.97	
Village Connectivity (Nos.)								
More than 1500	110	135	120	88.89	50	499	998.00	50
1499-1000	185	225	225	100.00	179	336	187.71	150
Less than 1000	3400	550	2575	468.18	1300	657	50.54	1202

Source: Annual Plan, 2004-05.

Table 3

Rural Connectivity by Mettle Roads during 9th and 10th plan (in Nos.)

Year	Total Village	Mettle Roads Level	Mettle Roads Additional	Remained Unconnected	Percent of total villages
9th plan	98248	43437	—	54811	55.79
2002-03	98248	46357	2920	51891	52.82
2003-04	98248	47849	1492	50399	51.30
2004-05	98248	50138	2289	48110	48.97

Source: Annual Report, 2004-05.

References

Banerji, P. and P.K. Chaubey (2004): Study of State Public Undertakings (SPSUs) and State Road Transport Undertakings (SRTUs), Submitted to Twelfth Finance Commission, Government of India.

Belli, Pedro et.al. (2001): *Economic Analysis of Investment Operations: Analytical Tools and Practical Applications*, World Bank Institute, The World Bank, Washington, D.C.

Government of Uttar Pradesh, (2002-03): *Tenth Five Year Plan (2002-07) and Annual Plan (2002-03)*, Vol. I, Part II, State Planning Commission.

Government of Uttar Pradesh, (2004-05): *Annual Plan (2004-05)*, Vol. I, Part II, State Planning Commission.

Kadiyali, et.al. (2003): *Study of Social and Economic Impact of Rural Roads*, under Uttar Pradesh Diversified Support Project, Public Works department, Government of Uttar Pradesh.

Singh, A.K., Yashvir Tyagi and Sanatan Nayak (2004): Project Report on *Economic and Financial Analysis*, Submitted to Uttar Pradesh Diversified Support Project, Giri Institute of Development Studies, Lucknow.

7

REGIONAL DISPARITIES AND AREA DEVELOPMENT PROGRAMMES

Y. Tyagi

I. Introduction

Uttar Pradesh is one of the largest states with diverse agro-climatic conditions, natural resource endowments, demographic features and historically uneven development of different regions. Traditionally, four economic regions, viz., Eastern, Western, Central and Bundelkhand are recognized in Uttar Pradesh comprising 27, 26, 10 and 7 districts respectively. Apart from inter-regional disparities there are wide spread intra-regional disparities too. Balanced regional development has been one of the objectives of successive Five Year Plans. Planned efforts through different schemes have also been made over the years to reduce regional disparities. Still, the problem of regional imbalances in Uttar Pradesh continues, as the Tenth Plan has commented, "Regional Disparity is still wide spread in the State" (Government of Uttar Pradesh, 2002-03). Uttar Pradesh as a whole has lagged behind other states in terms of development but within Uttar Pradesh regions and districts have fared differently in achieving the goal of development.

Some regions and districts have been left behind in the process of development. These areas need special attention of planners to accelerate the pace of development in the backward areas.

Objectives

Based on the above background, the present paper attempts to estimate the regional disparities in Uttar Pradesh on the basis of development indicators by taking the district level data in the state.

This paper is divided into seven sections. Section I deals with introduction, objectives of this study. Section II highlights the development indicators consisting demographic, social, infrastructure, industrial, agriculture. Section III describes the regional disparities, while, section IV analyses the programmes of the 10th plan. Section V deals with the reason of regional disparities, while section VI deals conclusions of the study. In the last, Section VII deals with policy recommendation for the study.

II. Development Indicators in Uttar Pradesh

Demographic Indicators

The density of population as per 2001 census was highest at 776 persons per sq. km. In Eastern region, followed by Western region (765), Central region (658) and the Bundelkhand region (280). Eastern region also registered highest population growth (26.35 per cent), closely followed by Western region (26.05 per cent), however, Central region (24.73 per cent) and Bundelkhand (22.32 per cent) marked lower rates of population growth during the decade of 1991-2001.

Urbanization is an important indicator of development. The 2001 Census showed that the degree of urbanization was highest at 28.25 per cent in Western region, followed by Central region (25.11 per cent), Bundelkhand (22.46 per cent) and only 11.78 per cent in Eastern region.

Social Indicators

Regional disparities are also revealed in terms of various

social indicators. For example, Bundelkhand registered the highest literacy percentage at 59.3 per cent followed by Central (57.58 per cent), Western (57.36 per cent) and Eastern (54.27 per cent). Number of beds in allopathic hospitals/dispensaries (including PHCs) per lakh of population for the year 2001-02 shows that Central region leads in this with 54.53 beds to the corresponding figures, for other regions are: Bundelkhand (47.25 per cent), Western (39.09 per cent) and Eastern (37.52 per cent).

Infrastructural Facilities

A sound economic infrastructure is must for economic development of any area. For regions of Uttar Pradesh the situation in this regard is as follows: The percentage of net irrigated area to net sown area was lowest in Bundelkhand region (45.17 per cent) and highest in Western region (91.49 per cent), the reference year is 2001-02. The length of pucca roads per thousand sq. km. of area is lowest in Bundelkhand region with a road length of 291.69 km. Western region with a road length of 467.64 is at the top. Availability of banking facilities is also the lowest in Eastern region 4.4 branches per lakh of population. Central region is ahead of other regions with 5.4 branches per lakh of population. Similarly, per capita power consumption (KWh) is found to be lowest in Bundelkhand with a figure of 143.3 KWh, whereas in Western region the same figure is 190.4 KWh.

Industrial Development

Lack of slow pace of industrial development contributes to backwardness of a region. Western region happens to be the most industrially developed region with 12.2 number of registered factories per lakh of population. In contrast Eastern region has only 1.9 factories per lakh of population.

Agricultural Development

All the regions of the State are agrarian economies. However, as per 2001 census, percentage of main workers engage din agriculture to total main workers is 56.8 per cent in Western region, whereas in Bundelkhand and Eastern regions this figure is very high at 74.52 per cent and 71.92 per cent respectively. Productivity of crops also varies across regions. Gross value of agricultural output per hectare of gross cropped area (2000-01) at current prices was Rs. 26037 in Western region, while it was only Rs. 11941 in Bundelkhand. There is preponderance of marginal holdings in Eastern region (83 per cent) as compared to 68.8 per cent in Western region.

III. Disparities in the State

Income Disparities

As a summary measure of overall regional disparities, per capita net domestic product is a frequently used indicator. Per capita net output from commodity producing sectors at current prices in 2000-01 was Rs. 11804 in Western region followed by Central region, Rs. 9387, Bundelkhand Rs. 9195 and Rs. 6788 in Eastern region, which is only 57.5 per cent of Western region's income (Table 1).

Intra-Regional Disparities

Within all the four regions, considerable intra-regional variation in the levels of development at the district level exists. For example, in the Western region, north-western districts that are in proximity of national capital Delhi are at a much higher level of development than the south-western districts. In the Central region, Lucknow-Kanpur region is far ahead of other districts. In the Eastern region Varanasi and Gorakhpur districts are relatively more developed in comparison to other districts Jhansi and to some extent Jalaun are comparatively developed in Bundelkhand region. Per capita Net Output from commodity producing sectors at constant prices of 1993-94 for 70 districts is given in the Table 1 & 2. It sheds light on inter-district disparities in per capita income. Significantly both co-efficient of variation and Gini-coefficient show an increase over the years. Hence, inter district disparities in per capita income can be said to have widened over time in Uttar Pradesh.

IV. Tenth Plan's Programmes

To tackle the special problems of the backward regions, a number of steps have been undertaken by the State Government. Since the Third Five Year Plan three regions of the State were declared backward, namely, Eastern region, Bundelkhand and Hill region (now Uttaranchal). Efforts were made to allocate a larger share of Plan funds to the backward regions of the State. The formula for distribution of district sector plan funds gave heavy weightage to socio-economic indicators of backwardness. Additionally, special schemes and funds have also been created to address the problem of backward regions. Under special area programmes a sum of Rs. 1047. 25 crores have been allocated for the duration of the 10th plan 2002-07. However, the district sector plan and other developmental programmes would also impact regional disparities. The main schemes for area development are described below:

Rastriya Sam Vikas Yojana (RSVY)

The Government of India in the year 2002-03, introduced a new initiative of RSVY for the development of backward districts in the country. The main objective of the scheme is to address the problems of low agricultural productivity, unemployment and to fill the critical gaps in physical and social infrastructure. Under the scheme, it was proposed to provide Rs. 15 crore per year to each of the districts for a period of 3 years. In the beginning of the scheme, five districts, namely, Rae Bareli, Unnao, Hardoi, Sitapur and Sonebhadra were selected. In the second phase of the scheme, five more districts, namely, Barabanki, Mirzapur, Banda, Fatehpur and Chitrakoot were selected. Finally, in the year, 2004-05, eleven more districts, namely, Jalaun, Hamirpur, Jaunpur, Kaushambi, Azamgarh, Pratapgarh, Mahoba, Gorakhpur, Kushi Nagar, Lalitpur and Chandauli were included in this scheme. This scheme could become operational only in the year 2004-05. In the Annual Plan of the State for 2004-05, a sum of Rs. 315 crore has been allocated for 21 backward districts of the State under RSVY. As per information available till October 2004 only Rs. 5.7 crores has been spend on this scheme. Financial and physical progress under this scheme has been weak.

Poorvanchal Vikas Nidhi and Bundelkhand Vikas Nidhi

To further the development of Eastern and Bundelkhand regions, State Government in 1990-91 created the Poorvanchal and Bundelkhand Vikas Nidhis. Under the Nidhis, schemes and projects are identified according to the local felt needs of the area at the district level. These are meant to provide infrastructural facilities to local people like construction of roads, minor bridges, drinking water facility, construction of Government buildings, installation of power sub-stations which, due to any reason, could not be funded from State or District Plans.

For the duration of the Tenth Plan, a sum of Rs. 750 crore has been provided for Poorvanchal Vikas Nidhi and Rs. 250 crore has been provided for Bundlekhand Vikas Nidhi. Under Poorvanchal Vikas Nidhi, in 2002-03 Rs. 147.74 crores were spend. For 2003-04, anticipated expenditure would be Rs. 149.30 crores. For 2004-05 an allocation of Rs. 150 crores has been made. Under Bundlekhand Vikas Nidhi, in the year 2002-03, Rs. 48.93 crores were spend, while anticipated expenditure for the year 2003-04 is Rs. 41.13 crores. For the year, 2004-05, Rs. 50 crores has been allocated. Financial progress under these Nidhi appears to be good.

V. Reasons for Regional Disparities

(1) Lack of industrialization in backward regions/districts is a prime cause of low level development in these areas. Poor socio-economic infrastructure and low entrepreneurial skills have hindered development.
(2) Lack of adequate irrigation facilities in Eastern and Bundlekhand regions has been mainly responsible for low agricultural productivity and little diversification of agriculture.
(3) Large flood prone areas in the Eastern region damage

the crops every year and thus putting the farmers to tremendous loss. This problem needs to be tackled on a war footing.

(4) Agriculture in the Bundlekhand region being largely rainfed, cropping intensity is low. The region is also drought-prone. In this area, programmes for watershed management should be given priority.

(5) Proportion of cash crops in the gross cropped area in the Eastern and Bundlekhand regions is very low. It depresses the value of agricultural produce per hectare. It also acts as a disincentive for private investment in agriculture.

(6) Some of the districts in the Western region are within or close to the National Capital Region. This results in higher pace of urbanization and industrialization in these districts. They also attract higher private investment The Districts falling in the NCR have grown at a faster rate because of better infrastructure facilities and large market outlets being available.

VI. Conclusions

(1) Uttar Pradesh is still afflicted by wide spread inter-regional and intra-regional disparities in levels of development.

(2) These disparities appeared to have grown over time.

(3) Efforts through special area programmes in Five Year Plans have been made to reduce disparities and ensure balanced development of the economy.

(4) However, planned efforts have not been commensurate with the severity of the problem.

(5) Implementation delays in some of the schemes (e.g. RSVY), have been noticed.

(6) Better coordination with other developmental programmes is required.

VII. Policy Recommendation

(1) Physical targets and corresponding achievements

under special area programmes should be laid down, properly monitored and evaluated on a yearly basis by the Planning Department.

(2) There is a need to dovetail special area programmes with other developmental programmes at the district level so that there is no duplication of effort and synergies among programmes are harnessed to optimize the use of resources.

(3) Infrastructural facilities in the backward districts should be augmented to give impetus to development.

(4) There should be evaluative studies to determine the effectiveness of various special area programmes in reducing regional disparities.

(5) The experience with the RSVY, that should have been launched in 2002-03 but could be launched only in 2004-05, shows that there is a need to have adequate capacity and capability to formulate, in time, plans/ programmes to take advantage of centrally sponsored schemes. For a poor and resource deficit state like Uttar Pradesh, such implementation delays are not appropriate.

(6) For balanced regional development, agro-climatic conditions, special problems and potential of development of different districts/regions should be properly assessed and taken into account while formulating area development plans.

Table 1

DISTRICT WISE PER CAPITA INCOME (IN Rs) AT 1993-94 PRICES

District	*1993-94*	*Ranking*	*1999-00*	*Ranking*	*2000-01*	*Ranking*
Saharanpur	7158	7	8581	6	8627	6
Mujaffar Nagar	7232	6	7887	11	7761	11
Bijnor	7026	9	8093	9	7987	10
Moradabad	5435	18	6380	24	8278	9
Rampur	5417	19	6077	25	5864	27
Jyotiba Phule Nagar	..		6983	17	7126	16
Meerut	8162	4	10632	2	10775	2
Bagpat			7473	13	7661	12

Ghaziabad	11587	1	8822	4	9061	5
Gautambudh Nagar			17912	1	18111	1
Bulandshahar	6780	10	8210	8	8309	8
Aligarh	5366	20	7130	16	6963	18
Hathras			5779	31	5903	26
Mathura	6504	11	8311	7	8352	7
Agra	6066	14	7806	12	7133	15
Firozabad	4212	37	5727	33	5975	25
Etah	4787	27	5748	32	5522	31
Mainpuri	4373	34	5405	37	5313	37
Badaun	4135	38	4997	40	5303	38
Bareilly	5832	15	6534	23	6631	20
Pilibhit	6242	13	6831	20	6991	17
Shahjahanpur	5620	16	6009	27	6261	22
Kheri	5236	22	6026	26	5729	29
Sitapur	4397	33	4654	45	5099	42
Hardoi	3703	43	4089	48	4048	51
Unnao	3965	42	4033	50	4220	49
Lucknow	7061	8	8692	5	9702	3
Raibareli	4010	40	4055	49	3972	53
Farrukhabad	4120	39	5885	30	5778	28
Kannauj			4736	43	4833	43
Etawah	4242	35	5901	29	5486	33
Auraiya			4744	42	4560	44
Kanpur Dehat	4899	25	6629	21	6139	23
Kanpur Nagar	7414	5	7362	14	7157	14
Jalaun	4991	23	6563	22	5499	32
Jhansi	9771	3	8013	10	7618	13
Lalitpur	5316	21	5624	34	5168	40
Hamirpur	5611	17	6840	19	5724	30
Mahoba			6929	18	6107	24
Banda	4641	30	5063	38	5340	36
Chitrakoot			3818	53	3522	59
Fatehpur	4644	29	5054	39	5343	35
Pratapgarh	3075	50	3529	60	3476	61
Kaushambi			3756	55	4081	50
Allahabad	4585	32	6007	28	6294	21
Barabanki	4645	28	5427	36	5115	41
Faizabad	3468	45	3926	51	3993	52
Ambedkar Nagar			3301	66	3269	68
Sultanpur	4958	24	3893	52	4236	48
Bahraich	3207	49	3400	65	3333	67
Shrawasti			2886	70	3142	69
Balrampur			3014	69	3379	65

District	1993-94	Ranking	1999-00	Ranking	2000-01	Ranking
Gonda	4844	26	3422	63	3473	62
Siddhartha Nagar	2458	54	3635	59	3343	66
Basti	3022	52	3658	57	3585	57
Sant Kabir Nagar			3054	68	2854	70
Maharajganj	3967	41	4710	44	4394	46
Gorakhpur	3520	44	4321	47	4268	47
Kushinagar			3636	58	3692	55
Deoria	3332	48	3517	61	3520	60
Azamgarh	3443	46	3798	54	3710	54
Mau	4225	36	4855	41	5397	34
Balia	3072	51	3421	64	3434	64
Jaunpur	2970	53	3488	62	3683	56
Ghazipur	3381	47	3756	55	3552	58
Chandauli			4589	46	4552	45
Varanasi	6333	12	7184	15	6742	19
Sant Ravidas Nagar			3155	67	3455	63
Mirzapur	4618	31	5553	35	5228	39
Sonebhadra	10855	2	9255	3	9095	4
Maximum	11587		17912		18111	
Minimum	2458		2886		2854	
Mean	5183.94		5716.90		5703.51	
SD	1901.17		2350.62		2376.81	
CV (%)	36.67		41.11698		41.67	
No of Districts	54		70		70	
GINI Co-efficient	0.19/		0.2/		0.2/65	

Source: Estimated From Various Volumes of Statistical Dairy, Government of Uttar Pradesh

Table 2

DISTRICTS ARRANGED IN DESCENDING ORDER OF PER CAPITA INCOME

Rank	*District*	*Per Capita Income (Rs.) at 1993/94 prices in 2000-01*
1	Gautambudh Nagar	18111
2	Meerut	10775
3	Lucknow	9702
4	Sonebhadra	9095
5	Ghaziabad	9061
6	Saharanpur	8627

7	Mathura	8352
8	Bulandshahar	8309
9	Moradabad	8278
10	Bijnor	7987
11	Mujaffar Nagar	7761
12	Bagpat	7661
13	Jhansi	7618
14	Kanpur Nagar	7157
15	Agra	7133
16	Jyotiba Phule Nagar	7126
17	Pilibhit	6991
18	Aligarh	6963
19	Varanasi	6742
20	Bareilly	6631
21	Allahabad	6294
22	Shahjahanpur	6261
23	Kanpur Dehat	6139
24	Mahoba	6107
25	Firozabad	5975
26	Hathras	5903
27	Rampur	5864
28	Farrukhabad	5778
29	Kheri	5729
30	Hamirpur	5724
31	Etah	5522
32	Jalaun	5499
33	Etawah	5486
34	Mau	5397
35	Fatehpur	5343
36	Banda	5340
37	Mainpuri	5313
38	Badaun	5303
39	Mirzapur	5228
40	Lalitpur	5168
41	Barabanki	5115
42	Sitapur	5099
43	Kannauj	4833
44	Auraiya	4560
45	Chandauli	4552
46	Maharajganj	4394
47	Gorakhpur	4268
48	Sultanpur	4236
49	Unnao	4220
50	Kaushambi	4081

Rank	*District*	*Per Capita Income (Rs.) at 1993/94 prices in 2000-01*
51	Hardoi	4048
52	Faizabad	3993
53	Raibareli	3972
54	Azamgarh	3710
55	Kushinagar	3692
56	Jaunpur	3683
57	Basti	3585
58	Ghazipur	3552
59	Chitrakoot	3522
60	Deoria	3520
61	Pratapgarh	3476
62	Gonda	3473
63	Sant Ravidas Nagar	3455
64	Balia	3434
65	Balrampur	3379
66	Siddhartha Nagar	3343
67	Bahraich	3333
68	Ambedkar Nagar	3269
69	Shrawasti	3142
70	Sant Kabir Nagar	2854

Source: Estimated From Various Volumes of Statistical Dairy, Government of Uttar Pradesh.

8

POVERTY AND UNEMPLOYMENT

Y. Tyagi

I. Profile of Poverty in Uttar Pradesh

Alleviation of poverty has been one of the prime objectives of planning and development policy operationalised through Five Year Plans at National and State level. Even the directive principles of state policy laid down in our constitution, inter-alia, require the state to minimize the inequalities in income, to provide facilities and opportunities, to ensure right to an adequate means of livelihood and equitable distribution of material resources, to prohibit concentration of wealth and means of production and to raise the level of nutrition and the standard of living. Therefore, raising standard of living of population and removal of poverty and unemployment continue to be the focus of planning in India. However, even after half a century of planned efforts, the twin problems of unemployment and poverty continue to demand high attention from planners. These problems are present in more acute form in a backward state like Uttar Pradesh. It would be instructive to have a look at the trend and pattern of incidence of poverty in the State. The estimates of poverty, based on minimum nutritional requirements of 2400 calorie per capita per day in rural areas and 2100 calorie in the urban areas, for the years, 1973-74 to 1999-2000, based on N.S.S.O. consumer surreys for the state as well as for All India are given in Annexure 1.

From a perusal of the table certain salient points can be inferred. These may be put as follows.

1. The Head Count Ratio (HCR), signifying the incidence of poverty in the state declined from about 57 percent in 1973-74 to about 31 percent in 1999-2000. In indicates a reduction of 26 percent points in this period i.e. on an average of 1 per cent decline every year. The corresponding reduction in rural and urban areas works out to be about 25 percent and 29 percent respectively.
2. The reduction in the absolute number of poor people has been highest (about 74 lakh) during the period 1993-2000.
3. The pace of decline in the incidence of poverty has been slower compared to that at the all India level.
4. The population below poverty line in the State in 1973-74 was 16.67 percent of the corresponding population of all India. However, the same increased 20.36 percent in 1999-2000. It indicates deterioration in Uttar Pradesh's relative poverty position over the years.
5. All through the period under review the absolute number of poor people in Uttar Pradesh continues to be above 500 lakh. It shown that the size of the poverty in the state is huge.
6. Rural poor still constitutes 78 percent of the total poor population in the state. The high incidence of poverty in the state can be attributed to the constellation of certain mutually reinforcing forces like low literacy, higher population growth. Excessive dependence on agriculture, low quality of human resources, disparities in the distribution of assets and income, low investment and sluggish economic growth.

Social Profile of Poverty in Uttar Pradesh

An analysis of the poverty estimates shows that social dimension of poverty is also important. There are certain social groups where incidence of poverty is very high. The following tables present the relevant information in this regard:

Table 1

SOCIAL PROFILE OF POOR (CASTE-WISE) (HCR) (IN PERCENT)

Year	*ST*	*SC*	*OBC*	*Others*	*Total*
1993-94	0.8	33.7		65.5	100
1999-2000	1.4	34.4	47.4	16.4	100

Source: Estimated from NSSO, 50th and 55th Round.

Table 2

SOCIAL PROFILE OF POOR (WORK-CATEGORY) (HCR) (IN PERCENT)

Category	*1993-94*	*1999-2000*
Artisan	14.1	17.2
Agricultural Labourer	26.5	29.9
Non-Agricultural Labourer	6.8	6.9
SE in Agriculture	49.5	40.0
Others	3.9	5.9
Total	100	100

Source: Estimated from NSSO, 50th and 55th Round.

Table 3

POVERTY IN DIFFERENT REGIONS (HCR) (IN PERCENT)

Region	*Urban*	*Rural*	*Over all*
Western	30.0	21.7	23.9
Central	33.4	42.2	39.7
Eastern	31.1	36.4	35.9
Bundelkhand	40.9	20.9	24.4
Gini- Coefficient	0.34	0.25	0.28

Source: Estimated from NSSO, 55th Round.

Table 4

POVERTY AMONG RELIGIOUS GROUPS HCR (1999-2000)

Category/Religion	*Hindu*	*Muslim*	*Total*
Rural	31.27	30.84	31.01
Urban	26.43	42.17	30.76

Source: Estimated from NSSO, 55th Round.

The above data imply that in poverty alleviation programmes social aspect of poverty should not be ignored. In rural areas artisans and agricultural laborers are most severely affected by poverty. Similarly Muslims in urban areas suffer greater degree of poverty. Therefore, these groups along with SC&ST need special attention.

Targets for the Tenth Five-Year Plan

The plan has targeted to bring down the HCR of poverty from 29.51 per cent in the base year 2001-02 to 25.41 per cent in the terminal year 2006-07. In absolute terms this translates to bringing down the number of poor people from 525.38 lakh in 2001-02 to 471.57 lakh in 2006-07. However, rural poor would still constitute 76 per cent of the total population of poor people. According to the preliminary results available from the N.S.S.O. 57th and 58th rounds of surveys it appears that poverty may have declined (Annexure IV & Annexure V)

Strategy for Poverty Alleviation

Strategy being followed at National and State level can be called a 'growth plus strategy' on the one hand it is built on the assumption that the 'trickle-down effects' of the general growth process will also reach poor people in some measure and on the other hand, this is sought to be supplemented by special poverty alleviation and employment generation Programmes targeted at specific poverty groups. Over the years, there has been a plethora of Programmes/schemes for poor people, launched by the central and State Governments. Indeed, the Governments seems to be suffering from excesses of

Programmes and are following a cycle of 'proliferation and then integration' of Programmes. Most of these Programmes suffer from poor implementation and faulty delivery mechanism. Hence the intended benefits suffer from many leakages and deprive the poor people of their legitimate gains.

In view of the enormity and complexity of the task of poverty alleviation, a multi-pronged approach is required which should ensure the following:

1. Acceleration of the present low rate of growth of the state's economy is a must to make a dent on poverty.
2. Programmes that enhance skills and capabilities of poor people should be given priority. This will enable them to participate fully in the market economy and benefit from the opportunities it offers. Sectors like health and education need more public investment.
3. Social security measures and safety nets that secure entitlements for poor people should be effectively implemented with full participation of the beneficiaries.
4. Emphasis should be given to creation of assets that would generate income to people on a sustainable basis.
5. Synergies among various developmental Programmes should be harnessed for optimum utilization of resources.
6. Urban local bodies and Panchayati Raj Institutions should be empowered and involved in greater degree in the execution of anti-poverty programmes.

II. Employment and Unemployment

Providing gainful employment to the growing labour force is a major challenge before the State's economy. Five Year Plans both at the national and state levels have taken cognizance of the problem and initiated many programmes to tackle the problem of unemployment in various segments of population. The Tenth Five Year Plan of U.P. has accorded the third highest priority (after agriculture and infrastructure) to generation of employment. It said, "measures designed to generate remunerative and productive employment to promote a shift of workforce from agriculture to other sectors and to contribute to growth in the economy at the same time will receive the next highest priority in the plan." Further, as part of the monitor able targets of Tenth Plan it has been listed as, "creation of 81 lakh employment opportunities during the Tenth Plan which would be sufficient to provide jobs to the backlog of unemployment at the end of the Ninth Plan and to the additional labour force during the Tenth Plan period."

A two-pronged strategy has by and large been followed in the Plans to generate employment opportunities and solve the problem of unemployment. One aspect of this is to accelerate the rate of growth of the economy to result in greater number of jobs in the economy. Another aspect of this is to initiate special employment programmes, e.g. Swarn Jayanti Gram Swarojgar Yojna, Sampoorna Gramin Rozgar Yojna, Indira Awas, PMGY, PMGSY etc. These programmes have been launched to tackle the twin problems of poverty and unemployment. These programmes have had moderate success in achieving their goals.

To grasp the situation in regard to employment growth in U.P. and prospects for employment generation during the Tenth Plan (2002-2007), we can look at the trends in employment growth in U.P., as per Census figures.

Trends in Employment Growth

According to 1991 Census, the number of main workers in the State was 388.81 lakh (excluding Uttaranchal). In 2001, the number of main workers in the State increased to 394.53 lakh (excluding Uttaranchal), thus recording a very low annual growth rate of 0.15 per cent in comparison to an annual growth rate of 2.47 per cent in 1981-91 (including Uttaranchal). However, marginal workers marked a high growth rate of 16.85 per cent during 1991-2001 (excluding Uttaranchal). In contrast the rate of growth of marginal workers was only 7.58 per cent (including Uttaranchal). The percentage of marginal workers increased to 27 per cent in 2001 from 7 per cent in 1991. It shows that there has been deterioration in the quality of employment in the last decade.

Occupational Structure of Workers

The activity-wise distribution of workers as per Census 2001 shows that agriculture sector still plays its main role in the economy of the state of the total workers, 65.60 per cent are agricultural workers and 34.60 per cent are non-agricultural workers. Among agricultural workers, there has been an absolute decline in the number of cultivators, whereas, rate of growth of agricultural labour has also declined between (1991-2001) compared to (1981-91). The rates of growth of workers in household industry and others have marked an increase in 1991-2001 compared to 1981-91. It can be said that a sectoral shift in favour of non-agricultural occupations can be discerned in Uttar Pradesh (Annexure 1).

These findings are also confirmed by the results of NSS surveys of 55th round (1999-2000) has brought out that during 1993-94 to 1999-2000, the number of persons engaged in agriculture declined absolutely. High annual rates of growth were registered in the sectors like, construction, wholesale and retail trade, restaurants and hotels as also in transport, storage and communication. However, there was a negative growth in services. Overall rate of growth of employment on the basis of usual status was only 1.02 per cent during 1993-94 to 1999-2000, as compared to 2.53 per cent during 1977-78 to 1987-88 (Annexure-II). This again shows that employment generation has not been commensurate with the requirements.

Information thrown by different rounds of NSS also shows a declining trend in self-employment and a definite trend of increase is found in the proportion of casual workers in the last more than two and a half decades. However, percentage of workers in regular employment shows a slight increase during 1993-94 to 1999-2000.

Trends in Unemployment

This can be ascertained from the information provided

by NSS surveys. Rates of unemployment on current daily status basis have been observed to be as follows:

Table 5

UNEMPLOYMENT RATE IN VARIOUS ROUND OF NSSO (IN PERCENT)

Rounds (Current Daily Status)	*Unemployment Rate (percent)*
27th (1972-1973)	3.75
32nd (1977-1978)	4.33
38th (1983)	4.71
43rd (1987-1988)	3.73
50th (1993-1994)	3.46
55th (1999-2000)	4.48

There seems to be an increase in unemployment during the last decade. According to 55th round of NSS, rate of unemployment on the usual status basis, was observed to be 2.09 per cent.

It should be kept in mind that in a poor, backward state like Uttar Pradesh besides, open unemployment, there is also large-scale underemployment. According to 55th round of NSS, the total number of underemployed in the state is about 112 lakh of which 96 lakh are in rural areas, and 16 lakh are in urban areas.

The number of persons registered on the live registers of Employment Exchanges stood at 18.64 lakh in 2001, in contrast to 20.38 lakh in 2000. Surprisingly in 1990, the number of job seekers was 31.9 lakh in 1990 as per Employment Exchange statistics. The lack of job opportunities through Employment Exchanges in the organised sector might have de-motivated unemployed youth to get themselves registered in the Employment Exchange.

Employment Generation during the Tenth Plan

The employment generation is directly linked with the growth of income. In broad terms, employment generation in the specific period can be calculated with the help of employment elasticity. The Tenth Plan assumed an employment elasticity of 0.38. Given the target rate of growth of income at 8 per cent per annum. The likely rate of growth of employment per annum can be taken to be 3.04 per cent. On this basis, the total employment generation during 2002-07 was expected to be 81 lakh. Given the low growth registered by State's economy, during the first two years' of Tenth Plan, it is unlikely that employment generation could have been of the order assumed at the beginning of the plan. This points to the fact that unemployment situation would have been further aggravated in the State.

III. Suggestions

Keeping in mind the requirements of employment generation during the Tenth Plan and need to have a viable strategy for tackling the twin problems of poverty and unemployment, the following suggestions may be relevant:

(1) During the remaining period of the Tenth Plan, all efforts should be made to achieve a higher rate of growth. Acceleration of growth is absolutely necessary for creation of adequate number of job opportunities.

(2) Public and private investment should be channelized into those sectors, where labour absorption is high. These sectors are, construction, livestock and dairy, food-processing industries, Information technology, communication, small and medium enterprises, trade and commerce etc. Private investment in these sectors should be encouraged through fiscal and administrative measures.

(3) There are large gaps in social and infra-structural facilities in the state. Education, health, power, irrigation, housing, road construction are the sectors in which there is a big scope for absorption of the skilled, semi-skilled and un-skilled labour force. Therefore, infrastructural sectors should receive more public investment.

(4) Expansion of rural non-farm employment through

diversification of agriculture and allied activities should be given priority.

(5) Generation of increased employment opportunities for rural and urban youth through self- employment Programmes should be emphasized.

(6) There is a great need to effect improvement in the quality of implementation of special employment Programmes by strengthening the planning, monitoring capabilities at the district and PRIs level.

(7) Special Programmes for the vulnerable sections of the society should be expanded and closely monitored

(8) The credit-deposit ratio in U.P. is very low hence micro-credit facilities should be expanded to encourage private investment especially by farmers, small and medium entrepreneurs.

Annexure 1

Number & Percent of Population living below Poverty Line during different NSSO Round

NSS Round	Uttar Pradesh						All India					
	Rural		Urban		Combined		Rural	Urban	Combined	Rural	Urban	Combined
	No. of persons	percent of persons	No. of persons	percent of persons	No. of persons	percent of persons	No. of persons	percent of persons	No. of persons	percent of persons	No. of persons	percent of persons
1973-74	449.99	56.23	85.74	60.09	535.73	57.07	2612.90	56.44	600.46	49.01	3213.36	54.88
1977-78	407.41	47.60	96.96	56.23	504.37	49.05	2642.47	53.07	646.48	45.24	3288.95	51.32
1983-84	448.03	46.45	108.71	49.82	556.74	47.07	2519.57	45.85	709.40	40.79	3228.97	44.48
1987-88	429.74	41.10	106.79	42.96	536.53	41.46	2318.79	39.09	751.69	38.20	3070.48	38.86
1993-94	496.18	42.28	108.28	35.39	604.46	40.85	2440.31	37.27	763.37	32.36	3203.68	35.97
1999-2000*	412.01	31.22	117.88	30.89	529.89	31.15	1932.43	27.09	670.07	23.62	2902.50	26.10

* Based on 30 days recall period

Annexure II

DISTRIBUTION OF WORKERS BY INDUSTRY (CENSUS 19981-1991)

Sector	Workers (in lakh)			Decadal Increase	Annual growth rate
	*1981**	*1991**	*1991***	*1981-91*	*1981-91*
Total Workers	323.97	413.61	388.81	89.64	2.47
1. Cultivators	189.58	220.31	206.86	30.73	1.51
2. Agricultural Labourers	51.77	78.33	76.09	26.56	4.23
3. Plantation/Forestry/ Fisheries Livestock and hunting	1.77	2.96	2.41	1.19	5.28
4. Mining/Quarring	0.20	0.35	0.3	0.15	5.76
5. Manufacturing including house-hold industry	29.22	32.05	30.57	2.83	0.93
6. Construction	3.30	5.11	4.35	1.81	4.47
7. Trade/Commerce	14.69	25.51	23.97	10.82	5.67
8. Transport Storage/ communication	6.50	7.71	7.15	1.21	1.72
9. Other services	26.79	41.28	37.11	14.49	4.42

* Including Uttaranchal
** Excluding Uttaranchal

Annexure III

DISTRIBUTION OF PERSONS ON THE BASIS OF USUAL STATUS (PS+SS) BY INDUSTRY IN UTTAR PRADESH

Sl. No.	*Industry*	*Number of persons (in lakhs)*				*Annual growth rate*	
0	Agriculture	262	322	354	347	2.08	-0.33
1	Mining and Quarrying	—	—	—	—	—	—
2 & 3	Manufacturing	35	44	48	60	2.31	3.79
4	Electricity	—	1	1	1	—	—
5	Construction	6	11	12	21	6.25	9.78
6	Whole sale and retail trades restaurant and hotels	22	31	37	54	3.49	6.50
7	Transport Storage and communication	8	10	13	17	2.26	4.57

8 & 9 Services	26	42	47	44	4.91	-1.09
Total	359	461	512	544	2.53	1.02

Annexure IV

Per 1000 Distribution of Persons by MPCE Classes

MPCE Class	*Urban*		*Cumulative Frequency*	
	57th Round	*58th Round*		
0-300	78	41	78	41
300-350	62	40	140	81
350-425	137	126	277	207
425-500	114	113	391	320
500-575	114	124	505	444
575-665	80	79	585	523
665-775	90	80	675	603
775-915	84	84	759	687
915-1120	88	97	847	784
1120-1500	86	96	933	880
1500-1925	35	53	968	933
1925+	32	68	1000	1001
all	1000	1000	78	41
Average MPCE	729	879	140	81

Annexure V

Per 1000 Distribution of Persons by MPCE Classes

MPCE Class	*Urban*		*Cumulative Frequency*	
	57th Round	*58th Round*		
0-300	82	35	82	35
300-350	26	41	108	76
350-425	153	90	261	166
425-500	127	107	388	273
500-575	192	112	580	385
575-665	81	103	661	488

MPCE Class	*Urban*		*Cumulative Frequency*	
	57th Round	*58th Round*		
665-775	94	116	755	604
775-915	40	94	795	698
915-1120	84	117	879	815
1120-1500	57	95	936	910
1500-1925	37	46	973	956
1925+	27	44	1000	1000
all	1000	1000		
Average MPCE	423	486		

9

POVERTY BEYOND OFFICIAL ESTIMATES
An Analysis with special Reference to Uttar Pradesh

D.M. Diwakar

Introduction

Debating poverty is an area of one of the most intensive discussions in economics. Differences in opinions, methodology, and analysis remained always debatable. And exercises to arrive at consensus for policy and action plan remained in focus of debates. Recent joint report on the Second Poverty and Social Monitoring Survey (PSMS-II) released by the Directorate of Economics and Statistics of the State's Planning Department and the World Bank has indicated that per capita expenditure of the poorest has increased sharply by 109 per cent between 1993-94 and 2003-04. And poverty has declined from 42.3 per cent to 28.5 per cent in rural areas despite disappointing growth rates of agriculture, growing unemployment, declining employment, poor delivery mechanism and undependable infrastructure including declining access to electricity, sanitation, non-access to PDS and non-sensitive credit support.

Now question arises as to what led to increase per capita expenditure of lowest strata of poor, which pushed them above poverty syndrome.

Debate on estimates of poverty became sharper with estimates of poverty during 1999-2000. The Planning Commission of India has brought estimates indicating significant decline of about 10 per cent in poverty during 1990s. Theses estimates have been derived by applying indirect method on data of the 55th Round of the NSS. According to official estimates, this holds good even in poor and backward states like Bihar, Rajasthan, and Uttar Pradesh. Although, many experts holding official line also did not agree among themselves (for example, Sen, 2001; Vaidyanathan, 2001; Kozel and Parker; 2003, Kozel and Deaton, 2005, etc.) there is consensus among them that present official estimates are not strictly comparable with earlier estimates without rationalization. Sen, Kozel and Deaton have tried to rationalize the indirect estimates of poverty in the framework of ruling class. However, applying Direct Method for estimating poverty from the same round of NSSO data for consumption and calorie intake suggests staggering figure of under consumption. And following the norms of 2400 kcal adopted by the Planning Commission, poverty in Rural India comes out to the level of about three fourth of its population. On the other hand, superiority of direct method has been pointed out by Patnaik (2004), Ram (2004), Diwakar (2005) and many others. They have questioned indirect method of poverty estimates and argued in favour of direct method of poverty estimates. This study is an attempt to review the situation of poverty in India with special reference to Uttar Pradesh. This exercise has been divided into six parts. Part one deals with the criteria adopted for the official estimates of poverty. Part two discusses official poverty estimates. Part three analyses alternative direct method for estimation of poverty, part four presents an introspective reflections, part five deals with vision and reality gaps, part six consolidates discussion with implications of indirect estimates of poverty.

I. Criteria for Official Estimates

If one goes in the details of the development of methodology adopted by the official experts, one looks back to All India Labour Conference 1957, when the issues of identifying poverty line was raised. The Planning Commission of the Government of India constituted a Task Force of Nutrition Expert Group in 1962 with a mandate to suggest desirable minimum consumption expenditure acceptable at national level. In the light of the recommendation of the Nutrition Advisory Committee 1958 of All India Council of Medical Research it was decided that minimum consumption expenditure should not be less than Rs. 100 per household with five persons for a month at the price of 1960-61 to meet the calorie for minimum nutrition and non-food requirement. In other words, per capita consumption expenditure should not be less than Rs. 20. Rs. 25 was suggested for urban area and Rs. 18.9 for rural areas (Gupta, Singh and Dutta, 1982:260). However, these estimates suffered from limitations, as it does not explain categorically the basis and difference for rural and urban area. Another study is of Dandekar and Rath (1971), which considered per capita requirement of 2250 calorie per diem for rural and urban areas. On the basis of NSSO data for consumption expenditure, Rs. 170.8 per annum or Rs. 14.2 per month at 1960-61 prices for rural areas and Rs. 271.4 per annum or Rs. 22.6 per month for urban areas was considered sufficient. In order to weed out inconsistency in the estimates of the Planning Commission consumption expenditure was raised to Rs. 180 per annum or Rs. 15 per month for rural areas and Rs. 270 per annum or Rs. 22.5 per month for urban areas. Still this estimates ignored the variation in calorie requirement on the basis of age, sex, occupation, region, etc. Sukhatma (1965) estimated poverty on the basis of the recommendation of Food and Agriculture Organization (FAO) of UNO and National Advisory Council but he rejected the criteria of average nutrition requirement later in his another exercise (Sukhatma, 1977) and estimated poverty on the basis of the minimum requirement of *reference person*. However, in absence of proper data and also because of official policy requirement average nutritional necessity remained at the centre stage.

Meanwhile, considering criteria of Task Force, 1962 of the Planning Commission, regional estimates of poverty were brought out by Chatterji and Bhattacharya (1969), Bardhan (1971), Rudra (1974), and many others. Applying all India criteria for poverty estimates followed by Dandekar and Rath and using state price indices Rajkrishna worked out state level poverty estimates. He included public consumption expenditure for estimation of poverty and introduced a concept if augmented poverty line. Public consumption expenditure was kept in five subheads—health and family planning, water supply and sanitation, education, jail, police and judiciary administration, road and social welfare. Thus, per capita public consumption expenditure was included with per capita private expenditure in 25th round of NSS (1970-71) and poverty estimates was worked out for every state. This estimate also has serious limitations, as this assumed equal access to public facility for all classes and thereby underestimated poverty. The Planning Commission constituted another Task Force in 1977 to prepare a report on minimum needs and effective consumption demand. This Task Force in its report worked out daily calorie requirement on the mid value of monthly per capita consumption expenditure. On the recommendation of the Nutrition Expert Group 1968 considering variation in requirement by age, sex, specific occupation, worker and non-worker category, nature of work, status of women in general and pregnancy, child and adult, etc., 2400 calorie for rural areas and 2100 calorie for urban area was fixed for poverty estimation. This was an effort to weed out inconsistencies in earlier estimates. On the basis of the data on per capita consumption expenditure including non-food consumption expenditure and corresponding calorie intake in 28th Round (1973-74) of NSS, Rs. 49.09 for rural areas and Rs. 56.64 for urban areas were fixed for poverty line expenditure (Gupta *et.al.* 1982:264). But this also did not include weight and physical efficiency (Tiwari, 1982:334). Needless to mention that estimating poverty through wholesale index has risk of over estimation and consumer index has every possibility of under estimation because of limited coverage. Despite these limitations, agriculture labour consumer index with base year of 1960-61 price index and industrial labour consumer index with base year of 1973-74 price index, poverty estimates have been worked out adjusting with inflation. Thus, up dated poverty line expenditure is merely an adjustment of inflation with old consumption basket of 1973-74. However, consumption expenditure data of NSS are available for corresponding rounds, and one finds no excuse for ignoring such data for estimating updated consumption expenditure and corresponding poverty estimates. Moreover, this is head count poverty based on consumption and not income and therefore it is consumption poverty line, which includes consumption out of borrowing also.

If one scrutiny the data sources, there are two sources for consumption expenditure to calculate poverty estimates- NSS and National Account Statistics (NAS). In case of NAS, consumption expenditure data are not collected separately rather they are extracted from the data collected for NAS, whereas, NSSO collects consumption expenditure data separately. Consumption expenditure data of NAS increase faster by 1 per cent than that of NSS data, which create extra ordinary difference in poverty estimates (Minhas, 1988). Another study suggests that this difference increased from 5 per cent in 1957-58 to 38 per cent in 1993-94 (Kulshreshta and Kar, 2005). Consensus prevails that consumption expenditure data collected through NSSO are more reliable than NAS data (Sunderam and Tendulkar, 2001). NSS collected consumption expenditure data along with data of employment and unemployment till 1993-94 (50th round), which were discontinued in 55th round (1999-2000). Now any analysis for relation between consumption and employment and unemployment needs a separate methodology. Moreover, there has been methodological shift in data collection of consumption expenditure. Conventionally data for consumption have been collected based on 30 day recall method but in 55th round 7 day, 30 day and 365 day recall method was adopted on the basis of specific commodity. Therefore consumption data between 50th and 55th round are not comparable. Consumption expenditure data based on 7 day recall method are 23 per cent higher than 30 day recall method but they are less inconsistent than the data based on large survey of thin sample. Moreover, it has been argued and substantiated that there is no apparent deficiencies in data, based on 30 day recall method (Deaton and Kozel, 2005: 8-9). Therefore, 30 day recall method appears better and acceptable for this purpose.

II. Official Poverty Estimates

Official estimates of poverty of the Planning Commission indicate that poverty in India has declined from 36 per cent of 1993-94 to 26.1 per cent in 1999-2000. Earlier estimates available from the Planning Commission suggest that the level of poverty was 53.4 per cent in 1957-58, which came down to 49.1 per cent in 1963-64 but it further increased to 57.9 per cent in 1967-68. This was the highest official estimates of poverty in India (Table 1). Since 1973-74 NSSO has been bringing poverty estimates at regular interval. The estimates reveal that poverty at all India level has come down from 54.9 per cent in 1973-74 to 36 per cent in 1993-94. Poverty estimates for rural and urban India for the corresponding period were 56.4, 37.3 and 49 and 32.4 per cent respectively. Poverty estimates in 1999-2000 calculated by the Planning Commission of the government of India suggests sharp decline in all India poverty to 26.1 per cent, in rural India 27.1 per cent and in urban India 23.4 per cent. However, methods adopted for the calculation of poverty in 1999-2000 are not comparable and remained controversial. Many experts in the official line also do not agree among themselves (for example, Sen, 2001; Vaidyanathan, 2001; Kozel and Parker, 2003; Kozel and Deaton, 2005). Consensus among them is that present official estimates are not strictly comparable with earlier estimates without rationalization. Sen, Kozel and Deaton have tried to rationalize the indirect estimates of poverty but did not come out of the boundary line significantly. Unfortunately, they could hardly cover up hard fact of the NSSO data, which suggest that 74.25 per cent of the poor population living in the rural areas.

Official data on poverty relating to Uttar Pradesh suggest

that during 1957-58 52.3 per cent population was living below poverty line. Poverty increased to 60.2 per cent within ten years (i.e., 1967-68). From 1973-74 poverty ratio started declining and until 1993-94 it came down to the level of 40.85 per cent and in 1999-2000 it was further reduced to 31.5 per cent. So far intensity of poverty in rural area of U.P is concerned, during 1973-74 it was to the tune of 84 per cent and witnessed marginal decline in concentration of poor in rural area until 1987-88. During 1993-94 concentration of poor in rural areas out of total poor in U.P. increased to 98.16 per cent. By 1999-2000 it marked a significant decline in concentration of poor to 77.75 per cent. Therefore, even official data suggest that majority of poor resides in rural areas. Table 2 suggests that during 1993-94 number of poor was 50.44 million, which increased to 52.99 million. Thus, about 2.55 million people were added in the lot of poor in U.P. Table 3 suggests that regional poverty has also declined significantly. Sharpest decline is found in the most backward region of the Uttar Pradesh, i.e., in Bundelkhand. Poverty in Bundelkhand region has declined from 68.9 per cent during 1993-94 to 24.4 per cent during 1999-2000. One has to be careful in his analysis asto what factor contributed so significantly in reducing poverty. If this is so, it can be a most successful model if at all these data have any meaning.

Occupation wise distribution of official poverty estimates displayed in table 5 suggest that poverty is at alarming height among agricultural labourer followed by other labourers. Among urban poor casual labourers were hard hit to the tune of 67.3 per cent which is almost stagnant to the position of 1993-94 with a marginal decline. Caste wise distribution of official estimates of poverty suggests that although there was significant decline in poverty, still most poverty-ridden people were from SCs irrespective of location. Religious community wise distribution of official poverty indicated in Table 6 reveals that there was hardly any difference in the incidence of poverty on the basis of religion. However, in urban areas, incidence of poverty was more among Muslims than Hindus. Looking at distribution of ownership of land and poverty, it was found that poverty has inverse relation with increasing size of land ownership (Table 7). A recent study on land redistribution and its impacts on human development suggests that state could not implement land reforms effectively but to the extent access to land resources was ensured through land redistribution, beneficiary could get rid of food insecurity, erected own house, acquired better health, children particularly girl child is also going to school, got access to institutional loan, liberated from bondage, etc. (Mishra and Diwakar, 2005; see also Diwakar, 2006). Thus, official estimates of poverty that agricultural and non-agricultural labourers, casual laborers, SCs, urban Muslims and people of central and eastern U.P. were more poor than others.

Now question arises if poverty has declined significantly, there must be enough ground to substantiate the basis for declining. There is hardly any disagreement that majority of the people stay in rural areas and depend on agriculture for their livelihood. The rate of change in per capita rural income has declined from 3.1 per cent during one decade of pre reforms (1981-82 to 1990-91) to 2.8 per cent during one decade of post reform (1991-92 to 1999-2000). Estimates of the government of India reveal that compound growth rates of area, production, and productivity of food grains declined. Growth rates of the production and productivity of non-food grains declined and overall growth rates of production and productivity of major crops have also declined. Percentage public expenditure on agriculture registered significant decline from 5.8 per cent in seventh five year plan to 5.2 per cent in eighth five year plan and 3.96 per cent in the ninth five year plan. Percentage public expenditure on irrigation and flood control has also been declining in consecutive five-year plans. Growth rate of industrial production for the period in reference has declined from 7.8 per cent to 5.7 per cent. Thus, material production of the Indian economy registered a sharp decline.

Examining growth scenario of U.P. in terms of NSDP one can see that U.P. economy grew by 5.1 per cent in 1980s but the rate of growth in 1990s declined to merely 3.86 per cent. Agriculture is undoubtedly mainstay for rural poor, which grew by 2.96 per cent in 1980s and 2.15 percent in post reform period.

Growth rates of area turned negative and that of production and productivity registered declining trend for total crops and food grains In case of non- food grains area recorded increasing trend, production registered positive but declining rate of growth and productivity turned negative. Growth rates of secondary sector declined sharply from double digit i.e., above 10 per cent in 1980s to 3.68 per cent in 1990s. Except construction, transport and communication, which witnessed increasing growth rates, remaining sectors witnessed declining growth rates in the economy of U.P. (Diwakar, 2005). Thus, in U.P. economy no strong basis of growth performance of the sectors was found, which could have been instrumental in reducing poverty of the state economy.

If one looks at employment scenario, which indicates source of income and basis for reduction of poverty, at the U.P. level employment during 1983 to 1993-94 was 1.4 per cent whereas during 1993-94 to 1999-2000 it remained stagnated to 1.4 per cent. At all India level, employment during 1983 to 1993-94 was 2.1 per cent whereas during 1993-94 to 1999-2000 was only 1.16 per cent (Table 8). For organized sector of agriculture growth rate was negative. Even unorganized sector registered merely 0.03 per cent growth rate in employment. Growth rate for Mining and Quarrying for the organized and unorganized sector remained negative. Employment elasticity for agriculture, which was 0.7 during 1983-93-94, turned to almost zero during 1993-94. If one takes economy as a whole, employment elasticity for pre reform period was 0.52, which declined to 0.16 in the post reform period. Annual growth rates of employed workers have declined from 2.04 per cent to merely 0.98 per cent. Growth rate of total employment was 2.7 for the pre reform period, which declined to 1.3 per cent during post reform period.

There was sharp increase in marginal workforce from 2.78 per cent to 11.96 per cent. Participation rate in case of main workforce has decreased from 0.18 to (-) 1.11 per cent but there is increase in participation of marginal workforce from 0.61 per cent to 9.85 per cent. This indicates that casualisation has increased sharply. If one looks at the NSS data, growth rate per annum of labour force, workforce and of unemployed persons, it is evident from data that during 1983 to 1993-94 rate of growth of workforce was higher than that of the labour force. Rate of growth of unemployed persons was almost negative. Unlike this during 1993-94 to 1999-2000 growth rate of work force was lower than that of labour force.

Growth rate of unemployed number of persons remained high. In case of U.P. NSS data suggest that rate of unemployment in U.P increased from 3.46 per cent during pre – reforms period to 4.48 per cent in post reforms period. Even at the national level it was of utter inconsistency that in the situation of discouraging employment and rising unemployment from (-) 1.19 to 5.26 per cent, official estimates of poverty was reporting decline. On the other hand payment of interest as percentage of national income has increased from 0.93 to 1.72. Share of profit and other outflow increased from 0.89 per cent to 2.18 per cent. Thus, total outflow increased by more than double from 1.82 per cent to 3.90 per cent. Domestic saving and total investment in the economy declined from 21 per cent to 18.4 per cent and 23.4 per cent to 21 per cent respectively. These are figures from the Ministry of Finance published in the various issues of the Economic Survey.

Human Development Report (HDR) 2005 reveals that incremental growth has negligible impacts on poverty reduction. Moreover, poverty is concentrated in rural areas of backward states like U.P., Bihar, M.P., etc. It may be mentioned that Human Development Index registered nominal improvement in the year 2005 (0.602) from the position of 2004 (0.595) and remained at the same position, i.e., at 127th ladder. In 2003 it was at 126th and in 2001 at 124th. It is an important indicator that economic reforms and economic growth could not render benefit towards improving HDI. In other words, there has been negligible progress in per capita income, literacy, and life expectancy in India in the recent years. These figures do not provide any basis for poverty reduction and therefore, data relating to poverty need a careful scrutiny.

III. Alternative Direct Methods for Estimation of Poverty

NSS publishes data on distribution of persons for monthly per capita expenditure in rupees and also distribution of persons for calorie intake by monthly per capita expenditure. These data are available for rural and urban areas in the Report Nos. 454 and 471 of 55th Round. These data do not need any expertise to understand the distribution of expenditure. In order to acquire 2400 calorie intake in rural areas and 2100 calories intake in urban areas data suggest that persons of the respective areas fall in expenditure group of rupees 525-615 and 575-665 respectively. In order to get exact figure if one draws ogive curve to find out cumulative percentage of the people up to this level rural area depicts 74.5 per cent of the people below 2400 calories intake. Similarly if one takes urban area for per capita monthly expenditure persons with 2100 calories intake fall in the expenditure group of 575-665. Drawing ogive curve for cumulative percentage crosses 50 per cent (Table 9).

Similarly if we do this exercise for Uttar Pradesh, Table 10 consumption of 2400 kcal requires expenditure class of Rs. 420-470 and using ogive curve as displayed in graph of the distribution of calorie intake, cumulative percentage come to about 64 per cent. Thus, we can find that official estimates have badly underestimated poverty. For example if one takes even for rural India Planning Commission has come out with 37.27 per cent of poor persons for which implied calories per capita per diem comes to 1970 only. For the 1999-2000 estimates indirect estimates of the Planning Commission brought the rural poverty to 27.1 per cent with Rs. 327.56 per capita monthly expenditure with which an individual can acquire 1890 calorie per diem. According to NSS data average expenditure for acquiring 2400 calories intake needs per capita monthly expenditure to the tune of Rs. 565. If one goes by NSS data and compromise at 2200 calories intake which required per capita monthly expenditure to the tune of Rs. 455, the figure of percentage of poverty at this ceiling of calories are 58 per cent. Even with 2000 calories intake, which require Rs. 380 per capita monthly expenditure the figure for poverty can not be less than 40 per cent.

Interstate variation is more alarming than general at national level. Table 11 suggests that as high as 94.5 per cent people in Tamil Nadu could not avail 2400 kcal calorie intake for which they required Rs. 970 against the calculation of per capita monthly expenditure the Planning Commission merely Rs. 307.64 and thereby only 20.55 per cent rural people were below the 2400 calorie intake norms. Second highest was the rural Maharastra with 92 per cent people with per capita monthly expenditure Rs. 870 to acquire 2400 calories against official estimates of Rs. 318.63 with which they could acquire merely 1760 calorie intake. Third highest poverty ridden state was rural Assam with 91 per cent people below 2400 calorie. Other states above 80 per cent rural people below 2400 kcal calorie norms were: Orissa (80 per cent: average per capita monthly expenditure Rs. 475 against official estimates 323.92), West Bengal (81: 575 against 350.17), Karnataka (82:650 against 309.59), Gujarat (83:735 against 318.94), A.P. (84:595:262.94), Kerala (82.5: 1105: 374.79). Similarly if one takes the estimates of other states, Bihar (77:455:333.07), M.P. (78.5:490:311.34), U.P. (61:455:336.88), Rajasthan (53.5:515:344.03), Punjab (58.5 : 715:362.68) and Haryana (47.5:615:362.81). Thus, there was huge under estimation of poverty. So long calorie norm is accepted for poverty estimation one can hardly deny the ground reality. However, official estimates ignored per capita monthly expenditure data with regards to calorie norms. If one adds education, health, sanitation, access to productive infrastructure, etc., in the definition of poverty, poverty figure may touch even a higher level. A careful analysis is required to reach a formidable conclusion in this regard.

IV. Introspective Reflection

Before independence Indian leaders were of the views that we were deprived because of colonial exploitation and transfer of resources from India to the British coffer. Even after independence we have been analyzing that hangover of colonial rule and persistence of policies and therefore exploitative resource transfer mechanism continues in sophisticated policies framework. Although this hypothesis has been debated at length and debate became sharper with the emergence of neo-colonial strategies and institutions pursuing liberalization and market oriented development as solution to all forms of deprivations. Now the results are coming up with clear results that poor has been bypassed in this process of development. "The blame for the poor performance on the employment front is usually apportioned on our choice of technique of production which has been failing to take into account the nature of resource endowment in the country. This is partly correct and may not be the whole truth. Our slow but steady movement toward dependence paradigm which is reflected in increasing foreign collaboration not only seriously undermined our self reliant growth strategy but is also to be squarely blamed for increasing unemployment in recent past" (Prasad, 1991).

Instead of going into the details of analysis here we would like to raise a simple question in this continuation. If these sets of policies and approaches for development did not produce desired results even at least for basic minimum level, is it not necessary to question the legitimacy of development approaches, justification of existing superstructures in their present forms, which have been unable to address the process of exclusion? Secondly, if the present structure and approaches of development continues, is it not the logical conclusion that any amount of efforts through this superstructure will lead to disappointment? Land reforms, poverty alleviation and rural development programmes, etc., are a few examples, where implementation has been distorted. There are many such examples, which can make an exhaustive list. Now with the same set of superstructure, if we are expecting to achieve miracle with new phrases and slogans, do we not need to reassess our strategies and approaches as, now inclusive development strategies are being forwarded for co-opting participatory development?

Since Independence the country has been putting various efforts together towards development to improve situation of employment – quantity as well as quality in order to reduce unemployment and eradicate poverty for better quality of life. Mixed economy model with coexistence of public and private sectors was accepted for development. Planned and community development were initiated. Main concern of the policy makers remained infrastructure building as facilitator of development through public sector keeping it away from the purview of profit motives. We have made progress also in many areas. GDP has substantially gone up. There has been substantial improvement in the infrastructure. Poverty ratio has declined. Dealing with plan wise strategies and results can be a meaningful exercise but constraints of the framework of this paper may not permit me to do so in details. Therefore instead of going into minute details we would like to draw your attention on the final results. The fact suggests that percentage per annum growth of employment has declined (GOI, 2002: 158-60) and incidence of rural unemployment has been increasing in the 1990s compared to 1980s (GOI, 2002: 161-63). Rural employment programmes have almost failed to create sustainable opportunities of rural employment for absorption of labour (Radhakrishna, 2002:245). Official documents also suggest that income gap between urban and rural has widened from 1:2 to 1:6 (Government of India, 2000). Rate of decline in rural poverty, which was 2.75 per cent in 1970s and 1980s has decreased to merely 0.73 per cent and hence rate of decrease in poverty is lower than the rate of increase in rural population (Radhakrishna, 2002). Despite all these depressing indications, official data claimed sharp decline in poverty in 1999-2000. Moreover, official documents of the Planning Commission of India also acknowledged. ..."it has yet to meet the challenge of generating sufficient employment opportunities to ensure that all its people have the purchasing power to obtain the food they require. Gainful employment is one of the most essential for food security and economic security" (GOI, 2003, p. 57).

Globalisation process has been gradually integrating world market. Liberalisaiton, privatisation and globalisation have allowed market to operate in the economy fast. Sources of revenue base have been shrinking on account of concessions to foreign investments. Disinvestment of public sector is added disadvantages as it reduces the base of employment in and revenue from public sector. Global competition in the labour market on the one hand requires sufficient number of skilled professional to enter into the global market, which developing countries in general do not have and on the other hand semi skilled professionals are not in a position to compete in the global market. Technical institutions to prepare skilled professionals are also not enough to meet demands of skilled professionals. Moreover, as government is withdrawing subsidies and financial support to these institutions, access to these institutions is becoming difficult to the potential professionals from the lot of common people. Voluntary retirement schemes, automation of enterprises, downsizing employment opportunities, labour laws reforms, curtailment in the right to democratic resistance, etc., have left little scope to improve the quantity and quality of employment. There is every possibility of penetrating crises of global deflation into the developing nations with foreign investment. Therefore, it is necessary to have a careful analysis on these dimensions while expecting too much from the planning in coming years.

V. Vision and Reality Gap

Our national vision, towards employment and poverty eradication emerged during freedom struggle of India against the British imperialism under colonial rule which systematically destroyed employment base of Indian economy and aggravated unemployment, misery and endemic poverty. This is correct also but not the whole truth. It is not the fact that people were not poor and unemployed before the British intrusion. One can trace back unemployment, poverty and helplessness of people earlier in middle ages also. One can link this to the context of unemployment with development process. Undoubtedly it was further aggravated during British colonial rule. National leaders of freedom movement were convinced that unless the issues of unemployment are addressed, meaningful and positive reconstruction and development of country would be difficult. As early as in 1925 Gandhi wrote: "Idleness is the great cause, the root of all evils, and if that root can be destroyed, most of the evils can be removed without further effort." (Gandhi: 1925: 299). He further emphasised: "Unless poverty and unemployment are wiped out from India, I would not agree that we have attained freedom." (CWMG, 87:463). These statements reflect deep rooted vision and meaning of freedom towards which India was to move with a comprehensive package of initiatives. It was not only Mahatma Gandhi, even Jawaharlal Nehru, who was an important architect of modern India and Gandhi had great expectations from his leadership. Nehru was also having strong view about unemployment eradication for the progress of the country. In 1929 Nehru wrote: "If we are to eradicate poverty, we must first do away with this wide spread unemployment. ... And see that the kisans are usefully employed in their spare time. They should be found some supplementary work" (Gopal, 1979: vol. 11, p. 156). Increasing number of farmers committing suicide speaks volumes of untold misery of the farmers. Gandhi emphasised on irrigation for the development of agriculture, which was the main source of employment: "The need for providing irrigation facilities to all villages can not but be emphasised too greatly. This is the foundation upon which agriculture depends for its progress, in absence of which it remains a gamble" (Gandhi, 1946). The country has not achieved irrigation cover more than 36 per cent and cropping intensity is still below 1.5. This indicates not only the neglects of agriculture but also lack of concern about peasantry. Employment potential of this sector is yet to be exploited through effective water management. As a result the agriculture is badly dependent on the vagaries of the monsoon and the fate of the peasantry in particular is hanging in balance amidst drought and floods. Not only Gandhi and Nehru, many other national leaders emphasised on providing employment as the responsibility of the State. There are many such evidences from other activists and leaders, who were equally important at that time. S.C. Bose was of the view that: "It is the duty of the state to provide employment to the citizens and where the state fails to perform this duty, it should accept the responsibility of maintaining them." However, the statements of Gandhi and Nehru are important, particularly of Nehru, who remained in the mainstream of the politics of power towards reconstruction of

Indian economy, polity and society. Today the state is shying away with its responsibilities and gradually adopting contradictory market oriented policies, which have narrowed the base of employment opportunities.

Visions were placed forward also when India got an environment of political freedom to a certain extent. At the outset of planning just after independence, India set a goal for reconstruction of the economy, polity and society with the basic objectives of growth with social justice through a combination of planning and community development strategies First Five Year Plan document clearly emphasised: "It is no longer possible to think of development as a process merely of increasing available supplies of material goods, it is necessary to ensure that simultaneously a steady advance is made towards the realization of wider objectives such as full employment and removal of economic inequalities. Maximum production, full employment, the attainment of economic equality and social justice, which constitute the accepted objectives of planning under present day conditions are not really so many different ideas but a series of selected aims which the country must work for ... even the limited objectives of increased production can not be achieved unless the wider objectives of social policy are constantly kept in mind and steadily pursued" (GOI, 1960: ch. ii, p. 25). Agriculture was on the top of priority list in the First Five Year Plan. In the Second Five Year Plan target was set to remove unemployment within a decade but the focus and priority was shifted from agriculture in First Plan to industry in Second Plan. Subsequently we moved to grow more to tackle food shortage through the Green Revolution in sixties. It was realised that trickle down effect of general development could not produce expected results therefore target approach was accepted to overcome poverty and unemployment. Poverty eradication through target group approach in seventies and minimum need programme in eighties followed by economic liberalisation, privatisation, and globalisation in nineties remained the course of policies to address the problems of unemployment and poverty. Results have never been very encouraging. On the contrary post reforms results have been very discouraging in terms of employment. State has been withdrawing from the responsibilities of providing employment contrary to the commitment of our national leaders who had a dream of self-reliant development and growth with distributive justice. Socialist approach to growth has been replaced by market oriented growth and therefore everything is gradually being left on market to be decided.

If this is the way to reduce poverty in order to achieve millennium development goals, this is a matter of serious concern. Under estimation of poverty has definite implication on policies and programmes. If the volume of poverty is reduced, budget allocations for poverty eradications and rural development will have weakened logic for state subsidies and special assistance. The grave danger posed by this approach is that it inevitably leads to misidentifying of the poor and subsequently to the adoption of targeting, monitoring, and evaluation criteria, which are equally narrow and thus, carrying the many blind spots in the concept of deprivation into the operational phase of interventions (Saith, 2005). By implication corporate governance will have free hand to exploit and expand against the interest of the poor. Comprador leadership with subservient bureaucracy has been facilitating their imperial masters. However, reducing public exchequer will have another significant inherent implication also. Comprador network of lackies, surviving on public expenditure leakages will have tough competition among them, which essentially aggravate continued infighting to expose each other.

VII. In lieu of conclusion

There could hardly be any disagreement that Indian experience of mainstream development process suggests: *(a)* trickle down hypothesis could not produce effective results *(b)* MacNmara approach of target oriented programmes for employment generation and poverty alleviation could achieve marginal success and *(c)* liberalization has by and large has bypassed the poor. Now inclusive development in the name of new strategy for development has been thrown up for so-called participatory development through partnership with support system. Contradictory expectations have been forwarded in the name of policies. There is every indication of promoting reforms despite unfavourable results. On the one hand privatisation and liberalisation is broadening its base and on the other hand labour intensive informal and non- farm employment is expected to tackle the problem of growing unemployment. These cannot go together. Looking into all these initiatives and paradigm shift at least in liberal sense and forms if not in contents, there is need to reflect and take a fresh look on development process and approaches.

Broadly there are two dominant streams of development practices in the world- one, capitalist path of development, which includes liberal reformist also and the other is communist experiment. Former despite its tall claims breathing its last amidst internal contradictions of stagnations, deflation, unemployment, and poverty. Even Asian Tiger of capitalist development could not survive in Asia despite extra ordinary support by international institutions and agencies. And latter, Communist practices, which collapsed in USSR after catering almost full employment for nearly seven decades which itself is a record and still exists in many countries with higher growth rates. China and Vietnam could be a few examples among others. In India there has been mixed economy with a hangover of Gandhian overtone and socialist touch, which has now lost its nominal current and now market oriented development has been gradually replacing all the egalitarian overtones in development processes of India. Now India has reached virtually to an irreversible situation, which needs strong political will power to get rid of this syndrome. However, Report on India vision 2020 gives very optimistic note but of course with many pros and cons. "Achieving full employment will require a reorientation of national priorities, technology policy and government action. Until now planning to achieve national goals has been largely done on a sector wise basis by respective ministries assigned with the responsibilities. These parallel lines of the planning need to be integrated around a central vision and set of goals, of which full employment must be one" (GOI, 2002, p. 59). It is an uphill task for any government to take risk of antagonising middle class and middle class will seldom volunteer to scarify present level of benefits and comfort at their own.

Moreover, ruling class has been busy in creating illusions and framing contradictory policies. On the one hand it has been facilitating imperial masters with concession after concessions in the name of reforms and narrowing down the base resources for state exchequer and on the other hand formulating popular policies for lip services towards employment generation and poverty eradication to contend resentment of the masses. Now agriculture, which has been the base of subsistence for poor and middle peasantries, has been opened for MNCs and TNCs through contract and corporate farming and WTO. Blind motivations for modernization and diversification of agriculture without proper infrastructure have resulted into policy driven deaths of the peasants even in the high growth regions of the country. Breakdown of institutional credit system has been proving strength to moneylenders for extracting exorbitant rate of interest even from the poor peasants. Inability to repay the loan because of crop failure and lack of effective insurance cover has been forcing them (peasants) to commit suicide. Humane gesture by announcing package for farmers of Vidarbha may not help them to sustain with non-viable agriculture, rather it will reinforce money-lending practices. Therefore, only option left before the people to get organized and resist against systematic design of exploitations adopted by the ruling compradors and their masters so that rebuilding a new world free from exploitation and inequality will be a possibility.

There must not be an iota of doubts that compradors occupying various positions from village to parliaments have been misleading the people in the name of poverty eradication. All the so-called efforts of poverty eradication from the beginning of land reforms, providing irrigation, creating infrastructures, so-called green revolution and diversification of agriculture, target oriented development programmes for poor, etc., failed because of inherent dishonest policies and their framework of implementations. At some places these programmes have shown positive results, as the pro poor social activists of radical movement did not allow them to siphon out the entire funds.

However, there is silver lining, which has emerged through 73rd and 74th amendments of Constitution of India. Panchayti Raj Institution (PRI) is coming up with a new sense of assertions. Particularly dalit and women participation in PRI extends hope for better rural leadership and change. Initially there might be some inconsistencies in the short run but in the long run this process may result into effective participation of rural poor in development process. One important point we would like to mention here is that no policy has been the result of the benevolent behaviour of the ruling class. For every initiative mass resistance through different forms and contents have forced them to legislate and implement those policies. It is also worth mentioning here that wherever, resistance has been stronger, implementation of programmes has been qualitatively different and better. If situation is going bad to worse there is need to conscientise and consolidate people's resistance to check exclusion and work out new institutions and strategies to address the issues of their own. Present ruling class appears completely subordinated to global finance. To expect something miracle from the ruling beneficiary class in favour of people and against global capital does not seem to have any basis. Solution therefore lies in consolidation of politically conscious organised democratic forces and their uncompromising resistance.

Table 1

PERCENTAGE DISTRIBUTION OF POVERTY IN INDIA AND UTTAR PRADESH

Year	*Percentage of Poverty in U.P.*		*Percentage of Poverty in India*	
	Total Poverty	*Rural Poverty*	*Total Poverty*	*Rural Poverty*
1957-58	52.3	—	53.4	—
1963-64	56.6	—	49.1	—
1967-68	60.2	—	57.9	—

Year	*Percentage of Poverty in U.P.*		*Percentage of Poverty in India*	
	Total Poverty	*Rural Poverty*	*Total Poverty*	*Rural Poverty*
1973-74	57.07	84.0	54.65	81.31
1977-78	49.05	80.78	51.82	62.10
1983	47.07	80.62	44-40	76.03
1987-88	41.40	79.91	35.80	75.52
1993-94	40.85	98.16	36.0	76.17
1999-2000	31.15	77.75	26.10	74.25

Source: Planning Commission, Government of India, New Delhi.

Table 2

NUMBER AND PERCENTAGE OF POOR IN INDIA AND UTTAR PRADESH

Region		*Rural*		*Urban*		*Total*	
		No. (lakh)	*%age*	*No. (lakh)*	*%age*	*No. (lakh)*	*%age*
1973 –74:	U.P.	449.99	56.53	85.74	60.09	535.73	57.07
	India	2612.90	55.44	500.46	49.01	3213.36	54.65
1973 –74:	U.P.	407.41	47.00	98.95	56.23	504.37	49.05
	India	2042.47	53.07	646.48	45.24	3288.9	51.82
1983:	U.P.	448.03	45.45	108.71	49.82	555.74	47.07
	India	2519.57	45.65	708.40	40.79	3228.97	44.40
1987-88:	U.P.	428.74	41.10	105.79	42.90	536.53	41.40
	India	2318.79	38.08	751.69	38.20	3070.48	35.80
1993-94:	U.P.	495.17	42:28	105.25	35.39	504.45	40.85
	India	2440.31	37.27	753.37	32.36	3203.65	36.0
1999-00:	U.P.	412.01	31.22	117.88	30.89	529.89	31.15
	India	1932.43	27.09	670.07	23.62	2602.50	26.10

Source: Planning Commission, Government of India, New Delhi.

Table 3

REGION WISE PERCENTAGE DISTRIBUTION OF OFFICIAL ESTIMATES OF POVERTY IN UNDIVIDED U.P.

	Urban		*Rural*		*Total*	
Region	*1993-94*	*1999-2000*	*1993-94*	*1999-2000*	*1993-94*	*1999-2000*
Hill	12.7	14.1	24.8	15.6	22.5	15.2
Western	31.1	30.0	29.3	21.7	29.8	23.9
Central	33.9	33.4	50.2	42.2	46.7	39.7
Eastern	38.6	31.1	48.8	36.4	47.5	35.9
Bundelkhand	74.4	40.9	67.4	20.9	68.9	24.4
U.P.	35.1	30.7	42.3	31.1	40.9	31.0

Source: World Bank and NSSO 50th and 55th Rounds.

Table 4

OCCUPATION WISE PERCENTAGE DISTRIBUTION OF RURAL AND URBAN POVERTY IN UTTAR PRADESH

Percentage Rural Poverty				*Percentage Urban Poverty*			
Year	*1983*	*1993-94*	*1999-2000*	*Year*	*1983*	*1993-94*	*1999-2000*
Non-Self Employment	52.3	44.3	33.7	Self Employment	51.6	39.9	34.3
Agricultural Labour	66.3	63.5	50.9	Regular Wage/Salary	—	17.4	14.4
Other Labour	48.2	52.3	36.9	Casual Labour	—	66.7	67.3
Ag. Self Employment	43.3	36.4	24.2	—	—	—	—
Others	30.4	25.9	21.3	Others	37.1	25.8	20.0
Total	47.4	42.3	31.1	Total	44.7	350	30.7

Source: World Bank and NSSO respective rounds.

Table 5

CASTE AND LOCATION WISE PERCENTAGE DISTRIBUTION OF POVERTY IN UTTAR PRADESH

	SCs/STs			*Others*			*Total*		
Year	*Urban*	*Rural*	*Total*	*Urban*	*Rural*	*Total*	*Urban*	*Rural*	*Total*
1987-88	48.3	56.2	55.3	35.7	37.5	37.2	37.4	42.3	41.5
1993-94	57.5	58.6	58.4	31.3	37.0	35.2	35.0	42.4	40.9
1999-2000	42.5	43.0	42.9	28.4	26.9	27.2	30.7	31.1	31.0

Source: World Bank and NSSO respective rounds.

Table 6

PERCENTAGE DISTRIBUTION OF POVERTY AMONG DIFFERENT RELIGIOUS COMMUNITIES IN U.P.

	Hindu	*Muslim*	*Total*
Rural	31.27	30.84	31.01
Urban	26.43	42.17	30.76

Source: John and Mutatkar, 2005.

Table 7

RELATIONSHIP BETWEEN OWNERSHIP OF LANDHOLDINGS AND RURAL POVERTY

Ownership Size of Land-holdings	*Percentage of Poverty, Population and Poor*								
	1983			*1993-94*			*1999-2000*		
Hectare	*Poverty*	*Popu-*	*Poor*	*Poverty*	*Popu-*	*Poor*	*Poverty*	*Popu-*	*Poor*
Landless	37.6	3	2	51.5	6	8	28.4	4	4
0-0-4	57.4	24	28	52.7	37	46	41.1	44	58
0-4-1-0	58.5	13	15	41.5	25	24	28.6	26	24
1-0-2-0	51.7	18	20	34.6	17	14	22.0	14	10
2-0-4-0	45.6	20	19	24.8	10	6	11.6	8	3
4+	30.7	23	15	19.8	5	2	6.8	3	1
All	47.5	100	100	42.4	100	100	31.0	100	100

Source: World Bank and NSSO respective rounds.
Note: Popu means Population.

Table 8

GROWTH RATE OF EMPLOYMENT IN BIMARU STATES OF INDIA

States	1983-93-94									1993-94-1999-2000								
	Rural			Urban			Combined			Rural			Urban			Combined		
	Male	Female	Person	Male	Female	Person	Male	Female	Person	Male	Female	Person	Male	Female	Person	Male	Female	Person
Bihar	1.9	-1.8	0.9	1.3	-1.4	0.9	1.8	-1.7	0.9	2.1	2.9	2.3	3.4	4.7	3.6	2.3	3.0	2.5
M.P.	2.2	1.6	1.9	3.2	3.7	3.3	2.4	1.7	2.2	1.4	1.4	1.4	3.5	2.3	3.3	1.9	1.5	1.8
Rajasthan	2.4	2.5	2.5	3.1	1.6	2.8	2.6	2.4	2.5	2.0	0.4	1.4	2.8	0.8	2.4	2.5	2.2	0.5
U.P.	2.2	0.8	1.8	2.7	4.1	2.9	2.3	1.1	2.0	1.4	1.3	1.4	3.5	2.3	3.3	2.0	1.8	1.4
India	2.0	1.5	1.8	2.8	3.2	2.9	2.2	1.7	2.1	1.6	0.8	1.3	2.6	1.5	2.4	1.9	0.9	1.6

Source: National Human Development Report 2001, pp. 158-60.

Table 9

PERCENTAGE DISTRIBUTION OF PERSONS BY PER CAPITA MONTHLY EXPENDITURE GROUP AND CALORIE INTAKE PER DIEM, (30 DAYS RECALL METHOD) 1999-2000: ALL INDIA

Monthly Per capita Expenditure	*Calorie Intake per diem*	*Persons %*	*Cumulative %*	*Monthly Per capita Expenditure*	*Calorie Intake per diem*	*Persons %*	*Cumulative %*
Below 225	1383	5.1	5.1	Below 300	1398	5.0	5.0
225- 255	1609	5.0	10.1	300- 350	1654	5.1	10.1
255- 300	1733	10.1	20.2	350- 425	1729	9.6	19.7
300- 340	1868	10.0	30.2	425- 500	1912	10.1	29.8
340- 380	1957	10.3	40.5	500- 575	1968	9.9	39.7
380-420	2054	9.7	50.2	**575- 665**	**2091**	**10.0**	**49.7**
420- 470	2173	10.2	60.4	665- 775	2187	10.1	59.8
470-525	2289	9.3	69.7	775- 915	2297	10.0	69.8
525- 615	**2403**	**10.3**	**80.0**	915- 1120	2467	10.0	79.8
615-775	2581	9.9	89.9	1120-1500	2536	10.1	89.9
775-900	2735	5.0	94.9	1500-1925	2736	5.0	94.0
900 +	3178	5.0	100.0	1925 +	2938	5.0	100.0

Source: NSSO (1999-2000), 55th Round, Report Nos 471 and 454.

Table 10

EXPENDITURE GROUP WISE CALORIE INTAKE AND DISTRIBUTION OF PERSONS (1999-2000), U.P. (RURAL)

Expenditure Class (Rs.)	*Average Expendi-ture (Rs.)*	*PC/day Kcal intake*	*% No. of Person*	*Cumulative %*
000-225	195	1466	4.4	4.4
225-255	243	1734	5.1	9.5
255-300	279	1893	11.3	20.8
300-340	320	1990	11.3	32.1
340- 380	361	2100	11.5	43.6
380-420	400	2226	10.6	54.2
420- 470	444	2375	9.8	64.0
470-525	496	2470	8.8	72.8
525-615	566	2631	10.1	82.9
615-775	687	2907	9.1	92.0
775-950	852	3190	4.3	96.3
950+	1386	3815	3.6	99.9
All Classes	467	2327	100	—

Source: NSS, 55th Round, 1999-2000, Report no. 454 and 471.

Distribution of Calorie Intake

by Average Expenditure in Rs

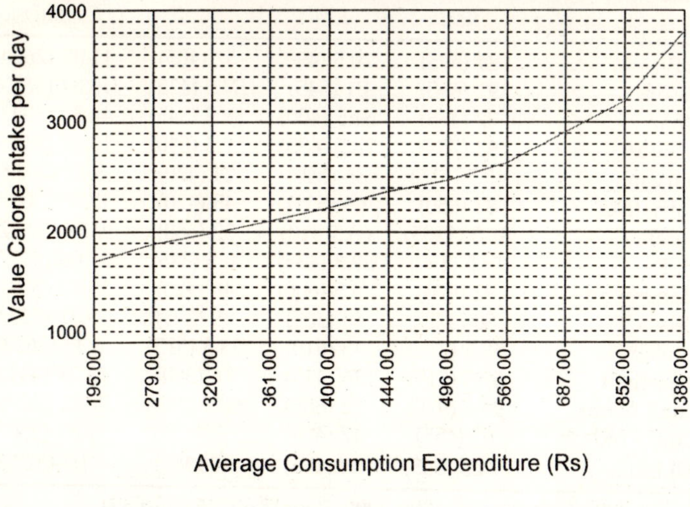

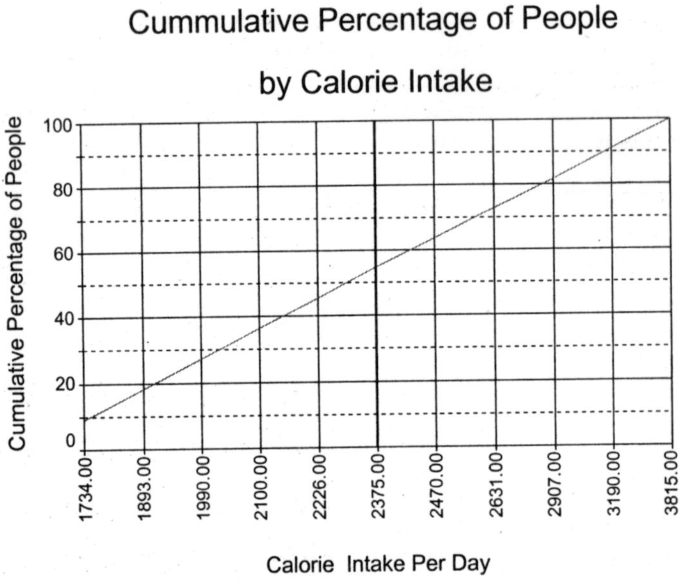

Table 11

INTERSTATE ESTIMATES OF RURAL POVERTY

State	*HCR-2400 Kcal*	*HCR-2200 Kcal*	*HCR-2000 Kcal*	*HCR-Planning Commission*
A.P.	84 (595)	70.5 (490)	52 (405)	11.05 (262.94)
Assam	91 (660)	81 (545)	57.5 (425)	40.04 (365.43)
Bihar	77 (455)	64.5 (400)	39.5 (345)	44.30 (333.07)
Gujarat	83 (735)	73.5 (635)	59.5 (540)	13.17 (318.94)
Haryana	47.5 (615)	36 (540)	24 (470)	8.27 (362.81)
Karnataka	82 (650)	69 (535)	45 (420)	17.38 (309.59)
Kerala	82.5 (1105)	68.5(810)	52 (660)	9.38 (374.79)
M. P.	78.5 (490)	69.5 (435)	465 (345)	37.06 (311.34)
Maharastra	92 (870)	76.5 (600)	46 (420)	23.72 (318.63)
Orissa	80 (475)	60 (365)	39 (295)	48.01 (323.92)
Punjab	58.5 (715)	45 (610)	28.5 (515)	6.35 (362.68)
Rajasthan	53.5 (515)	36 (445)	16 (360)	13.74 (344.03)
Tamil Nadu	94.5 (970)	82 (685)	68.5 (540)	20.55 (307.64)
Uttar Pradesh	61 (455)	47 (400)	27.5 (325)	31.85 (350.17)
All India	74.5 (565)	58 (455)	40 (380)	7.07 (327.56)

Source: NSS 55th Round, 1999-2000, Report no. 454 and 471.

References

Bardhan, P. K., (1971): "On the Minimum Level of Living and the Rural Poor: A Further Note," *Indian Economic Review*, April 6.

Chatterji, G.S. and Bhattacharya, (1969): "Rural Urban Differentials in Consumer Price in India," *Economic and Political Weekly*, May, 17.

Dandekar, V.M. and Rath, N., (1971): *Poverty in India*, Samiksha Trust, Bombay.

Sukhatma, P.V., (1965): *Feeding India's Growing Millions*, Asia Publishing House, Bombay.

Diwakar, D.M., (2005): *Abibhajit Uttar Pradesh Maen Garivi Ka Samikshatmak Vishleshhan* (Hindi), Conference Volume, Uttar Pradesh-Uttaranchal Economic Association, First Annual Conference, October 23-24.

Diwakar, D.M. (2006): "Status of Implementation of Land Reforms on Material and Human Deprivation in Uttar Pradesh," in Diwakar, D.M. and G.P. Mishra (ed), *Deprivation and Inclusive Development*, Manak Publications, Pvt. Ltd. New Delhi.

Gandhi, M.K., (1925): *Young India*, August 27.

Gandhi, M.K, (1946): *Harijan*, May 12.

Gandhi, M.K., *Collected Works*, Vol. 87.

Gopal, S., (1979): *Selected Works of Jawaharlal Nehru*, Orient Longmans, vol. 11.

Government of India, National Sample Survey Organisation

GOI, First Five Year Plan, 1960

Government of India (2000): Mid-Term Appraisal of Ninth Five Year Plan, Planning Commission, New Delhi.

Government of India (2001): Poverty Estimates for 1999-2000, Planning Commission, New Delhi, 22nd February.

Government of India (2002): National Human Development Report, 2001, Planning Commission, New Delhi.

Government of India (2003): Report of the Committee on India's Vision 2020, Planning Commission, Academic Foundation, New Delhi.

Gupta, S.P., P. Singh and K.L. Datta (1982): Measurement of Poverty, paper presented in a National Seminar on Regional Dimensions of India's Economic Development, Planning Commission, Government of India.

John, R.M. and R., Mutatkar, (2005): Statewise Estimates of Poverty among Religious Group in India, *Economic and Political Weekly*, March 24-April 1.

Kozel, D. and B. Parker; (2003): A Profile and Diagnostic of Poverty in Uttar Pradesh, *Economic and Political Weekly*, Vol. 38, No. 4, January 25.

Kozel and Deaton, (2005): *The Great India Poverty Debates*, MacMillan India.

Kulshreshta A.C., and A. Kar, (2005): "Estimates of Food Consumption Expenditure from Household Surveys and National Accounts," in Deaton and Kozel (ed.), *The Great India Poverty Debates*, Macmillan India.

Minhas, B. S., (1988): Validation of Large Scale Sample Survey Data: Case of NSS Estimates of Households Consumption Expenditure in Deaton and Kozel (ed.), (2005): *The Great India Poverty Debates*, Macmillan India.

Mishra, G.P. and D.M. Diwakar (2005): *Land Reforms and Human Development*, Manak Publications Pvt. Ltd., New Delhi.

Patnaik, U., (2004): "The Republic of Hunger," *Social Scientist*, Vol. 33, No. 9-10, September –October.

Prasad, P.H., (1991): *Lop Sided Growth*, Oxford, New Delhi.

Radhakrishna, R. (2002): "Agricultural Growth, Employment and Poverty : A Policy Perspective," *Economic and Political Weekly*, January 19.

Ram, Ramanand (2004): *Poverty Estimates in India: A Critical Appraisal*, Dissertation submitted to JNU, New Delhi.

Rudra, A., (1974): Minimum Level of Living: A Statistical Examination in Poverty and Income Distribution in Deaton and Kozel (ed.): *The Great India Poverty Debates*, Macmillan India, 2005.

Saith, A., (2005): Poverty Lines versus Poor: Method versus Meaning, *Economic and Political Weekly*, Vol. 40, no. 43, October 22-28.

Sen, A., (2001): "Estimates of Consumer Expenditure and its Distribution: Statistical Priorities after NSS 55th Round," *Economic and Political Weekly*, Vol. 35, No. 51, December 16.

Sukhatma, P.V., (1977): "Measurement of Poverty Based on Nutritions Needs," *Bulletin of the International Statistical Institute*, Vol. 47, book 4, contributed papers.

Sunderam, K. and S.D. Tendulkar, (2001): "NAS-NSS Estimates of Private Consumption for Poverty Estimation: A Disaggregate Comparison for 1993-94," *Economic and Political Weekly*, January 13.

The World Bank (2002a): "Poverty in India: The Challenges of Uttar Pradesh," Report No. 22323-IN. Washington, D.C.

Tiwari, J.N., (1982): "Note on Poverty Ratio and Development Index," in Planning Commission, (ed.), *Regional Dimensions of India's Economic Development*.

Vaidyanathan, A. (2001): "Poverty and Development Policy," *Economic & Political Weekly*, May 26.

10

SUSTAINABLE RURAL DEVELOPMENT

N.M.P. Verma

I. Introduction

Funds under this head include normal central assistance, open market borrowing, negotiated loans from financial institutions and additional central assistance for externally aided projects. In addition, special plan loans are given in those years when the State faced severe financial difficulties on account of disturbed conditions. There is a separate guideline for each programme The guidelines have been issued by Planning Commission, Government of India for centrally sponsored schemes. For State sponsored schemes, however, the concerned secretariat has issued such guidelines. These guidelines of the 10th plan have focused on objectives of the scheme, choice and selection mode of key activities, agency to screen the proposal, identification of area or beneficiaries, method of mobilization of either financial resources, or societal resources, release of grant, target fixation, utilization norm of the grant and all other relevant points which are essential and needs to be adhered to. For more detailed information of the specific guidelines the relevant materials may be referred to in the concerned document. The objectives of all the plans by and large confine to reduce rural unemployment and poverty through self and wage employment and also to create infrastructure. In the following analysis various rural development programmes under 10th plan will be dealt with one by one.

II. Various Rural Development Programmes

Swarn Jayanti Gram Swarozgar Yojana (SJGSY)

Swarn Jayanti Gram Swarozgar Yojana has been given due importance in the Annual Plans of Tenth Five Year Plan for generation of self-employment through micro enterprises. It has a vast coverage at all India level. Tenth Plan has targeted to cover 30 per cent of the rural poor in each block. It has also targeted most vulnerable group to bring them over the poverty line. As per the revised objective the programme would ultimately lead to strengthening and socio-economic empowerment of the rural poor as well as improve their collective bargaining power. Physical progress under SJGSY has been shown in Table 1. The table shows that during the first two years of the Tenth Five Year Plan the target for formation of self-help group (SHG) has remained constant. It was 120000 in both the years, 2002-03 and 2003-04.

Unfortunately the achievement came down in 2003-04 in comparison to 2002-03. The SHG formation to its target decreased from 73 per cent in 2002-03 to 71.0 per cent in 2003-04. This does not show a healthy trend. The achievement is also much lower to its target in both the years. So far as the issue of the loan distribution of SHG is concerned, the figures show a very pathetic situation. Only 23 per cent of targeted SHGs in 2002-03 and 11 per cent in 2003-04 has been covered for loan distribution. This way it may be added that there has been very slow progress in loan distribution in both the years and more slow in the later year. Such situation has taken place despite the fact that the amount was made available, which could not be spent. The percentage of expenditure, as shown in Table 2, has been 65 per cent in 2002-03 and 76 per cent in 2003-04. It may further be added that under this scheme the actual loan distribution as per cent of the target was just 27 per cent in 2002-03 which although doubled up to 55 per cent in 2003-04.

The major portion of expenditure has been on establishment. This needs to be rectified. Allocation for establishment is very less as per guidelines the govt. machineries may put some check on this issue through quick disposal of cases. As shown in Table 3 the actual expenditure on establishment as a percentage of its target has been lower in 2002-03 in comparison to 2003-04. Thus, from the above analysis, it may be concluded that under SJGSY achievements has been much lower than targets in the area of SHG formation, loan distribution and total expenditure. Targets can be achieved if available allocated amount is made available to the SHG. Therefore, more focus on formation of SHG may further be given. For this 70 key activities have been so far identified for self-employment and income generation especially in industry, service and business sectors, animal husbandry, horticulture, fish culture and minor irrigation. As a result during 2003-04, 1.41 lakh BPL families have been benefited against a target of 3.50 lakh BPL families. It shows that more than one lakh BPL families have not been benefited. In 2004-05 again the target is to assist 2.50 lakh BPL families and construct 8 Mandi yards, 4 sub-yards and a few (20) Haat Paths. Empowerment has gone up now. For example, in Sultanpur every number of Mahila SHG is able to earn Rs. 2000 per month per project. Poor loan distribution may be because of lack of entrepreneurship in BPL families, lack of coordination among banks, Government agencies and the BPL families. Requirements of guarantor and/or mortgaging of properties are also creating hurdles in loan delivery. Recovery of loan may also create sense of doubt for loan sanction.

Sampoorna Gramin Rozgar Yojana (SGRY)

This programme has been launched after November 2001 by merging Jawahar Gram Samridhi Yojana and Employment Assurance Scheme. For this 75 per cent resource is released by the Centre and 25 per cent by the State. Foodgrains are provided free of cost. The programme aims to create wage employment/

manual work around the villages. Poorest persons are preferred. The programme has been beneficial for the villagers in several respects. Firstly, contractors are not permitted to be engaged for execution of any of the work. Secondly, the Gram Panchayats have been involved for preparation of annual action plan, which is approved by the Gram Sabhas. The members of this Sabha are fully aware of the local surroundings. Thirdly, through this plan some infrastructure is also generated which has its effects on future development.

For the Tenth Plan period, state share outlay of Rs. 2092 crore has been fixed for generation of 8803 lakh man days of employment. Against the above target an outlay of Rs. 254 crore was released for generation of 1335 lakh man days of total employment including that of SC/ST. Adding both the shares of state and the centre, a sum of Rs. 130621 lakh in 2002-03 and 123506 lakh in 2003-04 were made available. But unfortunately expenditure was much less. Only 71 per cent was utilized in 2002-03 and 89 per cent in 2003-04. As a result, achievement of full targets has become a dream. Further, 9 lakh tonnes of foodgrain was targeted every year for distribution in terms of 6 kgs of wheat or 5 kgs of rice. But quality has not been maintained during distribution during first two annual plans. Even proper weighing is not done. During 2003-04 the target of employment generation was 1535 lakh man days, however, 1314 lakh man days was actually generated. During 2004-05 an outlay of Rs. 410.64 crore is proposed for further generation of 1700 lakh man days of employment. In order to increase expenditure advance planning is required so that by the time grants reach utilization can be efficiently done. This will make wage employment scheme more effective.

Pradhan Mantri Gramodaya Yojna (PMGY)

Under this special scheme rural social sectors such as water supply, housing, primary education, rural road, Primary health care and nutrition are covered. In the ninth plan the total expenditure in this scheme was 15253 crores. In the Tenth plan, however, against an outlay of Rs 1200.97 crore Rs 1112.13 crore is an anticipated expenditure during 2002-03 and Rs 1147.65

crore has been approved in 2003-04. But actual expenditure was only 845.32 crore in this year. During 2004-05 an outlay of Rs 1285 .978 crore has been proposed. In this plan for water supply there has been provision of safe drinking water for ten thousand quality problem houses. But the achievement has been very slow. Only 535 habitations were covered during 2002-03 and only 261 habitations are proposed in 2003-04. This way it is very difficult to achieve the plan target. According to the progress of physical targets satisfactory performance has been made under installation of New hand pump and Rebore hand pump schemes. By mid of tenth plan about 50 per cent of targets have been achieved. But under the scheme of check dams and piped water supply annual plan targets are not in consonance with Tenth plan targets. Therefore achievements will fall short of targets. In the following two annual plans special attention is required for check dams and piped water supply schemes.

The financial and physical achievements under Rural Housing scheme have been in conformity with plan targets. But annual plan targets are quite less. As per this trend Tenth plan targets cannot be achieved. The annual targets in the following two annual plan should be enhanced. In view of Tenth plan targets the annual plan targets for handpump installation and toilet construction in the school are low. These targets should be enhanced. No rural PHC has been installed in rural area under this scheme. This is also a very serious matter. But the construction of health centres has been completed as per plan target.

Under this programme, the expenditure during the year 2001-02 was Rs. 26.10 and Rs. 51.74 crore respectively. The level of beneficiaries by the end of the Ninth Plan was 52.85 lakh. The approved outlay for the Tenth Plan is Rs. 779.47 crore. The level of expenditure for the year 2002-03 is Rs. 144.42 crore through which the number of beneficiaries would be 4.36 lakh. During the Annual Plan 2003-04 against an outlay of Rs. 85.50 crore an amount of Rs. 98.56 crore was utilized. During 2004-05 an outlay of Rs. 86.28 crore is proposed for this programme to benefit 8.72 lakh children. Thus physical progress has not been satisfactory as per target in 2003-04 but expenditure was above targeted outlay in both the year 2002-04

An outlay of Rs. 1327.00 crore and Rs. 252.87 crore have been proposed for the Tenth Five Year Plan (2002-07) and the Annual Plan 2003-04 respectively for Road Electrification. Against the target of electrifying 3371 villages for the year 2002-03 and 2003-04 only 1839 and 428 villages respectively have been electrified. A target of 6000 villages have been again proposed for 2004-05. Although rural electrification is done but supply of electricity is not fully ensured. This needs special attention under power supply in rural area.

This is a centrally sponsored scheme for connecting every village. It is carried out by rural development department. At present there are 74673 unconnected habitations. For this 149346 km connectivity is required. During 2003-4 the projection of 2249 works having road length of 4540 km. with an amount of 1011.15 crores have been cleared by Government of India. During 2004-5 an outlay of Rs. 1000 crores is proposed as central share. The total requirement of fund is, however, 10600 crore. So far only 909.75 crore has been released by Govt of India upto the end of 2003-4. Thus 90 per cent of fund is still to be released. That is why there is slow progress of connectivity under this scheme. If there will be delay in fund release then cost of the project will escalate which may not be further compensated.

Other Specific Programmes

There are a few specific programmes for development of water disastrous area like Indira Awaas Yojana (IAY), Drought Prone are Programme (DPAP), Integrated Wasteland Development Programme (IWDP), Integrated Wasteland Development Programme (IWDP), Ambedkar Vishesh Rozgar Yojna (AVRY), Border Area Development Programme and Rastriya Sam Vikas Yojna.

Indira Awaas Yojana was started during 1985-86 for facilitating grant for construction of houses to members of SC/ST, freed bonded labourers and also non-SC/ST rural people, which are below the poverty line. Also more than 40 per cent of total IAY allocation should not be incurred for non-SC/ST in one financial year. Physical and financial progress has been shown in Table 4. It is to be mentioned with the help of the table that expenditure has been satisfactorily done because 93 per cent of expenditure has been incurred in 2002-03 and 95 per cent expenditure has been incurred in 2003-04. Achievements are even slightly more satisfactory in the sense that whatever was targeted was achieved fully in 2002-03 and also almost fully (95%) in 2003-04. But it is strange that the government has not revised unit cost per house upto 2002-03 and 2003-04. It was suddenly increased by 25 per cent in general region and around 25 per cent in Bundelkhand region. It means quality of construction must have been deteriorated in 2002-03 and 2003-04 because of increase in construction cost every year by at least 10 per cent. In this situation the plan should increase unit cost per house in every annual plan by at least 10 per cent.

Presently DPAP is in operation in 60 selected blocks of 15 districts in U.P. The programme aims at overall development of these drought prone areas. However, it has been noticed that targets are not being fulfilled. For instance, in 2003-04 against the target of 65000 hectares area, 42,162 hectares had been treated by different developmental measures. The expenditure was Rs. 369.90 lakh in 2003-04. However, in 2004-05 annual plan more thrust has been given on establishing sectoral linkages. In order to fulfill the target necessary adjustment will also be made in the plan especially in soil and water conservation, afforestation and water resource development.

IWDP is a centrally sponsored scheme. As per revised guidelines the resource is met at the ratio of 91.77 : 8.33 sharing basis by the Centre and the State. It is in operation in 35 districts of the State. During 2003-04 the government has taken several measures for capacity building and training, sustainability of assets and creation of SHG. During 2004-05, further emphasis has been given on sectoral linkages with concerned departments. In this plan the focus is on water harvesting through low cost farm ponds, Nallah bunds, check dam, percolation lakes, distillation of village tanks, fishery development, afforestation and pasture development.

This programme is a project based scheme for sustained employment generation. The AVRY is in take off stage and is in the process. Several projects executed under this scheme have yielded good results in generating self-employment. During 2003-04, employment was generated for 56,305 persons and further it has targeted to generate 120000 persons employment in 2004-05. In addition to this during the Tenth Plan, it is proposed to generate employment for 50 lakh persons under Rozgar Chhatri Yojana. During 2003-04, 1025248 person employment opportunities have been created under this scheme. Thus, it is proposed to generate employment opportunities for 1250000 persons in 2004-05. This seems essential for which more investment is required.

This programme is meant for 19 blocks of seven districts of the Indo-Nepal Border because of the distinct problem of the region. The length of International Border is 538 kms. But the fund allocation is very low. In 2002-3 the allocation was 8.32 crore in 2002-3, 17.45 crores in 2003-4 and again 8.32 crores in 2004-5. The expenditure was even less than annual allocation. The utilization was 25 per cent less in 2003-4 and 50 per cent less in 2003-4. This needs special attention because of the sensitiveness of the region.

Under Centrally Sponsored scheme Tenth Plan outlay is 39799.51 crores. It has been observed that annual allocation so far made is not enough to fulfill this target. Upto 2004-5 Rs 17352 crores have been proposed outlay. Expenditure has been even far less. In the first two annual plans the total expenditure was Rs. 8145.86 crores. This again is a matter of serious concern.

Under RSVY several rural development works are done. This relates to forest, health, education, dairy, animal husbandry, horticulture, irrigation, public works and several others. The program was started in three phases in order to cover several districts. But the unfortunate part has been only 22 per cent utilization of available fund. The total amount released was Rs 2492.79 lakhs upto October, 2004 out of which only Rs 547.12 lakh could be spent by this period. As a result, the set target in several sub sectors may not be fulfilled.

III. Employment, Income and Infrastructure

To create better environmental condition infrastructure

generation has also been considered inevitable through the following schemes:

1. Construction of Kharanjja/Nali
2. Construction of multipurpose Panchayat building/ welfare centre
3. Construction of Hatt Path.
4. Rural Sanitation

The financial targets of the Tenth Five Year Plan (2002-07) was Rs. 18625 lakh out of which Rs. 9544.66 lakh has been actually incurred in 2002-03 and Rs. 10569.55 lakh in 2003-04. Therefore, already in these two years the targets have been achieved. But again in 2004-05 additional financial expenditure of Rs. 7966.57 lakh has been estimated. This may be much more over and above the whole Tenth Plan target. It has also been observed that the physical target in the Tenth Plan for construction of Kharanja/Nali in Ambedkar Villages was 961 km. But the total construction was 7621 km. in 2002-03 and 1993 km. in 2003-04 totalling 9614 km. Thus again the target has already been achieved in the first two years of annual plan only.

The Tenth Plan has fixed the target of generation of employment upto 6422414 mandays through the above programmes out of which 2573245 was generated in 2002-03 and 3392757 in 2003-04. Hence this way again target of the tenth plan has been fully achieved during the first two years of the annual plan. It means lower target might have been fixed in the tenth plan document. This needs to be revised. Similarly it has been observed that the task of construction of multipurpose Panchayat Bhavan has also been realized during the first two years of Tenth plan. This also shows underestimation of the target. It may be construed that the above programs have been very successful for generation of rural employment and also for creation of infrastructure.

The backlog of unemployment in 2004-5 is 25 lakhs person. The total under employed persons in the state has been estimated 99 lakhs. In addition, new entrants in 2004-5 will be around 14 lakhs. Thus unemployed will be 39 lakhs and under employed would be 99 lakhs for whom employment has to be provided during the remaining two years of the tenth plan. The generation of employment is linked to growth of income. On the basis of employment elasticity (0.45) it has been estimated that targeted growth of 8% per annum would generate employment for about 14.64 lakh during annual plan period. This way the problem of backlog and new entrants in the labour force may be solved. The problems of under-employed will still remain unsolved for which extra effort is required in the next plan.

There is a huge literature on the assessment of rural development programmes in the State (Prasad, 1984). There is lots of expectation from the Government. The nature and size of the problem is also very vast and complicated. The situation of U.P. is worse. The plan expenditure (at constant prices) during the entire Eighth Five Year Plan fell short of the outlay by 26.3 per cent in U.P., which happens to be much less than Bihar (67.8%) and Orissa (46.9%). This situation continued in Ninth Plan and first two years of Tenth Plan also. The per capita plan expenditure also shows a decline with some fluctuations over the years. This was because of heavy shortfall in total plan expenditure as compared to the allocated outlay during the years. The huge hiatus between the approved outlay and expenditure in U.P. is alarming. U.P. was allocated more funds for energy sector at the time of allocation but it could not be implemented. The expenditure on irrigation was less than what was provided. The growth of per capita SDP in the 1990s was 1.2 per cent in U.P. that has further bearing on low growth in the Tenth Plan period. Vocational training of short duration may improve situation(Verma, 2005).

Several evaluation studies have been done on IRDP and other schemes. It has been pointed out that IRDP presented a matrix of multiple allied programmes without desired linkages. These were implemented as separate programmes without keeping in mind the overall objective of generating sustainable incomes. In addition to this there has been lack of coordination with other departments as well. In some cases works were executed as biased. Quality of work was bad in more than 60 percent cases. There has also been inadequacy of funds at Gram Panchayat level that led to rise of pressure group that created heterogeneous village economy. There was also lack of proper book keeping and transparency. For instance, an evaluation study of IRDP in Banda and Rae Bareli districts revealed that the programme continued to suffer from several shortcomings at the levels of planning and implementation. The study concluded that annual plans are prepared in a routine manner and proper integration of targets and their linking with local resources is not attempted. The process of beneficiary selection is defective and little after care support is provided to them. The borrowers were harassed by the cumbersome and dilatory procedures in obtaining loan. The required degree of cooperation between the development and financial institutions was found missing. The income of beneficiaries increased but the rise is not so significant. Only about 30 per cent of them could cross the poverty line (GIDS, Lucknow). Time to time, the Central and State government have also evaluated the developmental programs and even guidelines have been updated and revised. But at the implementation level there are socio-political hurdles that needs to be lessened in order to obtain the targets. Rules may also needs to be rationalised which may reduce bureaucratic delays in programme implementation. Coordination among various departments are also imperative for fast execution and success. Panchayati Raj institutions may be made transparent in order to solve local problems at the local level. Emphasis may be given on deciding priorities at the local level. Local planning may be cost effective also. Regional balancing is equally missing during target setting and fund allocation. This needs to be corrected through inter departmental coordination. Establishment cost may also be reduced and rationalized time to time. SHGs may be supported with motivation and basic infrastructure and liberal credit with due screening of cases. This will enhance success rate of beneficiaries. Mere formation of SHG may not be helpful. After construction of Awaas there should be quick distribution to beneficiaries. This may reduce maintenance cost.

IV. Conclusion

In the next Five Year Plan the Government should try to concentrate on quick release of central fund, efficient utilization of allocated fund, identification of right beneficiaries, reducing gap in target and achievement, putting right targets without any under or over estimation, focus on grass root planning, bureaucratic efficiency, perfect prioritization, center-state coordination, coordination among state departments, planning of gainful employment, road and communication connectivity, rural investment, smooth expenditure over the year, credit and marketing including storage and infrastructure, prompt implementation of programs and establishing vocational training centres in rural region especially in the Indo–Nepal border. Private investment in rural area should also be encouraged. It has also been observed that funds for several backwards districts are not made available in time. Funds are fully utilized in the areas that are politically strong. This attitude needs to be wiped out. Therefore, equity in fund allocation is required. As far as possible extra efforts may be also be made for involvement of the community and local area planning (Verma and Verma, 2004). Community participation in rural developmental programmes along with the interface with the Government can bring efficient results. The political intervention with economic planning may also be sidelined. The tendency of skewed expenditure in the last few months of a financial year may be avoided.

Table 1

PHYSICAL PROGRESS UNDER SJGSY

Year	*SHG Formation*			*Percent of Target SHG to whom Loan Provided*
	Target	*Achievement*	*Percent*	
2001-02	80000	80991	101.0	28.0
2002-03	120000	87549	73.0	23.0
2003-04	120000	85282	71.0	11.0

Table 2

FINANCIAL PROGRESS UNDER SJGSY (RS. IN LAKH)

Year	*Total Amount Available*	*Expenditure*	*Expenditure percentage*
2001-02	26379	15536	59.0
2002-03	22550	14721	65.0
2003-04	25606	19564	76.0

Table 3

HEAD WISE PERCENTAGE OF EXPENDITURE UNDER SJGSY

Year	*Actual Loan Distribution as per cent of Target*	*Actual Expenditure on Establishment as % of Target*
2001-02	33.0	73.0
2002-03	27.0	55.0
2003-04	55.0	78.0

Table 4

FINANCIAL AND PHYSICAL PROGRESS UNDER IAY

Year	*Percentage Expenditure*	*Percentage Achievement of Awaas to Target*	*Unit cost per house (Rs.)*	
			General Region	*Bundelkhand Region*
2001-02	93.0	100.0	20000	22000
2002-03	93.0	100.0	20000	22000
2003-04	95.0	95.0	20000	22000
2004-05	—	—	25000	27000

Table 5

FINANCIAL PROGRESS UNDER SGRY (RS. IN LAKH)

Year	*Total Amount Available*	*Expenditure*	*Expenditure percentage*
2001-02	101917	63989	63.0
2002-03	130621	92845	71.0
2003-04	123506	110527	89.0

Source: Office of the RD Commissioner, U.P. Government.

References

Government of Uttar Pradesh, (Various Years), *Annual Plans*, State Planning Institute, Lucknow.

Government of Uttar Pradesh, (1990): *Eighth Plan: Mid Term Appraisal*, GIDS, Lucknow.

Government of Uttar Pradesh, (2002): *Poverty and Social Monitoring in Uttar Pradesh*.

Government of Uttar Pradesh, (2002): *Tenth Five Year Plan*, State Planning Institute, Lucknow.

International Fund for Agricultural Development, (2002): *Assessment of Rural Poverty: Asia and the Pacific*, Rome, January.

Krishnaraj, Maithreyi, (2002): Growth and Rural Poverty, *Economic and Political Weekly*, Vol. XXXVII, No. 38.

Prasad, Kamta, (1984): *Planning for Poverty Alleviation*, Agricole, Delhi.

Robb, Peter, (1992): *Rural India: Land, Power and Society under British Rule*, OUP, Delhi.

Subuddhi, Karunamay, (2002): "Science and Technology for Rural Development", *Economic and Political Weekly*, Vol. XXXVII, No. 38.

Verma, N.M.P. and Verma, Lalit, (2004): "Sustainable Management of Flood Water through Community participation in India", *Sustainable Water Resources Management*, Proceedings of International Conference, Vol 1, United Nations University, Tokyo, Japan.

Verma, N.M.P., (2005): "Rural Development", *Report on Mid Term Appraisal of 10th Plan*, GIDS, Lucknow.

Verma, N.M.P. and Srivastava, Richa, (2006): "Deprivation and Empowerment Linkages in Development Discourse", DM Diwakar, GP Mishra (eds.) *Deprivation and Inclusive Development*, GIDS, Lucknow/Manak, Delhi.

Verma, N.M.P., (2005): *Economic Disparity and Industrial Development: A Case Study of SCs of Uttar Pradesh*, Classical Publishing House, New Delhi.

11

URBAN DEVELOPMENT AND POVERTY ALLEVIATION IN UTTAR PRADESH

A.N. Pandey

I. Introduction

Urban population of Uttar Pradesh, as per the census 2001, is 34.51 million, which accounts for 20.78 per cent of the total population. The decadal growth rate of urban population during the period of 1991-2001 was 32.8 per cent, which was greater than the growth rate of total population. It has been estimated that the annual growth rate of urban population in the state was 2.88 per cent, while the same at the national level was 2.75 per cent. As such, the urban population in U.P. has been growing at a faster rate. It has also been found that about 28 per cent of the total urban population in U.P. is located in six metropolitan cities of the state, viz. Kanpur, Lucknow, Agra, Varanasi, Allahabad and Meerut. The growth rate of population even in these cities is much higher and it has been estimated that the growth rate during the period of 1991-2001 was about 48.00 per cent. This suggested that almost one and half of the population of these cities were added during the last one decade.

The total number of house hold added to urban centers in U.P. during the period of 1991-2001 was as high as 14.23 lakh, out of which 10.75 lakh households were added due to the natural growth of population while the remaining 3.6 lakh households were added through migration of population. With such a high growth of urban population, it is obvious that there could be a variety of problems in the urban areas to be taken care during the 10th Plan period. The problems of urban areas could be with regard to dwelling units, infrastructure facilities and growing demand for goods and services. Also, with the migration of population from the rural areas there could be problems of urban poverty, unemployment and unhygienic living conditions. all these call for a planed development of urban amenities.

II. Department deal with Urban Development

Broadly there are three departments, in U.P. that deal with urban planning and development. These are as follows:

(i) Housing Department,
(ii) Urban Development Department,
(iii) Urban Employment and Poverty Alleviation Department.

1. Housing

Housing Need

In the urban areas, development of housing under the State Sector is taken care of by the Housing Department and actual implementation i.e. acquisition and development of plots, construction of houses and allotment are done by the local development authorities and the State Housing Board. It has been estimated that in U.P. there was a shortage of 7 lakh dwelling units in 2002 and additional 9.03 lakh dwelling units would be required during the Xth Plan Period (i.e. 2002-2007). Thus, there would be a shortage of 16.03 lakh dwelling units in U.P. during the Xth Plan Period.

Strategies for Housing

In order to meet this requirement, a sent of strategies were adopted for the Xth Five Year Plan. It has emphasized that the acquisition of land would be done through negotiations and about 12.5 per cent of land would be reserved for the people affected by projects. The 'consent award' would be initiated by amending either land acquisition Act or U.P. Urban Planning and Development Act. In order to facilitate the development of trunk infrastructure, development of land would be done through land pooling techniques would be applied. Also, involvement of private organized section and cooperative sector in housing would be increased and such organizations would be asked to set-aside 35.00 per cent of the land for people belonging to economically weaker sections (EWS) and low income group (LIG), while the remaining 65.00 per cent would be available for concerned organization to develop and allotted them as per their perceptions. Also, that no construction of housing would be done in state sector and only plots for economically weaker sections and low-income group people would be considered.

For meeting the housing requirement of urban areas during the Xth Five Year Plan, it was proposed that only 35 per cent of the dwelling units (i.e. 5.6 lakh dwelling units out of 16.03 lakh dwelling units) would be in the formal sector including the state sector, institutional sector, cooperative societies and private formal sector.

The development of these dwelling units could be in the form of construction of house as well as development of plots in the ratio of 70:30 respectively. The remaining dwelling units of 10.4 lakh would be developed through the informal sector.

Target for Housing & Non-Utilisation of Plan Outlay

Under the State Sector, 36000 LIG plots were propose to be developed for which Rs. 300.00 crores was required. Out of Rs. 300.00 crores, Rs. 150.00 crores was to be arranged from LIC&GIC and the remaining Rs. 150.00 crores was to come from the State Government. Accordingly, the outlay for housing during the Xth Five year Plan Period was fixed at Rs. 300.00 crores and an amount of Rs. 33.00 crore was allocated for the year 2002-03.

During the subsequent year 2003-04, 3700 LIG plots were propose to be developed for which an amount of Rs. 30.5 crores was required. Accordingly, outlay for the year 2003-04 was Rs. 30.5 crore and it was decided that Rs. 30.00 crore would be arranged from LIC and GIC and the balance Rs. 50.00 lakh would be met from the State Government resources.

However, it was reported the approved outlay for the Xth Five year Plan was only Rs. 110.00 crores and no fund could be released for the first two years of the Xth Plan and even the anticipated expenditure for 2004-05 was stated to be NIL. The main reason for the non-utilization of plan outlay was stated to be the lack of allotment of funds for housing sector in U.P. from the Life Insurance Corporation (LIC) and General Insurance Corporation (GIC) due to the default in repayment of loan and interest by some other departments of the Govt. of U.P.

However, the draft annual plan of 2003-04 showed that there was a provision of Rs. 230.00 crores for housing during the Xth Five Year Plan out of which Rs. 69.30 crore had been approved for the year 2002-03 against which the anticipated expenditure was to he tune of Rs. 88.34 crores. Further, the proposed outlay for the year 2003-04 was Rs. 19.00 crores.

It is obvious form the proceeding discussion that there is a lost of inconsistency in the figures of plan outlay for the Xth Five Year Plan as well as annual plans and the information furnished by the department concerned. As such, it is very difficult to make an appraisal of Xth Five Year Plan on the basis of these data for the development of urban housing in U.P. However, it is very much clear that there seems to be a major problem in this component of Xth Five Year Plan and it is doubtful whether the objective of Xth Five Year Plan with regard to development of urban housing would be achieved. Since a period of two years is still left, efforts should be made to take it seriously keeping in view the acute shortage of dwelling units in the urban areas of Uttar Pradesh. The approved outlay for the Xth Five Year Plan was stated to be Rs. 230.00 crores for this component and an amount of Rs. 105.43 crores was reported to have been utilized by March 2004. For the year 2004-05, the approved outlay was Rs. 20.50 crores out of which Rs. 3.09 crores had been utilized till Aug. 2004.

2. Urban Development

There are three major schemes under the urban development programme. These are as follows:

(i) National Capital Region (NCR)
(ii) Nagar Vikash Yojana (NVY),
(iii) Integrated Development of Small & Medium Town

The National Capital Region Programme is sponsored by the Government of India and it has three components, *(a)* National Capital Territory, *(b)* Delhi Metropolitan Area, and *(c)* Rest of National Capital Region.

While the objective of National Capital Territory is to control and restrict the growth of Delhi, the Delhi Metropolitan Area programme aims at moderate growth and the National Capital Region programme aims at induced growth in the National Capital Region. Under the NCR scheme, attempts are made to remove economic activities, like industry, offices and wholesale trading etc. from Delhi to the areas of National Capital Region on the one hand, and develop regional infrastructure, community facilities and other amenities and utilities in the neighborhood of Delhi comparable to those in the Delhi metropolitan area. Under this scheme, the urban centers of NOIDA, Greater NOIDA, Ghaziabad, Modinagar, Hapur, Pilakhua, Bulandshahar, Khurja and Meerut are covered. Attempts are also being made to develop Bareilly as the counter magnet city. The overall objective is to restrict the further growth of Delhi Metropolitan area and develop the urban centers in the neighborhood to attract the economic activities and migrating population which otherwise would have gone to Delhi.

Under the NCR schemes 75 per cent funds are made available by the Government of India and 25 per cent by the

State Government. As such only a nominal amount of Rs. 1.00 crore was proposed to be allocated during the year 2003-04 and it was assumed that the concerned implementing agencies, like housing Board, Development Authorities, UPSIDC, UPPCL and UPSRTC and others will arrange the remaining 25.00 per cent required as the share of the State Government. Since all these are centrally sponsored schemes, the concerned department has little information to furnish for appraisal of 10th Five Year Plan in this regard.

Nagar Vikas Yojana

Nagar Vikas Yojana aims at the development of parks, transit hostels, civil service institutes, community centers and so on. For this, funds are made available to the development authorities and local bodies. The allocation for the year 2002-03 was Rs. 4.00 crores. The same for the year 2003-04 was Rs. 4.00 crores and Rs. 5.5 crores had been proposed for the year 2003-05. Also, during the year 2002-03 there was a provision of Rs. 50.34 crores for the construction and development of "Dr. Ambedkar Antarrashtriya Samajik Parivartan Sahitya Sangrah Sansthan Evam Sangrahalaya". Similarly, during the year 2004-05 there was an allocation of Rs. 10.00 crores for the construction of "Indira Pratisthan". Thus, there was an allocation of Rs. 73.34 crores under the Nagar Vikas Yojana.

How casual approach to the city development schemes is obvious from the above figures. While a meager amount of Rs. 4.00 – 5.00 crores is allotted for the development of cities in the State for one year, a single institution claims a huge amount running into ten folds of the annual outlay. Could it be possible that funds for specific institutions are provided separately so that the availability of funds for city development scheme is not are not appropriated entirely by a single project of a particular city?

Integrated Development of Small & Medium Towns

This scheme was introduced during the 6th Plan period and is funded on matching basis by the Government of India and the State Government, Hudco and financial institutions on the basis of proportionate share which differ across the class of towns. Cities & towns having population up to 05 lakh are selected for this scheme. Accordingly to the Census of 2001, there were 670 such urban centers in U.P. till the end of March, 2002, 110 towns of the state of U.P. had been covered by this scheme and the target for the 10th Five Year Plan is to cover 150 additional towns. It is reported that 71 towns had benefited in a period of First two and half years of 10th Five Year Plan and it was hoped that the number of such town would go up to 91 against target of 90 towns by end of March 20054. Under this scheme, a total amount of Rs. 70.0 crores was proposed for the Xth Five Year Plan against which Rs. 10.58 crores was released during the year 2002-02 \3 and Rs. 6.75 crores during the year 2003-04. A sum of Rs. 13.88 crores had been received in 2002-03 and Rs. 10.92 crores in the year 2003-04 from the Government of India as their share. Further, there was an allocation of Rs. 15.00 crores for the year 2004-05 against which Rs. 3.09 lakh had been released by the State Government till September 2004 and Rs. 3.82 crores as a share of the Government of India. Thus, the State Government had released a total amount of Rs. 20.42 crores, and Rs. 28.62 crores had been received as the share of Govt. of India. However, it is not known as to how much has been contributed by the local bodies whose share ranges from 20.00 per cent to 40.00 per cent of the project cost depending on the size class of towns and cities.

While progress of the scheme during the Xth Plan period, on the basis of release of funds from the Govt. of U.P. and Govt. of India appear to be satisfactory, the outlay seem to be meager keeping in view the number of urban centers (150) to be covered during the Xth Plan period. As such, the impact of the scheme is bound to be marginal only.

3. Urban Employment and Poverty Alleviation (UEPA)

The third component of plan for Urban Development is the Urban Employment and Poverty Alleviation Programme which aims at tackling unemployment problem of urban poor and affords them congenial and hygienic living conditions. This component is implemented by the State Urban Development Agency through its field level organizations. It has been estimated that almost one-forth of urban population lives below the poverty line and urban unemployment in U.P. is estimated to be 4.8 per cent as against only 3.1 per cent in the rural areas. In order to tackle the twin problems of urban poverty and unemployment two major schemes are under operation while one is known as Swarn Jayanti Shahari Rozagar Yojana (SJSRY) and other is called National Slum Development Programme (NSDP). An outlay of Rs. 60.00 crores has been made for SJSY\RY and Rs. 200.50 crores for NSDP. Thus, the total outlay for these schemes under the Xth Fiver Year Plan is Rs. 260.50 crores. This outlay is substantially lower than the out of IXth Five Year Plan (Rs. 320.00 crores) against which the actual expenditure during the IXth Five Year Plan was Rs. 254.70 crores. Thus, there has been hardly any enhancement in the plan outlay for this component in comparison with the same in the IXth Five Year Plan.

Out of the total plan outlay, the allocation for the year 2003-04 was Rs. 48.10 crores i.e. Rs. 8.0 crores for SJSRY and Rs. 40.10 crores for NSDP. The outlay for the 2nd Year, i.e. 2003-04 was same but only Rs. 5.24 crores was reported to have been spent under SJSRY while the same under NSDP was Rs. 40.10 crores. The proposed out lay for the year 1004-05 was Rs. 8.0 crores for SJSRY while the same for NSDP had been enhanced to Rs. 42.80 crores. Thus, the annual outlay in the case of NSDP appeared to be quite normal but the same can not be said about the SJSRY as there was approved as well as proposed outlay of Rs. 24.00 crores only in three years and the total expenditure against outlay was Rs. 21.24 crores only. This would mean that the remaining plan outlay of about Rs. 39.00 crores would have to be spent in the remaining period of two years.

Swarn Jayanti Shahari Rozagar Yojana (SJSRY)

Within the scheme of SJSRY there are several sub-schemes known as urban Self-Employment Programme (USEP), Training Programme, Development of Women and Child in Urban Areas (DWACUA), Thrift and Credit Society (TCS), and Urban Wage-

Employment Programme (UWEP). USEP aims at providing financial assistance through banks for self-employment to the urban unemployed poor. Training Programmes aims at developing and upgrading the technical skills of urban poor so that they could get gainful employment for themselves. DWACUP aims at organization of urban poor women in groups for taking up self-employment ventures. Each DWACUA group can secure subsidy to the extent of either 50 per cent of project or Rs. 1.25 lakh whichever is less. TCS can be set up by DWACUA groups who could be eligible for a lump-sum amount of Rs. 25, 000.00 as revolving fund at the rate of Rs. 1, 000.00 per member but only after one year of the formation of the society. The fund can be used by the group of the society for a specific purpose. Another special scheme of SJSRY, Urban Wage Employment Programme (UWEP) aims at providing wage employment to urban poor living below the poverty line by utilizing their labour for construction of social and economical public assets. While 60.00 per cent of funds allocated under this scheme are to be utilized for materials, the remaining 40.00 per cent can be utilized for the payment of wages.

SJSRY is an innovative scheme planned to be implemented by the District Urban Development Agency (DUDA) with the help of community based organizations but the ground level situation is yet to be stabilized and made fully functional. As such, there is a need to strengthen the organizational set up both at the district level and community based organizational set ups in the urban centers. Manpower, funds, devolution of functional authorities, a substantial dose of training and retraining to the functionaries to government as well community organizations in order to upgrade their knowledge and skills as well as to bring about desirable attitudinal changes in them are some of the requirements to make them functionally effective. There is also a need to encourage the use of Information Technology (IT) among the functionaries and make the system transparent.

National Slum Development Programme (NSDP)

The second important component is the National Slum

Development Programme (NSDP), which aims at improving the living conditions in the slums by providing basis amenities, health facilities, dwelling units, education and awareness to the slum dwellers. NSDP is operational only in 88 out of about 676 urban centers in U.P.

Another sub-scheme is the Abolishing Scavenging and Rehabilitation of Scavengers. As per the Employment of Manual Scavengers and Construction of Dry Latrine (Prohibition) Act. 1993 of Govt. of India and its adoption by the State Government, the State has to be made Scavengers free within a specified period. This scheme encourages construction of low-cost sanitation scheme and provides for the rehabilitation for scavengers who would be liberated from the inhuman practice of carrying and cleaning night soil.

III. Observation

Though the aggregated performance data as well as amount spent have been indicated, it is not obvious from the available information as to what has been the progress within the period of last three years of the Xth Five Year Plan. As such it is difficult to go for physical and financial appraisal of each of the several schemes with regard to Xth Five Year Plan.

Though a number of financial institutions and banks have come forward to provide financial assistance for development of housing facilities in the private sector but the state sector seems to have suffered a lot, particularly during the Xth Five Year Plan period. As hardly any progress is reported in this regard, a systematic review and follow-up actions are required to put back the activities of Housing Department on the rail. As for the Nagar Vikas Yojana, it seems that pet personality oriented projects/monuments have taken precedence over the developmental need of cities. While there is a little allocation of funds (just about Rs. 4.00 – 5.00 crores for the State as a whole) for the development of cities, there does not seem to be any shortage of funds for the personality-oriented monuments. If at all such monuments and projects are considered necessary, requiring bulk of funds, they should be separated from the on-going schemes, and treated as independent projects. By doing so, the distortion in the planning for development and deprivation of on-going schemes from funds could be avoided.

While the progress with regard to integrated development of small and medium towns is appear to be reasonable, keeping in view the large number of towns and their requirements the allocation of funds seem to be inadequate. As for the Urban Employment and Poverty Alleviation Programme is concerned, the progress seems to be satisfactory. But of the field level organizations envisaged for the effective implementation of project is yet to be strengthened. A great deal of systematic and transparent efforts is required to make the impact of these schemes on urban poor visible. The best part of the SJSRY scheme is that scheme is being implemented through active participation of women functionaries at the community level and it this innovative mechanism is really takes off, it would help a lot not only in the mitigation of urban poverty but also in the empowerment of urban women and that too of weaker sections at the community level.

12

SOCIAL DEVELOPMENT
Education, Health, Planning, Population and Voluntary Sector

M.K. Agarwal

I. Introduction

In the changing socio-economic scenario of India, contours of development also undergoes through changes. As social development has been an important segment of economic development in the country, its significance has been increased tremendously in the recent years. Now the government is fast moving towards the directly productive activities to develop social and economic infrastructure. Keeping such pattern of changes, we shall be examining various aspects of social development in Uttar Pradesh during the early years of the Tenth Five Year Plan.

II. Education

At a time when literacy has become a major challenge in Uttar Pradesh, complexities in education are also on increasing trend. On the one hand, Uttar Pradesh has the binding of attaining the target of full employment; on the other hand, India has the credible challenge of establishing itself as the 'superpower of knowledge' by 2010. In such a challenge, role of Uttar Pradesh assumes great significance. The state not only resides one-sixth of the nation's population but also due to lagging of the state in terms of demographic transition behind other states of the country, share of the youth would be still higher.

To learn about the development of education in Uttar Pradesh, it becomes indispensable to learn about its various components. The progress of education can be reviewed by dividing into primary education, adult education, secondary education, higher education and technical education. According to 2001 census, the literacy rate in Uttar Pradesh was only 57.4 per cent, which is less than the national average of 65.4 per cent. However, it has been the highest at 90.9 per cent in Kerala. Within this it is a matter of greater concern due to further lower rate of literacy among the females in the state, which has been 43.0 per cent against the national average of 54.3 per cent, and the highest being recorded again in Kerala at 87.9 per cent. Despite such a grim scenario, there is lack of clear evidence about the well-defined strategy of take forward female literacy and their education in this most populous state of the country.

As far as primary education is concerned, government appears to have placed the maximum concentration on this because according to Sarva Shiksha Abhiyan (SSA) all are to be covered under primary education by 2007. According to this all children in the age group of 6-11 years will become literate. As per Annual Plan 2004-05, shortage of schools across the state is almost over. Furthermore, according to this Annual Plan, the desired teacher-pupil ratio of 1:45 would be attained by the end of 2004-05 by recruiting 20,000 Shiksha Mitras. Besides this the drop-out rate has been reduced to 34 per cent at the primary level and 45 per cent at the higher primary level of education. Even if we could derive inferences based on this information alone, the desired target would not be attainable by 2007 because teachers could not be recruited as per the need nor there has been any effective check on school drop-out rates.

Besides this we have also ignored growing population of children due to rising trend in population size in Uttar Pradesh.

There is provision for an outlay of Rs. 2795.65 crore during the Tenth Plan period for primary and upper primary education. But the actual expenditure is likely to be far below than this outlay. In the initial year of the Tenth Plan, i.e. 2002-03, the actual expenditure of Rs. 213.89 crore was less by 33 per cent from the outlay of Rs. 319.39 crore. Similarly in 2003-04, the actual expenditure of Rs. 198.68 crore was less by 29 per cent of the outlay size of Rs. 268.77 crore. An outlay of Rs. 415.94 crore was earmarked for 2004-05. It is a further serious matter that the total outlay on this account at current prices during the first three years was just 36 per cent of the overall outlay of the Tenth Plan on this account. Actual expenditure is still lower. Under such circumstances the states objectives are difficult to be achieved. Thus, the objective of the government seems to be more on attaining total literacy devoid of quality. However, even this is not easy to get. Under such circumstances, the government should fasten its belts to make it a success. In the urban areas, people prefer to send their kids in private schools instead of sending them to government run primary schools. This might be due to various reasons like growing income, social status, quality of education, etc. Therefore, it is expected of the government that it is reallocating the primary schools to such places where they are needed in true sense and this way the money spent on primary education bears more fruits.

Secondary education now needs greater thrust on qualitative improvement in the expansion in its horizons. It is so because the children start exploring their future avenues from this stage itself. At this stage, competition or differences between government and private education gets quite manifested. Moreover, at this stage impact of governmental policies and strategies have almost similar impacts on public and private educational institutions. However, it is this very stage where confusion and lack of proper strategy on the part of both central and state governments came to fore and they find helpless in getting their policies translated into action as per their desired ways. The Tenth Plan of Uttar Pradesh lays emphasis on providing quality education while providing the secondary education a new direction in the state. Firstly, it is not clear how far training to teachers during their service period has been actually given the shape of reality. It is also not clear how much new equipments and literatures have been provided to such schools for modernizing them. More than this, actual quality remains without any measurement due to lack of proper scaling. It becomes essential to mention such points that number of non-governmental and unaided private schools at the secondary level is increasing rapidly and in these institutions number of students is also increasing with rapid pace. However, quality of teachers in such institutions and thereby quality of education does not provide any sense of satisfaction. This becomes quite obvious if one goes through a study on noted secondary level schools in the state capital itself. On the other hand, in urban areas number of students in the erstwhile established and well-known governmental and government-aided non-governmental secondary schools has gone down sharply in recent years. Such students are getting attracted towards unaided private schools. Under such circumstances, teachers in the governmental and aided private schools have become in surplus. These teachers might be redeployed where they are actually needed so that with limited resources, expansion and quality of secondary education do not get sacrificed. Another major problem of the secondary education is mushrooming growth of private tuitions and coaching. This shows that the curriculum is not appropriate and teachers are not well trained and committed ones.

Higher education in the state is passing through a difficult phase. On the one hand, higher education is fast inviting private participation and at the same time there is sharp decline in its quality across the state. During the Tenth Plan period, enrolment rate of youths in the age groups of 18-23 years is targetted to be enhanced to 10 per cent from the existing 6 per cent. Besides, liberalization, quality and evaluation of curriculum quality are the other major features of higher education during the Tenth Plan. Along with this distance education has also been accorded due importance.

However, available indicators suggest that instead of getting qualitatively uplifted, higher education in the state seems to have fallen prey of crowd effect. It is so because most of the male and female youths are using it as a dormitory for males are not getting jobs and females are not getting married. The plight of the higher education can be understood if one analyses the fate of the major goal of the country which wishes to make the nation super-power of knowledge in the world by 2010. To achieve this ambitious target, colleges and universities require massive improvements in laboratories, modernization of libraries, while making world-standard books and journals, and proper enabling environment for research in all disciplines. However, available indicators only disappoint those who wish to review the real situation. This can be further understood from the fact that for the Tenth Plan, a small outlay of Rs. 168.18 crore has been made and even this does appear to be realized at the end of the plan period. During the year 2002-03, against an outlay of Rs. 17.11 crore, actual expenditure was lower at Rs. 12.12 crore. During 2003-04, against an outlay of Rs. 17.11 crore again, the actual expenditure was higher at Rs. 21.66 crore. For the year 2004-05, an outlay of Rs. 43.89 crore has been earmarked. Thus, in the first three years of the Tenth Plan outlay, less than half of the overall outlay was earmarked while actual expenditure is expected to be still lower. In fact, to make qualitative improvement in higher education, wherein the government has to make reforms that has very low component of political interference and help in creating an enabling environment. If we could pay proper attention, we can make Uttar Pradesh an important destination for foreign students interested in higher and technical education.

Along with higher education, role of technical education is also increasing in the fast changing socio-economic conditions wherein challenges are increasing due to globalisation of the country. With suitable and effective strategic planning, these challenges might be converted into opportunities. For this, to supply trained and skilled manpower to the changing needs of industry and business, quality-based diploma and degree courses must be made available. Realizing the growing demand for such pool of manpower, the government has opened the door for private participation. For this purpose in Uttar Pradesh an outlay of Rs. 989 crore has been made during the Tenth Plan period. In the year 2002-03, against an outlay of Rs. 15 crore, actual expenditure was lower at Rs. 11.64 crore. Similarly, in 2003-04, against an outlay of Rs. 75.10 crore, actual expenditure was just Rs. 8.75 crore. In 2004-05, the outlay was Rs. 78.19 crore. In the changing scenario of technical education, there is need to pay specific attention to research and quality. However, it is an irony that despite increased participation of the private sector, quality does not seem to move upward rather it is going down. Even in this regard, U.P. Technical University has not been able to establish itself upto the expected level and rather it has disappointed much. Here, research is lacking almost totally. Qualification of teachers is often not upto the required level. Here emphasis is more on minting money than on raising standard which is not in the interest of development of the state.

III. Population

Human resources turn into curse, when it harms the growth and development of the human kind itself. Every sixth Indian resides in Uttar Pradesh. Every thirty-seventh person of the world belongs to Uttar Pradesh. Already, we have seen snail's pace of economic development in this most populous state of the country. If we have a glance at Table 1, it gets obvious that in 2001, with a population size of 166 millions, it is not only the most populous state but also population growth rate is still getting higher. As against this, at the national level decline in the growth rate has already been witnessed. In terms of literacy rate, Uttar Pradesh ranks at the bottom among the states next only to Bihar and Jammu & Kashmir. Here more than half of the women are still illiterate. If we could look at some other indicators of development, it is found that low rate of urbanization and highly adverse sex-ratio speaks further about backwardness of the state. Inter-state differences on these counts are still persisting (Table 2).

In fact, Uttar Pradesh is still in the initial stages of the second phase (population explosion) of the demographic transition. This gets clear because birth and deaths rates are here higher than the national average. Crude death rate was 9.7 in 2002 which is close to the highest CBR (9.8) in Madhya Pradesh and Orissa. Crude birth rate is the highest in Uttar Pradesh at 31.6. This situation obtains both in rural as well as urban areas. In the state infant mortality rate was 80, which is the highest next only to Orissa (87) and Madhya Pradesh (85). The Tenth Plan aims to bring down the CBR to 7.2 at the end of the Plan, i.e. 2007. However, all these targets appear to unrealistic in our context. Such rapid decline could not be witnessed among other states so far. It is also difficult because literacy and particularly female literacy is at very low level. There is lack of proper strategy for birth control, as it lacks proper publicity and extension services in a society. Therefore, in such small time space birth rate cannot be brought down to this level. This gets clear to some extent, through the avoidance of state's population policy, 2000. Decline in death rate depends on health and medical facilities, nutrition, social awareness as well as gender equality among others. Despite this, if IMR comes down to 72 by 2007, neither birth rate nor death rate can be brought down upto the targetted level. All in all, there is need for special initiatives for population control. It is so because in the era of target free family planning approach, in the absence of sufficient awareness and health and family planning facilities, population growth rate cannot be checked as per the desire of the Tenth Plan in Uttar Pradesh.

Planning

Planning is such an exercise that works as an important and forceful link between information strategy and programme implementation. Here, we cannot deal in detail implicit problems and paradoxes of state level planning in the Indian context. However, for an effective planning mechanism in Uttar Pradesh, following points need attention of the planners.

- There is need for a suitable information system which is indispensable for guidance at different levels of planning process. It is an irony that once "Economic and Statistics Division" and "Perspective Planning Division" of the State were well established and reputed bodies which were not only compiling and presentating time series of data in excellent form, but also through research and analysis a proper analytical framework was getting prepared. Given this, now there is urgent need for proper collection and compilation of data as well as their updation with changing base years.

- Suitable awareness about resources and their timely exploitation not only becomes helpful in enhancing direct effectiveness of resources but also by increasing the indirect benefits rapidly, it can be instrumental in making the process of development sustainable and all-inclusive.
- A clear and objective target and appropriate strategy are indispensable for the success of any plan. But hazy picture of resources, lack of awareness about programmes among the people are not helpful in getting the desired results despite of favourable circumstances otherwise.
- For a successful strategy, it is essential that strategy and targets for any time schedule must be made known well in time. Generally such problems cannot be overcome in the absence f proper sequencing and coordination of various links.
- It is in-built deficiency in the planning mechanism of India and Uttar Pradesh that we plan our strategy based on any preceding population. This brings in tensions in the planning system since its very beginning. This is, in fact, away from reality.

IV. Health and Medical Facilities

In the process of economic development, it has been realized that it should be such that all are benefitted and these benefits are able to sustain the development in the long run. There, at the global level efforts are being made to bring in the focus such components of human development, that benefits every member of the society. In this sequence we can highlight annual effort of the UNDP initiated since 1990 in the form of Human Development Report. This report regularly analyses various dimensions of human development. This has special emphasis on health and medical facilities. Keeping this into account, we are evaluating the Tenth Plan of Uttar Pradesh.

In the Tenth Plan, it is claimed to provide special thrust to health and medical facilities. At the same time it is argued to frame its health strategy in the framework of National Health Policy. This makes clear that the state lacks its own suitable and effective health strategy, which needs to be chalked out. Besides this, the way needs have been pointed out and targets have been specified by the Tenth Plan, they appear to be only ritual lacking proper propelling force.

Still, if we make an attempt to examine resource position for health and medical facilities in Uttar Pradesh during the Tenth Plan period, it is noted that an outlay of Rs. 2044.8 crore has been approved. Out of this Rs. 993.9 crore is under the Externally Aided Programme (EAPs), whereas, Rs. 329.5 crore is under Prime Minister Gramodaya Yojana (PMGY) and another Rs. 21.4 crore has been under the Eleventh Finance Commission disbursement. Here, major doubt is raised over the exploitation of EAP at desired level because important source is not being exploited due to lack of proper strategy in Uttar Pradesh. In the year 2002-03, actual expenditure on health and medical facilities has been only 270.4 crore against an outlay of Rs. 313.3 crore. The situation got worse in the following year of 2003-04 when actual expenditure was lowered sharply at Rs. 197.5 crore against an outlay of Rs. 339.4 crore. The outlay for 2004-05 was Rs. 330.1 crore, lower than the preceding year. Thus, the total outlay of the first three years of the Tenth Plan itself has been only 48 per cent of the total outlay on this sub-sector. The actual expenditure has been still lower. Under such circumstances, targets for health and medical facilities are hard to be fulfilled. However, it is another fact that the expenditure on this sub-sector during the Ninth Plan was two per cent of the total, as against three per cent for the period from First to Ninth Plans. Against this, the outlay during the Tenth Plan is four per cent of the total plan outlay.

Although all the activities of the sub-sector would be hit due to shortfall of resources during the Tenth Plan, still the sectors which appear to get worst affected are required expansion of the health centres. Even, within this the most affected are the construction of mainly Community Health Centres. In fact, from the latter it is expected that by having one CHC at every block level, various health and medical facilities would be provided with sufficiently in the close vicinity of the villages. During the Tenth Plan period 200 CHCs are planned to be brought up. But in the first two years only 55 could be completed.

V. Voluntary Sector

Voluntary sector has existed in the society from early ages and these have played crucial social and economic roles successfully. However, in modern times role of voluntary agencies has increased manifold. In India also it is argued that the voluntary organizations have important role in development to play, which are as important as three levels of government and other private sector participation. Voluntary sector or organization is supposed to non-profit making, non-governmental and autonomous body, which is helped by general public and others in terms of resources. Voluntary agencies are engaged in various types of responsibilities like development, association and participation, and other short-term activities. Its activities are carried out by independent and other nominated/ selected persons by the members and these are financially independent agencies. IN fact, in contemporary context its relevance is felt because the gap between government's activities and public expectations is widening. This gap might be bridged by non-governmental voluntary agencies. There has been tremendous change in the activities of such organizations recently. These appear to incorporate emerging requirements.

In Uttar Pradesh also, role of voluntary agencies has been acknowledged. This gets obvious from the fact that in five year plans allocations, these are mentioned properly. The state government has taken many steps in recent years which are quite helpful to these organizations in terms of their promotions and acceptability. Moreover, in the plans, there is provision of outlays for carrying out activities only through voluntary agencies. However, the most important impediment in Uttar Pradesh, like elsewhere in the country, there is no proper and updated data bank about mushrooming growth of such organizations. To bridge this data gap, the State Planning Institute is seized of the matter but it also finds numerous difficulties in accomplishment of this task. By having a proper and updated data bank of voluntary agencies, the various arms of the government may have easy option of selecting the best ones to achieve the objectives of various government plans besides having effective coordination with them. However, the state still lacks any authentic and comprehensive list of such agencies. It is imperative to know various aspects of a voluntary organizations like what are its area of specialization; what are its experiences in various types of activities; what is the quality of the works accomplished so far by them; what is its image in the public; who are the persons and their images associated with it; and what are other efforts were made to mobilize resources other than the various organs of the government in fulfillment of their stated objectives. Outlays under plans for voluntary organizations are shown in Table 3. Following points come to the fore after going through it.

- Government has recognized the role of voluntary organizations and it is evident from the fact that there is provision for plan allocations.
- During the Ninth Plan an outlay of Rs. 169.3 crore (at 1996-97 prices) was approved to spent through voluntary organizations. However, actual expenditure was lower by 28 per cent.
- In the Tenth Plan, play outlay has been increased substantially to Rs. 536 crore as compared to the preceding plan. It is 0.9 per cent of the total plan outlay whereas it was 0.5 per cent in the Ninth Plan.
- During the Tenth Plan, out of the above plan outlay for the voluntary organizations, 80 per cent was

allocated for the agriculture sector whereas no provision has been made for social welfare, nutrition, etc.

- Even in the Tenth Plan also, there is no clear-cut resemblance between outlay and expenditure. This gets obvious from the experience of the first three years.

On the whole, it can be argued that for voluntary organizations the state government has no clear awareness and policy. Given this backdrop, it is difficult to derive any inference from the size and pattern of expenditures on or through such organizations. Therefore, there is no clear strategy about their monitoring and evaluation. Therefore, it becomes indispensable that there is proper and sufficient information about all aspects of voluntary organizations and it is also considered seriously that these agencies are mobilizing resources from non-governmental sector also. Otherwise, these will become another type of parasites on government's hard earned resources.

VI. A Synthesis

From the above discussion, it gets obvious that for long term development role of education, health, etc. is vital. Besides, it could exploit these avenues sufficiently, it would play decisive role in overall development of the state. Otherwise also, there is increased thrust on human capital at the national and international levels of strategy of formulations. Whereas it is a challenge in the given scenario, with prudent strategy formulation it can be converted into windows of opportunity. To provide them the shape of reality various forces are required to be synthesized whether there are governmental or non-governmental or even if there are through large public participation. We can sum up above discussion in the following points.

In Uttar Pradesh, increasing tendency of growth rate of population continues. Besides, birth rate, death rate and infant mortality rate are still very high.

- Growth of population makes the stagnating economic scenario further limited.
- Although improvement in education has been remarkable, still it is far behind the targeted range.
- There is need to pay special attention towards women literacy and education.
- From the view point of qualitative improvement, education at various levels needs to be given universality, be it medical education, technical education or the higher education in Uttar Pradesh.
- Lack of well-defined health policy comes to surface prominently in the state.
- It is indispensable to make qualitative improvements in health and medical areas. Pervasiveness of poverty and hunger, increasing population growth, illiteracy, etc. call for larger government participations and its pro-active role in this regard.
- Dynamic change in the planning system of the state along with encouraging larger public participation would become more fruitful and rewarding.

VII. Some Major Prospects

- Literacy would induce human development on the one hand and at the same it would be helpful in ameliorating poverty in the state.
- Whereas on the one hand quality embedded higher education, medical education and technical education is capable of attracting students from other parts of the country and abroad to enrich educational institutions and thus making financially viable, on the other hand this situation will equip the human resources to face the world successfully and exploit the situation in our favour.
- Quality embedded health and medical services would be instrumental in effective human resource development and this in turn would put a cap on growing population in the state.

- Whereas rapidly growing population in Uttar Pradesh is a big challenge presently as well as in future, this challenge might be turned into vital opportunity through effective human resource planning. It is because the state would be blessed with growing young population due to rising population in near future when many other parts of the country and other important countries would be facing scarcity of young population due to stagnant population.
- It would be more prudent to invite greater public participation to achieve desired rate of success instead of blindly increasing the dependency on voluntary organizations who have still to prove their worth and effectiveness. This can check misuse of public money and at the same time this would become effective tool of public faith through their active and responsible participation.

Table 1

SOME DEMOGRAPHIC FEATURES IN UTTAR PRADESH

India/UP Maximum/Minimum District	*Population Growth Rate (1991-2001 (%)*	*Average Size of Household (2001)*	*Sex Ratio (2001)*	*Sex ratio for 0-6 years (2001)*	*Literacy Rate (%) (2001)*	*Female Literacy Rate (%) (2001)*
India	21.30	5.3	933.0	927.0	64.8	53.7
Uttar Pradesh	25.85	6.5	898.0	915.6	56.3	42.2
Maximum Status (District)	47.19 (Ghaziabad)	8.4 (Sant Ravidas Nagar)	1020.0 (Azamgarh)	969.7 (Bahraich)	74.4 (Kanpur Nagar)	67.5 (Kanpur Nagar)
Minimum Status (District)	12.97 (Bagpat)	5.7 (Lucknow)	839.9 (Mathura)	850.4 (Bagpat)	33.8 (Sravasti)	18.6 (Sravasti)

Table 2

SOME INTER-SATE DEMOGRAPHIC FEATURES

State	Decadal Growth Rate		Sex Ratio	Literacy Rate	Ratio of Urban Population (%)
	1981-91	1991-2001			2001
Andhra Pradesh	24.2	13.9	978	61.1 (51.2)	27.1
Assam	24.2	18.9	932	64.3 (56.0)	12.7
Bihar	23.5	28.4	921	47.5 (33.6)	10.5
Gujarat	21.2	22.5	921	70.0 (58.6)	37.4
Haryana	27.4	28.1	861	68.6 (56.3)	29.0
Himachal Pradesh	20.8	17.5	970	77.1 (68.1)	9.8
Jammu & Kashmir	30.3	29.0	900	54.5 (41.8)	24.9
Karnataka	21.1	17.3	964	67.0 (57.5)	34.0
Kerala	14.3	9.4	1058	90.9 (87.9)	26.0
Madhya Pradesh	27.2	24.3	920	64.1 (50.3)	26.7
Maharastra	25.7	22.6	922	77.3 (67.5)	42.4
Orissa	20.1	15.9	972	63.6 (51.0)	15.0
Punjab	20.8	19.8	874	70.0 (63.6)	34.0
Rajasthan	28.4	28.3	922	61.0 (44.3)	23.4
Tamil Nadu	15.4	11.2	986	73.5 (64.6)	43.9
Uttar Pradesh	25.6	25.8	898	57.4 (43.0)	20.8
West Bengal	24.7	17.8	934	69.2 (60.2)	28.0
India	23.9	21.3	933	65.4(54.3)	27.8

Note: In parentheses, female, literacy rate has been given.

Table 3

PLAN OUTLAYS AND ACTUAL EXPENDITURE FOR VOLUNTARY ORGANIZATIONS (RS. LAKH)

	Ninth Five Year Plan (1997-2002)			*For Tenth 2005 (2002-07)*	*2002-03 (at current prices)*		*2003-04 (at current prices)*		*Plan Outlay (at current prices)*
	Outlay (1996-97 prices)	*Actual expenditure (Current Prices)*	*Actual expenditure (1996-97 prices)*	*Outlay (2001-02 prices)*	*Outlay*	*Actual Expenditure*	*Outlay*	*Actual Expenditure*	
Agriculture	—	1359.63	1040.19	42874.00	599.90	599.90	7683.00	7683.00	530.61
Soil and Water conservation	—	479.75	369.66	1963.00	546.00	276.00	545.00	228.00	591.00
Water supply and sanitation	13142.93	10631.68	8656.30	6750.00	6250.00	3478.04	1310.00	2440.82	300.00
Women welfare	522.53	1096.24	863.01	1591.91	544.01	444.45	—	170.74	713.02
SC/ST Welfare	3190.00	437.25	362.32	424.82	138.86	48.24	394.87	1.01	2434.94
Social Welfare	72.00	—	—	—	—	—	—	—	—
Nutrition	—	1116.01	856.38	—	—	560.23	—	452.25	—
Total	16927.46	15120.56	12147.85	53604.10	8078.97	5406.64	9932.57	10976.31	4569.07

13

LIVING CONDITION AND SURVIVAL STRATEGIES OF AGRICULTURAL LABOUR IN UTTAR PRADESH

D.M. Diwakar[1]

Introduction

Living condition of an individual or a household or a society depends mainly *inter-alia* on the level of access to and control over resources, i.e., land, labour and level of surplus (Bhardwaj, 1994:325) that one enjoys. Resources are although created by the labour of the society and should be owned by the society (Marx, 1954 : Vol. I: 47, 53 & 83), but they are hardly accessible and in the control of the producer directly except in socialist relations of production. Level of control over and access to resources are the reflection of the forms of ownership of the means of production, which also indicate the level of development that a society has acquired. In a predominantly agricultural economy like India where capitalist transformation in agriculture is yet to be a dominant form agricultural labourers are subordinated with various informal bondage in the syndrome of backward traditional agriculture where surplus labour with high intensity of poverty remains the general feature (Banerjee, 1993). Although green revolution has made a dent toward dynamising agricultural and resulted initially into higher wage and demand for labour (Jose, 1988; Acharya, 1989; Bhalla, 1993; Vaidyanathan, 1994) and it is also argued that total number of employment days and daily real wage has increased both in agriculture and non-agriculture across the state, which suggest an improvement in the economic status of agricultural labourers households (Sharma, 2001:37) but contrary to this, there is general agreement that labour absorption capacity in agriculture has declined (Bhalla, 1993). Mechanization has also played a role to reduce labour absorption capacity and wages in agriculture (Bharadwaj, 1994:342). Although, the data sources are different which may not be comparable but they have concluded that the increased wages could not be sustained (Parthasarthy, 1996: Unni, 1997). In absence of adequate employment opportunity, agricultural labourers being mostly from the lowest rung of a society have seldom control over the resources for livelihood. Agricultural labourers acquire their resources and means of livelihood in exchange of their wage labour. Wage labour employment opportunities in agriculture in the situation like India have always been subjected to vagaries of monsoon, as level of irrigation has still been very low. Besides this, there are other factors also, which decide the volume of employment opportunities to agricultural labourers, such as: technological development and level of mechanization, cropping intensity, nature of labour market and bargaining weaknesses of labour, etc. Since wage labour employment opportunities are the only important determinant factor for their income, which decides their living condition, prevailing wage rate, gender differentials and economic relations in the society, are important determinants. In this given situation agricultural labourers have to interact and work out their strategies for their survival.

This paper is an attempt to comprehend and analyse living condition and survival strategy of agricultural labourers. This exercise has been divided into four parts. Part one deals with macro overview and confessions of the broad indicators of living conditions of poor households and their determinants. Part two has covered micro variabilities from Uttar Pradesh dealing with labour participation, employment and access to basic amenities. Third part has focussed on case study from Kaushambi district of east U.P., which attempted to include living condition, consumption pattern, indebtedness, and labour market constraints with respect to survival strategies. And finally, fourth part underlines some policy options and concrete prescriptions and the strategies forwarded by the agricultural labourers households themselves to get rid of their hardships.

I. Macro Overview

Out of 49 Less Developed Countries (LDC) designated by the United Nations about 45 countries are importing food grains and 33 are net importers. Food, clothing and shelter still remain as major concern for the fundamental necessity for humanity despite all the tall claims of technological development and progress. An overview of the World Development Report (The World Bank, 2002) reflects global realization of the first among the basic issues of living conditions, i.e. food security. The report envisaged that it is not the declining production rather lack of purchasing power in the hands of the poor people is the core issue. Despite the fact that global food production has been declining demand for food grains has also been declining rapidly and resulting into depressing food prices. The alarming fact that document puts forward that about 820 million people of the world do not get enough food to lead their healthy and productive lives and about 160 million children are seriously under weight for their age (The World Bank, 2002:12). The Report confessed that despite great promise for improving the agriculture of the poor, bio-technology in general and transgenic research in particular have barely begun to be put to work to address the problems of the poor (*Ibid*, p. 24). As a result, people are not waiting to acquire resources and finance before migrating to urban areas. In many countries rural migrants have moved to the cities without the advantage of physical or financial assets or adequate human capital and in absence of effective institutions they are still away from development process. In this process they are alienated from the access to the basic resources particularly to the CPR. The report, however, uses all kinds of rhetoric for inclusive development, decentralization, co-operatives, redundancy of bureaucracy and governance of the state, etc. However, the Report carefully introduces contradictory proposition of private sector and NGOs as the promising agents of change and finally concludes 'the more people are heard the less assets wasted' (*Ibid*, p. 25). If one goes further to scan latest World Employment Report of ILO, there has been general trend of significant increase in rates of unemployment between 1990 and 2000. In some of the cases rate of unemployment has even gone much in the scale of double digit (ILO, 2001; 24, 26, 29, 32, 37). In case of India also incidence of rural unemployment has been increasing in the 1990s compared to 1980s (GOI, 2002: 162) and percentage per annum growth of rural employment has declined (GOI, 2002: 159). Rural employment programmes have failed to create sustainable opportunities of rural employment for absorption of labour (Radhakrishna, 2002:245). Official documents also suggest that income gap has widened from 1:2 to 1:6 (Government of India, 2000). There is apparent decline in annual compound growth rate of area production and yield of agriculture in the post reform decade (1990-91 to 2000-01) (Government of India, 2001-02: p. 186). There is widespread decline across the board in all the states in public sector capital expenditure for agriculture. The highest decline is observed in the resources allocated by the Union Government for agricultural infrastructure. The decline is not confined to investment in irrigation projects; it is rather sharper in other heads related to agricultural development (Chand, 2001:182). Rate of decline in rural poverty, which was 2.75 per cent in 1970s and 1980s has decreased to merely 0.73 per cent and hence rate of decrease in poverty is lower than the rate of increase in rural population (Radhakrishna, 2002). Rate of real consumption expenditure has declined (Rajuldevi, 2001). Despite all these depressing indications, sharp decline in poverty is claimed officially by 1999-2000. However, the methodology adopted for this calculation remained controversial (Vaidyanathan, 2001; Sundaram and Tendulkar, 2001; Sen, 2001).

National Human Development Report, 2001 considered longevity, i.e. ability to live long and healthy life, education, i.e. ability to read, write and acquire knowledge; and command over resources, i.e. ability to enjoy a decent standard of living and have a socially meaningful life as dimensions of well-being (Government of India, 2002: p. 10). Former two dimensions of well-being, i.e. longevity and education are very much determined by the third one, i.e., command over resources. The Report (NHDR, 2001) clearly indicated about considerable difference in the level of attainments of people depending upon their location (rural or urban), sex (male or female) and the social groups (SCs/STs or General) that the person belongs to. Specifically SCs/STs, women and people residing in rural areas have been found with lower level of attainments (NHDR, 2001, p. 11). Thus, it appears that living conditions of deprived sections of the society, women and people belonging to rural areas are yet to be uplifted to the extent that they could be brought to the mainstream of development.

II. Micro Variability

Labour Participation and Employment

In this backdrop of macro overview this paper is an attempt to examine micro context and variabilities. For this purpose Uttar Pradesh has been selected for many obvious reasons: *(i)* this is one of the largest and most populous states of the country; *(ii)* this state is a mix of modernisation and backwardness; *(iii)* its economic zones represents various development stages; (iv) this state represents the regions with agriculture as mainstay for livelihood. According to latest Census of India (2001), about 77.4 per cent of the main workforce in rural area are dependent on agriculture, as it is evident from Table 1. Another important fact that the table reveals is declining proportion of rural agricultural labour force. Particularly percentage of cultivators has decreased from about 72 per cent in 1961 to 49 per cent in 2001. But the percentage of agricultural labourers has gone up significantly. There was only 7 per cent main workers as agricultural labour in rural U.P., which has increased four times higher, i.e., 28.26 per cent in corresponding period in rural Uttar Pradesh. This may reflect increasing landlessness and polarisation in the rural economy of Uttar Pradesh. Labour force participation in general has also been declining if one goes by the data set of NSSO, as given in Table 2. Growth rate of employment has also been declining in rural India as well as in rural U.P. But unlike India as a whole female employment has increased in U.P.

Dealing further with labour participation and employment in agriculture, Rural Labour Enquiry Reports suggest that there was increase in percentage of labour force from 1974-75 to 1977-78, which remained almost stagnant in 1983 and again registered increase in 1987-88. However, there was sharp decline in 1993-94. Even the ratio of agricultural labour with land also declined from 79 per cent in 1987-88 to 62 per cent in 1993-94 (Table 3). Interestingly there is sharp decline in female self-employment and increase in male self-employment. Employment based on salary is almost insignificant. Dominant feature of employment remained as wage employment. Female wage employment in agriculture has slowly been increasing and approaching to equalize the male wage employment, as male wage employment has come down from 80.52 per cent in 1974-75 to 71.29 per cent in 1993-94. However, if one goes by round-wise details, there was sharp decline in male self-employment to the tune of about 11 per cent between 1974-75 and 1977-78 and thereafter improvement of about 5 per cent in 1983. Further decline was noticed in the next round. This shows that no clear picture emerged through round to round data on wage employment. On the one hand, backward agricultural zones with traditional agriculture and surplus labour resulted into lower wage rate and higher intensity of poverty, and on the other hand, green revolution area witnessed, mechanisation, high wage and higher demand for agricultural labour (Banerjee, 1993) initially. However, there is general agreement that labour absorption capacity of Indian agriculture as a whole has declined (Bhalla, 1993). Increase in family participation is another important factor, which reduced employment opportunities of agricultural labour (Government of India, 2000: 65).

It is not employment alone rather wage rate among many other factors are important determinants for living condition of agricultural labour. Rural Labour Enquiry Report on Wage and Earnings for various rounds since 1974-75 suggests that there is increase in daily real wage earnings in agriculture and non-agriculture (Table 4). However, gender difference persists and there is hardly any clear indication of decline in last twenty years so far daily real wage and earnings are concerned. However, data from agricultural wage in India suggest a contrary picture, i.e., there is hardly any increase in real wage (Sharma, 2001: pp. 27-38). Micro studies also suggests that there is an increase in nominal wage in Uttar Pradesh, but there is hardly any increase in real wage (Singh, 1984: 287; NCAER, 1996: 59). Moreover, NSS data for different rounds also indicates increase in incidence of rural unemployment in Uttar Pradesh (Table 5).

Thus, if there is declining trend in employment growth, increasing in incidence of unemployment and there is hardly any indication of increase in daily real wage, no are left for such romanticism that the living condition of agricultural labour has improved. However, one may argue the effects of infrastructure development and state intervention in terms of crash programmes for basic amenities for poor of which agricultural labour community may be the beneficiary. But there are findings that investment in infrastructure has been declining (Chand 2001). Another factor could be the benefit of the development of science and technology. Undoubtedly, technological development has reduced the hardship of lives of general masses and poor households to the extent that they could acquire access to the benefit of the development of science and technology. But it is still debatable, whether percolation of such factors could be effective to the households of the poor at the lowest rung of the society. This can be judged through a few indicators of basic amenities particularly households without access to these amenities, which indicate about the unfinished agenda and need to be taken up on priority basis.

Poverty and Access to Resources

Various rounds of NSS data show overall decline in poverty but if one goes with data for rural and social groups it is very much clear that 'rural poverty is becoming increasingly concentrated among households whose primary source of income is casual labour both in agriculture and rural non farm sector (The World Bank, 2002a:35). Poverty ratio is seen higher all through different rounds of the NSS data shown in table 5a. If one deals with poverty incidence and land ownership as an indicator of access to land resources, it is very much evident that land ownership and poverty incidence has inverse relationship. Table 5b suggests that as the size of ownership holdings above two hectares incidence of poverty declines significantly. It is found that 'access to well watered and fertile lands is constrained by the facts that their hamlets tend to be located in marginal land areas more prone to flooding or salanity' (The World Bank, 2002a:52).

Access to Basic Amenities

One of the significant determinants of living conditions for a household is access to basic amenities such as food, clothing, house, health and education. We can hardly escape the fact that despite efforts that have been made through community development programmes, target group approaches and general development, sizeable sections of the society are still to get their square meals and meaningful employment. As Table-6 shows, fairly large section of the households are surviving with kutcha and semi-pucca houses, practically no toilet facility and still waiting for safe drinking water and clean environment. The document of the World Bank records that 'in many rural villages, SC/Sts reside in separate hamlets at the edge of the village, and they are denied access to community infrastructure (especially clean water) and other common property resources shared by members of middle and upper castes' (The World Bank: 2002:52). This gives a general picture about the living condition of the poor households of the U.P. State as a whole. Further investigation through case study may provide basis to understand the ground realities in the context of living condition and survival strategies of agricultural labourers.

III. Case Study

Microscopic view through case study of living condition of agricultural labourers from Kaushambi district of East Uttar Pradesh may provide some basis to comprehend ground realities closely. Rationale to select this district may sound arbitrary but we depended much on district census details. According to 1991 census, a district having most labour concentration, i.e. Allahabad was selected for this purpose. At the second stage most agricultural labour populated tehsil and block, i.e. Chail and Nevada respectively was selected for case study purposes. This development block and Tehsil later carved out from Allahabad and now it is the part of a new district Kaushambi. Ten villages and ten households of agricultural labourers from each village, were selected for case study. This study since is confined to east U.P. lacks generalisation capacity for the state as a whole. However, it represents labour concentrated region of backward agriculture.

Sample study suggests that selected households mainly engaged in agriculture for wage labour (89 per cent of the household) however, sizeable income they derive from non-agriculture, i.e. 45 per cent. This also suggests that wage paid in agriculture is quite lower than that of non-agriculture, as they spend more days in agriculture than non-agriculture. It is also evident from wage rate prevailing in the sample district (Table 8). In most of the cases agricultural wage is less than half of the prescribed minimum wage in agriculture of U.P. (Rs. 58) for a day. If one goes by the demographic details it appears that there has been complementarities and overlapping in their employment and income in agriculture and non-agricultural work. It is evident from Table 7 that strength of total workforce is mainly of agricultural labourers who also work for non-agriculture activities. Total person days employment per household estimated are about 383.92, which comes to about 150 person days employment per worker in a year. These include, casual, seasonal, regular and other kinds of employment. Because of inadequate and the seasonality of the nature of employment mainly in agriculture and non-agriculture as well and lower wage rate in agriculture they move to non-agricultural rural employment in brick kiln and construction works. They hardly migrate to distant places for supplementing their earnings. On an average only Rs. 117 annually per household they earn through migrant labour work. They earn on an average Rs. 7077.44 per annum per household from agricultural wage (51 per cent) Rs. 6173.30 from non-agricultural wage, i.e. 45 per cent of annual income Rs. 117 from migration and Rs. 168.20 from other sources. From common property resources, they could extract about Rs. 285.34, i.e. 2.1 per cent of the household income. However, in per capita terms their income from agriculture is Rs. 1,222.93 and non-agriculture Rs. 1066.65 and thus, annual per capita income of the household is about Rs. 2387.09. In terms of per capita monthly income of the household for the survey year it is quite lower (Rs. 198.92) than the estimates of below poverty line expenditure for rural U.P., i.e. Rs. 336.88 per capita per month (GOI, 2001).

Household's Living Condition

With such a lower income of bare existence they reside in a pitiable condition. It was not possible to capture their details exhaustively. However, an attempt was made to collect some of the broad features of household's environment, which explain their living condition. Majority of the household (72 per cent) stay in mud built kutcha houses with straw thatched roof. Only 3 per cent of the households have semi-pucca houses and 25 per cent have pucca houses. Technology has undoubtedly played a significant role to improve the living condition of the poor. About 99 per cent households of the sample district have access to public hand pump for drinking water, but 97 per cent of households attend their natural call in the field of their owner farmers though unwillingly or often on the road side. About 47 per cent of the households do not have quilt, 35 per cent do not have even blanket to cope with chilly cold. Those who have blanket or quilt, most of them have only one quilt or blanket and they do not have mosquito net at all. On an average two pairs of shoes per household are with them. Most of the members of the households remain barefoot even in winter of hot summer. Only 3 per cent households have wooden cot. No other furniture was found with them. About 68 per cent of them do not have a lantern and 99 per cent do not have simple modern lamp. Only 3 per cent households have stove. About 50 per cent of the households have one bicycle, 15 per cent have one watch, 9 per cent have one torch. Most of them have more than one rope knit cot (char payee), one wooden door, and one water-collecting vessel. Mainly they have mix of mud, aluminium and steel utensils for domestic use. Even at the age of information explosion only 1 per cent households own radio, no one has television. Only 3 per cent of the households have Saving Bank Account.

Consumption Pattern Indebtedness and Survival Strategy

With the income of bare minimum to survive well below the income of poverty line estimate, there is hardly any need to undertake an exercise in order to understand consumption pattern. But with a view to know their deficit level and ability to cope with deficient environment it is important. Although, while calculating deficiency we depended on reporting of the household for requirement, which may sometimes suffer over estimation, one may not rule out the fact that they are only the best judge of their bare minimum requirement. It is evident from Table-9 that despite hard labour, in the syndrome of less employment opportunity and depressed wages they reported deficiency of about 22 per cent in cereals, 32 per cent in cotton clothes, 72 per cent in woollen and 20.5 per cent in housing maintenance expenditure. Common property resources (CPR) provide a great relief in meeting the expenditure of non-vegetable items, about 22 per cent other food items, and about 70 per cent expenditure on housing maintenance. Thus, CPR played an important role for the survival of the poor households.

Miserable income as a result of lower volume of employment amidst depressed wage and gender wage differential agricultural labour households are left with the only option, i.e. usury trap of moneylenders in absence of effective public credit support and state intervention. This may be with the condition of attached labour to secure labour supply, high rate of interest, to work at lower wage, access to owner farms field and CP.R (Bharadwaj, 1994: 334). There is strong positive correlation between value of livelihood extracted from CPR and attached and conditional labour loan. The loans are mainly used for consumption and health treatment. As it is evident from Table-10, on an average, there are Rs. 4540 as debt-burden on each household. Out of this loan over 61.56 per cent are from moneylenders. These are either attached or conditional loan whereas Rs. 1745 are the institutional loan. Although, institutional loans, in principle, are exclusively for production purposes under various schemes of employment and income generations, the amounts of loan have been used for consumption and health treatment purposes as well.

Labour Market Constraints and Survival Strategy

With the given situation of hardships and in absence of effective rescue from the public institution, labourers are forced to compromise and face economic as well as extra economic coercions. Labourers can hardly afford to resist. If they refuse to work at the lower wage rate, they are stopped to enter the farm of the owner farmer for collecting green fodder, their animals are restricted for grazing and their families are not allowed to attend their natural call. These strategies are adopted by the employer farmers to secure cheap labour supply at their demand (Lieten & Srivastava, 1999: 172). Since, there is hardly any alternative in the situation to under formation of labour market (Bharadwaj, 1994:333), agricultural labourers have to depend on their owner farmers to meet their crises. The situation has further been worsened due to subdivision and fragmentation of holdings, which has resulted into increased family participation of owner farmers. With a surplus labour, backward agricultural and lack of infrastructure particularly, cropping intensity and cropping pattern which has not changed significantly, not only the bargaining weakness but also the vulnerability of agricultural labourers has further been aggravated. Thus, the process of the expansion of employment opportunity has been blocked. Widespread drought in many states including U.P. will further aggravate misery of agricultural labourers. They are forced to accept below subsistence wage in absence of employment opportunity. Even for non-agricultural works in construction and brick kiln, influx of contract labour from the outside has depressing effect on labour household (Bhalla, 1993). Distribution of Gram Sabha land has been a point of hope for agricultural landless labourers to improve their living condition. But in most of the cases the possession is yet to be ensured. Strikingly when the agriculture of U.P. went for consolidation of holdings, Gram Sabha land was not consolidated. As a result, pieces of Gram Sabha land remained scattered and very much in the control of dominant class of the society, which are practically difficult for agricultural labourers to have meaningful possession. Even if they are ensured possession, their entry to that plot is always subjected to extra-economic coercion. It appears that strategically dominant landowners could successfully manipulated in their favour to retain their control on rural economy and polity directly or indirectly for all practical purposes, of course in absence of effective consolidation and assertion of agricultural labour households.

Some indications of strategies can be identified from the data presented in Table 11. It is evident from table that family size and workers have significantly positive correlation with non-agricultural earnings. Access to CPR is closely related to family size. This indicates non-workers role in collecting livelihood from CPR. CPR in general is in control of rich farmers and dominant people of the society. Attached labour gets better access than others. If labourers deny to be attached, they are restricted to get an access. This makes their life worse and left with no option but to compromise and attach themselves for which they get loan also at the lower rate of interest. So long farmers require their labour for their work, concession on interest continues but when the work is over the labourers are charged with higher rate of interest. Moreover, non-agricultural worker are significantly correlated with attached labour loan, as they are mostly working in brick kiln. Most strikingly there is negative correlation between money lending rate of interest and female labour participation. This suggests that increasing female labour participation ensures loan at lower rate of interest and vice-versa. In this sense female labour acquires more reliable position than male labour perhaps in terms of their bargaining weakness and vulnerability. However, these dimensions need to be investigated further. Thus, through all kinds of strategies, i.e. borrowing credit, tying in labour for lower wages and access to CPR, employment in non-agricultural sector to supplement income, etc., the labour households manage their survival possible despite all the heavy odds.

IV. Policy Options and Strategies

In the above analysis there are enough evidence to conclude that despite tall claims of development both at macro and micro levels there are enough indications that living conditions in the rural areas is still difficult and at subhuman level in absence of sustainable employment opportunities. The case study also suggests that agricultural labourers are yet to get access to their basic amenities. Their living condition is miserable and they have to struggle for their survival and subsistence livelihood and almost dependent on owners farmers strategies of production and investment as well as their choice of hire system (Bharadwaj, 1994: pp. 340-341). They are in the clutches of moneylender-cum-owner farmers in absence of effective state intervention and credit support from the public institutions. And the root of all these hardships lies in absence of meaningful adequate sustainable employment even if one takes note of second labour commission report because implementation of proper wage rate is a big question. Despite all features of depressing note and backwardness in agriculture, 'yet there is plenty of scope to increase employment in agriculture in this region. Efforts to push up the yields of existing crops by encouraging increased proper use of intermediate inputs specially fertilizer, and by improving agricultural infrastructure specially irrigation would be most productive of jobs in the low farm labour productivity regions' (Bhalla, 1993:462). Imperative need to expand effective irrigation network in agriculture is reinforced after severe failure of monsoon this year. Since the farm size is smaller in this region, under-formation of land market reinforces the under-formation of wage labour market (Bharadwaj, 1994: pp. 333-336), there is imperative need of expanding employment in rural areas through need based activities in non-agricultural sector as well. Diversification of agriculture and labour intensive technological upgrading may lead to expected agricultural productivity and employment. Thus, there is strong imperative to create wider economic opportunities, enhance capabilities and provide effective safety nets in order to protect the most vulnerable section of the society (The World Bank 2002a:53-54)

In order to get rid of unemployment and improve living condition, concrete prescriptions of activities for development, have been forwarded by the sample households through generating employment. The activities are: construction of road, ponds for irrigation and aquaculture, canals, dairy, bakery, carpet weaving, bidi making, training for stitching and embroidery, etc. The labourers of the sample village have argued mainly for expansion of employment opportunities. According to them rest would follow: such as, wage differential will be narrowed. With the implementation of minimum wage, income of the family will improve, which will not only lead to better living condition but also enhance capability and skills of rural labour. Needless to mention that enhancing the capabilities and skills of the rural labour is one of the major areas, which remained neglected grossly and need to be focussed (Vyas, 2002: 113-113). Vocational training for the required employment opportunities of their interest as they have suggested will be a valuable input in this direction.

Women can be the most effective agents of change to

improve living condition of the rural labour through their direct involvement in income generating schemes, health awareness collective initiatives, vocational training and social management. But the solution lies in improving purchasing power in the hands of poor through meaningful employment, direct access to land to the households, and self-managed co-operatives. Undoubtedly the welfare state has to play a significant role to organize, sensitise and train them with the help of identified sensitive and genuine catalyst agents from bureaucracy, NGOs and Society who will ultimately be ready to withdraw their presence in due course of direct participatory development. This will be in-built in their exercise. But with the growing market intervention this appears difficult in coming days. In a market economy, there would be market forces that drive the economy towards efficient capital utilization; but although labour power becomes a commodity there is no such inbuilt force on the market that tends to increase the participation of labourers providing them livelihood (Bharadwaj, 1994: L376).

Moreover, exception apart, developmental agents of state directly or indirectly have created dependence, siphoned out the resources and left them in lurch worsening their situation. Thus, welfares approach may not seem a viable solution but remain better than the market alternative, which is guided by the profit solely. Direct participation has potential strength to change the course of development. The need is to organize them for themselves until they start effective direct participation and exercising their power of check and balance to decide their destiny through their own institutional framework. This requires evolving a comprehensive package innovative institutional framework for establishing co-operation and co-ordination within labour intensive small-scale activities (Bharadwaj, 1994:362). However, this is an uphill task, which needs intensive reflection, action and social praxis.

Table 1

PERCENTAGE DISTRIBUTION OF RURAL MAIN WORKERS IN UTTAR PRADESH

Industrial Category	*1961*	*1971*	*1981*	*1991*	*2001**
Total Agricultural Workers	78.8	86.5	86.1	84.5	77.39
1. Cultivators	71.7	67.3	69.9	62.6	49.13
2. Agricultural Laboures	7.1	19.2	16.2	21.9	28.26
B. Household Industry	5.6	3.1	3.0	3.2	4.41
C. Other Workers	15.6	10.4	11.1	12.3	18.21

* Figures include Uttaranchal for Comparability.

Source: Census, Government of India, Various Issues.

Table 2

RURAL LABOUR FORCE PARTICIPATION AND GROWTH OF EMPLOYMENT IN INDIA AND U.P.

Year/	*India*			*Uttar Pradesh*		
Round	*Male*	*Female*	*Total*	*Male*	*Female*	*Total*
Labour Force Participation						
1983	88.7	51.0	70.3	89.7	39.7	66.0
1993-94	87.6	48.8	68.8	88.4	34.7	63.3
1999-2000	85.4	45.6	66.2	84.3	33.2	60.5
Growth Rate of Employment						
1983 to 1993-94	2.0	1.5	1.8	2.2	0.8	1.8
1993-94 to 1999-2000	1.6	0.8	1.3	1.4	1.3	1.4

Source : NSSO, 38th, 50th and 55th Rounds.

Table 3

CHANGING PROPORTION OF AGRICULTURAL LABOURERS AND PERCENTAGE CHANGE IN THEIR EMPLOYMENT STRUCTURE IN UTTAR PRADESH

Year	*Changing Proportion of:*		*Self-Employment*		*Wage Employment*		*Salary Basis*		*Total*	
	Agricultural Labour	*Agricultural Labourers with Land*	*Male*	*Female*	*Male*	*Female*	*Male*	*Female*	*Male*	*Female*
1974-75	15.81	56.80	19.10	47.09	80.52	52.91	0.38	—	100.00	100.00
1977-78	18.11	60.88	29.67	42.92	69.33	56.67	1.00	0.41	100.00	100.00
1983	18.01	53.62	24.26	30.04	74.75	69.13	0.99	0.83	100.00	100.00
1987-88	20.08	79.10	24.76	31.03	70.68	67.43	4.56	1.54	100.00	100.00
1993-94	15.31	62.14	27.10	29.30	71.29	69.96	1.61	0.74	100.00	100.00

Source: Rural Labour Enquiry, 1974-75 and 1977-78: Final Report on Wages and Earnings; 1983 and 1987-88 : Report on Consumption Expenditure; 1993-94 : Report on General Characteristics of Rural Labour Households and Report on Employment and Unemployment, Labour Bureau, Chandigarh, Shimla.

Table 4

DAILY REAL WAGE EARNINGS OF AGRICULTURAL LABOUR IN U.P.
(1980-81 = 100)

Year	In Agriculture		Non-Agriculture		Gender Wage Differentials (%)	
	Male	*Female*	*Male*	*Female*	*Agrl.*	*Non-Agrl.*
1974-75	3.85	3.01	4.42	2.59	78.18	58.60
1977-78	4.86	3.54	6.66	4.18	72.84	62.76
1983	3.71	2.75	5.05	2.11	74.12	41.78
1987-88	5.89	4.57	7.02	4.58	77.59	65.24
1993-94	7.49	5.70	10.37	6.15	76.10	59.31

Source: Rural Labour Enquiry : Report on Wage and Earnings, for respective years, Labour Bureau, Chandigarh, Shimla.

Table 5

INCIDENCE OF RURAL UNEMPLOYMENT IN INDIA AND U.P.

Year	India			Uttar Pradesh		
	Male	*Female*	*Total*	*Male*	*Female*	*Total*
1983	1.4	0.7	1.1	0.8	0.1	0.6
1993-94	1.5	0.8	1.2	0.9	0.0	0.7
1999-2000)	1.7	1.1	1.5	0.9	0.3	0.8

Source : NSSO, 38th, 50th and 55th Rounds.

Table 6

ACCESS TO BASIC AMENITIES IN RURAL, U.P.

Basic Amenities	*1981*	*1991*	*1993-94*
A. Housing			
(a) HH with Pucca House	21.56	32.70	32.20
(b) HH with Semi Pucca House	37.55	33.60	37.10
(c) HH with Kutcha House	40.89	33.70	30.80
B. Toilet Facility			
(a) HH with Toilet Facility	—	6.44	—
(b) SCs with Toilet Facility	—	2.60	—
C. Drinking Water			
(a) HH with Safe Drinking water	25.31	56.62	—
(b) SCs with Safe Drinking Water	—	51.94	—
(c) SCs without Safe Drinking Water and Toilet	—	45.58	—

Source: Government of India, National Human Development Report, Planning Commission, New Delhi.

Table 7

DEMOGRAPHIC FEATURE OF AGRICULTURAL LABOUR HOUSEHOLDS IN SAMPLE VILLAGES OF KAUSHAMBI DISTRICT

Item	*Male*	*Female*	*Children*	*Total*
Family Size	1.33	1.32	3.36	6.01
Total Workers	1.31	1.22	0.03	2.56
Agricultural Workers	1.31	1.22	0.03	2.56
Non-Agricultural Workers	1.23	0.13	0.00	1.36
Employment in Agriculture (Persondays/HH)	120.37	124.88	0.50	245.75
Employment in Non-Agriculture (Persondays/HH)	131.08	7.09	0.00	138.17
Total Employment (Persondays/HH)	251.45	131.97	0.50	383.92

Source: Field Survey, 2000-01.

Table 8

OPERATION-WISE EMPLOYMENT AND WAGE RATE IN AGRICULTURE OF SAMPLE DISTRICT OF U.P.

Agriculture Operation	*Person Days Employment*	*Wage Rate*	
		Male	*Female*
1. Ploughing and Sowing	8.81	25.50	20.00
2. Transplantation	44.07	29.00	35.70
3. Weeding	43.98	26.70	29.50
4. Harvesting	117.75	26.70	29.40
5. Threshing	10.03	60.62	3.86
6. Other Agriculture Works	21.11	38.08	16.16

Source: Field Survey, 2000-01.

Table 9

CONSUMPTION PATTERN AND DEFICIENCY IN AGRICULTURAL LABOUR HOUSEHOLD

Item	*Percentage Managed From*			*Percentage unattended Deficiency by any means*
	Wage Earnings and Loan and Advances	*CPR Access*	*Other source: public and Private*	
A. Basic Needs				
1. Food Items				
(a) Cereals	76.40	0.65	0.0	22.85
(b) Pulses	82.30	1.40	0.0	16.30
(c) Vegetables	45.00	20.00	10.0	25.0
(d) Meat, Fish & Eggs	22.30	32.70	0.0	45.00
(e) Milk & Fruits	13.00	00.00	0.0	87.00
(f) Other Food items	76.05	21.70	0.0	2.25
2. Clothing				
(a) Cotton	57.35	0.00	10.85	32.40
(b) Woolen	25.80	0.20	2.00	72.00
3. Housing	9.50	70.00	0.00	20.50
4. Health	84.35	0.50	0.00	15.15
5. Education				
(a) Boys	54.50	0.00	0.00	45.50
(b) Girls	17.50	0.00	0.00	82.50
6. Drinking Water	00.00	0.00	100.00	0.00
B. Supplementary				
1. Festivals	95.08	0.00	0.00	4.92
2. Social Function and Relation	99.50	0.00	0.00	0.50
3. Entertainments	90.00	0.00	0.00	10.0
4. Other Expenditure	86.50	0.00	0.00	13.50

Source: Field Survey, 2000-01.

Table 10

INDEBTEDNESS OF AGRICULTURAL LABOUR HOUSEHOLDS

Dimensions of Use of Loan	*Moneylender's Loan*			*Institutional Loan*	*Total*
	Attached Labour Loan	*Other Conditional Loan*	*Total Loan*		
Consumption	985	377	1362	400	1762
Production	176	60	236	1345	1581
Health Treatment	948	249	1197	--	1197
Total	2109	686	2795	1745	4540

Source: Field Survey, 2000-01

Table 11

CORRELATION MATRIX

	Family Size	*Female Labour Participation*	*Total Workers*	*Total Workers in Agriculture*	*Total Non-Agricultural Workers*
Annual Earning from Non-Ag. Wage Labour	0.288**	0.306**	0.422**	0.422**	0.493**
Value of Livelihood from CPR	0.321**	0.091	0.107	0.107	0.184
Attached Labour Loan	0.195	0.151	0.182	0.182	0.256*
Rate of Interest	0.00	-0.208*	-0.156	-0.156	-0.075

** Significant at 0.01 level (2-tailed).
* Significant at 0.05 level (2-tailed).

Source: Field Survey, 2000-01.

References

Acharya, S., (1989): Agricultural Wages India: A Disaggregated Analysis, *Indian Journal of Agricultural Economics,* Vol. 44, No. 2.

Banerjee, A. (1993): The Impact of New Economic Policy on Agricultural Labour, *Indian Journal of Agricultural Economics,* Vol. 48, No. 3, July-September.

Bhalla, Sheila (1993): The Dynamics of Wage Determination and Employment Generation in Indian Agriculture, *Indian Journal of agricultural Economics,* Vol. 48, No. 3, July-September.

Bharadwaj, K. (1994): "Accumulation, Exchange and Development," Sage, New Delhi.

Chand, R. (2002): "Emerging Trends and Issues in Public and Private Investments in Indian Agriculture : A State-wise Analysis," *Indian Journal of Agricultural Economics,* Vol. 56, No. 2, April-June.

Government of India (2002): *National Human Development Report, 2001,* Planning Commission, New Delh.

Government of India (2000): *Mid-Term Appraisal of Ninth Five Year Plan,* Planning Commission, New Delhi.

Government of India, *Economic Survey,* 2001-02, Ministry of Finance.

Government of India (2001): *Poverty Estimates for 1999-2000,* Planning Commission, New Delhi, 22nd February.

International Labour Organization (2002): *World Employment Report, 2001,* Geneva, pp. 16, 24, 26, 29, 32, 37.

Jose, A.V., (1988): "Trends in Real Wages of Agricultural Labourers," *Economic And Political Weekly,* Vol. 9, No. 12.

Lieten, G.K. and Ravi Srivastava (1999): *Unequal Partners,* Sage Publications, New Delhi.

Marx, K. (1954): *Capital,* Progress Publishers, Moscow, Vol. I, Reprint, 1986.

National Council of Applied Economic Research (1996): *Human Development Profile of India,* Main Report, Vol. I.

Radhakrishna, R. (2002): "Agricultural Growth, Employment and Poverty : A Policy Perspective," *Economic and Political Weekly,* January 19.

Sen, Abhijit (2001): "Estimates of Consumer Expenditure and Its Distribution : Statistical Priorities after NSS 55th Round," *Economic and Political Weekly,* Vol. 35, No. 51, December 16.

Sharma, H.R. (2001): "Employment and Earnings Agricultural Labourers : A State-wise Analysis," *The Indian Journal of Labour Economics,* Vol. 44, No. 1, January-March.

Singh, A.K. (1984): *Agricultural Development and Rural Poverty*, Ashish Publishing House, New Delhi.

Sundaram, K. and S.D. Tendulkar (2001): "NAS-NSS Estimates of Private Consumption for Poverty Estimation : A Disaggregated Comparison for 1993-94," *Economic and Political Weekly*, January 13.

The World Bank (2002): *World Development Report, Overview 2003: Sustainable Development in a Dynamic World Transforming Institutions, Growth and Quality of Life*, Washington, D.C.

The World Bank (2002a): *Poverty in India: The Challenges of Uttar Pradesh*, Report No. 22323-IN. Washington, D.C.

Vaidyanathan, A. (2001): "Poverty and Development Policy," *Economic & Political Weekly*, May 26.

Vyas, V.S. (2002): "Globalization : Hopes, Realities and Coping Strategy," *Economic and Political Weekly*, March 23.

14

EMPOWERMENT AND SOCIAL JUSTICE IN UTTAR PRADESH

D.R. Sahoo

I. Introduction

Women welfare can be considered as a consequential emergent of planned development. Women constitute the most significant section of general population because of their contribution in terms of both productive and reproductive roles. Women as a category in development process, who facilitate the élan vital owing to its multidimensional potential, ranging from its impact on health and nutrition of a population to the productive roles in the family structure of the society. Hence, women welfare has been comprehended as the most vital element for making development self-propellant.

Present Status

Females with 47.33 percent of total population constitute 7.86 crore in Uttar Pradesh as per 2001 census. Sex ratio has increased by 22 females since last decade, although it is still lower than sex ratio at national level, which stands at 933 in 2001. In comparison to 1991 figures, there is a slight improvement in literacy for females, i.e. 17.83 percent, which is also higher than the improved rate achieved in male literacy (13.98 percent). There are still scopes for improvement at all levels. On participatory level figures follow the same trend. In worker population ratio women comprise only 16.3 percent of the aggregate, against 47.4 percent male ratio in 2001. Index on reproductive health index places (RPI) Uttar-Pradesh at the bottom with score of 22.8.

Keeping in mind the above mentioned background, the objective of the present study is to focus on schemes taken by the government to step up the status of women. Secondly, to assess the performance of the special programmes taken by the government to upgrade the socially disadvantages groups, i.e., SCs and STs Women in the state.

FIGURE 1
NO. OF FEMALES PER ONE THOUSAND MALES IN UP AND INDIA IN DIFFERENT CENUSU

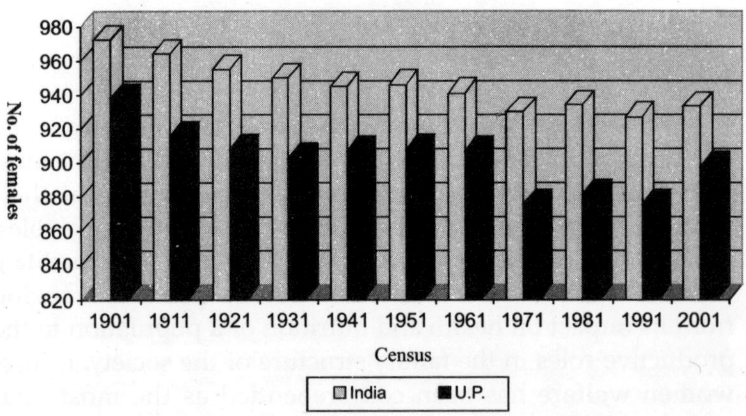

This paper is divided into seven sections. Section I deals with introduction, objectives of this study. Section II highlights the women welfare schemes in 10th plan; while section III describes empowerment of the socially disadvantaged groups in the state. Section IV analyses Empowerment of Scheduled Tribes, while section V deals with Welfare of Minorities. Section VI highlights about Welfare of other Backward Classes, while section VII deals with Summing up and Conclusion.

II. Women Welfare through the Tenth Plan

1. Elimination of all forms of discrimination against women.
2. Promotion of self-reliance through awareness generation at all levels and confidence building.
3. Special treatment on priority level to women of disadvantageous sections of society living below poverty line.
4. Promotion of women participation in decision making process by facilitating active involvement in the Panchayati Raj Institution.

Chairperson, Zila Panchayat	*53.62 percent*
Member, Zila Panchayat	*37.06 percent*
Chairperson, Kshettra Panchayat	*36.71 percent*
Member, Kshettra Panchayat	*35.82 percent*
Gram Pradhan	*35.32 percent*
Member, Gram Panchayat	*37.95 percent*

5. Effective implementation and monitoring of the women component Plan.
6. Accelerating process of women empowerment by organizing women's self help-groups.

Empowerment of women demands life cycle approach. In planning process every stage of their life needs special care, attention and priority. Depending upon the developmental needs at every stage female population is categorized in 5 sub groups. They include:

Girl children in the age group 0-14 years who are nearly 41 per cent of total female population. They deserve special care and attention because from the tender age they suffer gender bias and discrimination.

Adolescent girls in the age group 15-19 years, are nearly 9 per cent of total female population, are very sensitive. In this age group girls are in the preparatory stage for their future productive and reproductive roles in the society and family.

Women in the reproductive age group 15-44 years (nearly 42 per cent of female population) needs special care and attention because of their reproductive role.

Women in the working age group 15-59 years who are nearly 52 per cent of females have different demands like those of education,

Table 1

Financial Performance during 9th and 10th plan (Rs. Lakhs)

Sectors	*Expenditure during the Ninth Plant at 1996-97 prices*	*Tenth Plan Agreed Outlay*	*Annual Plan 2002-03 Approved Outlay*	*Annual Plan 2002-03 Anticipated Expenditure*	*Annual Plan 2003-04 proposed outlay*	*Annual Plan 2004-05 proposed outlay*
1	2	3	4	5	6	7
Social Security and Welfare						
Social Welfare	6027.20	17790.00	3453.00	3453.00	3453.00	
Welfare of Handicapped	990.64	225.00	219.12	219.12	227.12	
Women Welfare	8873.83	3000.00	710.00	344.79	600.00	
Nutrition	16440.86	77947.00	855.00	8550.00	8550.00	
Total-Social Security and Welfare	32332.53	98962.00	12932.12	12566.91	12830.12	
Grand Total: Women Component Plan	75386.30	149983.02	19207.58	18557.63	19131.45	

employment, income generation, decision-making and participation in the development process.

Women in the age group 60 and above (nearly 7 per cent) have limited needs basically related to health, financial emotional support.

Socio-Economic Empowerment

For women welfare sector, during tenth plan period 2002-07 total allocated outlay stands for Rs. 30.00 crores. For first annual plan i.e., 2002-03 it was Rs. 7.10 crores against which total expenditure was Rs. 4.22 crores. In 2003-04 expenditure was Rs. 9.25 crores though the outlay was Rs. 13.03 crores. Annual plan 2004-05 has provided an outlay of Rs. 14.22 crores. Tenth plan is specific and more focused on women welfare as it is aimed to treat development programmes with gender sensitivity.

Table 2

TOTAL OUTLAY AND EXPENDITURE IN 9TH AND 10TH PLAN (RS. IN LAKH)

Plan	*Outlay*	*Expenditure*
Tenth Plan (2002-2007)	3000.00	
Annual Plan (2002-2003)	710.00	422.98
Annual Plan (2003-2004)	1303.00	925.82
Annual Plan (2004-2005)	1422.18	

1. Government is aimed to tackle more deprived women on priority level by providing social security through grant-in-aid schemes. A Maintenance grant of Rs. 125.00 pm is provided to destitute women living below poverty line. In non-plan expenditure 457994 women are being covered. In addition 36591 women were selected from Ambedkar villages during 2002-03. For 2003-04 period proposed outlay for the scheme was Rs. 552.52 lakh Grant-in-aid is also provided up to Rs. 10,000.00 for marriage of widows' daughters. For 2003-04 outlay was proposed of Rs. 19.00 lakh.

2. Scholarship is also provided to girls of general category, who are pursuing higher technical and professional courses living below poverty line. Amount of scholarship is ranging from Rs. 50.00 to Rs. 425.00 pm. During 2003-04 outlay was proposed of Rs. 19.00 lakh for this purpose.
3. Provision is also made for construction and maintenance of observation Homes and Children Homes. These homes provide services like accommodation, medical facilities and opportunities for occupation as well. During 2003-04 period Rs. 18.48 lakh was proposed as an outlay.

   - Grant in aid to women of disadvantageous section of society living below the poverty line
   - Eliminate all forms of discrimination against women
   - Participation and active involvement of women in the Panchayati Raj Institutions
   - Awareness generation at all levels and their confidence building
   - Ensure effective inter-sectoral convergence.
   - Effective implementation and monitoring of the Women Component Plan.
   - Organize women's self-help-groups and thus mark the beginning of a major process of empowering women.
   - Shelter and protection to those who has no one to look after.
   - Effective enforcement of legislation made for their welfare.

4. Decision-making as well as financial assistance are incorporated with the active participation in project Swashakti. It is aimed to form Swashakti groups i.e. self-help groups, in which 10-20 members are included. Target group is provided financial assistance in the form of short-term loan on low interest rate. This is a centrally sponsored scheme for improving

quality of life of strata living below poverty line. Project is working in 18 districts. Implementation is being done by the UP women development corporation and UP land Development Corporation. More than 5200 groups have been formed.

5. Project Swayamsidha (IWEP) is another centrally sponsored scheme. Like Swashakti project it is also a scheme with women's orientation towards ownership of material, social and political resources. It is also working through SHGs and micro credit assistance. It was expected to cover all development blocks by the end of 2003-04 period.
6. Financial assistance to women's co-operative deals exclusively with economic empowerment. In this regard Mahila dairy programme is paving the way for women leadership. Aim of milk procurement was 118.08 litres during 2003 to 2004.

   - Increased self confidence, self esteem and autonomy
   - Ability to articulate needs, make demands and enforce rights both as an individual and in groups
   - Increased access to and control over economic and social resources and the political processes
   - Improved quality of life
   - Participation in planning and decision making process at family and community levels
   - Increased capacity of partner organizations and adoption of improved financial and managerial practices by them for dealing with socially meaningful projects.

7. Swarn Jayanti Gram Swarojgar Yojna is working also through SHGs with a blend of bank credit and government subsidy in rural areas for families living below poverty line. Proposed physical target for Tenth plan under this scheme is 90000 women. For 2003-04 allocation was of Rs. 17.60 crores.

- The vision of this project is to develop empowered women who will :
- Demand their rights from family, community and government;
- Have increased access to, and control over material, social and political resources;
- Have enhanced awareness and improved skills; and
- Be able to raise issues of common concern through mobilization and networking.

8. STEP i.e., Support to Training cum Employment Programme is also working for promotion of employment opportunities for women below poverty line. For annual plan 2002-03 outlay at Rs. 23.74 lakh was sanctioned by central government for covering 1200 beneficiaries.
9. National Maternity Benefit Scheme is launched under National Social Assistance Programme. A sum of Rs. 300.00 is provided to pregnant women for the first two live births. Old age pension scheme has made provision for pension up to Rs. 125.00 pm for women of 65 years and above. It was envisaged to cover 6.15 lakh old women during 2003 to 2004.
10. National Family Benefit Scheme is provided assistance of Rs. 5000 to Rs. 10000 in the event of death of the main bread earner of the family. 22000 families are proposed to get benefit during Tenth plan period.

    - Establishment of self-reliant women's Self-Help-Groups (SHGs);
    - Creation of confidence and awareness among members of SHGs regarding women's status, health, nutrition, education, sanitation and hygiene, legal rights, economic upliftment and other social, economic and political issues;
    - Strengthening and institutionalizing the savings habit in rural women and their control over economic resources;

- Improving access of women to micro-credit;
- Involving women in local level planning; and
- Convergence of services of DWCD and other departments.

11. The state government with the help of World Bank and care runs the Integrated Child Development Scheme. It is a programme for helping women technically and financially, in performing their roles in family especially as mothers. Anganwadi Centres provide institutional web for implementation of this programme, which provides assistance to improve nutritional, and health status of children below six years. It reduces malnutrition not only in children but also provide health security to pregnant and lactating mothers. Besides, early childhood education is another thrust area of this programme, in order to reduce drop out rate of school going children. Its last phase i.e. ICDS III was anticipated to be covered during a time span of five years for 1998-99 to 2003-04. For Tenth plan period an outlay of Rs. 779.47 crores. was proposed, including Rs. 312 crores for PMGY. Because child Nutrition programme has been included in the PMGY. During 2002-03 Rs. 85.50 crores was utilized in 17 projects and number of covered Anganwadi Centres (AWC) was 840. It was aimed to enlarge this figure up to 15600 AWCs during 2004-05 periods, covering 13.08 lakh beneficiaries.

III. Empowerment of the Socially Disadvantaged Groups

Empowerment of Scheduled Castes

The state of Uttar Pradesh has largest population of scheduled castes in India. SCs constitute for 21.4 per cent of the total population of the state, which accounts for 1661 lakh as per 2001 census. Besides, inclination of poverty ratio is much more pronounced as regards SCs. Population living below poverty line constitutes 37.4 per cent of total population of India, of which 48.9 per cent accounts for SCs population. In Uttar

Table 3

TOTAL OUTLAY AND EXPENDITURE FOR VARIOUS SCHEMES

Plan Year	*Outlay/ Expenditure (Rs. In Lakh)*	*No. of Projects*	*No. of AWC*	*Benefi ciaries in Lakh*
Tenth Plan Target/Achievement	77947.00	201	26010	21.85
Annual Plan (2002-03)				
Anticipated Achievement	8550	17	840	3.12
2003-04	8550.00	80	10400	8.72
2004-05	—	120	15600	13.08
2005-06	—	160	21800	17.44
2006-07	—	201	26010	21.85

Pradesh 40.85 per cent and 59.20 per cent stand for total population of BPL strata and SCs population of BPL strata respectively (1993-94 data).

Commitments of the 10th Plan

1. To remove social discrimination of SCs and to implement programmes for both social & economic upward mobility.
2. To take legislative and socio-economies measures for protection of civil rights of the SCs.
3. To implement self-employment generating programmes.
4. To establish Technical training Centres and Industrial Technical Institute to provide education to the students of SCs in the identified area.

Social Empowerment

1. Central core is formed by education, to accelerate the process of shifting concerns from welfare to upliftment where policy is aimed to ensure participation rather than making them beneficiaries merely. Total outlay for 10th plan is Rs. 90000 lakh, of which 61.97 per cent i.e., Rs. 55781 lakh is reserved for education.
2. But as we focus on trend in education at annual plan

level, picture is not quite satisfactory from 2002-05 during three plans expenditure for education shows only 45.66 per cent of the proposed outlay. Total expenditure of 2002-03 and 2003-04 while proposed expenditure for 2004-2005 accounts in aggregate of only Rs. 25472.73. That means 54.34 per cent of tenth plant outlay is reaming for next two plans.

3. As shown in table, education is considered as a whole term process in which desired targets are ranging from pre metric to post metric scholarships. Under the able of pre matric scholarships tenth plan target is aimed to reach to 4353565 SC's student. Against this target pace of annual plan 2002-03 & 2003-04 seems slow. Although state government seems determined to achieve the target, which can be seen in proposed target of 1077365 students for pre MS in 2004-05.
4. But conditions is not satisfactory as regards post MS. Achievement in 2002-03 and 2003-04 while proposed target of 2004-05 sum up only for 465631 students. There are 566369 students are more to attain the target of total 1032000 students in 10th plan. It is clear that for last two years of 10th plan target becomes too egregious.
5. Need oriented approach rationalizes a few schemes, which can be considered plan vital for development for disadvantaged group in general and SCs in particular.

I. Construction of Ashram Type School (ATS)

Students are provided free education with free fooding, clothing, stationary and medical facilities under this scheme. As this is aimed to children whose parents are victims of extreme poverty. Against the tenth plan target of 50 A.T.S annual plan of 2002-03 is quite better in comparison to 2003-04 where achievement is confined to just 4 A.T.S. Although target is improved for 2004-05, but it is 14 in numbers.

II. Hostel for Boys & Girls

This facility is available for students who are unable to continue their higher education from class IX and above on village level. Condition before 10th plan shows us that 170 hostels in operation of which only 38 for girls. Speed of 10th plan from 2002 to 2004 is quite slow] where only 25 hostels have constructed. In 2004-05 the target is aimed to construct 35 hostels. This accounts for total 60 hostels which is too marginal against the target of 450 hostels.

III. Establishments & Construction of centers under coaching and allied services

Pre-examination coaching facilities for IAS, PCS, Engineering, Medical & other services are provided too Sc student also.

IV. Discretionary Grant

Discretionary Grant s for marriage of daughters & treatment of persons suffering from severe diseases is provided to SCs.

Economic Empowerment

Central core to increase job opportunities by promotion of self-employment are of two folded strategy.

1. Financial Assistance
2. Skill development schemes

1. In order to speed up the empowerment of SCs, the Special Central Assistance (SCA) is also provided in addition to the state plan outlay. SCA is being facilitated to several schemes related to income generation. For 2002-03 and 2003-04 sanctioned amount for SCA stand for 164.95 cr. and Rs. 168.86 cr. respectively. For 2002-03 amount was utilized completely with total no of beneficiaries of 91077.

Ambedkar Village & Ambedkar Gram Vikas Yojna

Villages having largest SCs concentration are labeled as desired villages where various schemes of socio-economic development under Special Component Plan are being applied with in an integrated approach, entitled as Ambedkar Gram Vikas Yojna..

Specific Schemes of Employment Generation

Besides Ambedkar Village Yojna in which community approach is being emphasized, individual schemes are also provided to SCs and particularly those living below poverty line.

Self Employment Scheme

1. Schemes under this section are being financially assisted either by Banks i.e. Bankable SES or by National Schedule Castes Finance & Development Corporations (NSFDC). Though the provision of subsidy and margin money loan are same in both cases. In Which 50 percent of the project cost up to Rs. 10000/- is given as subsidy and 25 per cent is given as margin money loan at 4 per cent rate of interest or 2 per cent—9 per cent in case of NSFDC. For year 2004-05 physical target of bankable Self Employment Scheme is 111065 while it stands for 13935 in case of NSFDC scheme.
2. In urban areas persons with their own commercial land are provided financial assistance to construct shops. Besides, corporation (U.P. Schedule Castes Finance And Development Corporation) Also make purchase of shops from private builders and other development authorities from SCA funds, to be allotted to SCs. This is a subsidy cum interest free loan scheme. For 2004-05 physical target for construction of shops-2000. While 200 shops for purchase.
3. Various skill development schemes are also operating to cover unemployed SCs as well as scavengers & their

dependents, the focus is on the changing scenario of employment market. In accordance with the interest of choice training programmes are ranging from computer training to tractor repairing etc. Through Government and Non- government organization training would be free and stipend of Rs. 50-300 per month would be provided also. Physical target is 70819 (2004-05).

4. Employment opportunities for enlisted scavengers and their families by SUDA (state Urban Development Authority) would be implemented with the assistance of National Safai Karmachari Finance & Development Corporation (NSKFDC). This is a subsidy cum loan scheme] where loan for 15 per cent of the project cost is given as margin money loan while remaining is given from the NSKFDC. Physical target for 2004-05 is 5000 beneficiaries.

Social Justice

Under the Scheduled castes and Scheduled tribes (prevention of Atrocities) Act, 1989 incidences of atrocities against SC person are provided to be registered. Social justice is an unassailable component of empowerment of socially disadvantaged groups, as this is the underline principle of equal treatment and equal opportunities to raise one's quality of life. In 2002 number of atrocities registered against SCs are 1696. After 2002 data is not available but registration in such figure assure us a serious fault as regards empowerment of historically subjugated lot. It invokes for serious concern.

Table 4

TOTAL OUTLAY AND EXPENDITURE IN MAJOR HEADS DURING 10TH PLAN

Major Heads	*Tenth Plan outlay*	*Expenditure in 2002-03*	*Expenditure in 2003-04*
Direction and Administrating	2180.00	—	—
Economic Development	5000.00	100.00	1385.06

Major Heads	*Tenth Plan outlay*	*Expenditure in 2002-03*	*Expenditure in 2003-04*
Financial Assistance to Public sector under-takings	7889.00	500.00	—
Education	55781.00	4527.44	6417.31
Other Expenditure	4100.00	998.82	542.24
Other Schemes	15150.00	5458.19	1284.03
Total	90000.00	11584.45	9628.64

Table 5

PHYSICAL TARGETS AND ACHIEVEMENTS

Name of Scheme	*Unit*	*Tenth Plan Target*	*Achievement in 2002-03*	*Achievement in 2003-04*	*Achievement in 2004-05*
Pre-matric Scholarship					
(i) Scheduled Castes	No.	4353565	411554	913052	
(ii) Denotified Tribes	No.	180555	18988	33547	1077365
Post matric scholarship	No.	1032000	139888	125743	200000
Hostel for boys and girls	No.	450	18	7	35
A.T.S.	No.	50	15	4	14
(i) Grant for marriage of daughters	No.	57500	888	13468	12562
(ii) Grant for treatment against severe diseases	No.	5000	560	1496	

Table 6

FINANCIAL PERFORMANCE FOR SC AND ST UNDER VARIOUS HEADS

Programme	*S.C.*	*D.T.*	*Total*
Direction and administration	500.00	—	500.00
Economic development	1796.21	—	1796.21
Financial assistance to PSU	500.00	—	500.00
Education	14373.08	154.90	14527.98
Other expenditure	1012.24	—	1012.24
New Schemes	6063.50	—	6063.50
Total	24245.03	154.90	24399.93

Table 7

PHYSICAL ACHIEVEMENT OF VARIOUS EDUCATIONAL SCHEMES

Name of Scheme	*Unit*	*Target*
Pre-Matric Scholarship	No.	1077365
Post Matric Scholarship	No.	200000
Construction of Hostels for Boys & Girls	No.	35
Construction of A.T.S.	No.	14
Grant for marriage and treatment of severe diseases	No.	21562

IV. Empowerment of Scheduled Tribes

In 2003 with the inclusion of 10 new tribes, total number of scheduled tribes in the state of Uttar Pradesh has become 12. After the formation of Uttaranchal state in 2001, only Tharu & Buxa were remained in UP. 12 STs constitutes population of 380815 in Uttar Pradesh. In which Tharu comprises major portion of 78030 persons while Parahia has minimum population of 460 only.

Table 8

POPULATION UNDER VARIOUS CATEGORY OF TRIBES IN UP

S.No.	*Name of Tribes*	*Population of Scheduled Tribes*
1	Tharu	78030 (Max)
2	Buxa	1875
3	Gond, Dhuria, Nayak, Ojha, Pathari, Rajgond	148029
4	Kharwar, Khairwar	61692
5	Saharia	18267
6	Parahia	460 (Min)
7	Pankha, Panika	15059
8	Baiga	13800
9	Agariya	9553
10	Pathari	577
11	Chero	24406
12	Bhuyia, Bhuniya	9067
	Total	380815

Objectives of the 10th Plan

1. Development of critical infrastructure, particularly upgradation and enhancement of Ashram Type Schools and hostels for boys & girls of STs.
2. Development of infrastructure facilities like transportation etc. in the tribal areas.
3. Protection from exploitation in the field of land transfer, money lending, debt bondage etc.
4. Promotion of socio-economic measures to enable tribal people to reach on par with the levels of development of the general population.
5. To create an impact in the economic field of such an order which enable all tribal families to cross the poverty line.
6. Monitoring of the schemes would be undertaken at district, division and headquarter levels.

Socio-Economic Empowerment

1. As per 1993-94 data 37.4 per cent of total Indian population living below poverty line of which 57.1 per cent comprises for STs BPL population. While in Uttar Pradesh total BPL population is 45.3 per cent in which 66.6 per cent constitutes by tribal population living below poverty line. For economic upliftment of tribes different poverty line. For economic upliftment of tribals different poverty eradication schemes have been provided under Integrated Tribal Development Project, MADA projects etc. These schemes are associated with Agricultural, Horticulture, Animal Husbandry, Cottage & Village industries etc.
2. In order to solve socio-economic problems of tribes the state Government has applied the concept of Tribal Sub Plan (TSP) under the guidance of Govt. of India from 5th Five Year Plan. But to accelerate development process among tribes from 9th Five Year Plan allocation of outlays have been started in proportional terms of population.

3. In specific terms of 10 plan period from 2002-07, approach for tribal development is much more focused than previous. From 2002 onwards schemes which benefit the women & children are given priority. Besides schemes of non displacing manner are also preferred. Development of community assets, fund orientation under T.S.P. in terms of specific and felt needs of tribes are also among thrust areas. Protection of civil rights particularly in terms of proper rehabilitation of displaced tribes and effective control on transfer of land by tribes to others are recognized as the unassailable issues in 10th plan.
4. New scheme for intensified TSP has also adopted from 2002. Schemes which are aimed to provide cent percent benefit to the community of Sts shall be included under TSP. Besides, projects for infrastructure development in scheduled Tribes Basties shall be provided with cent percent outlay with TSP. As well as general schemes aimed at benefiting 0.06 per cent or more population of ST only additional percentage of outlay over & above 0.06 per cent would be counted towards TSP.
5. Out of Rs. 84233 crores of proposed outlay for state plan Rs. 5054 crores stands for allocated / quantified outlay under TSP during 10th plan period. For annual plan of 2002-03 and 2003-04 allocated/quantified outlay under TSP was Rs 4 crores each.
6. Besides, Special Central Assistance is also provided to the state for further support to the measures of upliftment of STs. SPA sanctioned for 10th plan is Rs. 2.78 crores. During first two annual plans of this period sanctioned amount of SCA is Rs. 32 crores each. While Annual plan 2004-05 has adopted strategy of promotion of participatory institution like SHGs and co-operations to harpen the edge of tribal development. For these purposes 10th plan's approved outlay is Rs. 3295.00 lakh and an outlay of Rs 473.00 lakh proposed for 2004-05 period.

7. Scheduled tribes constitutes most vulnerable and sensitive section of socially disadvantaged classes, as there are not only socioeconomic problems but a decisive question of tribal' integration into mainstream is also prevailing. Committed staff is another crucial factor in the implementation of welfare programmes so a need is haunting to check the potential of voluntary organization in this regard.
8. With a purpose of conducting action oriented research and survey for the socio-economic, educational and cultural development of SCs, STs, denotified tribes and other backward classes, 'State Institute of Research and Training For scheduled Castes & Scheduled Tribes' was established in 1986-87. For 10th plan an outlay of Rs. 50.00 lakh have been approved by the state government. Physical target accounts for 40 research and evaluation studies, 100 training courses to benefit 3000 officials, ten seminars, 10 publication work and construction of office building. Annual plan 2004-05 has proposed outlay of Rs. 5.00 lakh.

V. Welfare of Minorities

Being a secular and democratic state India has applied a socially equitable scheme for development process wherein minorities constitute that section of socially disadvantaged groups which need special attention and opportunities to overcome from backwardness either socio-economic or educational. As per 1991 census six religions groups viz. Muslims, Christian, Sikhs, Buddhists, Parsis & Jainies comprise more than 18 per cent of total population of the state as religions minorities.

Objectives assigned for Tenth Five Year Plan

1. To promote educational upliftment among minorities by providing them educational facilities, added with the incentives, like scholarship schemes as well as to check the tendency of dropouts.

2. Promotion of new education system by modernization of Madarsas, providing facilities and incentives for inclusion of modern subjects of science, computer and English, so that students of Minorities can be brought in mainstream.
3. To strengthen the Waqf by developing its properties and increased income so that it may serve as a community asset to accelerate social welfare and modernization.
4. To raise the standard of girl education in educationally backward areas of minorities.
5. To inculcate measures of economic development through promotion of schemes of self employment and Margin Money Loan & Term Loan etc.

Socio Economic Empowerment

1. As regards education facilities Pre-matric scholarship scheme has a proposed outlay of Rs. 1500 lakh for the tenth plan, while annual plan of 2002-03 it was Rs. 100 lakh. During second plan of 2003-04 expenditure for PMS was Rs. 1323.34 lakh aimed at physical target of 362570. For 2004-05 proposed outlay is Rs 1556.08 lakh for 425500 beneficiaries.
2. To provide new education system, expenditure for 'Opening Mini ITI in Madarsa Scheme' was Rs. 285.60 lakh during 2003-04 periods. Though it has reduced to Rs. 150 lakh for annual plan of 2004-05.
3. Grant is also provided by government to the Arabi-Farsi Madarsas for salary of teaching / non-teaching staff as these are primary education institutions preferred by minorities. Modernization of Madarsas is a centrally sponsored scheme wherein provision for Rs. 3000 for primary, Rs. 4000 for Madhayamik classes is being made as monthly scale. Besides Rs. 7000 is also provided for purchase of science/maths kit. Hietherto 772 Madarsas have been covered. In 2003-04 physical target was expected at 1,15,800 students including 46320 girls. During 2004-05 plan period Rs.

Table 9

TOTAL OUTLAY AND EXPENDITURE FOR MINORITY

S. No.	*Name of Scheme*	*Expenditure for 2003-2004*	*Physical Achievements*		
1	Pre-matric Scholarship (DS)	1323.34	362570	1556.08	425500
2	Share capital to U.P.W.D.C.	50.00	NA	50	
3	Opening of mini ITI in madarasa.	285.60	100	150	
4	Construction of vocational and professional training center at noida	110.72	1		
	Total	1769.66			

584.52 lakh is required to benefit 2.43 lakh students including 97200 girls.

4. For economic advancement Margin Money Loan is provided by the UP Minorities Finance & Development Corporation who desire the loan for industry, business or agriculture. MML is 15 per cent of the project cost, 75 percent of the total margin money by the bank as per rules or Rs. 45000 which ever is less at the rate of 7.5 percent per annum interest. Proposed target for MML in 2002-03 was Rs. 24.62 lakh. For 2003-04 and 2004-05 it scores for Rs. 400 lakh each.
5. Scheme for financial assistance are incorporated into Term Loan Scheme and Interest Free Loan, which stand for Rs. 175.07 lakh and Rs. 26.50 lakh respectively for 2002-03 period. During 2003-04 and 2004-05 period TLS account for Rs. 1000 lakh per year while IF loan remains also same at Rs. 50 lakh during both annual plans.
6. As distinguished from other items one trend seems frustrating in terms of self-employment. On one hand tenth plan is considered more specific because of its participatory orientation towards beneficiaries but proposed target and outlay has been reduced

Table 10

VARIOUS SCHEMES FOR MINORITIES

Scheme	*2002-2003*		*2003-2004*		*2004-2005*	
	Unit/ Std.	*Amt.*	*Unit/ Std.*	*Amt.*	*Unit/ Std.*	*Amt.*
Margin money Loan	118	24.62	400	400.00	400	400.00
Pre-examination coaching.	335	19.85	350	25.00	350	25.00
Skill Improvement and vocational training.	1000	25.00	1000	25.00	500	25.00
Term Loan scheme.	5215	175.07	2600	1000.00	2600	1000.00
Swyam sahayta samooh	300	300.00	138	138.00	100	50.00
Interest free Loan	100	26.50	100	50.00	100	50.00
Rikshaw Scheme					3000	180.00
Educational Loan Scheme					350	120.00

successively. In 2002-03 amount for Swayam Sahyata Samooh Rs. 300 lakh against physical target of 300. It reduced to Rs. 138 lakh in 2003-04 against target 138. While it comes down to Rs. 50 lakh with physical target of 100 units in 2004-05. Although Rs. 180 lakh has proposed for transformation of Rikshaw-pullers to Rikshaw-owners in 2004-05 period.

7. For further strengthening of waqfs, UP Waqf Development Corporation is being operated through which efforts are being made to improve financial condition of these institutions. During annual plan of 2003-04 expenditure of Rs. 50 lakh was made as share capital to UPWDC. The amount is same for period of 2004-05 i.e. Rs. 50 lakh.
8. During tenth plan period progress of some schemes are also not satisfactory. As construction of hostels for students and construction of Girls School Building are 100 per cent centrally sponsored scheme. For construction of 13 hostels are pending with the Govt. of India. Besides, central share was also not released during 2003-04 period. Proposals for construction of school building for girls are also pending. It can be examined that both these prorgrammes are crucial in

the sense that these are meaningful and significant for students living in remote area, where students of minorities are abundant but facilities are not available.

9. Despite a few schemes with slow pace ambit of development is multidimensional which can be seen easily through the diverse coverage of development programmes. For welfare schemes for minorities proposed outlay is Rs. 5342.08 lakh during 2004-05 period.

VI. Welfare of other Backward Classes

Other Backward classes refer to that section of socially disadvantaged groups excluding scheduled castes/scheduled tribes which is socially, economically as well as in terms of education deprived and backward, in comparison to other classes of general population. The estimation of the Social Justice Committee constituted by the State Government in 2000-01, the population of OBC accounts for 54 percent of the total population in rural areas of Uttar Pradesh. Estimating the population of OBCs in rural & urban areas as 54 percent of total population, it accounts for 8.966 crore in Uttar Pradesh.

Tenth Plan and Welfare of OBCs

1. Prevention against exploitation of OBCs by facilitating socio-economic measures for their upliftment.
2. To promote educational facilities to cover more and more students belonging to OBCs, like hostel facilities for boys & girls, to establish book bank, to provide educational loan to those living below poverty line etc.
3. To raise the self-reliance among the women of OBCs living bellow the poverty line.
4. To ensure proper utilization of funds earmarked under scholarships.

Socio-Economic Empowerment

1. As regards tenth plan for welfare of OBCs central

concern is education, which is considered as the most significant factor in the development process. Schemes like Pre-matric and Post-matric Scholarships, book bank, construction of hostels are working for the purpose.

2. For the welfare of SC/ST & OBC tenth plan's proposed outlay is Rs. 906.00 cr i.e. 1.08 percent of the total proposed outlay. For backward classes in 2002-03 approved outlay was Rs. 188.00 lakh while anticipated expenditure Rs. 2037 lakh.
3. Pre-matric scholarship is limited in its range as it is to be given to only those students whose parents' annual income does not exceed to Rs. 24000. But to deal the welfare of OBCs on par with social equity it has been decided to give pre-matric to OBC students on the same rate and same terms & condition as being currently given to SC/ST. So from class 1 to 5 scholarship of Rs. 25.00 is available, class 6 to 8 it is Rs. 40.00 and from class 9-10 it has an amount of Rs. 60.00 per month. For the annual plan 2003-04, under the centrally sponsored scheme an outlay was allocated of Rs. 1916.96 lakh but out of which only Rs. 608.9 lakh were spent on 168956 students. For annual plan 2004-05 physical target is about 12160211 students with the proposed outlay of Rs. 43749.00 lakh under pre-matric scholarships.

Table II

AMOUNT OF VARIOUS SCHOLARSHIPS TO DIFFERENT CATEGORY STUDENTS

Sl. No	*Course/Class*	*Scholarship Rate P.M.*	*Qualifying Criteria of annual Income*	*Eligibility in months*
1.	Class 1 to 5	Rs. 25.00	No limit	12 months
2.	Class 6 to 8	Rs. 40.00	No limit	12 months
3.	Class 9 to 10	Rs. 60.00	Rs. 30,000	12 months

4. For Post matric scholarship scheme, state government also decided to treat students of OBCs on the same criteria with same terms and condition as applied for SC/ST students. Owing to this effort now eligibility criteria expands from Rs. 24000 to Rs. 1 lakh per annum. Under this section proposed amount for annual plan 2003-04 was Rs. 5830. 71 lakh. For the year 2004-05 proposed outlay stands at Rs. 10971 lakh.
5. Construction of Hostels for OBCs is a centrally sponsored scheme of 50:50 ratio. Scheme is aimed to provide hostel facilities to OBC students who are below the creamy layer. Preference is given to the area where OBC students are in majority and also to those institutions, which provide land free of cost. During tenth plan physical target is 140 hostels. Speed of implementation is too slow under this scheme. For first year, i.e. 2002-03 expenditure was Rs. 200 lakh as state's share for construction of 11 hostels. During plan period of 2003-04 the amount and physical target both are same. While during 2004-05 proposed outlay is just Rs. 90.00 lakh. It is mainly due to paucity of funds and major population of this section. So serious efforts are still waiting.
6. Other schemes like book bank facilities specially for technical courses where books are too expensive, coaching institutes for pre-examination of different courses are also working to spread their coverage.
7. Programmes of economic development like Self Employment Programmes and Margin Money Assistance are being implemented through UP Backward Classes Finance Development Corporation. For first annual plan 2002-03 NBCFDC has approved action plan of Rs. 26.25 crores but amount received of only Rs. 7 crores. For year 2003-04, approved action plan was Rs. 23 crores but released Rs. 5.50 crores only. Target was 7000 beneficiaries but achieved target was 1174 beneficiaries by disbursing Rs. 5.69 crores. For 2004-05 period approved action plan is just Rs. 16

Table 12

COMPARISON SCHOLARSHIPS OF DAY SCHOLAR AND HOSTELLER

Group	*Previous Rate*				*Present Rate*			
	Rate P.M.				*Rate P.M.*			
	Day Scholar	*Hosteller*	*Income criteria*	*Duration in Month*	*Day Scholar*	*Hosteller*	*Income criteria*	*Duration in Month*
A	190.00	425.00	24000	10	330	740	1 lakh	10
B	190.00	290.00	Do	10	330	510	Do	10
C	190.00	290.00	Do	10	185	355	Do	10
D	90.00	150.00	Do	10	140	235	Do	10

crores for 3970 as physical target. But state government is aimed to achieve the target of 7000 beneficiaries. For which state government has made a budget provision of Rs. 1 crores for the purpose.

8. In Uttar Pradesh OBCs constitute a big lot so it is clear from the data, mentioned about that lack of adequate fund and big population of OBCs are intermingled in a big challenge to the development process. Therefore to raise funds for educational facilities to the desired strata, awareness towards corporate responsibility added with the incentives may facilitate an active potential in this regard by government.

Table 13

WELFARE OF SC/ST & OTHER BACKWARD CLASSES

Welfare of S.C. & others	*Welfare of Backward Classes*	*Welfare of Minorities*	*Tribal Welfare*	*Training Institute*
68701.33	5149.39	19729.81	358.68	5.89
2299.04	326.11	843.18	48.53	-
90000.00	15000.00	2500.00	3295.00	100.00
35952.82	500.00	750.00	2000.00	25.00
17904.00	1887.00	653.37	359.00	5.00
8975.80	85.00	50.00	200.00	1.25
17745.2	2037.00	653.37	359.00	5.00
8975.80	235.00	50.00	200.00	1.25
18000.00	1887.00	600.00	359.00	5.00
8587.37	85.00	100.00	200.00	1.25

VII. Summing up and Conclusion

Females with 47.33 percent of total population constitute 7.86 crore in Uttar Pradesh as per 2001 census. Sex ratio has increase up to 22 females since last decade, although it is still lower than sex ratio at national level, which stands at 933 in 2001 census. Sex ratio was 876 in 1991, which has increased to 898 in 2001. Figures of literacy rates also show a poor record that is 42.2 percent for female literacy agonist 68.8 per cent male literacy in Uttar Pradesh. In worker population ratio women comprise only 16.3 percent of the aggregate, against 47.4 percent male ratio in 2001. Index on reproductive health places (RPI) Uttar-Pradesh at the bottom with score of 22.8.

For women welfare sector, during tenth plan period 2002-07 total outlay stands for Rs. 30 crores. For first annual plan i.e., 2002-03 it was Rs. 7.10 crores against which total expenditure was Rs. 4.22 cr. In 2003-04 expenditure was Rs. 9.25 cr. Though the outlay was Rs. 13.03 crores, for annual plan 2004-05 has provided an outlay of Rs. 14.22 cr. The Tenth plan is specific and more focused on women welfare as it is aimed to treat development programmes with gender sensitivity to tackle more deprived women on priority level by providing social security through grant-in-aid schemes. Maintenance grants of Rs. 125.00 pm is provided to destitute women living below poverty line.

In non-plan expenditure 457994 women are being converted. In addition 36591 women were selected from Ambedkar villages during 2002-03. For 2003-04 period proposed outlay for the scheme was Rs. 552-52 lakh Grant-in-aid is also provided up to Rs. 10,000 for marriage of widows' daughters. For 2003-04 outlay was proposed of Rs. 19.00 lakh. Scholarship is also provided to girls of general category, who are pursuing higher technical and professional courses living below poverty line. Amount of scholarship is ranging from Rs. 50.00 to Rs. 425 pm. During 2003-04 outlay was proposed of Rs. 19.00 lakh for this purpose.

Provision is also made for construction and maintenance of observation Homes and Children Homes. These homes provide services like accommodation, medical facilities and opportunities for occupation as will. During 2003-04 period Rs. 18.48 lakh was proposed as an outlay. Decision-making as well as financial assistance are incorporated with the active participation in project Swashakti. It is aimed to form Swashakti groups i.e. self-help groups, in which 10-20 members are included. Target group is provided financial assistance in the form of short-term loan on low interest rate. This is a centrally sponsored scheme for improving quality of life of strata living below poverty line. Project is working in 18 districts.

Implementation is being done by the UP women development corporation and UP land Development Corporation. More than 5200 groups have been formed. Decision-making as well as financial assistance are incorporated with the active participation in project Swashakti

Decennial growth of SCs population is always higher than that of total population in the state. SCs population constitutes nearly 21 percent of the total population through out the planning era. Literacy rate of the SCs is substantially lower than that of total population. Moreover, literacy rate of both male and female within SCs is also low to the corresponding male and female literacy rate of the total population. Female literacy rate is nearly ¼ of that of male within the SCs category and nearly 1/3 of female in the total population category. Based on latest available information, population below poverty line in general and SCs in particular, score of UP remained always higher than that of all India level. Thus, poverty situation is very serious for SCs category, both at state and national level. Though the SCs constitute nearly 21 percent of the total population, yet the share of land holding (ownership in number) to total holding is only 16 percent and in area wise it is only 10 percent. It is evident from the fact that nearly 82 percent of SCs workers are engaged in primary sector, where as it is nearly 70 percent for general workers. In other words, nearly 18 per cent of SCs workers are engaged in both secondary and tertiary sector, whereas 30 per cent of the general workers are engaged on both the sector.

STs Population constitutes nearly 0.1 percent in 2001 and decennial growth arte is lower than that of total population. Literacy rate of STs is always lower than that of total population. Nearly 85 percent of STs engaged in primary sector and only 15 percent occupy in both secondary and tertiary sector. Nearly, 70 percent of total ST main workers are cultivators, 13 percent are agricultural labourers and rest 18 percent are non-agricultural labourers. However, nearly 66 percent Sts population live below the poverty line in 1993-94 in UP, whereas it is 57 percent at all India level.

Budget outlay and allocation

The budget allocation under state plan, the expenditure out of total outlay was nearly 91 percent in 9th plan, whereas it increased to 99 percent during 2002-03. The situation under special component plan (SCP) does not look bright, as only 56 percent of the outlay was spent during 9th plan, and it was 49 percent and 46 percent during 2002-03 and 2003-04 respectively. However, the share of SCP out of state plan outlay has increased from 19 percent in the 9th plan to 21 percent in 2002-03 and it remained constant at 21 percent 2003-04. On the other hand, the expenditure under SCP as a proportion to state plan has declined from 12 percent in 9th plan to 10 percent in 2002-03. Under state plan, the ratio of expenditure to outlay for STs similar to that of SCs, whereas under tribal sub-plan the ratio of expenditure has declined drastically from 62 percent in 9th plan to 6 percent in 2002-03 and 44 percent in 2003-04. However, TSP as a proportion to state plan varies from 4 percent to 7 percent during this period. Under Special Central Assistance (SCA) programme, there has been satisfactory performance between budget sanctioned and utilised. During the first two years of 10th plan shows nearly 132 percent and 94 percent of the budget sanctioned was utilised respectively.

Recommendations

Preferential planning for women can be considered as the most significant feature which may provide positive feedback to women empowerment constructively. Because empowerment defers from welfare in the sense of vibrant participation, measures regarding the policy mentioned above should be emphasized.

Either it is development programmes in general or women special programmes in particular, education and health have correctly been observed as basic areas for policy initiatives in the Tenth Five Year Plan. Both are big challenges for deprived class and specially in remote areas. But, our point is to mention education and health in process irrespective of output and outcome. In other words, measures regarding both these resources should be compiled with specific periodical training schedule, so that it can move in self - propellant way.

As regard to health specific measures, integrated approach has been applied in first three annual plans. The approach seems prolific in principle but in practice it is too much complex. There is a need to make cross verifications so that implementation can be made beneficial the same way.

As far as socio-economic measures are concerned, participation has increased through SHGs, etc., no doubt, but there is need to facilitate this process with proper training schedules by committed and specially trained personnel in which, approach must be integrated, i.e., from proper utilization of fund to storage and marketing facilities as well.

What seems more hampering is the lack of proper fund and committed staff. The need of hour is to make corporate socially responsible so that fund may be raised through private enterprises as well, while NGOs provide better options for committed staff.

Social justice is still far away. Only increased participation associated with training can provide practicable solution. Before initiation of any programmes in a given area, consciousness boost up initiatives are required not only for SCs, STs, and OBCs but also for general population so that space for acceptance may be created.

Development process has become more delicate and fragile once we focus on tribal development. Most significant point is to remember that this section requires specially designed programmes associated with their felt need. Nothing can be done in hasty manner, as for them development is not just empowerment but firstly it demands for commitment to transcendence. It may lead to their socio-economic and cultural confusion in lack of proper seriousness.

15

PLAN FINANCING, RESOURCE MOBILIZATION AND PRIVATE INVESTMENT

A.K. Singh

I. Introduction

In this chapter we have discussed issues related to plan expenditure, its link with growth rate, its composition, central plan assistance, resource mobilization by the state government and the trends in public debt, etc. and suggested measure for mobilizing resources. The chapter also discusses the recent trends in private sector investment in the state. We first start with a discussion of the trends in growth rate in SDP and their links with plan expenditure.

II. Growth Rate and Plan Expenditures

Growth rates in SDP in U.P. remained extremely sluggish during the first four five year plan periods, started picking up since the fifth plan period and caught up with the national growth rates in the sixth and the seventh plan period (Table 1). However, since the beginning of the nineties coinciding with the economic reform period, growth rate in U.P. dropped significantly and have not shown any signs of picking up in the current plan. These fluctuations in the SDP growth are closely related to the level of plan expenditures in the states as can be seen from Table 2. Thus, plan expenditure in U.P. as a percent of NSDP remained fairly low during the period 1951 to 1975. There was a quantum jump in plan expenditure levels from around 4.7 per cent of NSDP during the fourth Plan to over 7 per cent of NSDP during the Fifth, Sixth and the Seventh Five Year Plans. During this period growth rates also picked up. However, since early nineties there has been a sharp decline in the plan expenditure as per cent of NSDP, which is also reflected in a sharp decline in growth rates. There has taken places a marginal increase in plan expenditure ratio during the Tenth Five Year Plan. However, the ratio remains below the levels reached in the early seventies.

The decline in plan expenditure in its turn can be traced to the sharp deterioration in the fiscal situation in the state witnessed since early nineties. Due to the mounting pressure of non-developmental expenditure on salaries, pensions and interest payment the government budgets have been running

Table 1

COMPOUND ANNUAL GROWTH RATE OF TOTAL AND PER CAPITA INCOME IN UTTAR PRADESH AND INDIA SINCE 1951

Period	*CAGR of Total Income (%)*		*CAGR of Per Capita Income (%)*	
	Uttar Pradesh	*India*	*Uttar Pradesh*	*India*
1951-56	2.0	3.6	0.5	1.7
1956-61	1.9	4.0	0.3	1.9
1961-66	1.6	2.2	-0.2	0.0
1966-69	0.3	4.0	-1.5	1.8
1969-74	2.3	3.3	0.4	1.1
1974-79	5.7	5.3	3.3	2.9
1981-85	3.9	4.9	1.5	2.7
1985-90	5.7	5.8	3.3	3.6
1990-92	3.1	2.5	1.1	0.4
1992-97	3.2	6.8	1.4	4.9
1997-02	3.1	5.3	1.0	3.3

Source: Plan Documents, Government of Uttar Pradesh.

into continuous and high revenue deficit. Thus, the state government is not in a position to raise its expenditure on development plans and other priority sectors like education, health and infrastructure.

The economic slow down and fiscal crisis in the state are deeply interlinked. Low plan expenditure lead to low growth which in its turns reduces the growth in the government revenue. This further constrains the capacity of the state to increase plan expenditure, thus completing the vicious cycle. Thus, it is imperative to substantially raise the ratio of plan expenditure to SDP if growth rates are to be boosted up to meet the targeted growth rate.

Apart from the decline in plan investment levels in relation

Table 2

Total Plan Expenditure in Uttar Pradesh under Five Year Plans

Period	*Plan Expenditure (Rs. Crores)*	*Plan Expenditure as per cent of NSDP*
1951-56	153	2.05
1956-61	233	2.66
1961-66	561	4.53
1966-69	455	3.86
1969-74	1166	4.69
1974-79	2909	7.01
1979-85	7356	7.62
1985-90	11949	7.44
1990-92	7772	7.28
1992-97	21683	4.73
1997-98	5033	3.66
1998-99	5648	3.67
1999-00	5843	3.53
2000-01	5897	3.40
2001-02	5965	3.16
2002-03	6702	3.30
2003-04	7242	3.33
2004-05	9651	4.18

Source: Plan Documents, Government of Uttar Pradesh.
Note: Percentages from 1997-98 are in terms of GSDP.

to SDP is the fact that the quality of public expenditure has sharply deteriorated. Thus, capital expenditure constituted only 7-8 percent of total government expenditure (plan and non-plan) in the nineties (Table 3). There has been some improvement since 2000-01, when the ratio of capital expenditure improved to 10 per cent. However, since then it has stuck at the same level. Thus, even though the size of the budget has been going up, capital formation through the public expenditure is quite low leading to stagnation in the growth rate of the economy. For accelerating economic growth the capital content of government budget needs to be improved which will help in developing infrastructure in the state and attracting private investment.

Table 3

TRENDS IN CAPITAL EXPENDITURE IN UTTAR PRADESH

Year	*Capital Expenditure (in Rs. crore)*	*Capital Expen diture as % of Total Expenditure*	*Capital Expen-diture as % of GSDP*
1995-96	1129.35	6	1.06
1996-97	1435.41	7	1.12
1997-98	1667.64	7	1.21
1998-99	2096.96	7	1.36
1999-00	2533.34	8	1.53
2000-01	3267.55	10	1.88
2001-02	3555.56	10	1.88
2002-03	3794.39	10	1.87
2003-04	4985.22	11	2.29
2004-05	6320.15	10	2.74

Source: Computed from Budget Documents, UP Government

Apart from the overall decline of capital expenditure in the state budget, the composition of the plan expenditure has also undergone substantial change. Revenue expenditure now accounts for nearly half of the plan expenditure (Table 4). Thus, even the plan expenditure is not contributing much to the expansion of the productive capacity in the state. This situation needs to be rectified by raising the capital component of the plan expenditure.

Table 4

Revenue and Capital Component of Plan Expenditure in Uttar Pradesh (Rs. Crore)

Item	*2000-01*	*2001-02*	*2002-03*	*2003-04*	*2004-05 RE*	*2005-06 BE*
Revenue Expenditure	3686.01	3564.48	3574.82	3276.00	6416.45	7090.44
As % of total Expenditure	56.29	83.45	45.04	45.24	50.32	47.70
Capital Expenditure	2862.27	706.97	3361.37	3965.76	6334.70	7773.92
As % of total Expenditure	43.71	16.55	42.35	54.76	49.68	52.30
Total Plan Expenditure	6548.28	4271.45	7936.19	7241.76	12751.15	14864.36

Source: Plan Documents, Government of Uttar Pradesh.

III. Plan Outlays and Expenditure

An area of concern is the large and growing gap between plan outlays and plan expenditure (Table 5). Thus, during the Eighth Plan the plan expenditure as percent of plan outlay was only around 80 per cent. This ratio further declined to around 70 per cent in the Ninth Plan. The utilization ration increased to 90.95 per cent in 2002-03 but came down again to 79.26 percent in the following year. One reason for poor utilization of plan allocations is that the annual plan outlays are based on unrealistically high estimates of resource mobilization. This also reflects poorly on the ability of the government departments to fully utilize the plan allocations. Serious attention needs to be paid to identify the reasons for non-utilisation of plan funds and ensuring that plan outlays are fully utilized.

Total plan expenditure in the first two years of the Tenth Plan amounts to only 21.30 per cent of the total agreed outlay of Rs. 59,708 crore for the Tenth Plan. Even if the allocation for the year 2004-05 is fully utilised, total plan expenditure in the first three years of the Tenth Plan will not exceed 40 per cent of the plan size. Thus, in the remaining two years of the plan

TABLE 5
YEAR-WISE OUTLAY & EXPENDITURE (RS. CRORE)

Year	*Approved Outlay*	*Actual Expenditure*	*Expenditure as % of Outlay*
Seventh Plan			
1985-86	1750.55	1853.66	105.89
1986-87	2150.00	2163.02	100.61
1987-88	2629.65	2343.93	89.13
1988-89	2690.75	2664.82	99.04
1989-90	2970.81	2910.97	97.99
Annual Plans			
1990-91	3383.05	3208.22	94.83
1991-92	3892.01	3695.54	94.95
Eighth Plan			
1992-93	4039.92	3890.44	96.30
1993-94	4247.06	3432.78	80.83
1994-95	4760.06	4019.74	84.45
1995-96	5721.63	4436.25	77.53
1996-97	6774.03	5904.35	87.16
Ninth Plan	41910.00	28386.65	67.73
1997-98	6486.34	5032.92	77.59
1998-99	9234.96	5648.45	61.16
1999-00	10260.00	5843.24	56.95
2000-01	8122.00	5896.68	72.60
2001-02	8400.00	5965.36	71.10
Tenth Plan			
2002-03	7250.00	6593.74	90.95
2003-04	7728.00	6124.92	79.26
2004-05	9661.51	N.A.	N.A.

Source: Plan Documents, Government of Uttar Pradesh.
Note: Figures till Eighth Plan are for undivided U.P.

determined efforts will have to be made to substantially increase the annual plan expenditure.

IV. Pattern of Plan Financing

We will now discuss the pattern of plan financing and the related issues. A brief outline of the proposed financing pattern of the Tenth Five Year Plan is presented in Table 6. Out of the proposed outlay of Rs. 59,708 crores the state was to contribute

Table 6

PROPOSED FINANCING PATTERN OF THE TENTH FIVE YEAR PLAN AND AGREED RESOURCES FOR 2002-03 AND 2003-04 (RS. CRORE)

Sl. No.	*Item*	*Resources*	*Agreed Resources (2002-03)*	*Agreed Resources (2003-04)*
	State's Own Resources (1 to 9)	24297.88	1148.93	3499.47
1.	Balance from Current Revenue (BCR)	-9562.47	-6208.66	-3881.23
2.	Contribution of Public Enterprises	-1080.69	-883.29	25.59
	(i) SEB		-978.56	
	(ii) SRTC		104.27	
3.	State Provident Funds	8660.99	1784.48	1574.03
4.	Misc. Capital Receipts	-2687.61	-223.90	-126.75
5.	Small Saving	18281.17	3890.41	3480.00
6.	Upgradation grants for capital works	198.32	108.04	160.19
7.	Grant for Local Bodies	1207.99	279.01	
8.	Market Borrowings	4893.33	1489.55	1637.48
9.	Negotiated Loans	4386.85	913.29	630.26
	(a) Normal		446.86	
	LIC/GIC		343.23	
	REC		71.22	
	IDBI		32.41	
	(b) Additional (RIDF)		466.43	
	Central Support (10-24)	35410.12	6101.07	6162.04
10.	Normal Central Assistance	12680.62	2379.81	3120.26
11.	Additional CA for PMGY	2082.83	370.87	370.87
12.	Assistance Under AIBP	1825.00	365.00	275.00
13.	Additional CA for BADP	41.60	8.32	8.32
14.	Additional CA for Roads and Bridges	482.15	96.43	80.61
15.	Additional CA for EAP	14889.32	2085.00	1323.15
16.	Rashtriya Sam Vikas Yojana			315.00
17.	Assistance under Slum Development	200.50	40.10	42.79
18.	Additional CA for TSP	1.60	0.32	0.29
19.	Grand under Art.275(1)	1.35	0.27	0.30
20.	ACA for National Social Assistance Prog.	493.30	98.66	98.64
21.	ACA for Accelerated Power Dev. Restructuring Prog. (APDRP)	1512.20	302.44	179.82

22.	ACA for Rural Electrification	755.00	151.00	151.00
23.	ACA for Initiative for strengthening Urban Infrast. (ISUI)	302.25	60.45	60.45
23.	Nutrition Programme for Adolescent Girls			6.01
24	One time ACA	142.40	142.40	129.53
	Total Resources	59708.00	7250.00	9661.51

Source: Plan Documents, U.P. Government.

Rs. 24,298 crore or 40 per cent of the total outlay. However, in the agreed resource scheme the share of state amounted to only 16 per cent and 36 per cent during 20002-3 and 2003-04 respectively. The contribution of balance from current revenue was expected to be negative. The state proposed to raise resources mainly through withdrawals from provident fund, market borrowings and loans from financial institutions.

Against the proposed plan financing scheme, we find that in the first two years of the Tenth Five Year Plan negative BCR has exceeded the proposed BCR for the full plan. On the other hand, market loans have exceeded the proposed amount for the full period, whereas about 40 percent of PF and small borrowings have been utilized. Thus, while state's own contribution has been less than the proposed contribution, its dependence on borrowed sources of funds has exceeded the targets.

Central Plan Assistance

Plan assistance to U.P. has been shown in Table 7. Plan assistance in absolute terms shows a big jump after 2003-04. However, as a proportion of plan expenditure central plan assistance shows a marked decline in the current plan as compared to the ninth plan. While discussing the central assistance it is important to keep in mind the fact that central assistance consists of loans and grants in the ratio of 70:30. Figures for central plan loans have been shown in Table 8. Thus, a large size of plan outlay and larger amount of central plan assistance leads to an increase in the indebtedness of the state, which is very high. In fact, total repayments to the centre (loan plus interest) from U.P. now exceed what the state gets as central assistance. Thus, there is a reverse flow from the state to the centre.

Table 7

CENTRAL PLAN ASSISTANCE TO UTTAR PRADESH (RS. CRORE)

Item	*2000-01*	*2001-02*	*2002-03*	*2003-04*	*2004-05 RE*	*2005-06 BE*
Assistance for State Plan Schemes	1890.33	1994.15	1222.94	1346.53	1972.83	2283.11
Assistance for Central Plan Schemes	187.00	79.53	123.21	36.29	11.15	10.60
Assistance for Centrally Supported Schemes	391.16	764.72	537.62	529.66	1688.85	1454.74
Total Plan Assistance	2468.49	2838.40	1833.77	1912.48	3672.83	3748.45
Total Plan Expenditure	6548.28	4271.45	7728.00	7241.76	12751.15	14864.36
Plan Assistance as % of Plan Expenditure	37.70	66.45	24.38	26.41	28.80	25.22

Source: Plan and budget documents, U.P. government.

Contribution of Small Savings

As the state has been continuous incurring revenue deficit, there is no balance from the current revenue for plan financing. Thus, the state is relying upon borrowing to finance its share of plan expenditure mainly in the form of borrowings against national small saving schemes. The contribution of small savings to plan expenditure was 26.54 per cent and 35.28 percent of plan expenditure during the Eighth Plan and the Ninth Plan respectively. But it shot up to 62.14 percent in 2002-03 and further to 77.54 per cent during 2003-04 (Table 9). It is likely to come down to 56.32 per cent during 2004-05 and projected at 42.92 percent in the 2005-06 budgets.

Table 8

CENTRAL PLAN LOANS TO UTTAR PRADESH (RS. CRORE)

Item	*2000-01*	*2001-02*	*2002-03*	*2003-04*	*2004-05 RE*	*2005-06 BE*
For State Plan Schemes	3187.48	2613.50	3061.66	3058.70	3759.71	4343.95
For Central Plan Schemes	0.02	0.00	0.02	0.04	0.00	0.00
For Centrally Supported Schemes	66.83	84.28	0.00	20.53	0.00	4.00
Total Central Loans	3254.33	2697.78	3061.68	3079.27	3759.71	4347.95
Total Plan Expenditure	6548.28	4271.45	7728.00	7241.76	12751.15	14864.36
Central Loans as % of Plan Expenditure	49.70	63.16	39.62	42.52	29.49	29.25

Source: Plan and budget documents, U.P. Government.

Table 9

CONTRIBUTION OF SMALL SAVINGS TO PLAN EXPENDITURE IN UTTAR PRADESH

Item	*8th Plan (1992-97)*	*9th Plan (1997-02)*	*2002-03*	*2003-04*	*2004-05 RE*	*2005-06 BE*
Total Plan Expenditure/outlay	21683.56	46248.88	7241.76	7728.00	12751.15	14864.36
Loan against NSS	5841.56	16364.29	4500.00	5992.00	7181.50	6380.00
% of NSS loans to Total Plan Outlay	26.94	35.38	62.14	77.54	56.32	42.92

Source: Budget documents, U.P. Government

Taking the central government plan loans and other borrowings of the state government, we find that almost three-fourth of total plan expenditure in the state is being financed through borrowing and the remaining one-fourth through central grant. The plan expenditures are thus contributing to the increase in the public debt of the state, which is already very high. The situation is all the more worrisome because of the fact that almost half of the plan expenditure is in the nature of revenue expenditure, which is not likely to generate resources for repayment of the loans. This brings us to the issue of increasing public debt and its sustainability.

V. Sustainability of Public Debt

Due to its mounting expenditure the state government has been resorting to heavy borrowing. The state budgets for the past two decades have been continuously running huge revenue and fiscal deficits. The ratio of deficits to SDP has been going up (Table 10). In the recent years covering the Tenth Plan period the ratio of revenue deficit has hovered around 3 per cent and that of fiscal deficit around 5 per cent of SDP. A concerting feature of the deficits has been that a large part of the borrowings is being spent on revenue expenditure, which does not add to the productive capacity of the state or the revenue earnings of the government.

As a result of the continuous reliance on borrowings to meet state expenditure the indebtedness of the state has sharply increase both in the absolute and the relative terms. Total debt of the state government is projected to touch the figure of Rs. 1,30,000 crore (Table 11). The ratio of debt to SDP now is the highest among Indian states at over 50 per cent. Debt servicing ratio to revenue receipts is as high as 46 per cent during 2004-05. Interest payment alone now amounts to almost 30 per cent of the revenue expenditure, thereby, squeezing the capacity of the state to spend on priority sectors. The Twelfth finance Commission in its fiscal restructuring programme has suggested that the debt-SDP ratio of states should come down to 28 per cent and interest payment/ revenue expenditure ratio to 15 per cent by 2009-10.

The state has been gradually falling into debt trap as it has to borrow more to repay the past loans. This is obvious from the fact that debt serving as a ratio of debt receipts amounted to 87 per cent during 2000-01 and to 107 per cent of debt receipts in 2004-05. In other words the government is no longer in a position to service its debt from its own borrowing.

Table 10

TRENDS IN REVENUE AND FISCAL DEFICIT IN UTTAR PRADESH DURING 1991-2006

Year	*Revenue Deficit*			*Fiscal Deficit*	
	Rs. Crore	*As % of SDP*	*As % of FD*	*Rs. Crore*	*As % of SDP*
1991-92	724.59	1.1	26	2836.50	4.4
1992-93	1014.56	1.4	27	3710.93	5.2
1993-94	1148.72	1.4	36	3165.77	4.0
1994-95	2000.74	2.2	42	4766.50	7.3
1995-96	2340.65	2.3	53	4380.61	3.8
1996-97	3179.13	2.2	53	5956.20	4.3
1997-98	4623.91	3.6	61	7575.96	5.1
1998-99	8696.16	5.1	75	11632.53	6.8
1999-00	7252.61	3.9	65	11098.73	5.9
2000-01	6289.31	3.3	62	10179.52	5.6
2001-02	6181.80	3.4	62	9898.13	5.3
2002-03	5117.32	2.6	54	9496.91	4.9
2003-04	6305.75	2.8	59	10776.25	4.9
2004-05 (RE)	7176.47	3.1	52	13686.25	5.9
2005-06 (BE)	5403.47	2.1	40	13532.58	5.3

Source: U. P. Government, *White Paper on Budget 1998-99, Part-II and Budget Papers, 2005-06.*

Note: Revenue deficit figures for 2003-04 exclude the underwriting of loans of Rs. 12277.40 crore to UPSEB and Fiscal deficit figures for 2003-04 exclude the power bonds amounting to Rs. 5871.86 crores.

The present debt levels are clearly not sustainable. The state government is required to take firm and time bound measures to raise its resources and reduce the dependence on borrowing to finance its plan and non-plan expenditure. It is encouraging to note that the state government is aware of the gravity of the fiscal situation and has passed the Fiscal Responsibility and Budget management Act in the year 2004, becoming the fifth state to do so. What is needed is that the government should strictly adhere to the fiscal targets laid down in the FRBM Act.

Table 11

TRENDS IN LIABILITIES OF STATE OF UTTAR PRADESH DURING 1991-2006

Year	*Outstanding Liabilities (Rs. Crores)*	*As per cent of GSDP*
1990-91	17966	32.4
1991-92	21101	32.6
1992-93	24157	34.2
1993-94	26920	33.9
1994-95	31658	35.1
1995-96	36145	31.2
1996-97	41768	30.2
1997-98	48365	32.6
1998-99	55952	32.8
1999-00	65135	34.7
2000-01	72766	40.2
2001-02	83011	44.4
2002-03	91182	41.6
2003-04	106407	48.9
2004-05	116794	49.9
2005-06	129155	51.4

Source: U. P. Government, *White Paper on Budget 1998-99, Part-II and Budget Papers, 2005-06.*

Debt Relief Measures

Following the recommendations of the Eleventh Finance Commission Report a debt swap scheme was introduced under which the states were allowed to swap the earlier high cost debt by fresh low cost debts. Under the debt swap scheme U.P. government was able to swap total loans amounting to Rs. 11364.31 crore during the years 2002-03, 2003-04 and 2004-05 taken together. Out of this Rs. 5242.80 crore were out of small savings and Rs. 6121.51 through additional market borrowing. The debt swap will reduce the burden of interest payment in the years to come. However, it has added to the liquidity constraint on the state government in the short run. It has raised the debt servicing to new debt ratio on the one hand and restricted the availability of NSSF borrowings for plan purposes.

The Twelfth Finance Commission has recommended a

package of debt relief for the states. Under this package all the central loans to the state government as on 31st March 2005 will be merged and rescheduled with a maturing period of twenty years on which a rate of interest of 7.5 per cent will be charged. It has been estimated by the Finance Department, U.P. Government that this will lead to a saving in interest of Rs. 3133 crores and will reduce the annual repayment liability by Rs. 1533 crores over the award period. The states will be eligible for debt write off if they reduce their revenue deficit over the award period. U.P. can claim a debt write off to the tune of Rs. 4020 crores over the award period. To benefit from the debt write off scheme U.P. Government will have to make determined efforts to reduce its revenue deficit.

The New Debt Regime

It needs to be mentioned here that that the system of central assistance will undergo a change from the year 2005-06 following the recommendation of the Twelfth Finance Commission to stop on lending to states by the centre. No plan assistance will be only in terms of plan grants and on lending by centre swill be stopped. This may be a blessing in disguise as it will restrict the growth of public debt of the state. The window of loans from NSS Fund is open to the government to meet its debt requirements. However, it is a costly debt with current interest rate at 9.5 per cent.

The state government has now to gear itself for meeting the challenge of the new debt regime. It will have to go to the market for borrowing. The whole approach to plan financing has to undergo a change. Borrowing should be restricted to the economically and financially viable and bankable projects. There is no escape from mobilization of additional resources through non-debt sources to meet the expenditure requirement of the government for plan and non-plan purposes. We now turn to a discussion of the performance of the state government in resource mobilization.

VI. Resource Mobilization Efforts of the State Government

Table 12 shows the trends in revenue from different taxes since 2001-02, while Table 13 shows the annual increase from tax revenue. In the first three years of the Tenth Plan state governments tax revenue from own sources has gone up by about Rs. 5,350 crore or by Rs. 1700 crore annually. The state tax revenue has increased at a fairly high rate of about 15 per cent per annum, which can be termed as satisfactory. However, performance in terms of individual taxes has been uneven. While revenue from stamp and registration duties has increased at a rate of 21.5 per cent per annum, the rate of increase was around 13 per cent per annum in case of excise and trade tax and only 4.75 per cent per annum in case of entertainment tax. On the other hand, motor vehicles tax shows a negative trend.

Tax/SDP ratio continues to be very low in U.P. After registering an increase of about 0.75 per cent points in 2002-03, tax/SDP ratio has stagnated at around 6.3 per cent. Non-tax revenue, on the other hand, show a very modest growth of 6.11 per cent per annum and the ratio of non-tax revenue to SDP, which was slightly less than 1 per cent has declined further. The recent roll back in user charges in education and health sector has an adverse impact on state finances.

If the targets of reduction in revenue and fiscal deficits laid down in the FRBM ACT have to be met, a bold strategy of resource mobilization through tax and non-tax sources has to be adopted along with a restrain on the growth of non-development expenditure. A few suggestions are offered in this regard:

1. There is a vast unrealized potential of increasing land revenue, which has remained unchanged for quite some time. Even if 1 per cent of gross income from agriculture is realized as land revenue it can increase state revenue substantially.
2. The introduction of profession tax can yield substantial revenue.
3. There is large scale evasion of trade tax. Effective tax administration coupled with raids and seizures in case

of tax evaders can help raise revenue from this tax.

4. Revamp of property tax in the urban areas also holds promise for raising resources to strengthen the finances of the local bodies.
5. User charges for the economic and social services should be rationalized and gradually enhanced.
6. Subsidies of various types should be gradually phased out.
7. Government should adopt a transparent and time bound policy of privatization/closure of loss making undertakings and corporations.
8. Government should undertake strict measures for curbing its unproductive and wasteful expenditure and restrict the growth in public expenditure.

Table 12

TRENDS IN OWN TAX AND NON-TAX REVENUE DURING 2000-01 TO 2005-06

Items	*2001-02*	*2002-03*	*2003-04*	*2004-05 RE*	*2005-06 BE*
State Taxes and Fees					
Land Revenue	72.93	64.23	117.67	75.00	76.50
Stamp and Registration Fees	1429.29	2078.68	2296.06	2564.00	2928.00
Excise Duties	1961.38	2555.05	2472.37	2800.00	3200.00
Sales Tax/Trade Tax	6163.10	7123.74	7684.13	9000.00	10524.00
Taxes on Vehicles	503.04	618.84	676.96	429.77	588.74
Taxes on Goods and Passengers	76.65	77.33	80.21	494.47	653.00
Taxes and Duties on Electricity	9.22	145.29	174.72	191.51	194.99
Entertainment Tax	100.04	100.02	92.78	115.00	120.00
Total Tax Revenue	10319.32	12766.90	13601.22	15675.10	18290.58
Non- Tax Revenue	1787.07	1913.49	2282.08	2135.35	2247.19
Total Own revenue (A+B)	12106.39	14680.39	15883.30	17810.45	20537.77
GSDP (Rs. Crore)	188687.08	202903.95	217432.00	246829.00	279065.00

Source: U.P. Budget in Outline (Annual) and Budget Papers 2005-06.

Table 13

Annual Growth of Own Tax and Non-Tax Revenue during 2001-02 to 2005-06

Items	*2002-03*	*2003-04*	*2004-05 RE*	*2005-06 BE*	*CAGR(%) 2004-05 over 2001-02*
State Taxes and Fees					
Land Revenue	-11.93	83.20	-36.26	2.00	0.94
Stamp and Registration Fees	45.43	10.46	11.67	14.20	21.51
Excise Duties	30.27	-3.24	13.25	14.29	12.60
Sales Tax/Trade Tax	15.59	7.87	17.12	16.93	13.45
Taxes on Vehicles	23.02	9.39	-36.51	36.99	-5.11
Taxes on Goods and Passengers	0.89	3.72	516.47	32.06	86.16
Taxes and Duties on Electricity	1475.81	20.26	9.61	1.82	174.89
Entertainment Tax	-0.02	-7.24	23.95	4.35	4.75
Total Tax Revenue	23.72	6.54	15.25	16.69	14.95
Non- Tax Revenue	7.07	19.26	-6.43	5.24	6.11
Total Own revenue (A+B)	21.26	8.19	12.13	15.31	13.73
GSDP (Rs. Crore)	7.53	7.16	13.52	13.06	9.37

Source: U.P. Budget in Outline (Annual) and Budget Papers 2005-06.

VII. Private Investment

The Tenth Plan was based on the premise that 60 per cent of investment during the plan period will come from the private sector. It is not possible to have a full and clear picture of the total private investment in the state in the absence of the availability of the required data. Some assessment of the private investment activity can, however, be made with the help of the trends in the institutional loans and investment by the corporate sector on which some information is available.

Table 15 shows the trends in bank lending in U.P. in the past decade. Bank loans show an erratic trend. The growth in bank loans was 24.4 per cent during 2001-02. It came down to 15.5 per cent in 2002-03 and sharply fell next year to only 1.4 per cent. The table also reveals that the growth in bank credit

Table 14

TOTAL OWN REVENUE AS PERCENT OF GSDP: 2001-02 TO 2005-06

Items	*2001-02*	*2002-03*	*2003-04*	*2004-05* RE	*2005-06* BE
State Taxes and Fees					
Land Revenue	0.04	0.03	0.05	0.03	0.03
Stamp and Registration Fees	0.76	1.02	1.06	1.04	1.05
Excise Duties	1.04	1.26	1.14	1.13	1.15
Sales Tax/Trade Tax	3.27	3.51	3.53	3.65	3.77
Taxes on Vehicles	0.27	0.30	0.31	0.17	0.21
Taxes on Goods and Passengers	0.04	0.04	0.04	0.20	0.23
Taxes and Duties on Electricity	0.00	0.07	0.08	0.08	0.07
Entertainment Tax	0.05	0.05	0.04	0.05	0.04
Total Tax Revenue	5.47	6.29	6.26	6.35	6.55
Non- Tax Revenue	0.95	0.94	1.05	0.87	0.81
Total Own revenue (A+B)	6.42	7.24	7.30	7.22	7.36
GSDP (Rs. Crore)	100.00	100.00	100.00	100.00	100.00

Source: U.P. Budget in Outline (Annual) and Budget Papers 2005-06.

has in most of the years fallen short of the growth in bank deposits. This is reflected in the decline in credit-deposit ratio, which is hardly around 30-31 per cent much behind the national average. Another striking fact to be noted is that bank loans in U.P. amount to hardly 6-7 per cent of total bank loans in the country, whereas U.P. contributes to over 10 per cent of total deposits. These trends are indicative of the relatively low volume of economic activity in the state and its inability to utilize the savings beings generated in the state. *Concerted efforts are needed to improve the credit-deposit ratio in the state.*

The picture with respect to loans from the national term lending financial institutions is even more dismal. The level of loans sanctioned and disbursed by the financial institutions has come down to almost one-fourth of what it was in 2000-01. The share of U.P. in total loans disbursed by financial institutions has sharply declined from around 8 per cent in the mid-nineties

Table 15

TRENDS IN BANK LOANS AND DEPOSITS IN UTTAR PRADESH

Year	*Bank Branches (Nos.)*	*Bank Credit (Rs. Crore)*	*% change over previous year*	*As % to All India*	*Bank Deposit (Rs. Crore)*	*% change over previous year*	*As % to All India*	*Credit Deposit Ratio*	*(%) As% to All India*
1995-96	8854	14614	8.76	5.73	41777	15.85	9.8	34.20	55.25
1996-97	8897	17083	16.9	6.00	49260	17.91	9.84	33.68	59.29
1997-98	8978	19636	14.95	5.95	59992	21.79	10.05	32.73	59.18
1998-99	9072	21872	11.39	5.71	70358	17.28	10.07	31.09	56.75
1999-00	9063	25514	16.65	5.54	82675	17.51	10.06	30.86	55.10
2000-01	8254	27193	6.58	5.05	85373	3.26	8.99	31.06	54.77
2001-02	8324	33826	24.39	5.15	98520	15.4	8.76	33.46	57.31
2002-03	8312	39084	15.54	7.49	108685	10.32	11.32	29.02	53.40
2003-04	8213	39634	1.41	6.39	119333	9.8	10.47	31.37	57.68

Source: Reserve Bank of India, Handbook of Statistics on the Indian Economy.

to less than 4 per cent in the late nineties and stood at a paltry 3.17 per cent in 2002-03 and only 1.89 per cent in 2003-04. These figures are indicative of the poor investment climate in U.P.

Table 16

TRENDS IN CREDIT FROM FINANCIAL INSTITUTIONS TO UTTAR PRADESH

Year	*Sanctions*		*Disbursed*		*Uttar Pradesh as % of All India*
	Rs. Crore	*% change*	*Rs. Crore*	*% change*	
1995-96	4520	53.01	2773	41.97	7.97
1996-97	3363	-25.6	2962	14.47	6.94
1997-98	2724	-18.99	2411	-33.17	4.47
1998-99	3280	20.42	2176	-3.09	3.84
1999-00	3472	5.83	2602	11.7	3.87
2000-01	3588	3.33	2686	1.34	3.65
2001-02	1709	-52.35	1661	-39.49	2.79
2002-03	841	-50.79	813	-46.84	3.17
2003-04	869	3.23	659	-23.47	1.89

Source: Statistical Diary, U.P.

Proposed corporate investment registered a decline between the years 1996-97 and 2000-01, but shows signs of picking up after that (Table 17). Between 2001-02 and 2003-04 proposed investment jumped by as much as Rs. 20,000 crore. This is, however, not reflected in the actual investment as the rate of implementation shows a decline from around 47 per cent to around 36 per cent over this period. If the proposed investment fully materializes it will make a substantial impact on the state economy. Efforts should be made to identify the factors that are retarding the pace of implementation of proposed projects and to remove them expeditiously.

U.P. is attracting a very paltry amount of investment by domestic and foreign investors. As on August 2004, the number of projects being implemented in U.P. was 438 involving an investment of Rs. 18,098 crore, amounting to 7.8 per cent and 9.5 per cent respectively of total projects and investment in India as a whole (Table 18). However, during 2003-04 U.P. share in

Table 17

PROJECT INVESTMENTS OUTSTANDING IN UTTAR PRADESH DURING 1995-2004

Year	*Proposed Investment (Rs. crore)*	*Change over Previous Year (Rs. crore)*	*Under implementation (Rs. crore)*	*Rate of Implementation (%)*
1995-96	58928		22363	37.95
1996-97	62077	3149	28229	45.47
1997-98	50680	-11397	19808	39.08
1998-99	48473	-2207	15257	31.48
1999-00	54514	6041	23425	42.97
2000-01	53464	-1050	23841	44.59
2001-02	59739	6275	28050	46.95
2002-03	69404	9665	24275	34.98
2003-04	72906	3502	26710	36.64

Source: Centre for Monitoring Indian Economy, Monthly Reports, U.P.

IEMs was only 5.62 per cent and that of investment only 1.4 per cent.

Table 18

IEMs BEING IMPLEMENTED IN UTTAR PRADESH AND INDIA

Number and Type of Projects and Proposed Investment	*Uttar Pradesh*	*All India*	*All India % share to*
IEM's Filed (April 2003-March 2004)			
Number	232	4130	5.62
Investment (Rs. Crore)	2149	154931	1.39
Under Implementation as of August 2004			
Number	438	5631	7.78
Investment (Rs. Crore)	18098	189867	9.53

Source: Centre for Monitoring Indian Economy, Monthly Reports, U.P.

U.P.'s share in foreign direct investment is even less. Thus U.P. attracted only 38 FDI proposals during 2003-04 involving an investment of Rs. 102.32 crore. Thus, the number of proposals and investment involved were hardly 2.0 per cent and 1.5 per cent of all India proposals and investment respectively (Table

19). *Our analysis indicates that the efforts to attract outside investment to U.P. are not showing the desired results. An in-depth analysis of the factors involved is urgently called for.*

Table 19

FOREIGN DIRECT INVESTMENT APPROVALS IN UTTAR PRADESH AND INDIA DURING 2003-04

Number and Type of Projects and Proposed Investment	*Uttar Pradesh*	*All India*	*% share to All India*
Technical (Nos.)	13	299	4.35
Financial (Nos.)	25	1630	1.53
Total (Nos.)	38	1929	1.97
Investment (Rs. Crore)	102.32	6833.31	1.50

Source: Centre for Monitoring Indian Economy, Monthly Reports, U.P.

VIII. Summing Up

Our analysis of the plan investment and their financing leads to the following conclusions:

- Since early nineties there has been a sharp decline in the plan expenditure as per cent of NSDP, which is also reflected in a sharp decline in growth rates. The decline in plan expenditure in its turn can be traced to the sharp deterioration in the fiscal situation in the state witnessed since early nineties. The economic slow down and fiscal crisis in the state are deeply interlinked.
- An area of concern is the large and growing gap between plan outlays and plan expenditure. Even if the allocation for the year 2004-05 is fully utlilised, total plan expenditure in the first three years of the Tenth Plan will not exceed 40 per cent of the plan size.
- Taking the central government plan loans and other borrowings of the state government, we find that almost three-fourth of total plan expenditure in the state is being financed through borrowing and the remaining one-fourth through central grant. The plan

expenditures are thus contributing to the increase in the public debt of the state, which is already very high.

- The ratio of debt to SDP now is the highest among Indian states at over 50 per cent. Debt servicing ratio to revenue receipts is as high as 46 per cent during 2004-05. Interest payment alone now amounts to almost 30 per cent of the revenue expenditure, thereby, squeezing the capacity of the state to spend on priority sectors. The whole approach to plan financing has to undergo a change. Borrowing should be restricted to the economically and financially viable and bankable projects.
- The situation with respect to institutional finance in U.P. is not satisfactory. Bank loans in U.P. amount to hardly 6-7 per cent of total bank loans in the country, whereas U.P. contributes to over 10 per cent of total deposits. The picture with respect to loans from the national term lending financial institutions is even more dismal.
- U.P. is attracting a very paltry amount of investment by domestic and foreign investors.
- A bold strategy of resource mobilization through tax and non-tax sources has to be adopted along with a restrain on the growth of non-development expenditure so that development expenditure in the vital sectors can be increased.
- Factors responsible for low rate of domestic and foreign investment and for their poor implementation rate should be identified and corrective measures introduced urgently the boost the level of investment needed to boost up the growth rate of the state economy.

16

GOVERNANCE REFORMS IN UTTAR PRADESH

T.N. Dhar

I. Introduction

The link between good governance on the one hand and sustainable as well as equitable economic and social progress on the other has become increasingly evident world over in recent decades. Whatever be the political and economic choices made by the state, good political and administrative governance. Good economic governance and good civic governance are the *sine quo non* of human development. This is where governance reforms assume significance, import and urgency.

What is governance? How can we broadly define it? There is wide-based recognition amongst experts of the proposition that governance is how an organization steers itself and the institutions, processes and structures that are used to achieve its goals. Governance is also, in broader and integrated contexts, crucially concerned with how organizations (e.g. institutions, departments. hierarchies security and enforcement agencies, legal entities service providers, etc.) relate to each other, how they relate to citizens and the way in which citizens are given a voice.

The notion that too much government is not good may have some merit but let us be very clear here that good governance is unexceptionable. Good government does not necessarily mean less government. It is true that governments need not do those things that people can better do themselves. The essential duty of a government is to provide security, ensure peace and order, and create conditions for knowledge. Good health, entrepreneurship and people's advancement, and, effectively and equitably, implement what is called the social contract and deliver it at efficient costs, without discrimination and within determined time frames. Unfortunately governments have tended to become sluggish. Vast, much layered and proliferating organisations that often are centralised political systems and bureaucracies preoccupied with hierarchies, rules, procedures, and compartmentalized decision-making, and subject to incessant political pressures and manipulations. In the process they have become less responsive, highly costly and poorly accountable. The critical issue, therefore, is how can governments and institutions be made flexible, performing, caring, equity-led, transparent, responsive and readily accountable? How can government at all levels and their institutional arms become innovative, participatory and decentralized? These are the important questions that need to be asked and answered if reformed governance is to be sought and achieved.

II. The National Scene

When India became independent it chose parliamentary democracy as the mode of its polity. To the goals of democracy and republicanism were later added two distinct markers, namely secularism and socialism. We started with the mixed-economy model which was underpinned by strong foundations of central planning and a powerful, commanding public sector. This model did not deliver growth in the required measure; nor equity either. In 1980s a gradual but perceptible shift began in the direction of opening up the economy. Then came a distinct, vigorous and path-breaking push in 1991 towards a liberalised economic model. The 73rd & 74th Amendments were enacted in 1992 to give constitutional recognition to PRIs/ULBs and indicate their functional assignment, It was felt that unless multi-sectoral and multi-institutional reforms were undertaken parallely with speed, determination and dynamism, the country I s economy could not accelerate and the problems of poverty inequity, unemployment and deprivation could not be solved) nor the challenge of globalization met. In the middle and late nineties the dominant thinking amongst the highest political and administrative echelons was that of co-operative federalism, of a sustained liberalization policy, of institutional empowerment of people in decentralised modes, of fiscal stabilisation and of effective administrative reforms. The areas of concern included decentralisation and delegation accountability, openness in governance, social justice respect for citizen's rights, constitutional, legal and electoral reforms and reforms in civil services in the widest sense of that term. The NDA coalition came into existence at the Centre after the 12th Lok Sabha was constituted in 1999. It came up with a National Agenda. The Agenda spoke of the times as a "political age of reconciliation" and "consensual mode of governance". It declared its commitment to a stable honest efficient and transparent government. It talked of self-reliance, of removal of unemployment and of a higher economic growth of 7-8 per cent a year. It promised new policies in areas like food security. Water, judicial reforms, environment, social justice, etc. The Agenda was affirmed to be a sincere and solemn covenant aimed at changing the content and culture of governance of this great nation freeing it from the triple causes of hunger, fear and corruption'. A dream, alas that did not materialize!

Then followed the UPA coalition in 2004 which came out with its CNP (Common Minimum Programme) that has emphasized social harmony and enforcement of *law* without fear or favour, enhancement of the welfare of dalits. SCs/STs/ OBCs, farmers and farm labour, empowerment of women, attention to child development, education, health, democratic decentralisation, development of physical and social infrastructure, generation of employment and "the unleashing of the creative energies of our entrepreneurs, businessmen, scientists, engineers, and all other professionals and productive forces of society". It also laid great stress on governance reforms and further opening up of the country's economy so as to achieve a high growth path of 7 to 8 per cent a year in a sustained way "that generates employment so that each family is assured of a safe and viable livelihood". The reforms agenda is on. A fiscal responsibility law had been enacted centrally already and so also a freedom of information law. An Employment Guarantee Law is on the anvil. The freedom of information law is proposed to be converted into a more effective people-friendly right to information law. Many tax and non-tax regime corrections. Have been made and regulatory mechanisms set up in some important areas of economic activities like, for example, fiscal stabilization, financial marketing, corporate governance, power tariffs, etc. The process is afoot but facing some ideological barriers and coalition compulsions. The nation is awaiting outcomes with fingers crossed!

In 1996 the Central Government convened an important Chief Secretaries' Conference on "Effective and Responsive Administration". Its contexts were decentralisation and delegation, reform of civil services, accountability, transparency, legal reforms, citizens' rights, etc. However, no one talked about political reforms at the time. Many important suggestions emerged out of the high level nineties conferences which, inter alia, included a Charter of Ethics for Government Officials, an Independent Commission against Corruption. Codes of Conduct for Public Servants and Politicians, High Powered Civil Services Boards for processing postings, transfers and promotions of Senior Officers and the appointment of a Civil Services Ombudsman. Effective decentralisation of funds, functionaries and finances to rural and urban local bodies (PRIs and ULBs) was strongly advocated. A suggested action plan for fighting corruption emerged from the Central Vigilance Commissioner (CVC) that proposed many specific steps like the evolving of a CPI (Corruption Perception Index), zero tolerance of corruption, annual property returns by ministers/ parliamentarians. Mobilizing youth to fight corruption laying of traps and speedy disciplinary action, a whistle blowing law according of statutory status to the CVC, a freedom of information law, e-governance enactment of a Corrupt Public Servants (Forfeiture of Property) law and the implementation of the Benami Transactions Prohibition) Act which had already been passed by the Parliament in 1988. Election reform was another area of priority flagged. A Constitutional Review Commission gave its detailed report that has yet to see any action-taken measures. The Kelkar Committee has made wide ranging recommendations in tax and non-tax areas. Other Committees headed by Hota, Surendra Nath, Yugandhar and Alagh offered their recommendations. The Central Government is now setting up a Second Administrative Reforms Commission (the first one was constituted in 1966; to go into several areas of public administration including suggesting ways for right sizing manpower, cost control, functional reorganization of ministries, review of rules and procedures for quick and efficient service, management of cadres performance appraisal systems, outsourcing, strengthening of Panchayat and municipal governments etc.

III. Emerging Scenario in Uttar Pradesh

The issues of governance have been receiving attention in U.P. for many years now. Following the CM's Conference of 1997 an assessment was made within the government of the factors that were impinging negatively on the economic growth of the State. A diagnostic appraisal brought out the following weaknesses:

- *(a)* Weak governance that manifested itself in poor service delivery.
- *(b)* Excessive regulation and uncoordinated and wasteful public spending.
- *(c)* Inadequate transparency accountability and integrity of public services,
- *(d)* High fiscal deficits forcing the State to resort to debt financing.
- *(e)* Low level of human development
- *(f)* Over stretched public sector that was unable to discharge to responsibilities effectively.

(g) Infrastructure bottlenecks especially in power sector.

In November 1998 the Poverty Reduction and Economic Management Unit (S.A. Region) of the World Bank brought out a report about the fiscal crisis faced by U.P. It observed that) in its budget statement of June 1998, the State Govt. had signalled a 'commitment to improve the quality of governance in the State to increase accountability and to reduce the incidence of administrative misconduct or corruption. With the slogan of the four D's-delivery, discipline dovetailing and determination to collect revenues-GOUP wishes to energies the administration and develop a new work culture. As a part of this initiative, measures have been announced to simplify complex laws and regulations. Improve transparency in civil service recruitment, to increase decentralisation in order to bring government to the doorstep of the people, to increase right to access to information about government policies and activities and to establish policy making cells in each department to improve the focus and quality of administration". The Report further went on to make a telling comment. "One problem that has plagued U.P. is acute political instability. Over the last decade, the state has witnessed eleven changes in government. As a result there has been a tendency to maximize short-term gains rather than addressing the long-term strategic issues concerning economic development of the state. Unstable coalitions and frequent charges in political leadership have been accompanied by frequent transfers of senior bureaucrats resulting in extremely limited tenures that have played havoc with all public organizations" (W.B. Report No. 18633N dated 30.11.1998). The key areas flagged for reform in the report included governance fiscal adjustments, deregulation, divestment, restructuring, of public enterprises, civil services renewal, work appraisal systems, open government, anti-corruption strategy, down-sizing of government departments, decentrallsatlon and local government reform, and removal of bottlenecks in respect of both social (health, education, etc.) and physical (power, irrigation, roads. etc.) infrastructure.

Sensing the acute financial crisis facing the State the Government brought out a white paper in 1998-99 calling for quick and multiple responses to correct the situation. In March. 2000, GOUP came out with a Policy Paper on Reforms in Governance that importantly, sought to redefine the government. It came out with a paradigm shift while stating that "the role of the State Government will progressively change with less emphasis on direct provision of goods and services and more on setting policy, contracting out, mandating, regulating, facilitating or financing economic and social services through private sector". Deregulation and divestment were identified as thrust areas for which high level bodies (High Powered Deregulation Committee and Divestment Commission) were set up. The essential strategies included *(a)* role redefinition of the government, *(b)* bringing transparency and accountability to government functioning by increasing people's access to information quick grievance removal and vigorously combating corruption, *(c)* renewal of civil services through right-sizing, restructuring and strict performance appraisals, *(d)* institutional as well as administrative decentralisation, *(e)* financial management reforms, *(f)* public participation in governance through NGO mobilization, etc. The policy document also spelt out the government's intention to bring down its personnel numbers by 2 per cent a year till 2004) constitute Policy Planning Cells (PPCs) in all departments, develop and implement organisational performance indicators, give high priority to HRD issues like training, tenure security and transfer norms and modernise office technology in terms of computerisation e-governance and quick communication systems. Sound financial management, budgeting and expenditure reforms and effective auditing were the other needed quick intervention areas flagged. Taking into account the wide scope and importance of the reform agenda, a Cabinet. Committee, headed by the Chief Minister was also constituted for 'providing guidance and direction to the overall implementation of the Governance Reform Policy'.

While outlining the wide ranging reforms agenda the U.P. Government also prioritized some of its important tasks. These were, economy measures, taxation and revenue regime changes developing a Medium Term Expenditure Framework, doing away with the Personal Ledger A/c system rationalizing user charges and reducing subsidies to make these pointedly targeted to the intended beneficiaries. A high level implementation team headed by the Chief Secretary to the Government was to spearhead the implementation of the policy while the Cabinet Committee on Economic Development was to review every quarter policies issued by different Departments. In addition to general matters, sectoral reforms for power, industrial development, PSUs, demography and health matters, and empowerment of local bodies were also envisaged.

Following the announcement of the new Governance Policy (2000), many consequential measures were taken by the State Government but~ in the meanwhile, between 1999 and 2003 three governments changed hands in Lucknow. Inevitably the reforms agenda suffered many discontinuities. On the positive side the following steps, illustratively speaking, were initiated:

(i) A ban on recruitment of government staff was put in place so as to move towards right-sizing through the normal attrition process.

(ii) High level bodies for divestment, deregulation and expenditure efficiencies were constituted who submitted their reports and recommendations.

(iii) The State Government issued orders for the setting up Policy Planning Cells in 56 Departments which, in addition to their membership of highest level administrative and technical officials also provided for induction of external experts from scientific, engineering, academic, economic, social and public administration disciplines.

(iv) More functions and powers were decentralised to Panchayati Raj bodies and some of the functionaries of departments transferred to them, namely, for example primary and upper primary education, state tube wells, hand pumps, medical and health, women and child welfare, livestock, social welfare rural development, etc.

(v) Several PSUs were wound up; efforts also began to privatise others. By early 2004, 19 units of 5 selected corporations had been closed. The PSE restructuring programme involves identification of' units with a view to determining the need for the State Govt. to continue as owners. For loss-making PSE.s., VRS packages have to be a drawn up and a road map for winding up such units to be laid down. Restructuring the activities of operating enterprises was yet another option pursued. From over 50 the number of PSEs had come down to 41 by 2002-03. By way disinvestment this process has been initiated in respect of 24 closed/ sick sugar mills. Similar action in respect of 27 other such enterprises is reported to be under way.

(vi) Each service providing department/agency was required prepare and disseminate widely Citizen Charters that would indicate in clear terms, the kind of service available its quality, price, location and grievance removal system set-up, including names, addresses and phone numbers of the officials at different levels to be contacted for quick complaint redressal. The Charters were to include, monitoring, feed-back and correction mechanisms.

(vii) The GOUP signed an MOU with the GOI in June, 1999 that contained a broad diagnosis of the fiscal situation of the State and mutually agreed upon a set of specific reform measures in key areas to restructure the finances of the State with a view "to reducing revenue and fiscal deficits by enhancing resources and curbing non-productive revenue expenditure. Emphasis was also laid on protecting and enhancing high priority development expenditure". In the same context the GOUP initiated the "U.P. Fiscal Reform and Public Sector Restructuring Programme". The GOI agreed to catalyse World Bank assistance for the reform programme. A Project Agreement was signed with the W.B. in May, 2000, and Rs. 1101 crore were received as Programme Loan-I in June 2001. An key step in this

respect was the preparation of a Medium Term Fiscal Policy (MTFP) that was placed before the State Legislature.

(viii) The major components of the MTFP provided for medium term specific fiscal targets, including Medium Term Expenditure Framework (MTEF) improving financial management and audit functions and taxation reforms. Later on, the MTEF was revised. Certain steps in respect of expenditure management were put in place like prioritising expenditure, accurate accounting, monitoring and control measures. As a result of reform measures fiscal deficit came down from 5.9 per cent of the GSDP in 99-2000 to 4.7 per cent in 2002-03. The revenue deficit also came down from about Rs. 7252 crore to Rs. 5117 crore in the same period. A revenue enhancement strategy is also being pursued which includes trade tax reforms, levy of entry tax} user charges rationalisation and debt swapping.

(ix) Power sector reforms constitute a high thrust policy area. The U.P. Electricity Reforms Act 1999 was enforced from January. 14, 2000. Earlier, the U.P. Electricity Regulatory Commission had been set up in 1998. The unbundling of the UPSEB commenced in 2000. The U.P. Electricity Supply Code came into being in 2002 in the form of an anti-theft law. Several separate electricity distribution companies (DISCOMS) were formed as a part of the unbundling process. A Financial Restructuring Plan (FRP) was also evolved with a view to help the power sector companies to progressively consolidate their financial position. This process is still on. It is facing many difficulties on account of staff resistance and other factors and has yet to pick up pace and dynamism in the needed measure.

(x) One of the most important measures taken in 2004 was the enactment of Fiscal Responsibility and Budget Management law, the main objectives of which are to

induct strict fiscal discipline within the state government, lay down fiscal management principles and bring about transparency in financial matters. It mandates the elimination of revenue deficit within five years (by 2009), reduction of the fiscal deficit to 3 per cent in the same time horizon and reduction of the debt liability of the State to 25 per cent of its GSDP by 2018. Each year the government is required by law to lay before the legislature its medium term fiscal restructuring policy (MTFRP). There is provision for half yearly reviews. Relaxation from deficit reduction targets is permitted only on account any natural calamity or national security needs.

(xi) The treasury system in the State was computerized right down from the state to the district level. The process had begun as far back as in the eighties but was completed in late nineties. The system has very considerably achieved the objective of timely and account compilation of accounts. It has since been extended to cover other important areas like salary and pension disbursements, on-line cheque generation, budget control, etc.

(xii) In many areas, the State Government developed new policies. Thus, for example the State Water Policy was brought out in 1999 and the U.P. Agriculture Policy brought out were Tourism Policy (in 2000), Public Services Reforms Policy (2000), IT Policy (1999), Export Policy (2002), the U.P. Forest Policy (1998), Road Development Policy (1998), Good Governance Policy (2000), the Industrial and Service Sector Investment Policy (2004) and the new Housing Policy (2005). The Sugar Policy was revised in 2004. This listing is not comprehensive.

(xiii) For bringing about transparency executive orders were issued for providing access to public documents with suitable exceptions listed. Orders for setting up departmental cells and cells in collectorate for this purpose were issued and reportedly 51 departments

agencies came out with Citizen Charters.

(xiv) In the transport sector private participation was invited and transport development was sought to be linked with a massive programme of strengthening the road network with WB support.

(xv) A Special Economic Zone legislation was engaged and four new SEZs planned for Agra, Kanpur, Badohi, Varanasi and Moradabad locations. Similarly five special Development Zones were to be developed, namely, a Medi City, a Web City, a Bio City, a NRI City and a Shopping Mall cluster. A new Industrial Policy was announced in 2004 and a high level U.P. Development Council set up to push forward U.P.'s industrial development with vigour and dynamism.

The above listing of measures taken is only illustrative. The main question to ask is what have been the results at the ground level of various policy, legal, procedural, technical and administrative initiatives taken.

The Balance Sheet

Let us take a look some of the intervention areas for a brief assessment here :

(a) Fiscal Scenario

First, the fiscal management scenario. The following table reflects the fiscal scene in the State as it has emerged from 2001-02 onwards :

The above table in brief shows both positives as well as negatives. Thus, we can see that on the whole the BCR has improved and interest ratio come down. The tax-GSDP ratio has also shown improvement. An effort is being made to reverse the capital expenditure compression as from 2005-06. The revenue deficit has also shown a downward trend. But two areas of concern subsist, namely, a persisting high fiscal deficit and the sharply rising debt burden. Debt servicing burden alone in 2004-05 was high as Rs. 19327 crore. The total size of the debt by the end 2005-06 is estimated to be very high at about Rs.

Table 1

SOME CORE INDICATORS OF U.P.'S FISCAL HEALTH (IN CRORE RUPEES) (ROUNDED)

	2001-02 (actual)	2002-03 (actual)	2003-04 (actual)	2004-05 (B.E.)	2004-05 (Revised CST)	2005-06 (B.E.)
1. Balance from Current Revenue (BCR)	-5456	-3426	-17219 (-4942) A	-4578	-4432	-2061
2. Interest Ratio (in percent)	31	24	31	30	27	24
3. Total Tax Receipts/GSDP Ratio (in percent)	11.3	12.1	12.4	13.3	13.4	14.1
4. State's Own Tax Income/ GSDP Ratio (in percent)	5.7	6.5	6.3	6.9	6.7	7.3
5. Capital Outlay/Capital Receipts Ratio (in percent)	32	30	27	35	35	52
6. Debt/GSDP Ratio (in percent)	44	41	48.9	49.1	49.9	51.4
7. Revenue Deficit	6181	5117	18583 (6306) B	5527	7176	5403
8. Fiscal Deficit	9898	9497	16648 (10776) C	10398	13686	13533
9. Rev. Deficit/Fiscal Deficit Ratio (in percent)	62.5	53.9	11.5 (58.5) D	53.2	52.4	39.9

Notes : (*i*) Figures at A&B exclude the written off loan amount of Rs.12227.40 crore of the erstwhile U.P. State Electricity Board

(*ii*) Figures C&D exclude the amount of Rs.5871.86 crore representing Power Bonds issued.

Source: U.P. Budget Documents for 2005-06, Volume II, Part-I, P. 33

1,29,155 crore i.e. 51.4 per cent of the GSDP. Expenditure on salaries, pensions and interest comprises over 80 per cent of the State's total revenue receipts that include central tax share transfers. This burden is expected to go up considerably if the 50 per cent DA merger demand by employees is agreed to by the Government, as appears to be likely. Computerisation of departmental accounts is yet to be achieved unto the DDO level which is essential for improving financial management and accountability right across the departmental domains and down to the ground level. There is also need for the setting up of a well-staffed and competent Cash and Debt Management wing in the Finance Department.

The process of budgeting has to undergo many corrections and improvements. For example, the budget calendar needs changing to ensure proper pre-budget SND scrutiny— The size of supplementary demands has been ballooning making the very process of budgeting dimensionally inaccurate and adhoc. The Contingency Fund Management, too, is far too loose. The PLA and DCL arrangements have been curbed but not phased out wholly. Budget releases are even now not spaced out to harmonies resource inflow and expenditure streams. The tendency to incessantly draw down the public account is by no means fiscally a prudent path. That is why there is a rising demand for entrusting PF accruals and withdrawals to a fiscally autonomous body. In fact future pensions also need to be made contributory on a sharing basis as has been one by the Centre for new employees. Some of the states have already taken this path. Transparency in budget preparation, decentralisation, effective audit, a law on procurement and awarding of contracts, limits on state guarantees on different types of loans raised by non-governmental bodies, and prompt follow-up and disposal of audit paras are some of the other matters that demand quick attention in better financial management contexts. Performance budgeting and measurement systems are weak or not adequately implemented. There is certainly need for greater legislative oversight through the mechanisms of the Estimates and Public Account Committees, the Committee on Public Undertakings (COPU), the questions asked in the legislature and full discussions on budget proposals. Since the time available for in-depth budget discussions in the legislature if often limited a committee system may be considered for this purpose as is the practice followed by the Parliament.

(b) Policies and their Implementations: Some Examples

Let us now consider the general situation that obtains in the State in relation to the development and announcement of various sectoral policies. Here, the picture is rather discouraging. Between policies and their successful implementation vast gaping gaps subsist. It would be appropriate to cite some examples here. The U.P. Agriculture Policy of 1999 emphasized effective land and water management, diversification of agriculture regional planning special attention to rural infrastructure and development of agro-based industries. Amongst other things it flagged a 20 per cent seed replacement rate extensive soil testing, balanced use of fertilizers, greater use of biological and organic fertilizers and integrated pest control and nutrition management. Not much of all this has happened on the ground. A proper land use policy has yet to be evolved and announced. The seed replacement rate hovers between 10-12 per cent only. The NPK use imbalance continues; so does the disequilibrium between inorganic and organic fertilizers. Value additions to agricultural produce are abysmally low and marketing support poor. Similarly, the lab-land interface is as yet very deficient in reach, extension and adaptations crumbling. Agriculture credit is low because of the weak and co-operative structure. Delivery systems for technology transfer, inputs, credit, etc. are of very poor quality. The result is that we have an agricultural sector of the state's economy that grew only at a lowly 2.3 per cent per annum between 1993-94 and 2001-02. This situation has not changed much since 2001-02. That is perhaps why the need for a revised policy has been felt.

One more telling example would be that relating to yet another critical sector, namely water. The U.P. State Water Policy was announced in May 1999. It contained the estimates of surface and ground water availability in the State in utilizable terms and its future needs, indicated water allocative priorities and laid down some of its broad objectives. These objectives, inter alia highlight preservation of scarce water resources optimization of the uses of available water, conservation, better management, sustainability, equity in water uses flood and drainage issues conflict resolution in water uses and HRD/ R&D. Improving data-base, factoring in environmental and ecological impacts conjunctive uses of water, water harvesting, participatory irrigation management, private sector participation, appropriate institutional and legal framework and water pricing are some other areas of action emphasized. A State Water Board had already been established in 1996 under the Chairmanship of the Chief Secretary. The State Water Resources Agency (SWARA) and a State Water Resources Data and Analysis Centre (SWRDAC) were constituted in June 2001. Two Sub-Basin Development and Water Management Boards were notified for Jaunpur and Imamganj canal distributaries under the Chairpersonship of the State Irrigation Minister.

What, however, is the ground situation? The fact of the matter is that most of the policy announcements have yet to become operationalised. Serious gaps between irrigation potential claimed to have been created and actual irrigation persist. Ground water regimes have been very poorly managed by unregulated tapping on the one hand and absence of conjunctive water use on the other. In 2002-03 the potential created was claimed to be 27,890 thousand ha while utilization was only 19,766 thousand ha. Of 805 development blocks, nearly 70% have been affected by ground water level depletion. In nearly one third of the affected blocks depletion is above 2 meters (in 19 blocks it is above 5 meters). Contrarily, there is simultaneous sub-surface water-logging by which, according to groundwater experts nearly 79 lakh ha area was affected in 2000 if post-monsoon below ground water levels are taken into account. This is a creeping disaster crying for quick interventions. Water use efficiency (WUE) is low. According to WAPCO, taking into account various kinds of losses (evaporation leakage, seepage, etc.), the overall WUE for unlined water courses ranges between 48 to 52 per cent only.

The State Tube Well (STW) management is in a mess. Per STW irrigated area has shown sharp fall over time. It was only 24 ha in 2000, down from over 70 ha in the seventies. Maintenance expenditure on STWs is in the region of about Rs. 400 crore or so a year. Revenue collection was only Rs. 0.73 crore in 2001-02. In most cases STW jamabandis had not been prepared, nor demand raised. In respect of canals the revenue is only about a quarter of the O&M expenditure. Conjunctive water use as an effective instrument of State water policy is yet to be adopted in any meaningful way. Water pricing and water use regulation have still to be legislated though it is informally learnt that a Commission is proposed to be set up for the purpose. The State Water Board has, frankly speaking, not become a vigorous, effective body.

Nearly a dozen departments and agencies are concerned with water management and between them the needed dynamic and constructive interface is wanting. Expenditure on establishment in the Irrigation Dept. is very high in comparison to the work load. Participatory irrigation management and water harvesting are the two other critical components of the State Water Policy that have still to become realities.

The examples of the State Agriculture and Water Policies have been cited here to underline the general deficiencies and wide gaps between policy and implementation in the State. That is certainly a critical and generic governance reform issue that needs to be squarely and speedily addressed. Lack of convergence between policy and implementation is a negativity widely prevailing across the board in most sectors of development planning in Uttar Pradesh.

Several important State policies adopted in recent years have gone into disuse or have been even partially reversed. Take the example of Citizen Charters. It is said that 41 departments/agencies have prepared the charters. The cold fact is that hardly any of these are operational. The public is simply not aware of them. For transparency and accessibility Special Cells were set up at the government level in various departments and even in district collectorates. Most of these have become defunct or have been closed. So have the departmental Policy Planning Cells. There are, however, a few bright patches to be seen in the area of grievance removal These are some local initiatives taken. Thus, for example, at the instance of D.M. Sitapur, the LOKVANI programme got going in the district in Nov. 2004. It is an internet access-based grievance removal and information-obtaining system available to all citizens of the district. Already over 7000 complaints and requests for information had been received in the first three months of the project and over 60% are reported to have been attended to. Such initiatives are welcome and need support, dissemination and replication.

Many development functions and departmental functionaries were transferred to Gram Panchayats in 1999 (about 11 functions and staff of 8 deptts). This process has in effect been reversed in various degrees.

Proliferation

Keeping a check on the proliferation of government departments and their personnel is a matter of accepted policy in the State (see Up's Annual Plan Document 2005-06, Vol. I, Part-I, page 113). Here, only a couple of examples will reflect the ground situation as it is obtaining in real terms. The first relates to the U.P. Secretariate the second to the number of state government employees.

In 1965, when Uttaranchal was also part of U.P., apart from the Chief Secretary, the number of Secretaries to the Govt. was only 21 who were supported by 114 Special/Addl./Joint/ Deputy and Under Secretaries. By 1998 the number of Principal Secys/Secys had gone up to 88 and that of other categories to 359. The number of sections had risen from 251 to 385. The number of levels that officers occupied in the Secretariat had shot up by 33%. The number of the ministerial staff, too, rose from 2252 to 3348. The Sectt. set-up continues to be top heavy and growing!

Let us also take a look at the number of government employees. In 1971 the number of government employees was about 5.44 lakhs. This number had shot up to about 9.33 lakhs by 1999 when U.P. and Uttaranchal were still one. The policy of the government has been to down-size the strength of staff by 2 per cent a year and 'reduction in recruitment in departments other than education, police and medical and health'. The annual budget documents of the State Government (year 2002-03 to 2005-2006) show that, over a three year period (2001-2004), the strength of gazetted officers had gone up by 16.3 per cent, while that of the non-gazetted personnel had marginally come down by about 4.5 per cent. The following table would reflect the situation as it has emerged:

Table 2

SANCTIONED STRENGTH OF GAZETTED AND NON-GAZETTED GOVERNMENT PERSONNEL IN U.P.

Date	*No. of Gazetted Employees*	*No. of Non-Gazetted Employees*	*Total Government Employees*
1-4-2001	50,857	8,02,283	8,53,140
1-4-2002	54,415	8,24,067	8,78,482
1-4-2003	57,006	8,35,833	8,92,839
1-4-2004	59,125	7,66,358	8,25,483

Source : U.P. Budget Documents (2002-03 to 2005-06).

In a period of three years the total sanctioned strength had fallen by less than 3.25 per cent. Apart from this, there are several lakh teachers who are not government employees but whose salaries have to be borne be the government.

Administration of Justice

The accumulation of civil) criminal and revenue cases in various courts in the State are well known. Their number has gone up to millions. There is great clogging at all levels. Many undertrials have to wait years in jails before their cases are taken up or decided. The incidence of delays in civil and revenue cases is legend. This is an important area of governance reform where many approaches are needed to speed up processes and decision-making. Alternate dispute resolution methods and quick arbitration and compounding arrangements are required. The Lok Adalats have to playa greater role. So have Consumer

Forums. It is perhaps time to think of cleaning, refining and reviving the Nyaya Panchayat System to reach justice to people nearer their homes.

Law and Order

Development planning, in order to succeed requires peace and order. This is an important aspect of governance that demands high priority attention at the hands of the government. Efforts in this direction have been made but much more remains to be done. Some recent figures about the incidence of main crimes in the State would be relevant here. The following table reflects the trends during last three years:

Table 3

INCIDENCE OF MAIN CRIMES IN U.P. (2002-2004)

Sl. No.	*Type of Crime*	*Year 2002*	*Year 2003*	*Year 2004*
1.	Dacoities	340	230	260
2.	Loots	2206	1607	2031
3.	Murders	6802	5421	6068
4.	Riots	4184	2059	3539
5.	Burglaries	4968	3122	4277
6.	Road Hold-ups	13	11	6
7.	Kidnappings for ransom	180	142	223
8.	Dowry Deaths	1797	1311	1624
9.	Rapes	1289	858	1263
10.*	Bank Dacoities and Loots	19	17	12

Note: * Bank dacoity loot numbers are included in general dacoity and loot numbers given in the horizontal columns No. 1 and 2.

The number of crimes against SCs/STs has corned own from 5435 in 2002 to 2677 in 2004. The number of crimes against women is also down though very marginally, from 14814 in 2002 to 14136 in 20D4 While the overall trends are of some decline, in absolute terms, the situation is still one that has to J improve. In the; area of policing several reform measures need to be taken to improve things that would include more force numbers, better training and better equipment. Also a very considerable proportion of the police force is doing non-police duties. This situation needs to be corrected.

Ultimately, the perception of order and security has to inform the mind of the common man and the investor who wants to come to U.P. to put in his or her money. Some of the other areas that need special attention are the growing menace of land mafias, the increasing use of illegal arms, the Naxalite problems in Eastern U.P. and the growing sensitivity of the U.P.-Nepal border.

Transparency, Right to Information and Grievance Removal

Transparency in decision-making is an essential ingredient of good governance. Public needs to be kept informed about government policies and decisions taken at all levels. What we have today in Uttar Pradesh is an executive dispensation regarding people's access to government documents and to grievance removal mechanisms. The people's right to know has been recognized by courts as a fundamental right under articles 19 and 21 of our Constitution. In our country, we have had, in the past, the dark cloud of secrecy hanging over the systems of governance. Its symbol was, and is, the Official Secrets Act of 1923 that excludes people from information and lays down the penal regime of penalties for anyone who seeks to obtain it. The demand for right to information began emerging in the country in recent years.

Among the Indian States, Tamil Nadu became a pioneer in this context. It enacted a right to information law in 1997. Later on, similar laws were adopted by M.P" Gujarat; Rajasthan, Karnataka and Delhi. The Government of India also enacted of Freedom of Information law in December 2002 but it did not provide for any penalty for an official if she or he refused to give information to which an applicant has a legitimate claim except that of a departmental appeal. This central law is now proposed to be replaced by a Right to Information law with a view to ensure that the proposed right becomes more of a reality. In the State of U.P no right to information law has as yet been legislated, The State Government has passed only administrative orders that do not have a statutory basis as of now. Such a law needs to be enacted as early as possible.

The right to information' is a valuable device for preventing or reducing corruption, empowering people and improving both citizen participation and citizen satisfaction. There are many other ways in which openness, accountability and responsiveness in administration can be achieved. The Citizen Charters need to be fully activated, made effective and given wide publicity through media. One window systems need to be introduced where services and facilities are provided or people are directly affected by decisions. Clear and criterion-based openness is required in functional areas like for example, payment of pensions and scholarships, tax assessments/ recoveries, loaning, tenders, government purchases, allotments of land, building plan approvals, water and power connections, billing, etc. In government offices, and that of public service providers bill boards should be put up indicating in simple words procedures and giving names, addresses and phone numbers of grievance removal officers at different levels. Token systems can be introduced at public service counters. Such and similar measures can promote cleaner governance and become preventive antidotes for reducing corruption. The Udhyog Bandhu and Awas Bandhu are two State level set-ups that have assisted many people in the sectors of industry and housing. Similar initiatives for other sectors are called for. Such facilitation must travel down to district and block levels, too.

Democratic Decentralization

Following the enactment of the 73rd and 74th Constitutional Amendments, and adoption of the needed conformity laws by the State Government) U.P. set up the Bajaj Commission in 1994 to go into the issues of strengthening panchayati raj. Consequent to its Report, in 1999, the State government amended the panchayat related laws and transferred functions of 11 Departments and functionaries of 8 to Gram Panchayats. The ZP Adhyaksha was made the Chairperson of the DRDA as well as the Sinchai Bandhu. At the time, it seemed the State Government had recognized the importance of the participatory process as a key element of good governance. The Golfs Task

Force on Devolution of Powers and Functions to PRIs (2001) had flagged some of the essential elements of devolution like, for example, allocation of funds, functions and functionaries, administrative control over staff made available to Panchayats, transfer of programmes with budgets, capacity building and freedom to take administrative and financial decisions at local levels. Training and linkages between PRI tiers were stressed. Unfortunately, the process of decentralisation in U.P. has not proceeded ahead as intended. In fact it has suffered several reverses. Staff of many of the departments transferred to PRIs (including teachers) has been reverted back. Budgets are still controlled by respective government departments and agencies. So is staff PRIs in effect, remain disempowered !

Democratic decentralisation is most certainly an essential and important area of governance reform and everything possible needs to be done to make PRIs, rural as well urban, effective institutions of local governance. To make Gram Panchayats viable administrative and economic units their demographic size would need to be raised to 10,000 or so.

The Government also enacted the District Planning Committee law in 1999 as mandatory required by the 74th Constitutional Amendment. Again, it is very disappointing to observe that DPCs have not become operational entities. The Central Govt. has now indicated in no uncertain terms that plans consolidated by DPCs in each State would form the basis of the 11th Five Year Plan. The Union Minister of Panchayats is reported to have stated recently in a day-long meeting of Chief Secys and Principal Secys *(PRJ* that (wherever DPCs are constituted and prepare district plans, the State will be in a position to get its share of Rs. 20.000 crore a year' (TOI-LKW-12—04- 05). It is high time that OPCs are made effective, operational and performing bodies in real terms.

Delivery Systems and Need of Convergence: A Critical Area of Action

If governance at the tool-meets.-object level is to improve, (and that is undeniably the most critical level) and benefits of development and anti-poverty programmes reached effectually to those who need these most) it is the delivery systems that need to be tightened up and vastly improved. Most development programmes launched at considerable costs and with lot of enthusiasm flounder for lack of properly worked out delivery systems.

Government and its agencies deliver various types of programmes, services, materials, benefits, facilitation subsidies, subventions, scholarships, pensions, credit, etc. to people. These can relate to physical infrastructure like roads power, irrigation, housing, drinking water, transportation, communication, etc. In the social infrastructure area services would include education, health, family welfare, nutrition, etc. Other types of deliveries could include credit, public distribution, procurement, subsidies, input supplies, financial assistance, technology transfer, etc. These are just some sample sets of activity types. An efficient delivery system requires convergence of related facilities, services, staff, institutional arrangements, materials and input supplies, credit and other assistance-disbursing arrangements, facilities for deposit of tax, non-tax and user charge dues, knowledge transfer, and a host of similar other components.

We may quickly glance here at some of the rural development linkages that have to be factored into the delivery systems in a diagramatic form (see diagram at Annexure-I). This diagram roughly reflects the position at the district level. The diagram at Annexure-II indicates the levels at which deliveries would have to be provided. The delivery points would, in actuality; be located at many levels, e.g. district, block, sub-block and gram panchayat. The delivery systems at all these levels will have to be both convergent as' well as decentralized, keeping in view the roughly indicated linkages. Convergence will have to be achieved at these levels and point s for all types of facilities and services that are provided—

The key requirements for improving the Delivery Systems world include :

(a) Decentralisation – democratic, institutional, financial and administrative,

(*b*) Convergence of services and facilities at points of delivery,
(*c*) Community participation, stakeholder involvement and citizen oversight,
(*d*) Right to information, transparency, open decision-making,
(*e*) One- window arrangements,
(*f*) Quick grievance removal systems,
(*g*) A credible and operative Citizen Charter system linked with social audit,
(*h*) Effective field inspections, monitoring, feed-back and corrective action,
(*i*) Careful targeting of benefits, subsidies, financial assistance, concessional prices, etc.
(*j*) Outsource deliveries where feasible under supervision and quality-cum-cost control measures,
(*k*) Use Information Technology for improving deliveries, reducing costs and for ensuring smoothly operating supply lines, distribution, inventory control, monitoring, etc.

Corruption

A great enemy of human development is corruption. It is both a menace and a challenge. Nearly two centuries ago Edmund Burke had said. "Among the people generally corrupt liberty cannot long exist". The virus of corruption has spread through out the social, political, economic and administrative fabric of the country. Servants of the state have become servants of pelf and power It has just about become a way of life. It needs to be tackled firmly and ruthlessly. There is political corruption and criminalization of politics. This is the area that needs to be cleaned first. Then there is large scale corruption in government departments and its agencies. Recently a TOI survey asking for the most serious problem faced by the country brought out the response from 60% of respondents that it was corruption.

Corruption has two aspects—preventive and curative. The need is to concentrate on preventive measures like transparency, right to information, open decision- making and making systems less prone to mal-practices. Prevention would also include vigilance/ surveillance, regular declaration of as sets by public servants with periodic verification on random basis, performance audit and strict follow-up, and citizen participation land citizen oversight wherever possible). At the curative level there is need for quick investigations, prompt booking of the corrupt and speedy legal process to 'bring the culprits to book. There should be a whistle blowing law enacted. Also, a Corrupt Public Servants (Forfeiture of Property) law needs to be legislated. Corruption is a dangerous threat that needs to be met through all means available—social, political, legal, judicial, penal and administrative.

Non-Governmental Organizations

NGOs voice and represent the voluntary sector which can be constructively mainstreamed into the strengthening of the processes of development at grass-root levels. Voluntary organizations can act as catalyzing agent bridges and facilitators in delivering development in villages, hamlets and urban mohallas/basties. They are more flexible in approach, less rule-bound and simpler in managerial structures. If these bodies are carefully screened, selected and mobilised they can provide more efficient delivery of services at lesser costs, with greater involvement of people and better utilization of funds.

The NGO movement in Uttar Pradesh is weak. It needs to be strengthened and fully and effectively co-opted into the streams of planned development. A note of caution would, however, be very appropriate here. Many spurious organizations claiming to be NGOs for public interest have mushroomed. Such organizations have to be firmly excluded through rigorous screening, proper verification and black listing where required.

E-Governance

The role of Information Technology as an instrument of efficiency, speed, progress and development has been acknowledged widely. Computers, internet, electronic connectivity, GIS, satellite mapping and other information collecting, processing and storing devices and systems are already very advantageously and powerfully employed in areas like science, education, data collection, processing and transmission, transportation, crime control, travel, communications, banking, billing, finance, insurance and a host of other economic activities. Other fields where IT can make powerful impacts are e-governance, training, HRD modernization of government offices (including that of its agencies and institutions) and their work environment, setting up of LAN/WAN net-works 'for quick communication, consultation and decision-making, tax, non-tax and user charge collections, transfer of knowledge to citizens (especially farmers and small entrepreneurs), project and programme monitoring and many other important service and delivery-related functions. This is clearly an area where Uttar Pradesh has yet to make strides in the required measure. Andhra Pradesh. Karnataka and some other States have already moved ahead. Some important initiatives have been taken by the NIC which has set the tone of e-governance in the rural development sector through 'rural informatics'. A wide range of software applications has been developed supported by ICT infrastructure to aid planning, monitoring and sharing of information amongst various agencies. Back-end computerisation has made it possible to bring widely usable information and services into the public domain. A very vigorous, multi-pronged thrust towards endowing e-governance with an umbrella nature in administrative contexts is called for in U.P. That has surely and undeniably to be a high priority area of reform in governance in the State.

IV. Summarizing the Priority: Areas of Governance Reforms

(a) Political Arena

Unless the political system is cleaned up, the hope for other interventions, improvements and reforms that are certainly necessary and essential, is difficult of realization. For bringing about political reforms the essential requirements, are will and consensus amongst political parties on a reasoned position. Time has come when they should rise above their narrow, short-term, parochial interests and arrive at an agreement for the cleaning up of the political system (including electoral reforms).

(b) Administrative Domain:

(a) Reducing the costs of governance,
(b) Capacity building of government and PSU personnel,
(c) Insulate government officials and police from recurrent political interference. Depoliticize police force. Ensure tenure security.
(d) Enact law for citizen's Right to Information,
(e) Strengthen anti-corruption laws/machinery/institutions,
(f) Introduction of quick and efficient grievance removal systems. High emphasis on E-governance. Transparency and open decision-making,
(g) Introduce financial/budgetary discipline and fiscal responsibility at all levels,
(h) Reform the Administration of Justice System,
(i) Strengthen democratic decentralization and, importantly, bring about convergence in delivery systems,
(j) Factor in environment safety and sustainability in all developmental processes.

(c) Fiscal and Financial Management

(a) Reduction of the high fiscal and revenue deficits,
(b) Strict enforcement Fiscal Responsibility Law.
(c) Review of the subsidy regime. Subsidies should be restricted to merit goods and specifically targeted only to properly identified, deserving and eligible groups.
(d) Widening and deepening of the tax base. Rationalizing user charges and moving to cost-based pricing with provision for cross-subsidization where necessary.
(e) Set up Statutory Regulatory Authorities for those service or supply sectors where these do not exist now,

e.g. transport, irrigation, water, municipal services, etc.

(f) Curb on State Guarantees through statutory means.

(g) Reform the Pension and Provident Fund Systems.

(d) *Infrastructure and Rural/Urban Development*

(a) Step up investments on power, roads, irrigation and transportation substantially. At the same time there must be high emphasis on strengthening social infrastructure in areas like health, education, nutrition and women and child welfare.

(b) Maintenance of assets already created.

(c) Power tariffs need to be rationalized and depoliticized. Water pricing is equally important.

(d) For pricing infrastructure related services independent regulatory bodies should be set up.

(e) The legal, financial and managerial environment has to be made conducive to public-private partnerships in infrastructure projects.

(f) Special attention to problems of Urban Development.

(e) *Employment and Manpower Planning*

(a) Tackling the huge back-log of unemployment and absorbing additions to labour force. While employment guarantee can be a distant goal, social security needs to be improved.

(b) The present labour laws need to be amended. It is self-employment that must be given high priority.

(c) Skill formation has to be upgraded at all levels.

V. Conclusion

In a fast moving world governments have to live with and respond to change. And, governance has to ensure that such change does not cause disparities to increase or give rise to social unrest and dislocations. We need a middle path whereby empowerment of people and freedom of choice can stimulate entrepreneurship, where development creates incomes work and opportunities and it becomes equitable as well as sustainable. The Government has to become catalytic. It should steer, not row. The Government has to be efficient open, mission-driven and result-oriented. It has to be citizen-friendly, specially for those who are weak and poor. It has to move from centralization to decentralisation, delegation and devolution. It should become committed to the deepening of democracy and strive for greater equity amongst and empowerment of, people. All this will necessarily demand clean and—competent political management, efficient honest and accountable bureaucracies (general as well as technical), an administration with compassion and outreach, sound fiscal policies, ethics-led businesses, rule of law, strong institutions and informed citizenry. The challenges are onerous. The answer lies in positive and determined responses.

In the present age of globalization liberalization and competition there is at times an impression created that the role of government is on the decline. This is certainly not true of a country like India or a State like U.P. where poverty, deprivation and want still prevail in a very considerable measure. In the pursuit of a widely shared and sustainable growth the market forces would have need to be tempered by enabling, equity-oriented policies and laws, good governance, strong institutions and vibrant people's democratic bodies. The market and the state have to complement and supplement each other.

Over eight decades ago Gandhiji listed seven sins of public life. These were: politics without principles, wealth without work, pleasure without conscience, knowledge without character, commerce without morality, science without humanity and worship without sacrifice. The lessons that we can draw from this listing are never as valid as now for ushering in good governance.

INDEX